Globalization:
The International HRD
Consultant
and Practitioner

Angus Reynolds & Leonard Nadler

Human Resource Development Press, Inc.
Amherst, Massachusetts

CONTENTS

PART FOUR:

Preface

We set out to present a book that would be useful to those involved with any aspect of the global HRD, a practical rather than an academic or theoretical book. It does not represent warmed-over research reports or other-worldly concepts that bear no relationship to the real world of work.

Our contributors have been generous in supplying their expertise, and the result is a broad diversity of thought throughout the book. We have not tried to resolve conflicts in the positions taken by chapter authors, since this would destroy the value of diversity. Where differences do exist, they are essentially minor — there is broad agreement on the important points.

A problem for people who are or want to be active in global HRD is that they are often unaware of the complexities involved. Our challenge was to help you understand those complexities, so we asked our contributors to provide practical information about how to apply various HRD concepts in real-world situations. They have met our expectations — and in many cases exceeded them!

How the Book Is Organized

The major thrust of the book is to present relevant information and pertinent practices concerning the client-consultant relationship in HRD, as well as the experiences of HRD practitioners. To that end, the book begins with a glossary of important global HRD terms and their meanings that will help you better understand the message of the experts who contribute their ideas and experiences.

Part One provides background and lays out the basic information needed to work effectively no matter what the country, situation, setting, or method involved.

Part Two presents a variety of approaches to understanding and applying the "global HRD view." The chapters address the global situation from varying positions and setting, but in general terms rather than in terms of specific countries.

Part Three deals with specific projects, countries, and regions. This section provides a sense of "what it's all about."

Part Four sums up the knowledge and experience found in the book. A detailed index at the end will help you locate the particular information you need.

How to Use the Book

This book should have a prominent place on the bookshelf of anybody concerned with global HRD. You are urged to first scan it from start to finish, to get a comprehensive view of global HRD. Then return to it whenever you need information about a specific topic, locale, or method—the book was designed to be a ready reference that will save you many wearisome hours of research.

Although the book is primarily for those who are, or want to be, involved in global HRD, it can also be useful for managers and the growing number of other kinds of professionals who provide help to clients in global situations.

Thanks to Our Many Colleagues, Past and Present

This book is the product of the help and encouragement of many people. Naturally, we are indebted to the staff and management of HRD Press, who gave us the opportunity to meet some important needs of those involved in global HRD. We are specifically grateful to Bob Carkhuff. He supplied the support and encouragement we needed to bring the work to completion.

We are also grateful for the cooperation and help of many other individuals. Some helped us specifically with this book. Others enabled us to see important ideas in particular countries and projects. People's willingness to share information and make valuable suggestions made it possible for us to present a coherent picture of global HRD.

In some ways, those who have helped us and the chapter authors to reach our current understanding are legion. Many nameless people have helped us in a broad range of ways. This book would be incomplete without special tribute to all whose help has been invaluable. We dedicate this book to them.

Angus Reynolds   Leonard Nadler
New York, New York   College Park, Maryland

January, 1993

About the Authors

The experience of this book's editors is certainly relevant: Both have long years of experience in other countries, cultures, and languages on both a temporary and long-term basis. Also, each has served as Director of the American Society for Training and Development's International Professional Practice Area.

DR. ANGUS REYNOLDS is Professor of Instructional Technology at the New York Institute of Technology. He built that institution's graduate programs to serve the needs of students employed in various HRD capacities by major organizations in the greater metropolitan New York area. For the previous decade he was Control Data Corporation's senior corporate HRD consultant. As Chief Consultant for CDC's Instructional Technology Consulting Center, his major work centered around high-level technology transfer consulting assistance to client organizations worldwide. A long-time consultant, he has identified and implemented solutions to problems in major multinational organizations in the aluminum, automotive, chemical, computer, food, hospitality, law enforcement, market research, nuclear, petroleum, power, steel, and telecommunication industries, as well as for the United Nations. He edited *Technology Transfer: A Project Guide for International HRD* and coauthored *Selecting and Developing Media for Instruction*, Third Edition. He has contributed to a number of important works, including *Handbook of Human Resource Development, Instructional Technology Guidebook,* and the *AMA Handbook of Human Resource Management and Development*. His doctoral dissertation, concerning cross-cultural training for employees of multinational corporations for work in China, was completed under the guidance of the man he considers his personal mentor—Leonard Nadler.

DR. LEONARD NADLER is HRD Professor Emeritus of The George Washington University and a partner in Nadler Associates. He is probably the best known American international HRD figure because of his many books, long and short international assignments in a wide range of countries over a span of 25 years, and long and widely known leadership of the graduate HRD degree programs at The George Washington University. His professional contributions have been recognized many times. He has received the Gordon Bliss Memorial Award of ASTD, was the first recipient of the Distinguished Contribution to Human Resource Development Award of ASTD, was selected by the readers of *Training Magazine* as one of the 10 outstanding trainers, and was elected to the HRD Hall of Fame of *Training Magazine*.

Dr. Nadler has worked in 34 different countries. In addition, he has published over 150 articles in a wide variety of professional publications and chapters in various professional books. He is the author of nine books and is the Series Editor of the Gulf Publishing Company series on Releasing Human Potential; consultant to Jossey-Bass Publishers on their Human Resource Series; and consultant to the HRD Press on *The Trainer's Resource*.

PART ONE

Essentials for Success in Global HRD

Essentials for Success in Global HRD

You will need certain information to be effective in any setting or country in which you work. This section first presents a Global HRD Glossary and then further explores the defined terms. It depicts HRD in a global setting, laying out the basic information you must have to work effectively with others and prepare media or technology-based HRD activities for them.

Chapter 1, "Semantics and Concepts," explains the terminology consistently used throughout the book. It is essential for effective communication because there are still no generally accepted definitions of some frequently and casually used HRD words. By using the Glossary definitions throughout the book you will be able to understand what is being communicated.

In Chapter 2, "Establishing a Sound Foundation for Global Consulting," we discuss personal and professional preparation for managing global HRD or acting as a consultant or practitioner. This chapter should give you a clear understanding of the consulting process and setting.

Chapter 3, "Working Internationally," is also our contribution. It serves as a transition to the global setting by briefly presenting some basic ideas that will be echoed and expanded upon by all the chapter authors.

Robert Kohls is well-known to all experienced global HRD professionals, and is accessible to aspiring ones. He wrote Chapter 4, "Preparing Yourself for Work Overseas," especially for this book. It provides his latest insights into the problems of preparing for work overseas. Even those who know Bob's work well will also want to read his ideas here.

Chapter 5, "Coping With the Language Barrier: Using Interpreters Effectively," is presented by Zeace Nadler. She addresses the important issue of how to function in situations where you must work with people through an interpreter. She draws the distinction between translation and interpretation and then concentrates on the latter. This chapter is a good example of our practical "toolkit" concept. You can take its suggestions and apply them immediately.

Michael Pellett has been translating media-based instruction for 12 years. In Chapter 6, "Adapting U.S. Instructional Media for Foreign Users," Pellett shows how you can translate existing English learning programs and adapt them to other cultures by following eight simple rules. He provides vivid examples of how to do it right as well as examples of flawed methods, and misplaced concerns.

Angus Reynolds provides similar help for "Adapting Technology-Based Instruction" in Chapter 7. The chapter covers the technical side of HRD but is presented non-technically. This chapter will prove a useful introduction to this area for nontechnical managers and practitioners involved in projects with a Technology-Based HRD component.

When you have finished this section you will be well-prepared for a better understanding of global HRD presented in the later chapters. Now, we invite you to launch your preparation.

CHAPTER 1

Semantics and Concepts

Angus Reynolds
Leonard Nadler

We hope that each reader will start this book by reading this chapter! In a book of readings, you may not always do so, but in this case it will help you get the most out of the remaining chapters.

Throughout the book, we have tried to ensure consistency in the use of terms and their definitions. We believe this is essential if the book is to communicate effectively with the different kinds of people who will read it. Too often we have seen similar books that lack standard definitions. The result is that in each chapter you must seek out what the author meant by some of the key words. Worse, you may not realize that different writers are using the same words to mean different things. Because we do have standard definitions, you can turn to any chapter in this book and find that the words (e.g., *training, education*) mean the same thing. Each prospective author received a set of definitions, which we discuss below. Of course, not all the authors were able to follow these definitions exactly as described here; for example, because of the particular years they are describing. Where there are deviations, we will call them to your attention.

One major difficulty concerns language. English is not the first language of all the authors. To the degree possible, we have tried to edit their writing to make their ideas emerge more clearly.

One example of language difficulty arises in Spanish. In standard dictionaries, "training" is translated into several different words: *instrucción*, *educación*, *entrenamiento*, and *adiestramiento*. In several languages, some words used in HRD have different meanings. We have tried to minimize any confusion that it might cause.

A second, even more important difficulty is that there are still no generally accepted definitions of some words frequently and casually used in the HRD field. Therefore, we are presenting the definitions here that apply throughout the book. You may disagree with these definitions, but at least you will know what is being communicated and then you can draw your own conclusions.

Defining HRD

The basic HRD-related definitions in this book can be found in more depth in another source (Nadler and Nadler, 1989). Briefly, Human Resource Development (HRD) can be defined as:
- Organized learning experiences provided by employers
  within a specified period of time
  to bring about the possibility of
- Performance improvement and
- Personal growth.

Let us look at each of these elements.

Organized learning experiences provided by employers

The essence of HRD is *learning*. There are other ways to achieve performance improvement, but when learning is the approach, it is HRD. Although *organized*, it can be formal (classroom, computer) or informal (on-the-job learning). Although *provided* by the employer, it can be delivered through a variety of approaches, both internal and external. There is also non-employee HRD, but that will not be covered to any extent in this book.

Within a specified period of time

The actual time that the organized learning is to start and stop is specific. There are many reasons for this, but the emphasis is on the factor that HRD is identifiable by a commitment of time by the organization/employer and the individual.

To bring about the possibility of performance improvement and personal growth

The major focus of HRD is on *performance improvement*, usually on the present job but sometimes to assure appropriate performance on a future job. *Personal growth* can also be provided, although it is not usually a major HRD activity. Within HRD, there are three different types of activity areas: training, education, and development.

Defining the Activity Areas

Some of the semantic difficulties arise in defining the activity areas. We caution you to focus on the *concepts* instead of the labels, which are merely a convenient way to communicate. Arguing about the labels generally causes people to lose sight of the basic concepts and the real differences among the three activity areas.

The first area is concerned with learning that is focused on the *present* job of the learner, and is labelled *training*.

The second area is concerned with learning that is focused on an *identified* job of the learner. The label for this learning is *education*. Unfortunately, it is sometimes called "retraining," but that fogs up the focus, because it does not tell us if the learner already knew the material and had to learn it again or the learner will be now moving on to a new job.

The third area is *not job focused,* which can sometimes present some difficulties, as most HRD people are very job focused. The label for this learning is *development*.

Part of the possible confusion comes from differences in how these words are used in other contexts and in various countries. For example, we found that in Venezuela the concepts did not present any problem, but the labels did! The client we worked with there tended to reverse education and development, so we had to reverse our use of the labels to be consistent in the concepts.

For this book, however, it was not possible to adjust for such differences in the use of these labels. If it presents any difficulties, we ask you to accept the labels as you read, in order to get the most out of the significant contributions of these authors.

Consultant and Practitioner

Research since 1958 in the United States and other countries has produced a role-model approach to what people do in HRD. Essentially, the major roles and the sub-roles are as follows:

Learning Specialist
Facilitator of learning (instructor, group leader, etc.)
Designer of learning programs
Developer of instructional strategies

Manager of HRD
Supervisor of HRD programs
Developer of HRD personnel/staff
Arranger of facilities and finance
Maintainer of relations

Consultant
Expert
Advocate
Stimulator
Change agent

For purposes of this book, we have left out the *Manager of HRD*. This book focuses mainly on external people who serve HRD managers under a written or implied contract. Generally, HRD managers are not contracted from outside the organization.

It is important to clarify the term "consultant". It is too often misused, both inside and outside the United States, to mean anybody who comes from outside the organization. This is incorrect usage for two reasons: First, it is possible for a consultant to be internal to the organization, and second, the "consultant" is often really serving as a Learning Specialist or Practitioner—designing a learning program or delivering it.

Some people tend to use the word "trainer" without any definition. It is not possible for the reader (or client) to know if they mean instructor, designer, or whatever. Therefore, we were tempted to title this book *Consultants and Learning Specialists*. We realized, however, that "Learning Specialists" in a title might not adequately communicate, so we used "Practitioner."

Global HRD Glossary

Jargon is vocabulary from someone else's field. Sometimes specialized words convey a meaning much better than common English. However, when specialized words are in common use, it is necessary to learn their meaning to communicate effectively with others who use them. This specialized glossary for global HRD is intended to help you get past the strange words and on to the points discussed.

Specific chapters also use a wide variety of other terms. The ones we list here appear in more than one chapter. People who work internationally sometimes forget that other HRD and non-HRD people do not necessarily know them, so we want you to know the consistent meaning they have here. No matter what your level of experience, you might simply skim over the words in the glossary in sequence. We suggest that you carefully read the definitions and note how the words will be used.

Client
The client is the person responsible for the result of the consultation. This is not necessarily the person who served as the initial contact, go-between, or sponsor in securing a particular consultant.

Client System
The client system is the organizational unit most directly affected by the consultation and is generally lead by the client.

Consultant
See page 8 for discussion of this word's meaning.

Cross-Cultural
Incorporating information and values of a second culture on an equal basis with the original culture.

Culture Shock
An adverse reaction experienced by persons who travel or work in an unfamiliar place.

Development
See page 7 for discussion of this word's meaning.

Education
See page 7 discussion of this word's meaning.

Expatriate
An employee who works for an extended time in a country other than the one in which citizenship is held.

Foreign
A person or organization from anywhere outside the country in question.

Global
The all-encompassing term for international, multinational, and transnational activities emerged in the early 1990s. Considered the ultimate and most desirable phase in the range from domestic, export, international/multinational, to global. Is generally considered to require a higher level of competence and commitment than the other activities on the list.

Home Country
Any country where the person or organization involved in the international HRD activity or project originates.

Host Country
Any country where the international HRD activity or project will be carried out.

HRD
See page 6 for discussion of this word's meaning.

Indigenous
A person with origins in the country in which he or she currently resides. Compare with *native*.

Intercultural
In this book, synonymous with cross-cultural.

International
A person or organization with origin in one country with intent on personal and business success in at least one other country.

Learning Specialist
See page 8 for discussion of this word's meaning.

Manager of HRD
See page 8 for discussion of this word's meaning.

Multinational
Business term describing an organization with origin in one country incorporating intent on success, focus on realities, and adaptation to conditions in several others in addition to the original country.

National
A person who retains his or her original citizenship despite the country in which work is carried out, or time involved. An organization with the origin, focus, and behavior of one country.

Native
A person with origin in the country where currently located. This is not a degrading term and has nothing to do with "natives in grass huts." An American originating and living in New York City is a *native*. Your experience must suggest to you that aside from being a native of a country, there are probably regional differences.

Parent Company
Company with ownership and control of the investment.

Practitioner
See page 8 for discussion of this word's meaning.

Reentry
Return to the home country by an employee after service in a foreign country.

Third Country National (TCN)
A person with citizenship in a country other than the host country or the country of origin of the organization involved.

Trainer
See page 8 for discussion of this word's meaning.

Training
Learning that focuses on the present job of the learner.

Transnational
Business term describing an organization with origin in one country incorporating intent on success in several other countries, integrating focus on realities, and adapting to conditions to the exclusion of only the original country.

Conclusion

We hope this clarifies the questions of terminology as used in this book. Keeping these definitions in mind should help you to better understand and use of the material.

References

Bell, C., and Nadler, L. *Clients & Consultants.* Houston, TX: Gulf Publishing Company, 1979.

Nadler, L., and Nadler, Z. *Developing Human Resources* (Third Edition). San Francisco, CA: Jossey-Bass Inc., Publishers, 1989.

CHAPTER 2

Establishing a Sound Foundation for Global Consulting

Angus Reynolds
Leonard Nadler

Optimum application of HRD knowledge and skills in a modern organization calls for the simultaneous deployment or use of various specialties and roles. All contemporary analyses of the HRD function include the consulting role. Nadler and Nadler (1989) distinguish the three major roles: learning specialist, HRD manager, and consultant, shown in Figure 2.1 (also, see Chapter 1 of this book). Epstein (1976) includes learning specialist, program manager, training administrator, and consultant. Bennis (1966) identifies three roles for a change agent: training, consulting, and applied research. Lawrence and Lorch (1969) suggest a three-fold role for the organization development specialist: educator, diagnostician, and consultant. Lippitt (1979) describes the training and development department of an organization as including four major roles: learning specialist, administrator, information coordinator, and internal consultant to management.

The work of an internal consultant in an organization differs in many respects from an external consultant. However, in the context of a developmental or change-oriented relationship with a client, the work of both has many aspects and processes in common, whether the client is an individual, manager, group, department, or whole organization. Writers differ in their terminology for the process steps and in the models or conceptual frameworks they use.

Figure 2.1: Roles of the human resource developer

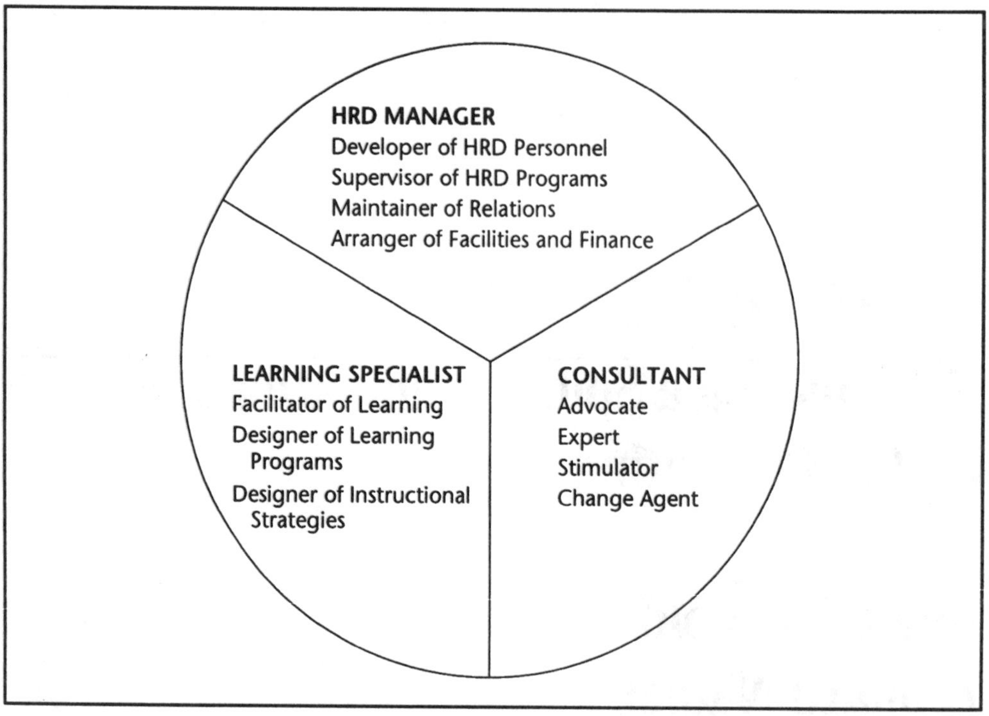

HRD MANAGER
Developer of HRD Personnel
Supervisor of HRD Programs
Maintainer of Relations
Arranger of Facilities and Finance

LEARNING SPECIALIST
Facilitator of Learning
Designer of Learning
   Programs
Designer of Instructional
   Strategies

CONSULTANT
Advocate
Expert
Stimulator
Change Agent

This chapter will synthesize the complete process into a simple, useful framework of logical and practical steps. While models reflect distinct phases, in reality these distinctions are less precise, with much overlap and fusion. The sequence, emphasis, and appropriateness of each step vary from situation to situation. To succeed as a global consultant, one obviously must be flexible and able to adapt.

Global Consulting

Consultation is a two-way process aimed at aiding and helping a person, group, organization, or larger social system in mobilizing internal and external resources to deal with problem confrontations and change efforts (Lippitt and Lippitt, 1978). The values, intentions, and behaviors of consultative interaction differ from those of management, supervision, and evaluation, as well as from those of therapy and friendship. It's true that many people, especially in the contemporary context of change, necessarily use consultative postures and interaction. These are valid in carrying out some functions of their primary roles as managers, administrators, supervisors, counselors, and staff specialists, but this book does not focus on such informal behavior. Our interest here is in formal, professional consultation.

Bell and Nadler (1979) tell us that consulting is the provision of information or help by a professional helper (consultant) to a help-needing person or system (client) in the context of a voluntary temporary relationship that is mutually advantageous (see additional information in the Global HRD Glossary in Chapter 1).

Because of competence, experience, status, regulation, or a combination of these, the client views the consultant as capable of providing needed information, support, or help. The consultant is always external to the client system; i.e., the unit, group, or person seeking help. However, the consultant may be internal to the larger organization in which the client is an employee. Therefore, sometimes the consultant is a physical outsider but always a psychological outsider. The power of the internal organizational consultant, while influenced by the political or structural focus of the professional group or unit, is determined primarily by earned influence:

- Competence
- Ideas
- Acceptance
- One's role

There are many different types of consultant, varying types of relevant behavior, and diverse expectations. For example, the client of a consulting financial expert, engineer, or medical specialist expects an educated opinion on or direct answer to the problem at hand. However, in the global HRD area the consultant is nearly always in a helping relationship. Consultants function to release the potential of the client with whom they are working. Their emphasis is on how to

- Generate and use resources
- Establish collaborative efforts
- Solve problems

What Schein calls process consultation is included in one particular dimension of this approach. It is a set of activities by the consultant that help the client to perceive, understand, and act upon process events in the client's environment (Schein, 1969). However, we will not address process consultation.

The global consultant must achieve the same results as a domestic consultant. The overall process, the general relationships are the same, and so should be the results. The important difference is that a global consultant will always operate in a more complex setting. In this chapter we will describe these overall conditions so you can appreciate consultation. The remaining chapters also will explore many of these significant differences.

Consultant Roles

The designation "consultant" describes a range of behaviors. Consultants behave in several roles depending on the needs of the client, situation, and the helper's own style and expertise. Arguing that the human-resource consultant must be flexible and mobile, Nadler and Nadler (1989) distinguish between the resource person and the facilitator. The client expects that in the former role, as advocate or expert, the consultant will provide specific, definite responses to identified problems. In the latter role, the consultant acts proactively as stimulator or change agent in identifying goals and strategies for change, development, and learning (see Figure 2.2).

The rationale for this distinction is that the only learning that importantly influences behavior is self-learning. Therefore, the consultant sometimes operates best as facilitator of discovery rather than dispenser of information.

These competencies may be deployed in a directive or nondirective mode, depending on necessity and desired goals. In the more directive mode, the consultant assumes leadership and directs the activity. In the non-directive mode, the consultant provides data as a resource or guide for the client's self-started problem solving.

The Consulting Process

There are many ways of perceiving the consulting process. Most writers agree there is entry, some type of diagnosis, some response or action, and lastly, ending of the consultation. Most agree there is a defined beginning and a defined end. Bell and Nadler (1979) view the consulting process as having five phases: entry, diagnosis, response, disengagement, closure. Lippitt and Lippitt (1978) identify six major phases in a consultant-client working relationship: first contact or entry; formulating a contract and establishing a helping relationship; problem identification and diagnostic analysis; setting goals and planning for action; taking action and cycling feedback; contract completion, continuity support and termination. The remainder of this chapter follows the Bell and Nadler five-step framework of the consulting process.

Entry

Initial contact
Any developmental relationship has a starting point that can significantly influence the later interactions. In the global context, you may receive a phone call from a department head seeking advice. You may have a chance conversation with a manager in a social setting that develops into a mutual exchange of views on a work problem. You may visit another country on other business, or attend a conference. The process may start with any inquiry after you publish an article or book, or with attendance at a course or seminar you conducted. Obviously, you may also conduct a well-planned, thorough marketing campaign.

Figure 2.2: Sub-roles of the HRD consultant

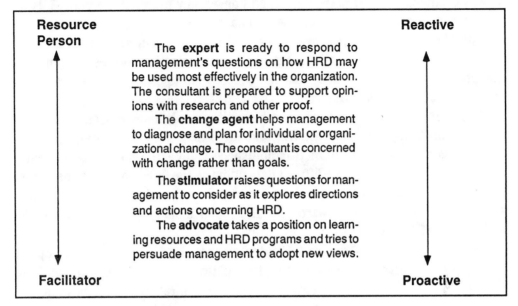

There are three principal modes of initial contact:

- The client looks for a consultant
- The consultant looks for a client
- The chance meeting

The intentions, attitudes, perceptions, and quality of interaction between the parties during early contact can lead to positive or negative orientations later in the relationship. Physical and psychological contact and entry of one person into the life-space of another is normally an event with unique implications. In the global setting this is even more complex. Among the crucial issues in any potential relationship are such factors as territoriality and dissonance associated with a fear of the unknown. Early contact and entry together create a more general problem: the attachment of a new person to an existing system. By whatever means, you have identified and established contact and at least a minimal relationship with the potential client.

Formal entry

Your first essential task is to establish awareness and perception of your competence, reliability, and usefulness in the current situation or problem in the workplace. Basically, this calls for building trust and confidence. It is a two-way process in which you mutually explore the potential for working together. You also explore the readiness for and commitment to change and learning within the client system.

Your aim is to gain the client's temporary attention and acceptance—that is, to achieve psychological entry with the client by showing and convincing the client that you have something positive and necessary to offer. You may do this by citing your specialized knowledge or skills, insight, expertise, and successful experience. The impact communicated by personality, and nonverbally between the parties, is an important dimension at this stage. A perfect balance between competence and trust is desirable. For example, your overconcern with proving your knowledge and skill can so threaten the proposed client that mistrust and rejection may result. Managing this process comes more readily to some people than to others, but everyone can improve through conscious effort.

The client is normally concerned with simultaneously improving organizational results, enhancing individual growth, and increasing personal power. This is a complex agenda for any consultant to handle successfully at the entry stage. The entry problem becomes more or less difficult depending on the fit between the consultant and the client systems. Factors include: perceived need, assignment of values, role expectation, resource and reward allocation, and feelings about the control of dependency (Glidewell, 1979).

You will have achieved successful "entry" when there is a readiness to accept, or at least explore, further the possibility and usefulness of your services. You seek here to develop an active work relationship through mutual role exploration, value and stereotype testing, and norm and expectation setting. This establishes trust and confidence as the basis for your later co-partnership and mutual influence. Simply put, you must agree to explore the situation before you can determine whether there will be a consultation. The expected result of the entry stage is agreement to go on to diagnosis of the problem and situation.

Diagnosis

Initial diagnosis

Many unsuccessful work assignments are caused by ignoring this important stage. In practice, exploring or diagnosing the feasibility of the work or project may sometimes be an inherent part of "entry."

Whether a task is feasible depends on many variables, including:

- Constraints of time and money
- Usefulness of the proposed task to a wider, more long-term goal (whether of the client or consultant)
- Degree of cooperation
- Both the need and readiness for change
- Learning and development
- Commitment and motivation of personnel who will be involved during the relationship

Tentative entry into a working relationship includes exploration of these and other issues. Schein (1969) identifies four main issues for the consultant at this stage:

- Feelings of identification with the new client and client system
- Needs regarding acceptance, not only by the client system as a whole, but by individuals and groups
- The control and influence the consultant may be able to exert through the relationship
- Whether the goals and needs of the client and individual groups will allow for satisfaction of own needs–emotional, intellectual, or otherwise

Throughout the "feasibility" stage, security within the client system will be an important issue for the consultant. (This also should be relevant as the "entry" stage.) It is not uncommon that the client with a high degree of self-assurance and certainty about the current systems, structures, knowledge, skills, relationships, and problems adopts aggressively negative postures. The client may show a low degree of readiness to change.

On the other hand, too low a degree of security may indicate excessive dependency needs. A level of reasonable security results in the client being open to exploration of alternatives and acceptance of feedback and new data. Also, there is usually a general readiness to listen, reflect, and experiment. Important forces affecting the client's security include: the status of the individual client within the organization, motivation to achieve, understanding of technical and economic "constraints" operating in the situation, and tolerance of ambiguity. These and other factors will influence the complete conclusions and feelings the consultant brings to bear on the diagnosis.

Initial diagnosis at this stage eases exploration of the situation and the various implications of proceeding with the project or work. It also helps to build trust between the parties and can stimulate a readiness for change, learning, and development from the client. The "feasibility" stage is best used to establish early awareness and growth in the client and influencing the client to feel responsible for ensuring a successful result. Change really starts at this early stage, not after it. Lastly, some valid, objective data are collected, commitment is tested and built, and decisions are made that lead to the formulation of a contract.

Contract for full diagnosis
Eventually, the period of mutual acquaintance, testing, and early factual exploration and feedback is finished. The parties enter the stage of more formal agreement on the precise nature of the assignment and the explicit stages and procedures to the completed. Among the areas for negotiated agreement are

- Targets and objectives
- Desired outcomes of the proposed work in terms of behavior change, interpersonal skills, knowledge

- Resources to be deployed
- Time frame
- Individual roles with responsibilities and accountability

Either party may draft the contract. Often, large organizations have standard contracting documents and procedures. They may cover the economic and administrative aspects of professional services. More important—and often not clarified—is the psychological dimension of human commitment and responsibility. This is related to mutual understanding and trust, with established rapport, loyalty, and credibility. At least some elements of the psychological contract should be committed to records to establish an atmosphere of security and predictability. This provides a means of evaluating later performance and success.

In the global setting there is a diverse range of contracting practices. There are also differences in reaching the point of contract, the importance associated with the contract, and the personal (psychological) component. Sometimes the personal contract may be all-important. In other cases, the letter of the document rules. Differences always reflect the society and culture of the host country. Part of your job as a global consultant is to know which combinations of factors is in effect.

Diagnosis and feedback

In some cases, this activity may be a part, or even all, of the response phase. At the end of the diagnosis the consultant typically can present the client with a variety of choices that the client will have helped to generate. During the diagnostic stage, the goal is to explore the situation in detail, assess through objective, and obtain valid information and data. The diagnosis should not be a one-way process. Actively involve the client in the diagnosis, so that while working with you on the problem the client gradually becomes sensitive to and aware of the total situation. The goal is that ultimately your client will assume "ownership" of the problem and its solution.

Also, when possible, those who will be involved in the implementation of change or who will be effected by it should be part of the diagnostic activity. Participating in the diagnosis creates an increased awareness of what is wrong. In turn, this can lead to steps to change the situation.

Beware of the situation in which the client has ostensibly performed a diagnosis and is ready to draw up a fulfillment contract. If you initially accept the client's diagnosis, you must accept the results of your change in efforts. All too often a misdiagnosis produces HRD activities that cannot solve the underlying problems(s). You must accept all blame for such failure. (You'll get the blame anyway.)

There are six interrelated goals of diagnosis (Furr, 1979):

- To produce learning and change itself
- To assess the variables relevant to the overall goal
- To create an expanded awareness and growth in the client

- To create in the client a personal value from the relationship separate from objective organizational purpose
- To energize momentum towards learning and change
- To focus the client's attention on the variables necessary to facilitate learning and change, and achieve the goal

At the feedback stage, you should present the data in a lucid, understandable form, preferably with some quantification if possible. The data should help in reaching objective interpretation and deducing possible courses of action. However, in the early stages, it is important that feedback be non-directive and non-evaluative. As the project moves nearer the actual implementation of actions, or remedial steps, more direct feedback is appropriate.

Contracting for action
Often, this may be covered during the early contract phase. In this case, after the diagnosis it may be wise to review and clarify the contract's terms and conditions–particularly those of a psychological nature. These include issues of authority and power that may have become better defined during the diagnosis phase. For example: Who will have access to the data? Who will have responsibility for implementation? Experience shows that internal consultants working within organizations tend to overlook the importance of these matters. They risk an increase of misunderstanding, doubt, and intensity of issues at a later stage. This phase merges closely with the following one–response.

Response

Action planning
It is precisely at this stage that the unique nature of the global HRD consultant-client relationship can be seen most clearly. Here are the important steps:

- Begin a process of joint planning for implementing of actions and changes based on the various diagnoses and information available from the data-collection stages. One of your prime responsibilities is ensuring the greatest likelihood that the actions will be successful instead of abortive. A good approach is to plan for small successes on a step-by-step path of action. By this point, your client has become the "owner" of the problem, and you should gradually adopt client-centered style. For example: suggesting, probing, clarifying, and reflecting instead of identifying, proposing, recommending, and prescribing. Elements of this later style may be necessary until the very end. However, the more successful and developmental the relationship, the less you will need to use the more directive support styles.

- Consider the data for possible alternative solutions and future change and behavior (of individuals, groups, and the overall organization, as appropriate).

- Set precise aims and choose specific actions to work towards these objectives. You are now ready to make specific, remedial, action-oriented decisions.

- Determine the necessary resources (time, people, materials, etc.) for implementing the decisions.

- Agree upon specific criteria by which the success of the action will be gauged and evaluated.

- Evaluate commitment to the whole project and implementation of plans.

To sum up, this stage implies concerted joint, but client-centered efforts to define specific changes to be undertaken and allocation of the needed resources. At this point, recontracting may be necessary: to reclarify roles, responsibilities, authority, and commitment.

Though often overlooked at this stage, plans for the withdrawal of, or later relationship with, the consultant should be an integral part of action planning.

Lastly, during the action-planning stages (and throughout the whole consulting process) you should be concerned with the need to gauge interventions at the proper level. Harrison (1979) makes two relevant suggestions:
- Intervene at a level no deeper than needed to produce enduring solutions to the problems at hand.
- Intervene at a level no deeper than that at which the energy and resources of the client can be committed to problem solving and change.

Implementation

This is the core "action" stage of the whole consulting process—the actual doing or effecting of the jointly agreed and planned activities or changes. Obviously, the specific action can be anything that has been the subject of this project. The payoff is in the successful taking of action. The continuity of the long-term gains after the first bursts of energy and effort is crucial. Experience has shown that close monitoring of the action and changes are essential, with a continuing supportive relationship and feedback about progress.

Counseling and advice, even occasional direction, may be required to reduce anxiety and tension as new learning happens and client behavior changes. Doubt, new experiences, and ongoing difficulties are an inherent part of the change process. During implementation of changes, joint monitoring of developments by consultant and client may lead to revisions in the original action plans. Revising action and mobilizing added resources are often necessary to ensure goal achievement and best results.

Disengagement

Withdrawal
Withdrawal from the consulting relationship is often a difficult task, especially when you have been working within your own organization. The aim of the whole process is to help the client become an autonomous, self-directing agent of the new situation or ongoing processes within the organizational environment. The more this was achieved, the greater will have been your effectiveness, and the smoother the withdrawal stage.

Evaluation
Evaluation is too often omitted from global HRD projects, because the client may be reluctant to pay for evaluation activities. Nevertheless, evaluation of results and effectiveness of the work can help to ensure that the project and changes have been implemented adequately. Evaluation also allows you to check your own performance, the effectiveness of the diagnosis and planning, and the techniques and methods used. Finally, evaluation can demonstrate results that can lead to future work for you.

You should discuss the criteria and overall goals for evaluation during earlier stages of the consulting process. For example, determine evaluation plans in the contract-setting stage.

When standards and criteria are established and agreed upon at an early stage, the most successful evaluation results. When you conduct the evaluation jointly, it can lead to further learning by the client. Among the areas for review in any evaluation are the client-consultant relationship itself, specific consulting and HRD activities undertaken, and progress towards specific goals.

Closure

Closure implies that the client is now to continue independently, or there is an explicit decision between the client and you to stop or you might agree to continue the relationship in a different manner. An example is a phasing-out relationship over time to gradually increase the client's autonomy and control over later activities.

To ensure the best long-term change and development, you and the client must establish a plan for follow-up support and continuity of change efforts. Provision for gradual ending in this fashion is a significant test of your competence and professional quality as a consultant. Every consultation relationship must have some agreed plan for a healthy, mutually satisfying termination of the working relationship.

Prepare for Global Consulting

We wish all consultants and would-be consultants success in their chosen areas. The global arena is incredibly complex, diverse, and satisfying. You might ask, "In which aspect of HRD is the consultant-client relationship more critical?" We would answer without hesitation: in the global arena.

Your aim in all global consulting activities should be to help the client explore the situation and problems. You should become aware of and sensitive to the various casual factors and issues affecting the situation. You must prepare to adopt varying styles, postures, and competencies to enable the client to become "owner" of the problem and situation—that is, to gradually assume responsibilities for diagnosis, action planning, and implementation of remedial or change-directed activities. An overall client-centered (nondirective), developmental relationship leads to ultimate withdrawal once the client has become autonomous and self-regulating.

Even in technical projects, you must be attentive to the "process" as well as to the "content" of the problem or situation. Where appropriate, give material support in resources, information, direction, systems, and HRD activities.

It is crucial in global consulting for you to be able to

- Empathize with the client
- Perceive the problem or situation
- View and assess from varying alternative stances and perspectives

What's needed is "unobtrusive constant attention," the capability for self-appraisal, self-possession, and self-use without the loss of one's identity, emotionality, or competence.

Remember, you operate in a socio-technical-economic system. Therefore, a purely mechanistic, clinical relationship is both inappropriate and counter-productive. Likewise, you must avoid loss of self to the client, and loss of perceptiveness, control or objectivity through over-identification or over-empathizing. Try to maintain an optimum balance between involvement and detachment. You should constantly reappraise your own behavior, skills, and motives in a client-centered, but self-restraining posture.

Finally, the five phases just outlined are for your convenience in understanding the process. Adapt them in a flexible, dynamic manner. In some consultant/client interactions not all phases will necessarily be completed. Likewise, the sequence may vary and sometimes a particular stage, for example "contracting" or "diagnosing," may recur during the overall relationship.

References

Argyris, C. *Intervention Theory and Method: A Behavior Science View*. Reading, MA: Addison-Wesley, 1970, *page* 379.

Bell, C., and Nadler, L. *The Client-Consultant Handbook*, Houston, TX: Gulf Publishing, 1979.

Bennis, W. *Changing Organizations*. New York, NY: McGraw-Hill, 1966.

Blake, R.R., and Mouton, J.S. *Consultation*. Reading, MA: Addison Wesley, 1976. p. 484.

Epstein, J. *The Employee Development Specialist Curriculum Plan*. Washington, DC: Bureau of Training, U.S. Civil Service Commission, 1976.

Furr, R.T. "Serving as a Messenger: The Client-Consultant Relationship During Diagnosis". In *The Client-Consultant Handbook*, Bell, C., and Nadler, L. (Eds.). Houston, TX: Gulf Publishing, 1979.

Glidewell, J. "The Entry Problem in Consultation". In the *Client-Consultant Handbook*, Bell, C., and Nadler, L. (Eds.). Houston, TX: Gulf Publishing, 1979.

Harrison, R. "Choosing the Depth of Organization Intervention". In *The Client-Consultant Handbook*, Bell, C., and Nadler, L. (Eds.). Houston, TX: Gulf Publishing, 1979.

Lawrence, P., and Lorch, J. *Developing Organizations: Diagnosis and Action*. Reading, MA: Addison-Wesley, 1969.

Lippitt, G., and Lippitt, R. *The Consulting Process in Action*. La Jolla, CA: University Associates, 1978.

Lippitt, G. "The Trainer's Role as an Internal Consultant". In *The Client-Consultant Handbook*, Bell, C., and Nadler, L. (Eds.) Houston, TX: Gulf Publishing, 1979.

Nadler, L., and Nadler, Z. *Developing Human Resources*, (Third Edition). San Francisco, CA: Jossey-Bass Inc., Publishers, 1989.

Schein, E. *Process Consultation: Its Role in Organizational Development*. Reading, MA: Addison-Wesley, 1969.

CHAPTER 3
Working Internationally

Angus Reynolds
Leonard Nadler

"Live long and prosper!" So says the nonhuman, Vulcan Mr. Spock of the starship *Enterprise*. We can imagine a business person who sees someone with very long pointed ears, coming out of a spaceship. We think that business person would realize that this person is different, that effort must be expended to understand it, and that dealings with it must be undertaken carefully.

Unfortunately, otherwise sophisticated domestic business people often fail to take this approach in a global setting. Once they find they can communicate, they are too quick to fall back on the old law, "We are all the same." The worst thing about such naiveté is that people don't know they have it. Angus was very disappointed several years ago when he saw one of his international HRD articles published in a magazine. The article pointed out how there could be many different learning situations for a single project involving two different countries. He went on to describe how people differ in different cultures and the care that must be taken for any global project. But the magazine editor included another article in the same issue that took the "everyone is the same" approach. Each author in this book knows better. It is true that we all belong to the same species—but we are *very* different. These differences are sustained in the ways we undertake business, government, and just living. The worst thing about naiveté is that people don't know they have it.

This is a challenge that one must accept when deciding to enter the global HRD arena. One must understand that there is an increase in complexity that must be mastered. That increase is not arithmetic (such as 5+5=10), but logarithmic (such as 5 x 5=25). You should be aware of the level of effort needed to manage this problem. It can be done—many people around the world manage this problem quite well.

The problem has several components. There are those who are totally naive and simply blunder. There are those who understand that something must be learned, but learn too little and blunder. The problem is so complex that even quite experienced people make or almost make mistakes in a new situation.

Despite the problem, working with diverse people in varied situations around the world should be fun. If it isn't, you may be considering the wrong field.

Overcome Naiveté

Naiveté as stupidity

Angus recently had the unhappy experience of visiting a New York hospital emergency room. A notice was posted prominently on the door in two languages. In English the sign proclaimed: "If you have a febrile rash illness, please do not enter."

This sign would communicate to a reader who knows the word "febrile," which means "marked by fever" or "feverish." We estimate that this word is at the graduate school level. Why not just say fever? Clearly, the sign was written for the doctors—not the patients.

Angus does not claim to know Spanish but he could decide what the Spanish version announced. It said:

"Si usted tiene ronch acompanada con fievre o tiene alguna enfermeda contadina: por favor no entre."

Angus decided that the Spanish version meant something like: "If you have a rash accompanied with fever or contagious sickness, please do not enter." We think it is interesting that the Spanish version is clear and written at a level that communicates just what is needed to the people who were likely to read it. Evidently, the Spanish translator was not as dumb as the person who wrote the English notice.

You don't have to leave your own backyard to see people who don't understand their target population. Our hospital notice example shows how people can be totally insensitive to their customers. How much more complex will the situation be when your topic is totally unknown to the target population? Now put your population thousands of kilometers away. Possibly remove the ready availability of competent translators. Make it a new product, system, or technique—one that is not well established, even in the home country. Can you expect to succeed with the same level of execution as the New York hospital? We doubt it, and we believe that if you are reading this book, you already know better.

Global naiveté

One case in point is Japan. The Japanese culture is fascinating to most Americans. They often admire the Japanese and the more superficial the contact, the likelier they are to decide that "they are the same as we are." What is probably unconsciously meant is: "I'm a nice person. I'm likable. These people are nice and I like them. We must be the same as each other (I'm willing to overlook any differences that might exist)."

We both have lived and worked in Japan. We both admired the country, the culture, and the people, and we learned something of the language. Still, we agree with Hiroshi Wagatsuma, the author of *Nihon-jin to America-jin Koko ga Dai Chigai,* a very popular book in Japan. Its title might be translated freely as "Japanese and Americans Are Completely Different!" There is no crime in saying, "We are all different!" It may not sound as pleasant as "We are all the same," but it is far more accurate.

Accept the Challenge

Are you ready to find out what it takes to succeed? We assume you are competent in your field. There is no country in the world where you can succeed with incompetence. We know of many cases where people on projects were sent home, even after they had been brought to another country at great expense. Perhaps there were more that should have been. Everyone should know their strengths, weaknesses, and limitations, and we should all try to apply our strengths to situations within our limits.

Introduction to SUCCESS

Just how complex is work involving only two countries? Situations involving human beings are often hard to quantify, but some people appreciate finite numbers. Let's look at just how complex such a case might be. Several models have tried to explain the complexity of international HRD, among them Skinner (1964), Reynolds (1979), and Schnapper (1980). None of which seemed adequate to the task. However, the SUCCESS model (Reynolds, 1984) does approximate the complexity of global HRD for situations involving two countries. It is not a linear or system model, but taxonomical, based on the five concepts of people, global programs, HRD activities, time, and human concern. The first three concepts are viewed in three dimensions. These are then viewed over time, the fourth dimension. The fifth element, human concern, is assumed to be omnipresent.

The usefulness of complex models often depends on the ability to visualize them. The SUCCESS model is presented graphically in a form similar to Guilford's classic Structure of the Intellect model (Guilford, 1959), which is a cube made up of smaller cubes, looking like a more complex version of the popular Rubik's Cube ™ toy. In SUCCESS, each of the small cubes is called a "cell" and each cell is defined by the combination of the first three concepts: people, global programs, and HRD activities.

A Realization of global HRD's complexity

Each of the concepts is broken down further. The people component is called "human," and includes hosts, expatriates, and nonemployees. The global programs component is called "content," and comprises area, expertise, and culture. The HRD activities component is called "content," and includes training, education, and development. This component was originally based on Nadler (1980), but is completely consistent with Nadler and Nadler (1989) and the descriptions given in the first chapter of this book. The HRD activity is the focus of the SUCCESS model. The result is a 3 x 3 x 3 cell cube with exactly the same appearance as a Rubik's Cube™. There are 91 cells as shown in Figure 3.1.

Figure 3.1: Global HRD at a Single Point in Time

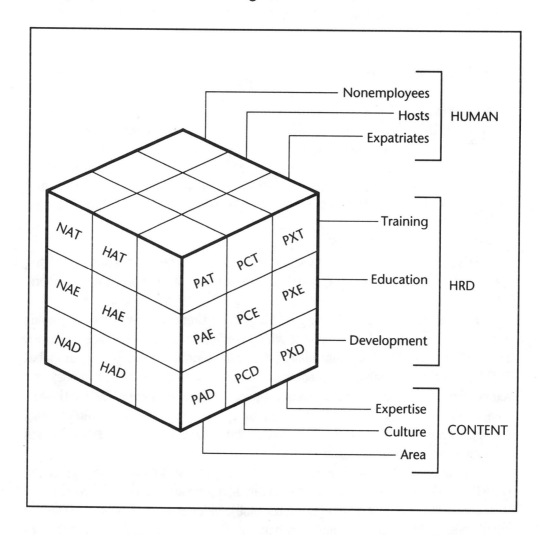

Source: *Training and Development Journal*, June 1981. Used with permission.

Each cell represents a possible global HRD situation involving two countries. At a point in time, global HRD in each of the 91 cells could represent the content of the global HRD project. Remember that time is also a consideration. The components of time are before, during, and after. These represent the periods in the relationship before the expatriates arrive in the host country, during the stay, and after departure. This creates 273 (3 x 91) possibilities for this particular project. Imagine the possibilities with people from third countries and with truly multinational projects.

To be honest we do not believe there *are* 273 possibilities on every given project. There must be many more than that! One purpose of the model is to serve as a descriptive analog of reality. However, its prime purpose is to shock the reader into a perception of the potential level of complexity that must be mastered. It can be used prescriptively, by determining the "active" cell for a given employee and project. Then identify the

- Affected person as host, expatriate, or nonemployee
- Expertise required, characteristics of the pertinent area, and the culture of the host country
- HRD activities as training, education, or development
- Time as before the expatriates arrive in the host country, during the stay, or after departure

The result is, in effect, the identity of the applicable cell. With this information you can make appropriate inquiry and preparation in each of the components identified.

People who care about people

What, then, separates the successful experienced global consultant and practitioner from those who fail? In part, it is the SUCCESS model's fifth dimension—human concern. Human concern is the "glue" that holds the whole encounter together. Some global projects may work based on simple mutual self-interest or commercial benefits. To persist, HRD projects and the HRD component of commercial projects must evidence human concern. If it exists, it will be evident without any effort to show it off. If it is lacking, no pretense will be an adequate substitute.

The other part of human concern drives good HRD consultants and practitioners to make sure they understand the dimensional components of the project's cell(s). Many experienced and successful global HRD consultants and practitioners have never heard of the SUCCESS model. That is because it was created to describe the considerations that they already recognize. Successful international people simply go about their business making sure that they know all they can about the components of their program or project.

Joi de Vivre

Birds of a feather flock together

The petty jealousies and rivalries that exist in any other endeavor also plague the global scene. However, we have found that "international people" seem to enjoy each other's company. We think that international people are more fun! Could this be related to the human concern that successful clients and practitioners seem to incorporate into their work? We think that when people who have this trait in common come together they are likelier to get along.

The other side of the mountain

Some people don't want to leave their emotional village. They aren't interested in what's on the other side of the mountain. We know an HRD professional who said frankly that he wasn't interested in international work. Much to his credit, he put his money where his mouth was — he didn't attempt to do any. We have also seen people who *were* overseas but who really didn't want to be. It wasn't a pretty sight.

Somewhere between these two extremes are those who are overseas, but shouldn't be. They find that they don't like the culture, customs, architecture, music, food, handicrafts, or anything about the place where they are. We have never seen a successful global HRD practitioner or consultant who didn't actively develop an interest in one or more of these. We would suggest that if that seems impossible, it is best to go home.

If it tastes like chicken, should you avoid it?

Irma Bombeck is often fun to read. Part of her humorous advice is that: Beware of food that is described as "Some Americans say it tastes like chicken" should be printed on the passports of the gastronomically timid. It is hard to disagree with the advice considering that she limited it to the timid. However, you can carry your caution too far. Would you miss out on grilled eel at the Japanese summer "lover's festival"? Would you want to miss the duck's feet soup with fried morning glories in the shade of the Wat Arun in Bangkok? Would you try the "dancing sushi" in Taipei?

If you apply similar caution to opportunities to know the host country people and their culture better you will miss much that could help both your personal development and your business development. Worse, if you have limited understanding of the host country, no matter how successful you are, you will never know what might have been had you taken the time and effort to know more.

This whole book tells you the what, when, where, who, why, and how to go overseas. In this chapter, we leave it to the title of Irma Bombeck's recent book to provide some interesting and sage-sounding advice for the would-be global person. It is *When You Look Like Your Passport Photo, It's Time to Go Home*.

References

Bombeck, I. *When You Look Like Your Passport Photo, It's Time to Go Home*. New York, NY: Harper-Collins, 1991.

Guilford, J. "The Three Faces of Intellect." *American Psychologist* ,14, (1959), p. 469.

Nadler, L. *Corporate Human Resources Development*. New York, NY: Van Nostrand Reinhold, 1980.

Nadler, L., and Nadler, Z. *Developing Human Resources* (Third Edition). San Francisco, CA: Jossey-Bass Inc., Publishers, 1989.

Reynolds, A. *The Intercultural Impact of Multinational Organizations in Latin America*. Presentation with another scholar at Society for Intercultural Education Training and Research conference, Mexico City, 1979.

Reynolds, A. "SUCCESS in International HRD". In *Technology Transfer: A Project Guide for International HRD*. Reynolds, A. (Ed.). Boston, MA: International Human Resource Development Corporation, 1984.

Schnapper, M. *International Training*. Presentation at Interagency Roundtable for Area Studies and Intercultural Training, Washington, DC: May, 1980.

Skinner, C. "Management of International Production". *Harvard Business Review*, Sept.- Oct. 1964, p. 132.

Wagatsuma, H. *Nihon-jin to America-jin Koko ga Dai Chigai*. Tokyo: Nesco Books, 1985.

CHAPTER 4
Preparing Yourself for Work Overseas

L. Robert Kohls

As the chapter title suggests preparation is necessary for an overseas position. No matter how successful you have been in the United States, everyone needs to be prepared to live and work productively in a foreign country. In fact, if, in the country where you have been assigned, you continue to do everything that has made you so successful in the United States, in exactly the same way, you will most likely fail in your new country. What defines success in each country is completely different. It is essential to adapt to your new country's ways of doing business if you are also to succeed there.

Although this chapter focuses on what you can do to prepare yourself for your foreign assignment, it does not absolve your employer from the responsibility of at least sending you and your spouse for a week of predeparture training aimed at your specific country of assignment and providing you with ongoing language training.

However, the ultimate responsibility for becoming knowledgeable about your new home (which hereafter will be referred to as your "host country") is yours, both before you go and after you arrive. You and your spouse should begin by checking out every major library in whatever city you are now living and talking personally (equipped with a set of questions you have prepared in advance) with every single person your research can turn up who is from or has worked in your host country. Tape these interviews for later relistening or take notes during the meeting for your own personal file on your host country.

It is an amazing and alarming fact that there are only eight countries in the world—the United States, England, France, Spain, Germany, Italy, China and Japan—for which there are already a sufficient number of travel books in English. So something that either you or your spouse could profitably do with your spare time while you're acclimating yourself to your host country is to write a travel guide to help other Americans also get to know it. But the main purpose for starting a personal file on your host country is to make sure you are collecting information on its every conceivable aspect. The file will also become a convenient way to collect and take with you articles you lack time to read before you go.

Professional Predeparture Training

Professional cross-cultural training is available, but you may have to insist that your corporation send both you and your spouse to receive it. Many studies show it is the spouse who is most often responsible for the couple deciding to terminate their foreign assignment early, so the spouse should always be included in predeparture cross-cultural and language training before and after arrival.

You will need facts and figures as you argue your case, because many American employers erroneously believe that whoever has done a good job back home is automatically equipped to do a repeat performance anywhere in the world. Actually, without cross-cultural training, only 20 percent of the Americans sent overseas will do well, and even they would do much better with such preparation. The normal failure rate of Americans sent to work overseas without cross-cultural training runs between 40 and 60 percent, depending on which country they are going to.

With adequate predeparture training, that failure rate can be reduced dramatically. The Business Council for International Understanding (BCIU), working with the Shell Oil Company, has figures that prove the effectiveness of cross-cultural training. Before providing any training for the employees it sent to Saudi Arabia, Shell was experiencing a 60 percent early return rate. With three days of training, that rate dropped to 5 percent. With a six-day predeparture program, the figure dropped to 1.5 percent. When this percentage is coupled with the estimated cost of bringing a mid-to-upper-level executive and his or her family home early—anywhere from $150,000 to $250,000—your boss would be a fool not to send you and your spouse for such training. If your boss needs further convincing, point out that no one can estimate the damage an early returnee might have done to your company's reputation in the host country before finally being evacuated.

Now, for the brighter side of the story. Here is a brief rundown of what predeparture training can be expected to do to prepare you for the assignment. This list first appeared in *Intercultural Training: Don't Leave Home Without It*. (Kohls, 1984).

Predeparture training can help you to:

- Prepare for the move overseas (and it is a whole different matter than merely moving within the continental United States)

- Master the logistical skills of surviving in the host country (e.g., marketing, housing, transportation, schooling for your young children, even knowing beforehand what necessary items you can buy easily in your host country and what should be taken with you)

- Communicate, verbally and nonverbally, with nationals of the host country. (Obviously, this will vary, depending on whether the predeparture program includes language training, and even if it does, one cannot learn much of the language in one or two weeks. This means you will have to continue language learning in-country.)

- Minimize your social blunders in the host country

- Make sense out of a totally different set of operative values, implicit cultural assumptions (about the way the world works, or should ideally work), as well as an unfamiliar reasoning process and system of logic

- Apply the indigenous values, cultural assumptions, reasoning process, and logic system (rather than the ones you brought with you) to interpret all that is seen and heard in the new culture

- Successfully weather the trauma of culture shock (which is very real, very debilitating, and must be dealt with). I recommend that for working your way through culture shock you also take along a copy of my book *Survival Kit for Overseas Living* (Kohls, 1984)

- Facilitate a rapid and successful adjustment of each family member to the host country, enabling them to have a positive, productive overseas experience

- Move toward becoming bicultural. Of course, one cannot become fully bicultural in a two- or three-year assignment, but you should be able to function appropriately in both cultures and to feel comfortable in doing it

- Better understand your own country—and yourself (an unexpected side benefit of cross-cultural training)

Predeparture Programs

The best predeparture programs follow a certain sequence, and many authorities such as Moran, Harris, Adler, Loewenthal, and Ferraro insist that all the individual parts and their precise order are absolutely vital to the success of any predeparture cross-cultural training.

Phase one is generally referred to as training in cross-cultural awareness. Although the points included in this initial phase may sound academic, they must be presented in a most unacademic way. To make the remaining phases effective, this first phase should familiarize the learner with such concepts as ethnocentrism, perception, stereotypes and stereotyping, the "development" concept, the "culture" concept, biculturalism, culture shock, and the adjustment cycle.

Phase two, surprisingly, makes the learner aware of our own American culture and how we have been enculturated into doing things in our own peculiar way (from other countries' points of view). To make the final phase work, this is an absolutely necessary second step and must not be eliminated or sloughed over.

After these first two phases, the learners are ready to move on to what they thought they came to get—information regarding the host country.

Where to get Cross-Cultural Training

A quarter of a century ago, if companies about to send a representative overseas thought of giving any training at all, it tended to be, "Let's send 'em to Berlitz for language classes." Or "Let's send 'em upstairs to talk to Joe. He worked there five or six years ago."

Professional cross-cultural training is essential. It is available (and has been for more than a quarter of a century). It is effective. It is readily available. Insist on receiving it.

Throughout this chapter, I have used the term "sending the employee out" for cross-cultural training. Of course, there may be someone in your own city equipped to provide such training, and this possibility should be investigated. Most major companies send their personnel for a week-long custom-designed program at one of the companies providing the bulk of cross-cultural training. *You will find several listed in Resources at the end of this chapter. I urge you to contact them for information to present to your International HRD department if it is not currently sending overseas-assigned personnel out for such training.*

Preparing Yourself

In addition to the formal cross-cultural preparation provided by your company, there is much you and your family can do to prepare yourselves.

Mental Preparation

Not even the best predeparture training program in the world can do as much to ensure you will have a rewarding overseas living/working experience as a positive, expectant attitude. Wanting to go and experience the foreign culture is the best insurance policy possible.

Mild apprehension is normal, but if either you or your spouse desperately fears, dreads, despises, or detests the idea of going to live in another country, the foreign assignment is not for you. If, on the other hand, it sounds stimulating, exciting, challenging; if you feel you are ready for a change of scenery; if you have always wanted to travel to exotic places (not only to your host country but to all the vacation spots in the larger region and every place between here and there), the foreign assignment can become the most exciting thing that has ever happened to you and your family, and the one thing that all of you will soon be saying is "the most important and influential experience of your whole life," as so many Americans before you now claim.

Although most Americans do not realize it until the foreign assignment is over and they are back home, the overseas experience also has a positive effect on your subsequent stateside work performance. It increases one's ability to "psych out" a situation where you do not know the ground rules beforehand; it develops an ability to think yourself into someone else's shoes; it develops the ability to make decisions when the situation is ambiguous, unclear, and confusing. In short, the overseas assignment provides one of the best proving grounds for taking on a more responsible job back home. Those skills you have picked up in Abu Dhabi can be just as useful back in Oshkosh!

Language Classes

Americans have never had a reputation for much facility in foreign languages. Most Americans speak no other language than English with any fluency. Until now, we have not even valued those who grew up in a bicultural home and ended up speaking English and, perhaps, Spanish with equal fluency. That is all changing very rapidly, and as you learn a foreign language on a foreign assignment, you begin to see how your own life has expanded to incorporate two worlds and the two realities they encompass.

Perhaps the singly most important thing you can begin to learn about your host country is its language. Even when you begin, and you have only a dozen useful sentences in your head or on your tongue, you will be amazed at how it will open doors in the new culture. For speaking even a few phrases says far more than the content of the sentence you have just spoken. It says, first and foremost, "I respect your culture as equal to mine." It says, too, "I'm trying to learn all about it."

As already mentioned, a one-week or two-week predeparture program can only briefly introduce the language and its sound system, let you begin to hear what the spoken language sounds like, and give you 20 or 25 of the more useful phrases. Most of your language learning will have to take place overseas. Most companies find that it is worth the cost to provide a private tutor a couple of hours per day for their overseas executives. But even if your company will not pick up the tab, you can always find an English-speaking national willing to exchange an hour of conversational English lessons for an hour of tutoring in his/her native language.

Information Preparation

Once you learn of your foreign assignment, it should become a pleasant and instructional assignment for you and/or your spouse to begin collecting information about your host country. Some of the categories listed below (e.g., Category One) will, by their very nature, have more information available in English in U.S. libraries than others (e.g., Category Two), but digging and prying out information should be equally enjoyable and valuable. You should explore the following eight areas.

Factual Background Data. This type of information is easily collected in any well-stocked city library. You will probably find it useful to prepare file folders for each of the following categories, into which you can place your notes and photocopies of articles as you collect them:

- Historical Data
- Demographic Data
- Geographic Data
- Political Data
- Economic Data
- Religious/Philosophical Data
- Social Data
- Aesthetic Data

Profile Information on the People. Although there are fewer books that include such information, it is absolutely vital. You will probably discover that "people resources" will be much better than books, once you have identified the knowledgeable and sympathetic people to use as resources.

In this category you should learn all you can about the host country's:
- Customs and Traditions (including holidays)
- Beliefs and Values
- Cultural Assumptions (about work, education, and every other aspect of life)
- Cultural Taboos
- Non verbal Communication Thought Processes
- Nonverbal Communication

Any variations of values, etc., among the various ethnic groups that make up the country should, of course, be researched as well as the mainstream culture.

Famous People and Places. Every country has its heroes and its places of historic and scenic interest. These are always a matter of great national pride. We would find it absolutely inexcusable for a foreign visitor to come to the United States and not know who George Washington or Abraham Lincoln were. It is equally inexcusable for us to go to their country and not know who the George Washingtons and the Abraham Lincolns of their country are. These heroes, of course, include contemporary officials and dignitaries as well. Of course you can, and will, learn more about them once you are there, but you ought to care enough to go with at least the basics.

Problems Currently Faced by the People of the Country. Every country, including our own, has a minimum of twenty or thirty identifiable problems faced by the country at any given time. Some may be problems of long standing, others more recent. They will cover all aspects of life—economic, political, social, developmental, and environmental. It is most important for you to collect data on the separate problems you are able to identify from their point of view (rather than from ours).

Integration Problems Faced by Americans Living in the Host Country. If you were to talk to one hundred Americans who have lived at least one continuous year in the host country, nearly all of them would give you an almost identical list of what most annoyed them about the host country. The reason is that the expatriate always carries his/her own culture to the foreign country. Most of the items on this "Integration Problems" list are not troubling for the country's nationals (unless, of course, they have spent a considerable amount of time in the United States and been influenced by American culture). Because of the consistency of these lists, you shouldn't need to interview more than three to five Americans with experience in the host country to gather or verify this information.

Indigenous Practices and Business Procedures. To some extent, international business procedures are becoming homogenized. Yet it will astound you how sometimes the simplest procedures can be done in such an endless variety of ways around the world.

There are many business practices and requirements with which the American expatriate will need to become familiar. The following random items are merely a beginning, but they are enough to indicate the complexity of the task:

- Work Force
- Natural Resources
- Major Exports
- Major Imports

- Major Trading Partners
- Transportation Systems
- Communication Systems
- Energy Systems
- Number of National Holidays
- Affiliation with International Organizations
- Recruitment Procedures
- Initial Job Assignment(s)
- Training
- Job Rotation
- Performance Evaluation
- Promotion
- Salary Criteria
- Incentive Systems
- Job Assignment and Reassignment
- Welfare
- Employee Layoffs
- Retirement
- Labor Relations/Unions
- Internal Structure of Local Corporations
- National Labor Laws
- Tariffs and Duties
- Import Quotas
- Export Commitments
- Limits on Expansion
- Price Controls
- Financing Restrictions
- Restrictions on Nationality of Management
- Foreign Ownership Limitations
- Local Sourcing Requirements
- Nationalization and Expropriation
- Local Manufacturing Requirements
- Dealing With the Bureaucracy
- Local Environmental Restrictions
- Capital Repatriation Restrictions
- Dividend Remittance Restrictions
- Abrogation of Rights of Royalties
- Restrictions on Spouse Working

Political and Economic Risk Factors. It has become common practice for corporations contemplating a business venture with a foreign company to commission a risk analysis firm to prepare a Political Risk Assessment and an Economic Risk

Assessment. Have these assessments brought up to date before taking a particular in-country assignment. Even if there are estimated to be considerable risks involved, you might still decide to accept the assignment, but you would want to know fully what you were getting into.

Terrorism and Security Factors. These factors will vary in relevancy, depending on the current political situation in your country of assignment and the surrounding countries.

If the factors are relevant, your company can obtain excellent instructional materials developed by the Foreign Service Institute of the U.S. Department of State and the U.S. Navy, since these are in the public domain.

Logistical Preparation

Even in the most modern and cosmopolitan cities around the world, there are likely to be a few items you will wish you had brought with you that you were not informed about. With careful predeparture sleuthing you will know precisely what you can easily get in-country and what you should bring with you or arrange to have sent periodically via a stateside relative or friend.

For information, try to find a couple who have recently returned from living and working in the same city you are about to depart for. Situations do change, so someone who left the host city more than a year ago may have such outdated information as to be of questionable value to you for this task. You should have your own list of questions to ask these resource people, but here are some of the obvious categories to help you start your investigation:

- Setting Up a Household In-Country
- Best Areas of the City to Live In
- Living Off the Local Economy
- Residence and Work Documents
- Housing
- Utilities
- Electric Current
- Mail
- Telephone, Faxes, Cables, etc.
- Transportation (inter-city and intra-city)
- Banking
- Insurance
- Schools
- Religious Facilities
- Health Facilities
- Currency

- Legal Holidays
- Support Systems
- Making Friends
- Establishing a Daily Routine
- Managing Servants (if applicable)
- Finding Where to Buy Necessary Items
- Exploring the Host City and its Resources
- Entertainment/Leisure Activities
- Not-to-Be-Missed Restaurants
- Making Contacts for Children
- And anything else you should know about

Preparing to Manage Culture Shock

Unless you are already a veteran at living overseas, you can count on one thing: culture shock. In one of my other writings, I have called culture shock "the occupational hazard of overseas living through which one has to be willing to go in order to have the pleasures of experiencing other countries and cultures in depth." And anyone who has had a positive overseas living experience can tell you, with full, unrestricted animation, what a "once-in-a-lifetime," "you-can't-imagine-it-until-you-have-done-it" kind of experience it is! In truth, it is well worth the temporary inconvenience of culture shock.

At the same time, culture shock should not be underestimated. For while you are in the depths of its throes, you will definitely consider it one of the worst things that has ever happened to you. However, you do not have to sit helplessly by while culture shock is being inflicted upon you. There are specifications you can take to work your way out of culture shock. They may be of little interest or use to you at the moment, but when you are in the midst of culture shock, reread this list and adopt as many of the suggestions as you can:

- By simply realizing that you are going to experience some degree of culture shock and recognizing when it happens, you can alleviate its severity. Tell yourself that it is natural, and it doesn't mean you are deficient or strange. It happens in some degree to all adults who go to live and work in a culture other than the one in which they were raised. You will survive if you accept it as a temporary inconvenience and wait it out. Thousands before you have lived through it and are all the better for the experience, for they now have learned the incredible lesson that we do not seem capable of learning in any other way: that our culture is not the single right way, nor is it even the superior way, to do things. It is merely one of thousands of equally valid ways that the world's people have invented for solving the challenge of providing our basic needs and enjoyments.

- Borrow a copy of *Survival Kit for Overseas Living* to read and reread whenever you need it as you become enculturated to your host country. It will help you begin to see things from a new perspective.
- Work hard to gather information about your host country—especially when you are in known culture shock. This is when you will feel least like doing it, but work all the harder at it during this time. Develop a structured plan and schedule to do your information gathering. Use native informants, sympathetic expatriates, and books as sources.
- Select one or, at most, two area(s) of interest and investigate them even more thoroughly than other topics. For example, if you are a football fan in the United States, do not sit around complaining because the Super Bowl game is not shown on TV in your host country. Instead, turn your interest to soccer. Learn all you can about soccer, how it compares and how it contrasts with football, what the rules are, which are the best teams (locally and internationally), and who the best players are.
- Look for the underlying logic in everything you can observe in the new culture. Many Americans are good at this. It does not matter whether you are wrong in your assumptions—you can always correct them later as you get more and better information. But you will have reinforced in your mind that these are intelligent and logical people with whom you are dealing—people worthy of respect. This, more than anything else, will help you expel the ethnocentric idea that anything that is different is, ipso facto, inferior. You will soon come to see it is only different, and from time to time you will learn to actually prefer the host culture's ways to our own.
- Try to trace every "strange" action in the host culture to its underlying value(s). An illustration in reverse, out of our own culture, will make the point. An Egyptian visitor to the United States was shocked at what he witnessed in the gift shop at Washington, D.C.'s Air and Space Museum. There, he saw a young American mother, squatting to bring herself down to the height of her six-year-old son. She said, "Now, Tommy, if you buy that model airplane now, then you're not going to have enough money to buy a Coke when your sister wants to stop and have a Coke later in the morning, and then you're going to be very unhappy." The Egyptian visitor was shocked because no Egyptian mother would ever have said such a thing to her son. In the first place, the Egyptian mother would not have given the little boy his own money to manage or have intervened to teach him how best to spend it. But he could see, from what he had learned American values to be, that it was absolutely natural for the American mother to act the way she did. He could further see that the mother and the little boy were having a very important lesson in American values. And from this enlightening observation, he could see that several American values were being reinforced, first giving Tommy his own allowance to spend, and then by advising him on how to spend it. These values were

1. Independence
2. Self-Help and Responsibility
3. Future Orientation and Planning for the Future
4. Delayed Gratification
5. Control Over the Environment

In the same way, every interaction you observe in the foreign culture can reveal that country's values—provided you are as skilled as the Egyptian visitor in analyzing what you see:

• As uncomfortable as culture shock makes you feel, force yourself to see the good things about your situation. Sit down and make a list of all the pluses of your current situation. You will be surprised to see how many are on your list. Then concentrate on the good things rather than on the bad.

• Avoid like the plague those Americans who are not adjusted to the host country and are, therefore, in a rather permanent state of culture shock. It is absolutely essential for them to spend their days with others who are equally maladjusted so they can sit around and commiserate with one another. People who are inflicted with this illness constantly need to find new people to infect with their own negative interpretation of the host culture. Consequently, they sit and wait for each incoming boatload of "Gringos" so they can pounce on them and demonstrate the many ways in which the "natives" are inferior. They have to constantly keep proving it is not they themselves who are wrong. Do whatever you have to do to get out of their way. You do not need someone else's second-hand prejudices.

• Never allow yourself to gripe and complain and make jokes about how stupid the "natives" are. It will eventually make the job of achieving a positive adjustment nearly impossible.

• Never stay around to join in a laugh as your countrymen (and women) and other foreigners make such jokes. Get out fast. It is sheer poison.

• Keep your sense of humor—especially the ability to laugh at yourself. Laughing at yourself and the silly mistakes you will inevitably make as you learn to function in a foreign culture may be the best medicine there is.

• Find another American who has already gone through the process of adjusting to this new culture and has a positive attitude toward the people of the host country. Talking your cultural adjustment problems out with such a person can be extremely helpful.

- Become acquainted with as many host nationals as you can. Get to know them as people and try to develop a deeper friendship with one or two of them. After you get to know them fairly well, you might also be able to discuss your adjustment problems with them. Certainly you can ask their advice and assistance on how to act in specific situations with which you are unfamiliar. Overseas Americans who spend all their time only with other Americans never adjust to the host country.

- In the discussions suggested in the previous two items, emphasize how the differences you are experiencing make you feel. Focus on how you are being affected rather than on the causes and, therefore, on how "wrong" the foreign ways are.

- Do not worry that, as you adjust and learn to function in your host country, you will lose the personal values you came with. Your basic values are much deeper and more permanent than that, so they probably will not change that much (at least they do not have to). You are in control of that. To function according to the customs of your host country (where that is appropriate) does not make you less of an American. It only makes you more comfortable and "at home."

- Keep busy. Keep active. Keep your mind occupied. Do not sit around and mope and feel sorry for yourself. Fill any spare time with studying the new culture, exploring your new city, or strenuous athletic activity, anything to keep busy.

- During the lowest points in your culture shock experience, travel to a neighboring country—or to a scenic spot in your host country. The diversion will be "just what the doctor ordered," and even a few days away will make you happy to get "home" again.

- As you gradually begin to work your way out of culture shock, start a program to talk about the U.S.A. to local groups. Show slides of your homeland (and maybe some commercial slides of New York City, Washington, D.C., and San Francisco). Become an "unofficial ambassador" (see Vetter, 1984) to correct some of the misinformation which _Dallas_, _Dynasty_ and _Falcon Crest_ have created in the minds of host-country nationals.

- Even at the "darkest hour"—and especially at the darkest hour—have faith that there are brighter days ahead and that you will survive culture shock— even if you do nothing but simply wait for it to pass. Time alone will bring you through.

- If your spouse has accompanied you, be concerned about his/her welfare too. Spouses are even more susceptible to culture shock because they do not have a full-time job to occupy their time and their minds. They have more free time, and if they lack the self-motivation to fill it with useful activities (like investigating the exotic foreign culture in which they find themselves), life can get mighty boring. They may long for home and the friends they left behind, until they reach the point where only going home can relieve their distress. Take the time to provide caring support to make sure that does not happen.

Special Problems Faced by Men/Women/Children Overseas

While everyone—man, woman, and child—will experience some degree of culture shock as they adjust to the foreign environment, there are also special adjustment problems facing each of the sexes and different problems which adults and children may expect.

Problems Facing Foreign Men in Adjusting to the Host Country. In the last decade of the 20th century, virtually all executives sent by American companies to represent their interests overseas are still male; therefore, this section assumes it is the male of the couple who has the work assignment and is responsible for the overseas posting. As such, he is the one most likely to receive the blame (and the guilt associated with it) if the family does not like being in that country.

He must adjust to new working conditions and a new staff. There will probably be a language problem, even if his staff speaks English and even if the country of assignment is England. As an overseas representative for his company, he is also the "man caught in the middle." He must bear the responsibility of supervising a staff whose customs and values he does not yet thoroughly understand, and he must try to communicate these differences to a home office which naively expects American-type production schedules to be met just as they would be back home.

He is likely (especially if he is inclined to be a workaholic) to concentrate too much on his work and neglect his family and their needs. He may feel the pressure to spend more quality time with his family without succeeding in doing so. This is a classic situation for developing guilt.

His wife, if she does not have an outside job of her own, may out-explore her husband and learn more and more quickly about the host country than her husband is able to do. If the couple is well adjusted, this is not problem; the wife can share her new discoveries with her spouse as she makes them. But if there is the slightest bit of jealousy or competition in the relationship, this situation may cause considerable trouble and resentment.

The unmarried male executive will encounter more problems in many foreign countries than he is likely to experience in the United States. To be unmarried much beyond the age of 30 is, in many countries, thought to be "unnatural" and, if nothing else, will probably cause the nationals to constantly ask him why he is not married. No answer, of which I am aware, has been found which will satisfy this curiosity and concern.

In America, even upper-level managers feel free to conduct their off-the-job lives in leisure clothing, perhaps working in the garden if they enjoy doing that. In many Third World countries, a high-level executive is expected to stay in that role 24 hours of every day, never "letting his hair down." This is not something an American can adjust to easily.

In some Muslim countries, of course, there are restrictions on the use of alcohol, even if you are a non-Muslim.

Problems Facing Foreign Women in Adjusting to the Host Country. Even more than in the United States, women overseas often are identified only as "the wife of so and so" or "the mother of so and so." This is not easy for the American woman to accept. Certainly, the second-class status of women in a host country will become a problem for the American woman who has lived with the hard-won achievements of the women's liberation movement. Limited as those achievements appear to be in the U.S., they seem far too liberal to be brought about in many countries where American women find themselves stationed.

If it is the wife who has the job of running the household in the foreign country, it can be either an exciting challenge or an incomprehensible nightmare. Certainly it is most often the wife who must confront the culture most directly, buying unfamiliar produce, haggling and bargaining to get a fair price, never sure at first whether she is being cheated.

If she is in a country where she is expected to have servants, this is likely to be a first-time experience for which her past experience as a housewife has not prepared her. Most egalitarian Americans find it difficult to establish the necessary sense of superiority to enable them to control most servants in countries where it is the norm to have servants. At best, they will find that having servants is a mixed blessing. They will also surely soon discover that they must develop a different, and often "unnatural," personality in order to manage servants effectively.

If the wife does not work outside the home, and particularly if she has spent the entire day unable to communicate with another adult, she may want to talk and talk once her husband arrives home. The husband may not find this to be an equally enjoyable activity, particularly if much of what she talks about is the endless number of unresolved problems that she encountered during her day.

The American woman may find herself in a culture where women are treated grossly differently from men. For example, she may be expected to go outside only when accompanied by an adult, male escort. Such restrictions on freedom of movement may make her feel that she is living in a prison.

Many American women who are pursuing a career in their own country often do not have the freedom or opportunity to continue their careers in the country of their husband's assignment. To some this is frustrating; to others it may be totally unacceptable.

Almost nowhere, other than in Western Europe, do American women feel they have the independence they generally have in the United States. Unless they are willing to temporarily exchange a degree of their freedom for the opportunities to experience exotic cultures and to travel in foreign lands they may have only been able to dream about, they will probably feel they have been asked to give up too much for the good of their husband's career.

In some cultures, if American women continue to dress as would be acceptable in the United States, their dress (or more accurately, their undress) may send signals to the males of their host country that they are "loose" women making themselves available for sexual advances.

If it is the American woman who has received the professional assignment overseas, all of the challenges that an American man in her position could be expected to encounter will likely be increased by 200 or 300 percent for her. It can be exciting to pioneer social changes of this magnitude, but unless she has been realistically prepared for what the situation will be like, she is likely to discover much too late that it is worse than she had imagined.

The solution for the spouse who is not expected to work outside the home is to completely throw herself into uncovering the new culture, but this is possible only if she can conceive it as the opportunity of a lifetime. And only if she has the full support of an understanding husband who is not too stressed out by the challenges of his own job and the foreign environment to give her the time and attention she needs.

Problems Facing American Children in Adjusting to the Host Country. American children who spend most of their adolescent years in foreign countries, as the offspring of businessmen, foreign-service officers, missionaries, or military personnel, invariably share a common experience. They end up not knowing where "home" is. They are American, yet America does not feel like their home since they have only been there on furlough. They do not know where their roots are.

Of course, most of them are quick to add that the advantages of this "rootless" existence far outweigh the disadvantages. They are truly citizens of the world—much more cosmopolitan and aware than most of the American young people who have never left the United States. Most of them become more introverted than they might have been if they had stayed home: introverted and introspective, philosophical, and profound, extremely "serious" people with high values and high ethical standards.

The "short termer," the child who shares his/her parents' two–or three-year assignment overseas, also absorbs a few of these same attributes. And, almost without exception, he or she will, after the experience is long past, be heard to say, "Living overseas was the best, most influential experience of my life. It changed my whole life for the better. I wouldn't trade that experience for anything!" In fact, if you as a parent had any inkling of what a positive effect your foreign assignment would likely have on your son's or daughter's life, you probably would grab the next overseas assignment you could get your hands on.

Yet the least likely member of your family to want to go overseas is your teenage son or daughter. It is not easy for them to leave their high school and their friends. They will resist it to the end, and in the end, will only agree to go under coercion and duress. If, like many American children, they have been raised to believe that America is the best country in the world, and especially if they have been raised in an extremely affluent America, they won't want to throw all that aside to go to "some Third World country," or even, for that matter, to Western Europe.

Whatever foreign-based school you decide to enroll them in, it will probably be extremely competitive and they will have to work a whole lot harder to keep up than they do in the average American public school. They may run into more frequent and more difficult tests, more rote memorization, harsher discipline, and even the expectation that they are to show more respect for their teachers. Their education will undoubtedly be more advanced and less creative.

So many things about the foreign environment seem so terribly "unAmerican." People walk more, or use more public transportation; many countries may have only one or two TV stations, that may only broadcast for a few hours every evening; they are surely not likely to be able to watch their favorite TV shows or to play their favorite video games; they can count on not knowing, for the next two or three years, what the latest hit songs and movies are. From their point of view, the next few years are going to be "mighty grim." And yet, the hardest part of the experience is at the end, when they must say endless goodbyes to the new friends they worked so hard to make and whom they will never see again.

One of the few real advantages that American children living in a foreign country have is their ability to learn a foreign language more easily than adults, so it is not uncommon for them to be able to outspeak their parents in a short time. Yet, they are not likely to see that as an achievement greatly to be desired, and certainly not one worth leaving the comforts of home to experience.

Parents bound for an overseas assignment need to prepare, before they go, by taking along such things as sparklers for the Fourth of July, Christmas ornaments, Easter egg dyes, and birthday candles and balloons so that American holidays can still be celebrated in familiar ways.

Preparing for Regional Excursions from Your Overseas Base

Realizing that wherever your overseas posting may be, you will be able to take numerous R&Rs in all directions. Prepare by taking along tourist guidebooks for the possible places you might want to visit. It would be a pity to waste your opportunity to "see the world" next door.

Preparing for the Physical Move Overseas

By the time they receive an overseas assignment, most American executives have experienced many household moves within the continental United States, perhaps even a move clear across the whole country. In spite of all this experience, they are usually totally unprepared for their first overseas move.

In moving across the United States, chances are they would sell their home and buy a new one in their new city. Most Americans moving overseas would be well advised not to sell their home but to sell their car. Another important difference is deciding what personal effects to take with you overseas and which ones to put in storage (at company expense, of course) until you return. And particularly for an overseas move, it is important to hire the best movers rather than the cheapest ones.

More specific information should be provided to you either by the International HRD division of your corporation or by the contractor who handles your predeparture orientation.

Selecting a Mentor to Represent Your Interests While You Are Gone

For many, the most dangerous aspect of the overseas assignment is that when the assignment is over and you return to the home office, it is like you have been dead for three years. Nearly everyone has forgotten you. Those who do remember you have the vague impression that you have been on a three-year boondoggle! "Out of sight, out of mind."

Only you can be counted on to see that you are not forgotten back at home base. And the best way to do that is to hand pick the right person to be your own personal mentor while you are gone. This executive will make it a point to bring up your name from time to time. "I just heard from Harvey. From all reports, he's doing a great job for us in Bangkok. He'll be returning home next year, and we've got to keep him in mind to be sure to pick a good assignment for him." If you have chosen well, this person will be your back-home press agent while you are unable to look out for your own interests. He, or she, can also keep you informed about changes in personnel and policies as they occur, so there will be no surprises waiting for you when you return home.

Even so, coming home can have its problems. Some studies indicate that 20 percent of those who return are so maladjusted that they leave their companies within a year. The reason for this high dropout rate is called "Reverse Culture Shock" or "Re-Entry Shock." Since it is not the subject of this chapter, we cannot deal with it here, but you should definitely investigate the phenomenon as you prepare to return home, and request re-entry training as soon as you return.

Saying Your Farewells

Modern American life has become so devoid of rituals, ceremonies, and "rites of passage" that we tend to totally ignore or make light of the major transitions in our lives. Leaving the United States for a couple of years to live in a foreign country for the first time is, indeed, a major transition, and you ignore it at your own peril. Taking this transition seriously and putting closure on one chapter of your life allows you to begin the new chapter with the best possible chances of success. A farewell party, with formal speeches, gift giving, and tearful, heartfelt goodbyes—all of these are proper ways of celebrating such a momentous occasion.

Future Possibilities

The miracles of modern technology are far more available in today's video games than they are in providing genuinely educational materials. The technology is available, but it has not yet been applied on a grand scale for the kinds of audio visual materials needed to prepare you for your overseas assignment. The advances that are already possible must wait for the future. Those possibilities include software data bases, edited electronically to include the latest up-to-the-minute corrections and changes for every country in the world. They also include interactive video, allowing the HRD to slant the learning in the direction which would be of greatest personal benefit and gratification.

An urgently needed type of assistance to personnel newly assigned overseas is "In-Country/Settling-In Assistance," which would be available on the spot in 100 or more major cities around the world. This program would take over where predeparture training leaves off. It would provide immediate assistance to the newly arrived expatriate, tailored to the specific needs of each family, for the first month or two after arrival. Such a service is currently provided for a limited number of countries by Moran, Stahl, & Boyer, but it could easily be offered by other companies as well, in these days of immediate fax communication, by utilizing U.S. Foreign Service spouses on site in each of the 100 cities where the services could be made available. This idea awaits the organizational skills of an eager entrepreneur who will "run with it." All I ask in return is that you let me know when and through whom the service is available so that I can make potential users aware of its availability, thus sending business your way.

Resources

BCIU (The Business Council for International Understanding–affiliated with American University), Suite 244, Foxhall Square, 3301 New Mexico Avenue NW, Washington, D.C. 20011, (202) 686-2771.

Clarke Consulting Group, One Lagoon Drive, Suite 230, Redwood City, California 94065, (415) 591-8100.

Moran, Stahl, & Boyer, 900 28th Street, Suite 200, Boulder, Colorado 80383, (303) 449-8440.

References

Adler, N. *International Dimensions of Organizational Behavior*. Boston, MA: Kent Publishing Company (Wadsworth), 1986.

Austin, C. *Cross-Cultural Re-Entry: A Book of Readings*. Abilene,TX: Abilene Christian University Press, 1986.

Brislin, R. K., Cherrie, C., and Yong, M. *Intercultural Interactions: A Practical Guide*. Beverly Hills,CA: Sage Publications, 1986.

Ferraro, B. P. *The Cultural Dimension of International Business*. Englewood Cliffs, NJ: Prentice Hall, 1990.

Harris, P. R., and Moran, R. T. *Managing Cultural Differences*, Houston,TX: Gulf Publishing Company, 1987.

Kohls, L. R. *Intercultural Training: Don't Leave Home Without It*. Washington, DC: International Society for Intercultural Education, Training and Research, 1984.

Kohls, L. R. and Tyler, V. L. *A Select Guide to Area Studies Resources*, Provo,UT: Brigham Young University, 1988.

McKay, V. *Moving Abroad: A Guide to International Living*. Yarmouth,ME: Intercultural Press, 1984

Storti, C. *The Art of Crossing Cultures*. Yarmouth, ME : Intercultural Press, 1990.

Torbiorn, I. *Living Abroad: Personal Adjustment and Personnel Policy in the Overseas Setting*. New York, NY: John Wiley and Sons, 1982.

Vetter, C. T. *Citizen Ambassadors: Guidelines for Responding to Questions About America*. Provo,UT: Brigham Young University, 1983.

Ward, T. *Living Overseas: A Book of Preparations*. New York, NY: Free Press (Macmillan),1984.

About the Author

L. **Robert Kohls** is Professor of International Business at San Francisco State University. Previously, he was Director of Training and Development at the U.S. Information Agency and Director of the Washington International Center. He completed is doctoral studies at New York University. He is a founding member and member of the Governing Council of the International Society for Intercultural Education, Training and Research. He received the 1986 Primus Inter Pares Award in Amsterdam, and is the author of the well-known *Survival Kit for Overseas Living*.

CHAPTER 5

Coping With the Language Barrier: Using Interpreters Effectively

Zeace Nadler

One of the questions that constantly arises in international work is whether you need to know the language of the country you are working in. For many HRD people this does not pose any problem, since they speak many languages. Despite that, however, they may still get assignments in countries where the language is foreign to them.

For many U.S. HRD people, it can be a real problem. The frequently heard joke is

"What do you call a person who speaks three languages? Trilingual.
What do you call a person who speaks two languages? Bilingual.
What do you call a person who speaks one language? An American!"

Unfortunately, there is a sound basis for the last response. It is only in recent years that U.S. schools have been requiring at least one foreign language. Therefore, some HRD people who graduated earlier may speak only English.

Do you really need to know the language to work in another country? That has been the focus of arguments for many years and there is still no complete agreement. It is, perhaps, a valid need when you will be spending a long time in a country where English is not generally spoken. For a short stay, it is almost impossible for most of us to learn enough to really function in another language.

You may be involved at various levels of the organization or the government with whom you are working. Even if some of those counterparts can speak English, there may be cultural and political reasons for them to speak in their own language.

Learning something of the language of the other country can help in two ways. First, it shows that you have an interest in the other country, and it is a good idea to be able to use some polite words and phrases such as "please," "thank you," " hello," and "good-bye." Even these may not be easy to learn because of pronunciations strange to you or tonal inflections that may not exist in your own language. Generally, your hosts will excuse your mispronunciations, and give you some credit for just trying.

Second, language is a manifestation of culture. Learning some of the language can help you to better understand your clients. For example, there may be different words appropriate for males and females, or different words to be used depending on the level of the people you are speaking to, or some words not permissible at all in polite society.

Note that this discussion is limited to language, and does not bear on using any form of gestures or sign language. That is an altogether different issue that must be considered, but not in this chapter.

HRD people in the United States must recognize that the flow is no longer in one direction, ie., from the United States to other countries. There are people coming from many countries to do business in the United States who are not fluent in English. Therefore, interpreters become a necessity, yet very little has been done to train HRD people to work *through* an interpreter. One reason is our traditional way of identifying training needs by looking for the difference between expected performance and actual performance. In the case of using interpreters, how can that be done? Most people who use interpreters have very little idea of what is expected from an interpreter and little or no way of knowing whether the interpreter has functioned effectively. In the case of a breakdown in communications or relationships it is usually, though not always, the fault of the person using the interpreter, who often does not even know that something has gone wrong. Therefore, there is no "need," in our usual usage of that word.

This became evident when my husband and I made a presentation on this subject at the 1986 ASTD Conference. Those at the session were involved in international work and had used interpreters, but almost all said that they had never had any training in using interpreters. Still, they could cite examples of how a situation broke down, or goals were not met, because of ineffective use of interpreters.

Defining Terms

One problem is that even some people who work internationally have not fully understood that success or disaster can result when working in two languages. In seeking help, they should realize the differences between two kinds of people:

- Interpreters, who work with the spoken word and live people in action-oriented situations.
- Translators, who work with the written word and can work in isolation without seeing either the writer or the reader.

It is possible for an interpreter to also do translating, but very unusual for a translator also to do interpreting.

There is another important distinction, in the kind of interpreting:

- Simultaneous: You and the interpreter speak at the same time.
- Consecutive: You speak, and then the interpreter speaks.

Simultaneous is preferred when working with a large group such as when making a speech or conducting a learning situation. It requires special equipment so that the interpreter can hear you and at the same time put the ideas and words into the host-country language.

Consecutive can be used in any situation, but it is preferred for small groups or one-on-one, as in consulting. No equipment is needed, but the language exchange takes twice as long.

I will first discuss guidelines that apply to both simultaneous and consecutive interpreting, and then those applicable only to simultaneous and those only to consecutive. There will be some oversimplification since I will be discussing guidelines that are useful worldwide, but there are differences, depending on the country and the culture. At times, I will refer to some of these differences, but by no means can they all be considered in a brief chapter.

Using an Interpreter–General

There are some factors to consider any time an interpreter is being used, as listed in Figure 5.1.

Select an interpreter

It is not enough to select a person who is familiar, or even fluent, in both languages. Interpreting is a skill that goes far beyond language facility. In part, the interpreter must be able to become submerged in the personality and style of the speaker.

In some countries, you will be expected to provide your own interpreter even though the host has one. This does not signify distrust, but merely a respectful consideration for the parity between both parties. It is always possible, of course, that an interpreter provided by your client will feel a strong sense of loyalty to that client. That can influence the nature and content of the communication process, so you should consider providing your own interpreter, although this can be very costly.

Figure 5.1: Using an Interpreter – General

- Select an Interpreter
- Brief an Interpreter
- Speak clearly and slowly
- Speak only in English
- Avoid unusual words
- Provide the Interpreter with copies of your outline
- Provide a vocabulary of special words
- Create feedback

Brief the interpreter

If this is the first time you are using a particular interpreter, a briefing is essential. It allows the interpreter to get a feel of your language, style, and pace. If the interpreter has any questions or suggestions, they can be discussed during the briefing. Although pertinent for all situations, it is particularly important for consecutive interpretation.

Speak clearly and slowly

Many of us tend to speak rapidly. Though perhaps not a significant problem when we are talking to others in English, it can become one when working through an interpreter. Since there is a time lag even with simultaneous interpreting you may not be getting immediate feedback through nonverbal signals such as nods or grunts. This can raise your anxiety level, and your feeling that there is no communication may cause you to speak even more rapidly. This only provides additional pressure on the interpreter, leading to less effective work.

There are situations when your clients will understand some English but they cannot or will not engage in English conversation. If you speak clearly and slowly, your client will be able to understand some of what is being said and the interpreter functions as an aid.

Speak only in English

It is useful and polite to know some words and phrases in the host country language, but when using an interpreter this should generally be limited to: "hello", "good-bye," "please," and "thank you." Even here there can be difficulty if the host language reflects status. In Japanese, "Doozo Yoroshiku" is a greeting between equals or friends. When greeting a higher level person, particularly for the first time, "Hajimete Ome Ni Kakarimasu" would be expected. In some languages, saying "hello" can take several minutes!

Therefore, limit your conversation to English. A good interpreter will put your "hello" into the proper cultural and linguistic context for the situation. Of course, you may never know if this has been done correctly, but your clients will recognize the shortcoming on the part of the interpreter, if there is one, and not attribute it to you.

It can also be confusing when you take certain words into another context. Several years ago, the word "honcho" was commonly used in the U.S., brought back by military personnel who had served in Japan. They used it to mean the boss or supervisor, though that is not the actual meaning in Japan—there are many different words for those positions in Japan, depending on a variety of factors. For a Spanish interpreter in South America, for example, the word "honcho" would not be a known English word.

Avoid unusual words

This does not apply to technical or product vocabulary, since your clients will generally know those words. If not briefed, the interpreter may have some difficulty with the vocabulary of a particular profession, but your client will probably not.

A problem arises when you try to use English slang, regionalisms, and words that are arcane and uncommon. Do you realize that in the U.S. we have words that are common in some parts of the country and unknown in others, such as "all-overish," "can't hardlies," "bumfidgets," and "belly-clapper"? (Source: *Dictionary of American Regional English.*)

I remember one situation in Brazil where I was at an international conference. As my husband and I would be making a presentation later, I sat in the large auditorium with a Brazilian counterpart. A speaker from the U.S., working through interpreters, was describing a situation and said in English, "You have to take the ball and run with it as you do in football." His reference was obviously to U.S. football, for football in Brazil is really soccer. My Brazilian counterpart, who knew English very well but was listening on the earphones, told me that the interpreter got completely lost on that one. It took the interpreter about two minutes to try to explain the problem. During that time everything the speaker said was completely lost to that part of the audience who had to rely on interpretation.

Some interpreters will have been schooled in British English, which is different from American English. This becomes apparent in words such as "lift," "chemist," "boot," "Wellingtons," and "nosh."

Provide the interpreter with copies of your outline

This would not apply to a consulting situation, but is certainly relevant for a speech or learning session. A good interpreter will not give your talk for you, but knowing what is coming can facilitate the interpreter's work. The outline will not tell the interpreter the exact words you will use, but will give some idea of the flow.

Provide a vocabulary of special words

There may be some words or phrases that the interpreter should know beforehand. When planning to speak of Human Resource Development (HRD), for example, let the interpreter know that in Spanish this becomes *Desarollo de Recursos Humanos* (DRH). This is relatively easy, though I have had some interpreters who chose other words until the clients corrected them!

Create feedback

Continually determine if there has been effective communication. One way is to ask questions, but here you must consider culture. In the U.S. and some other countries, it is not only permissible but expected that questions will be sharp and direct. A confronting question is considered a good one, but that is not the case in every part of the world. There are countries where non-confronting behavior is the norm and a direct question can be considered an insult. Even though the question will go through the interpreter, who will ask it, you should be sensitive to a non-confronting society and phrase the question closer to its cultural norm.

You can also create other forms of feedback, such as exercises or asking the client to do something. What you want is observable behavior to check out the communication. When working in Malaysia (a non-confronting society), I planned to ask a group of leaders to "List the needs you have ..." (regarding the particular objective). It took several hours working with the client to find the correct words that would give me this feedback without being confronting.

You can obtain written feedback by having the client put responses to the feedback situation on newsprint and have the interpreter translate them.

Using an Interpreter – Simultaneous

The items discussed under general interpretation also have application for simultaneous. In addition, as listed in Figure 5.2, there are some factors peculiar to simultaneous interpretation.

Figure 5.2: Using an Interpreter – Simultaneous

- Have good working equipment
- Select professional interpreters
- Use more than one interpreter
- Allow for language differences
- Prepare visual aids with special
- Create feedback

Have good working equipment

In simultaneous interpreting, the equipment is another intervening factor. Even the best interpreter can be severely hampered by ineffective or poorly designed equipment. However, the advances in the field over the past decades have been phenomenal. Today, the parties can all use lavaliere microphones and earpieces, so that it is almost impossible for the casual observer to even know that simultaneous interpreting is going on.

If possible, check out the equipment under the conditions in which it will be used. The interpreter can be in a different part of the room from you, so that visual attention will be focused on you. Sometimes there will be fixed equipment with an interpreter's booth set somewhere in the back of the room or even in another room.

Select professional interpreters

Simultaneous interpreters must be proficient and comfortable with the equipment. When a professional interpreting firm is hired to do the work, it will provide the equipment and you can expect that the interpreters will be competent in its use. When the interpreter is an individual, or usually a two person partnership, they may not be able to afford the equipment. They will use what is available or rent what they can get, and in some situations the equipment may be unfamiliar to them. If those interpreters must be used, give them an opportunity to become familiar with the equipment before using it.

Use more than one interpreter

Simultaneous interpreting requires at least two interpreters. In most situations, each interpreter cannot work for more than 20 minutes to a half of an hour, because simultaneous interpreting is grueling work. The interpreter hears one language and speaks another, at the same time! A good interpreter also tries to emulate your vocal mannerisms including the tone and emphasis. This is extremely difficult, and one person cannot do it efficiently for an extended period—over 30 minutes.

Allow for language differences

This is more for the benefit of the interpreter than the audience. In many languages, it takes longer to say what has been said briefly in English. This is partly a factor of grammar, but also one of culture. For example, when you fly to Japan you can expect to hear the following announcement made in English:

"Ladies and gentlemen, we will soon be landing at Narita airport outside of Tokyo. Please fasten your seat belts, bring your seats to an upright position, and stop smoking. Do not stand up until the aircraft comes to a complete halt."

The same announcement will then be made in Japanese. If translated into English it would read as follows:

"My esteemed customers, in about twenty minutes we will have the honor of bringing you to Narita airport. It would be very much appreciated and considerate of you to now put out your tobacco and place your tables back in the upright position. We would also be very grateful if you would condescend, most respected customers, to put your chairs upright, and you could also fasten your seat belts. We respectfully request that you do not arise from your seat until the airplane has come to a complete stop at the terminal. This would be very much appreciated and we are deeply grateful that you have selected our humble airline to fly. You have done us a great honor."

Prepare visual aids with special words or phrases

This has two advantages. First, in developing the visual you may find that some of the words or phrases cannot be translated in their existing form. In working with an interpreter in Venezuela, I was preparing an overhead transparency in Spanish and in English that included the words "cultural baggage." The first attempt at translation produced "suitcases that carry culture." It took almost half an hour, and two interpreters, to find exactly the right words in Spanish.

This produced the second advantage. When I did speak, using the overhead transparency, the interpreter knew exactly what I meant to say and had the appropriate Spanish words ready.

As noted earlier, in some countries your clients can read and write English, since it is taught in many schools. Many, however, have not had the opportunity of speaking English, so their skills in that area are limited. The English visuals, even if not translated, can be helpful to clients in some situations.

Create feedback

Even in simultaneous interpreting situations, it is possible to create feedback. Time must be allowed, however, for the clients to respond. There are times when humor can be used, but it must be done very cautiously, as people do not perceive humor the same way in all parts of the world. I do not tell jokes, for example, but sometimes rely on "one-liners"—statements that I know will encourage laughter from the audience.

At the IFTDO Conference in Mexico City in 1978, my husband, Len, was giving a talk to the general session with simultaneous interpretation. He delivered a one-liner and waited for the interpreter to finish to see if there was any laughter. Before the interpreter even stopped talking there was a wave of laughter from the participants who understood English. As expected, there was a second wave when the interpreter finished. But as he got ready to move ahead, there was a third wave of laughter! And for the rest of his talk each of his one-liners was followed by three waves.

After his talk, we asked some Mexican friends about this mysterious third wave of laughter. They explained that it was from those who prided themselves on their knowledge of English, and so did not use the earphones to avail themselves of the interpretation. They did not really understand English so they did not laugh with the first wave. They were not using the earphones, so they did not laugh with the second wave. However, as laughter seemed to be appropriate, and to show that they did understand English (even if they didn't), they too laughed, causing the third wave of laughter.

This provided confusing feedback, but now we are aware of this and listen for it.

Using an Interpreter – Consecutive

In the consecutive situation, no equipment is used. If it is a consulting situation, or one involving a small group, the interpreter stands with the group, and usually takes notes. Some special factors also must be considered, as listed in Figure 5.3.

Figure 5.3: Using an Interpreter – Consecutive

- Talk to the host
- Pause after every two or three sentences
- Allow interpreters to make notes
- Allow intrepreters to use a dictionary
- Use words, avoid gestures
- Speak in your normal voice

Talk to the client

When using a consecutive interpreter, speak directly to the client or group, even though it is the interpreter who is listening for the English. Almost everybody knows this, but many find it difficult to do it in an actual situation. This is partly due to our mainstream U.S. culture, where we have been brought up to look at the person we are talking to. In this situation, you are not talking *to* the interpreter but *through* the interpreter, and it can be difficult to make that adjustment.

Pause after every 2 or 3 sentences

In simultaneous interpreting, you can talk in your usual sentence pattern, though more slowly. With consecutive interpreting, you must stop talking to allow the interpreter to talk. The consecutive interpreter cannot translate each word, but deals with your ideas. Therefore, you should speak in short sentences with no more than one subordinate clause and stop after an idea has been presented. This should usually be in no more than three sentences. When an interpreter asks you to say more, it does not mean that the interpreter is more proficient, but rather that you may not have adequately communicated an idea.

You can have difficulty dealing with consecutive interpreting simply because you do not know what to do after you have finished talking while the interpreter is working. Generally, it's best just to smile and look friendly and interested! Anything else can interfere with communication from the interpreter to the client.

Allow the interpreter to make notes

You may think that if the interpreter is making notes, it signifies a poor memory and an inability to handle the assignment. Quite the contrary. A good interpreter develops a personal shorthand of symbols or words to facilitate recalling the idea. You should generally ignore the note-taking and maintain eye contact with the client. However, if you see that the interpreter is making many notes, it could signify that you are talking too long before allowing for interpretation.

Allow the interpreter to use a dictionary

There are times when an interpreter will open a dictionary during the exchange. If so, stop talking, for the interpreter cannot really be listening. Without embarrassing the interpreter, you might ask what word is causing a problem. Usually, it will be an English word that is unfamiliar to the interpreter. The difficulty may also be finding the right word in the host language, particularly when it represents an idea.

If the interpreter is forced to use the dictionary repeatedly during the conversation, you might request a break and ask the interpreter to identify the problem. It could be you, the interpreter, or the nature of the material. If only one interpreter is being used to interpret both ways, it could be the client who is using words for which the interpreter is having difficulty finding English equivalents. There is little you can do about that except to recognize the interpreter's problem.

Use words—avoid gestures

It is amazing how many of us in the U.S. use gestures to supplement their words. At one time, this was a criticism made about immigrants from the Mediterranean area and of certain ethnic groups, who extensively used gestures in conversation. Perhaps they have influenced the rest of the population, for gesturing is now quite common.

There are two problems connected with gestures. First, a gesture can have different meanings in different countries and cultures. A frequently cited example is the U.S. gesture of forming a circle with the thumb and adjoining finger. In the U.S. this means "O.K." and is a generally accepted gesture of approval. In Brazil, however, exactly the same gesture has sexual significance that is best avoided.

Second, there is an element of dissonance even when the gesture might be appropriate. You make the gesture while speaking, but the words to accompany that gesture are not heard by your client until later. At that point, the client must either try to relate the gesture to the words being spoken, or ignore the gesture as being irrelevant. If so, what else might the client have to ignore in the communication?

Speak in your normal voice

Many people unfortunately try to break through a language barrier by shouting. Even people who know that shouting will do no good have difficulty in constraining themselves when there is a communication problem. You cannot expect the interpreter to shout. Indeed, in some countries shouting is considered extremely impolite and can cause the client to terminate the situation.

Using your normal voice does not mean sounding as if you are speaking to a child. Rather, it is the usual voice level that you would be expected to use given the size of the group being addressed, and the relative status of participants.

Conclusion

Working through interpreters is a skill that you must develop if you want to function effectively in situations where your own language will not suffice. Do not wait for the day when the whole world will be speaking the same language. It certainly will not happen in our lifetime, and it is doubtful if one language will ever suffice in parts of the world where you may want to provide services.

About the Author

Zeace Nadler is a Partner in Nadler Associates in College Park, MD. She taught for the School of Education and Human Development at George Washington University. She has travelled in more than 50 countries and worked in more than 30, mainly on programs concerning adult education and HRD. She has written, edited, or coauthored *Developing Human Resources, The Comprehensive Guide to Successful Meetings and Conference, The Conference Book,* and *The Handbook of Human Resource Development.*

CHAPTER 6
Adapting U.S. Instructional Media for Foreign Users

Michael R. Pellet

In Human Resource Development, learner homogeneity means cost-savings and predictable results of a given instructional program. Allowing for some regional variations, in the United States it is possible to identify many common factors within a particular group of learners. This enables the HRD professional to predict the effectiveness of HRD activities, identify a learning curve, and determine the correlation between HRD and productivity and safety. Sometimes if a program was developed–and proven to be effective—in the United States, it may be a good candidate for use in another country. The response can range from: "No problem! Anybody can translate it into . . . ." to "What about cultural sensitivity? No way! Let's let our people in . . . do it in-country!"

Adapting U.S. instructional media for use in foreign countries is a very effective way to stretch the HRD dollar. It is an ideal way of accomplishing the transfer of technology. Furthermore, it is successful at the most effective level: the worker who needs the information to perform the job. However, the adaptation process requires more than simply translating. On the other hand, it does not call for becoming an anthropologist or a sociologist. In converting instructional media for foreign users, the key concept should be common sense. The following eight rules should give the U.S.-based HRD professional a good handle on what the process involves.

Rule 1:
Develop a Sound Learner Profile

This is a cardinal rule in developing all instructional materials, yet many instructors ignore it when adapting existing programs for use in another country. Knowing about the learners was essential for developing the original program and is just as essential for selecting and adapting the program for foreign use. Many organizations go to the expense of converting a program into another language only to find that it languishes on a shelf somewhere. Worse yet, it may be presented and offend or amuse the target audience — all because that audience wasn't researched.

Over the years we have developed an M² Ltd. questionnaire which can be easily adapted to various circumstances. Depending on the replies, it is possible to create a one-page profile containing the basic information listed in Table 6.1.

Table 6.1: Learner Profile Items

• Sex
• Age range
• Ethnic background
• Length of employment
• Education
• Motivation
• Interests
• Information source

Sex. In many countries, the gender of the target audience determines the language and tone used.

Age range. Again, the tone and style of the language depend on the relative ages of the speaker and the audience.

Ethnic background. Few countries have the plurality of backgrounds that exist in the U.S. However, there are distinct differences in Latin America. For instance, a person may be a "mestizo" of mixed Indian and European blood, a "mulatto," or "European." There are specific class distinctions associated with those backgrounds. Even when you adapt a program for U.S. use, the term "Hispanic"—which is only a U.S. creation—is not enough. A full-blooded Indian from El Salvador has absolutely nothing in common with an Argentinean descendant of Spaniards.

Length of employment. In many countries long-term employees are treated with deference. This is true, even if their jobs are essentially lower level. For instance, a long-employed foreman may be treated as "Don" in Mexico and must be spoken to with consideration. This is particularly important when converting instructional media that contains role-playing. Excessive use of first names and unwelcome familiarity may cause the target audience to dismiss the contents because they are unable to associate with the situation.

Education. The importance of education in converting instructional media has to do with vocabulary and delivery. Regardless of the word used in the original English, the translated word must be one accessible to the learners at their educational level. Unfortunately, many companies emphasize accurate translation at the expense of understanding the idea. One example that we experienced personally was with the use of the word "procedure" in a videotape for training mechanics. We accurately translated the word as "procedimiento" every time the original videotape referred to "the Pump Alignment Procedure . . . . Know your procedure . . . . The procedure contains the following steps . . . ." It was only when we actually taught the program that we discovered what our target audience thought of our accuracy. We remember a young first-level mechanic who expressed his frustration when trying to remember the answer. He said: "I know how to do it, I just can't remember the fancy word you used!"

Motivation. There are many very good instruments for measuring motivational level. However, what we need here is general information of the type you can get through a simple self-test or questionnaire. We base our Motivation Rating on Maslow's Pyramid but any similar system would do the job. The value of knowing the motivational level of a learner has to do with the way in which we present the information. For instance, the original HRD program presentation may be straight and factual. If the adapted program is to instruct foreign workers who are at the survival level, it will be necessary to reformat the text and add graphics.

Our form also includes a space for listing interests and the information source. Interests may or may not be relevant. We have found the source of information to be essential. Often, a supervisor will tell us that all the employees are literate. Then we find out in class that this is not the case. Let's say you have the basic facts about the learner and have developed a profile. Before adapting an HRD program, conduct some basic research on the geographic location, standard of living, and educational system of the target countries. An ideal source is a good encyclopedia. You might also call the consulates of the countries involved or use your neighborhood library. There is no need to launch a full-scale research operation but the few hours you will spend beforehand can be extremely valuable afterwards. One anecdote comes to mind of a videotape translated to instruct truck maintenance mechanics. The tape flawlessly explained how to change antifreeze and talked about cold and snow in Buffalo, New York. The translation was perfect. However, when mechanics in El Salvador saw the tape, they were mystified. They couldn't understand the obscure reference. They had never seen snow nor experienced freezing cold.

Rule 2:
Do Not Try to Adapt an HRD Program That Is "Somebody's Baby"

There are programs developed in the U.S. that are successful because they rely on the cult of personality. They might have been developed and presented by a charismatic specialist, or by someone who developed a specific theory or technique. Those programs may work very well in the United States or in other English-speaking countries because they rely on the individual's presentation. But they will not succeed when adapted into another language if the information they contain cannot stand alone.

One of the most difficult adaptation jobs is to translate and dub a management program in which the creator was videotaped giving a live presentation. Since the presentation has been ad-libbed, the transcribed text may sound ridiculous. When people are speaking, we are not disturbed if they repeat themselves or use made up words and convoluted logic. Since the speaker is animated, we understand the meaning, even if it is not presented accurately. However, the cold eye of the translator makes short shrift of sentences such as "You've .... You've just made a sale .... You're on top! Now, er . . . er . . . What you need is something that goes . . . goes through the loop . . . you and me. Get it?"

Regardless of how good foreign language actors are, they will sound like idiots trying to say something like that. Even if you create a new translated sentence to cover that gap, the sentence has to occupy that same space and have the same breaks. If not, the "charismatic" English speaker will be reduced to a hilarious out-of-synch opening and closing of the mouth.

Often, it is very difficult to tell the creators of an English-language program that their presentation will not enthrall the foreign natives — it's like telling a doting mother she has an ugly baby. Many program creators are highly-motivated, action-oriented, individuals who find it difficult to take someone else's advice about their program. The result will be a disappointment to all concerned.

Rule 3:
Use Only Professional Translators to Translate Instructional Media

There is an old Italian phrase that says "Traduttori traditori." It means, "Translators are traitors." Of course that is not the case, but twelve years of seeing hair-raising translations by well-meaning people convinced us the old Italian aphorism has some truth in it. The United States has long been a one-language country. Even now, there is a surprising amount of naiveté regarding foreign languages. Smart business people would not dream of having their next-door neighbor write a technical paper on power generation. Yet, they think nothing of asking their Aunt Sally to translate a program into German. Translation is not something that people can do just because they happen to be bilingual, no more than good writing is something you do because you happen to speak English.

Under no circumstance should using friends or relatives be an option. There are three approaches that you can choose for doing the translation:

- Use free-lance translators.
- Use a translation house in the United States.
- Translate in the foreign country.

What is the difference between these three approaches?

Free-lancers are usually cheaper than translation houses because only one person does the work. Good professional translators will have the appropriate reference books, the word-processing equipment, and the commitment to the schedules desired. With a free-lancer, the owner of the English-language program generally has responsibility for the ultimate product. The program owner will also be responsible for any required layout and graphics.

U.S.-based translation houses are more costly than a free-lancers because they normally have more than one person work on a translation—and they accept responsibility for the final product. The price can vary widely depending on what you expect them to do and their level of expertise. For example, some can recreate graphics, change languages, do multiple languages, etc.

Foreign translation houses can be very good, but European ones may be much more costly than those in the U.S. One problem we encountered early on is that while the foreign language may be flawless, the translators may be deficient in English, particularly technical or idiomatic English. An added problem may be scheduling and an unnecessary slavishness to the English material.

Out of necessity, we evolved into a combination translation house and HRD company that has retained the best of both worlds. This combination allows us to assure that we have the best translators and the knowledge of what should be the ultimate objective. This has come in quite handy, even when adapting a program that is not our own. For example, we translated a videotape on the latest technological advances of a large equipment manufacturer. We instructed the translators to replace the simple sentence "the equipment will be ready in the early Spring" with "the equipment will be ready by April." This was important because the manufacturer would send the video to Italy, Spain, Germany, Argentina, and Brazil. They do not all experience Spring in the same months.

Rule 4:
Develop a Standard Procedure for Translation

A standard procedure for translation is necessary to avoid simply translating the words and missing the HRD dimension. As mentioned before, the translation can be faultless and still not serve the needs of the learner. You should develop a fixed written procedure together with those responsible for the actual translation. Then it will be possible for the translator(s) to follow the same steps every time. This will ensure uniform quality and effective information transfer. A typical procedure might contain the following items:

- List the HRD pitfalls.
- Identify the learner.
- Review the material to be translated.
- Divide the material into idea blocks.
- After completing the translation, have somebody enact the instructions.
- Special handling for video scripts.
- Send the translated material to a subject-expert in the country.

List the HRD pitfalls

The first step in developing a procedure is to create a list of all the HRD pitfalls of the particular languages, words that are perfectly innocent but have evolved into vernacular epithets in some groups or countries. Other examples include simple directional words that have ambiguous meanings, such as: "up," "down," "sideways;" and technical words that have become a dialect. Stress that the translator must pay particular attention to false cognates. For instance, in a translation into Spanish for Latin America, the word *discussion* should not be translated as *discusión*. If it is, the learners may understand that they are being told to argue with their instructor.

Identify the learner

One way to do this is to give the translator a copy of the learner profile. Then the translator can confirm that the level of the translated language will be appropriate for the target audience.

Review the material to be translated

This is something that almost every good translator does before beginning the translation. It can consist of a simple reading of the material and highlighting of potential trouble areas. These may be technical terms, company-specific expressions, or specialized techniques.

Divide the material into idea blocks

Whether the material to be translated is a manual or a video script, the objective is to transmit blocks of information. Ask the translator to break down the material into idea blocks. That way, you can identify the idea that absolutely has to be transmitted to the learner. In many instances, a translation will concentrate on the accuracy of the words and neglect the importance of the idea.

An interesting example is the prevalence of the words "clockwise" and "counterclockwise." They appear in English-language manuals to indicate the way a pump or valve must be tightened or removed. In English, the terms are accepted as an unambiguous way of giving instructions. However, in Spanish or Portuguese these terms are incredibly long and cumbersome. Furthermore, if the learners are third-world mechanics or electricians, they might not have made the connection between right and clockwise and left and counterclockwise. This instruction calls for a specific way of viewing time, a cultural familiarity with time and clocks, and the conversion of an abstract concept—time. This must be related to a physical device—a clock. Then it must be related to another abstract concept—direction—and finally, back to the tangible pump or valve. Since tightening the valve may be the main idea, simply use the words that will permit the learner to accomplish that objective. For example, "turn the valve to the left to tighten."

After completing the translation, have somebody enact the instructions

Whoever reviews the translation should do what the learner is supposed to do. For example, a paragraph states: "He uses the proper hand tool to prevent the gears from moving . . . then reaches inside and manually rotates the scale and fastens the cover plate on the housing." There is something terribly wrong here, because the mechanic has to have three hands to carry out this operation.

Special handling for video scripts

Translations for video scripts require all the above steps and another important one: pay attention to the time. English can tolerate almost any compression and there are fascinatingly rich expressions that can be reduced to two syllables. When translating instructional scripts, you must remember how people in the target language actually speak. The English must not be followed so closely that the actor sounds like a hilarious Godzilla movie, ie., racing to squeeze a language that is almost twice as long as English into the space provided by a casual remark like "kind of." Streamline the translation and, particularly, avoid using the entire name of a procedure more than once every two paragraphs. This is done very often in English instructional material but in translated material it is unnecessary. For example, saying "changing the packing in a two-way valve" can consume a great deal of time. In the foreign language, it is possible to make use of gender, pronouns, and nouns. And, last, stress to everybody involved in the translation not to use the passive form. It deadens a presentation and increases the amount of words. For example, instead of saying "The compressor is charged by injection,—" the translation should say, "Charge the compressor by injecting."

Send the translated material to a subject-expert in the country

This is always a good final review of the translation, before finalizing the HRD program. A word of caution is appropriate here. Do not send the material on an open-ended schedule because the review might take anywhere from one month to a year.

Rule 5:
Don't Fall Into the "Egotistical" Approach to HRD

Don't take the attitude "We're going to teach them the right way to do X." While this rule may seem to be another aspect of knowing the learner, it really concerns a sensitivity to the reality of the daily existence of the learner. Much has been made of cultural sensitivity. In many ways, the concept itself has become obscured by thousands of experts. Basically, the "egotistical" approach is that the only way to do things is the American way or that American technology is the only one around. This is particularly annoying to other industrial nations because it implies that their technology, of which they are reasonably proud, is not worth considering. Similarly, the so-called Third World countries do not take kindly to being treated as if they were in the Stone Age simply because their technology may not be the most advanced. Many instructional programs which, as some say, try to teach the natives to wear clothes are immediately rejected—even when the technical information is sound. The whole world thinks that Americans have a very high opinion of themselves. To translate a program that makes excessive use of the royal "we" will give the impression that the Americans are speaking about themselves. The way to avoid this is to identify the speaker of the text or video at once. "We, the creators of this program ...." When possible, use the first person voice. Wherever possible, establish the reason for doing a specific task. For example, instead of saying, "We keep the surface extremely clean," the translated version could say ,"Keep the surface very clean in order to ...." This should be done even if the English does not contain the complete information.

To give an even more powerful example of what can happen by thoughtlessly falling into the egotistical approach, a major U.S. corporation that had produced a very good instructional program wanted to translate it into Portuguese. They had spent much money hiring translators and experts, in addition to a full production house, to create a truly good program. Indeed, the program was excellent. The only problem was that in trying to produce the best program possible, they had used beautiful office sets for recreating the work scenes. When the Brazilian employees were asked why the program did not succeed, they replied: "Because that's just to show us how the Americans do things. That's very interesting, but it doesn't apply to us." Why? Because the offices did not look anything like the offices in their company. So, in effect, it was like watching *Dynasty,* without the fancy clothes.

Rule 6:
Keep an Eye on the "Small" Issues of Cultural Sensitivity

Not many years ago few people in the United States were concerned about cultural sensitivity because, in truth, there were few possibilities for exporting instructional materials. Nowadays, however, almost everybody is aware of the need for cultural sensitivity, whether they have it or not. Unfortunately, sometimes those who are adapting English instructional materials for another culture may concentrate so much on the large issues that they overlook the smaller ones. Recently, a very good HRD activity was converted into Korean. The contents had been analyzed and cross-checked for all possible nuances that might offend the Korean learners. The text had been read very carefully to ensure full comprehension; colors were chosen to ensure maximum acceptability; graphics were specially designed for the videotape. In short, all that could be done had been done, except that the videotape was totally faithful to the English, including using first names and addressing the people as " you"—something that is never done in Korea.

Rule 7:
Make Sure That Your Text Layout is Not Inhibiting

When the instructional medium is a text, some liberties should be taken with the original English text. Make sure that the translation is "learner friendly." This means that you should use pictures, graphics, and white space wherever possible to make the text easier to understand. If measurements are not converted, include a conversion table. If references are made to organizations or people who are widely known in the United States but not anywhere else, you must explain them. Almost all languages need more space than English, so it may be necessary to change the layout rather than try to cram everything into the same number of pages.

Rule 8:
Always Include an Instructor's Guide

This rule has proven itself time and time again. Rather than assume there will be a formal instructor in charge of administering the program, you must include a guide in every program. It is often impossible to determine who will be giving the instruction and what their level of skill will be. Even if it is only a few pages long, the guide should at least answer the following questions:

- What materials are included in the program?
- How are they supposed to be used?
- What are the main objectives?
- What are the key points to be stressed?

Conclusion

By following these eight basic rules, we have enjoyed the ultimate mark of success in HRD: to watch the learner's face light up and say, "Ah! I understand!" Those simple words—which indicate the instant in which a message has been successfully transmitted—are the ultimate goal of all international HRD practitioners and consultants. That moment when a listener, reader, or viewer thousands of miles away expresses total enlightenment should be both our objective and our stimulus as HRD professionals.

About the Author

Michael R. Pellet is President of M² Ltd. in Gaithersburg, MD. Previously, he was manager of international operations for a major consulting engineering firm and an operations consultant for international power projects. He has a B.S. in engineering and is a Registered Professional Engineer. He is a member of the Suburban Maryland International Trade Association. Since founding M² Ltd. he has converted more than 300 hours of videotape and text courseware into Spanish, and it has been estimated that these programs have been used by 10,000 learners in 17 countries.

CHAPTER 7

Adapting Technology-Based Instruction

Angus Reynolds

In some cases, a simple mistranslation can have dire results. I recall one when former President Nixon was talking with the Prime Minister of Japan, who made a comment that his interpreter translated as, "I'll take care of it." A correct translation would have been, "I'll take it under advisement," a different matter altogether. The mistranslation caused a major international incident.

Correct translation is terribly important in HRD. However, it is only one part of good instructional adaptation for foreign users.

Many U.S. organizations "export" their seminar-based instruction to non-English speaking countries. Somehow it seems to survive the trip. Why would automated HRD be any different?

Actually, the exported instruction "survives" the trip only because the local national who delivers the "foreign" seminar provides more than simple translation. Not wanting to appear like a fool, the indigenous presenter applies a natural sense of the local setting and provides both preplanned and spontaneous cultural adaptation in judicious amounts. As a result, the "foreign" instructional materials are made acceptable to the local learners.

I once asked the former Director of Training of Xerox do Brasil how he employed instructional packages sent from the Rochester, N.Y. Headquarters. Xerox packages were, and are, well done. He replied, "We never use them as they arrive. We always have to adapt them to fit in with our own circumstances." This agrees with accounts I hear all around the globe.

Technology-based instructional programs include multimedia self-study packages, computer-assisted instruction (CAI), and interactive video. This courseware obviously lacks the local national to provide key cultural adaptation. More significantly, on-the-spot adaptation will not be done. Local subsidiaries or customers may lack the technical capability to adapt them to fit in with their own circumstances. The only recourse is to adapt them *before* they are sent overseas. This chapter deals with why various aspects of automated materials must be changed, how, and how much it will cost. The major areas for consideration are illustrated in Figure 7.1.

Figure 7.1: The Technology-Based Instruction Adaptation Wheel

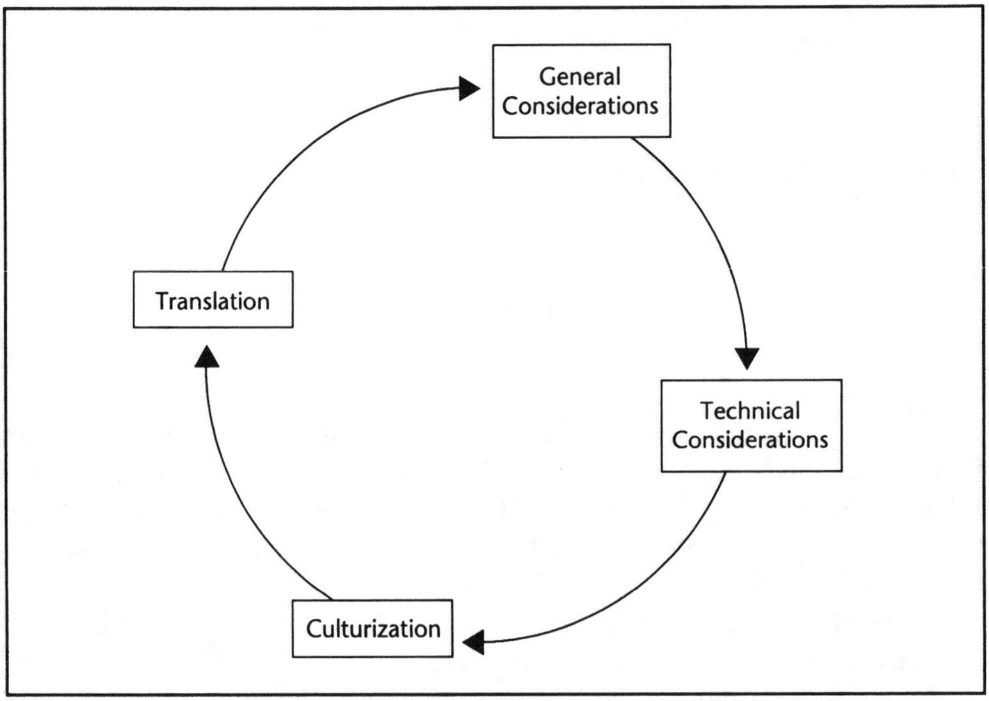

A prime consideration is the sequence of the items in the wheel.   Many practitioners would consider these items in order of their technical complexity, thus considering translation first. Actually, translation is the *last* consideration. You must first get the technology straight, then proceed to culturization and translation. We will address each of these considerations.

General Considerations

You must deal with the "mechanics" of presenting the technology-based program before you can focus on contents. Figure 7.2 shows the general and technical factors you must consider.

Figure 7.2: General and Technical Considerations

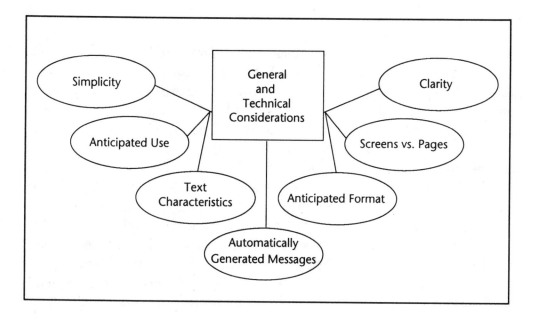

Keep it simple – but interesting

Obviously, this advice transcends global HRD. A simple lesson is easier to adapt. The problem is that in the hands of a less than skillful designer, simple sometimes equals boring. Design rules such as "keep it simple" may limit creative freedom. It is especially difficult to hold back on a good idea for a lesson in English just because the lesson might someday be translated.

Ordinarily, anyone designing an automated lesson should want it to be as effective and interesting as possible. I once visited a colleague who was "cranking out" CAI lessons. In that case, simplicity was ensured by a tight budget and short schedule. The resulting lessons were certainly simple, but she wasn't happy because she wanted to produce more stimulating learning materials. This story's instructional-development lesson is this: Remember that simplicity must be balanced with other considerations. You can't have the best of both worlds. Nevertheless, strive to ensure that keeping it simple does not mean making it dull.

Insure clarity

This rule is also applicable beyond the international realm. Fortunately, it is easier to achieve than simplicity. A vague or obscure English narrative or explanation will be equally obscure in Italian or Tamil. If you have unclear HRD materials, don't consider exporting them. The best advice here is to think about redeveloping anything that isn't clear in the original. It is a good move, whether the materials are exported or not.

Technical Considerations

Anticipate foreign use

There may be foreign marketing opportunities for your courseware. If so, standardization can help to avoid difficulty. You should establish certain format standards in advance for the designers who create the originals for any development project. Additional standards can be established based on the anticipated foreign audience. One might specify the size of borders or the positioning of certain information on displays. Others might apply to the display of specifically U.S. things, such as coins, dollar signs, and famous U.S. landmarks.

Generic standardization can be done before you identify any particular project or target country for foreign delivery. Perhaps you can anticipate that a module might be used in Saudi Arabia or China. If so, make the best creative use of that knowledge.

Space is one of the most important factors to consider. Many HRD people aren't aware that some written languages take far more space than others to convey the same information. For U.S. developers, German provides the most frequently encountered space limitation, because it requires about 30 percent more space than English. Other languages have similar requirements.

Adaptation of automated instruction benefits more from foresight than printed texts. Perhaps you will later translate a program into another language for which foreign markets might be ripe. If so, pay particular attention to the potential space problems when laying out frames. This is seldom a major problem in translating a printed text or manual—you can just add pages. Not so in a well-conceived automated lesson, because the entire design could be ruined. A more advanced anticipation concept is to produce a "modular" basic design that provides for developing country-, industry-, and company-specific modules according to user need and demand.

Think screens vs. pages

If you decide to translate *an awful* automated program where screen after screen of text follow one another, no one will ever notice. It can't get worse. In contrast, a well-designed program can get worse from translation. Many good programs present much of their information on one or more discrete screen displays, or "frames." Often creative and interesting programs teach the learner in a single frame simulation. If the designer has to divide a uni-frame design to accommodate the new language, the integrity (and probably the impact) of the lesson will be lost.

Moreover, the frame may tend to become cluttered, even though you try to keep it simple. Equipment diagrams or other diagrams with labels or informational boxes are a prime example. A frame that is crowded in English just isn't going to succeed in German.

Anticipate display format

The foreign language may not lend itself to presentation in the preplanned space. A common example is the translation of English material into Arabic or Hebrew. In some frames, English text accompanies a graphic display. Usually you place it to the left of the related graphic or answer space. In a Semitic language (written from right to left), the "natural" positions for the text is reversed.

To prevent such problems, you should establish standards. For example, save space on both sides of graphics, or consistently place the text either above or below them. Such standards work. The price is that such limitations impair your creative freedom.

Consider text characteristics

A worst-case illustration of the format problem arises when you try to translate automated instruction into Japanese or Chinese. Japanese and Chinese are character-oriented languages. They require much different keyboard input and display.

I once created a Japanese computer-assisted instruction lesson by converting an existing program from English to Japanese. The system I used did not have Japanese characters available, so I had to create those I would need—dot by dot. This was made much harder by the greater number of dots needed. Simple ASCII English characters can be displayed in a 6 x 8 matrix. The system I used at the time could accommodate all alphabetic language letters in an 8 x 16 matrix. I needed four times more to display the complex Japanese Kanji characters, so I created a 16 x 32 character matrix and then filled in every character I needed. Figure 7.3 shows these matrices.

Figure 7.3: Alphabet-Character Matrix Comparison

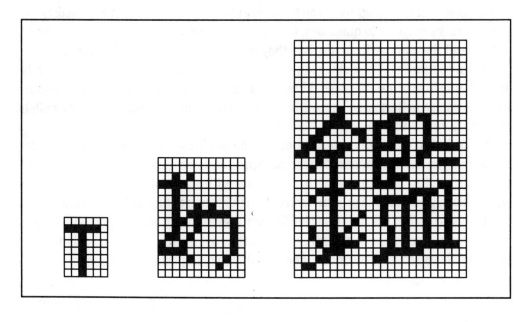

It would have been possible, but not simple, to make a one-for-one trade of keyboard keys as can be done for other alphabetic languages, such as the Cyrillic alphabet used in Russia. To make characters display requires eight keystrokes each.

Also, I found that the format used in the original lesson was not suitable for Japanese. Many of the displays looked "funny," even before cultural considerations. At the same time, it became clear that some of the material just wasn't right for Japanese users. Both problems led to a heavy dose of cultural adaptation. By the time I finished, almost nothing remained of the original lesson but the concept. I redesigned the program starting with the first *shoshomachi kudasai* "please wait a moment" message, that displayed while the computer was preparing the lesson. Changes went through to the *sayonara* "good-bye" page. Remember this story when you negotiate with a foreign buyer for a translated version of your automated instructional programs. Don't commit to a price on the assumption that all you will have to do is turn the English program over to a translator. In the real global HRD world, such thinking is foolhardy at best.

Deal with system- and application-generated messages

Think of the familiar Lotus 1-2-3™ spreadsheet. It is "application software." You can buy special software that enables your computer to display "foreign" letters and numbers in the spreadsheet, so your customer could then type on special key caps, to display letters of the Armenian alphabet. But doing that doesn't change the spreadsheet's *own* software. The spreadsheet's own menus and messages will still display in English. This example can help you appreciate software considerations in automated instructional development for users in other countries.

Today, lessons are usually created with menu-oriented development "systems" as opposed to being written in a computer language. Designers do not write "code," but fill out menus. It is conceptually the same as entering information in a spreadsheet. After learners respond to questions, the system generates the desired effect. These menus, and the standardized displays they generate, make things simpler for users in the United States. They obviously do not make things simple when the user is literate only in another language. I know of a case where the learners were Turks in an organization in Germany. There is little reason to think they could read the English comments on the screen.

If you haven't thought about it before, you don't *own* the Lotus 1-2-3™ *code*. Neither do you have the access to alter it. Typically, you will not own the code for the programs used to develop and deliver automated instruction. The problem for an organization that wants to present instruction in French or Slovak is not so much that the menus are in English. It is that the displays they automatically display will remain in English in Quebec or Bratislava, because they are generated by the application software. So you must answer one, and possibly two, important questions:

- Is the system available in the target language?
- If not, can you translate it?

Training a whole courseware-development group in instructional design is an unusual step. However, I had the delightful experience of doing this with Kingsley Wanigasundera and his Sri Lankan team. When they finished their training, they designed and developed computer and video lessons – and since they were granted access to change the automatic displays, they created a beautiful Sinhalese character set. The lessons were eventually driven as far into rural Sri Lanka as the roads go, then "manpacked" to remote villages and delivered on battery-powered equipment.

Development involving such special complex character sets always takes comparatively long. Multiple step text entry is required, rather than simple input.

Jim Glish of Computer Teaching Corporation experienced the size problem. It is also operative in application-generated cases. He correctly anticipated that the lesson model software he was designing would eventually be used in Germany. He planned for and provided 30 percent additional space. Unfortunately, the particular topics and lessons that were ultimately translated exceeded even that extra space. His foresight was correct, but proved to be insufficient for the particular instruction eventually adapted.

Culturalization

Consider culturalization as *total* translation. Len Nadler likes to point out that culture and language are inextricably linked. Experienced international HRD practitioners understand the need to consider cultural as well as linguistic differences when adapting an instructional program for another country.

Any international HRD pro can tell you that a speech or course must be both translated and adapted to function effectively for a particular foreign audience. Technology-based program delivery is no different. Ignoring the need for adaptation when translating a program from English into Spanish—or Arabic or Japanese— invites disaster. Potential exists for 273 different sets of conditions that pertain to individuals in technology transfer situations (Al Romaithy and Reynolds, 1981; Reynolds, 1984). Most of them can be resolved by competent culturalization.

The need for cultural adaptation can arise even when the language remains the same. Ethnocentrism places cultural blinders upon us all. Have you thought about translating English into American? It's difficult to recognize the extent to which you may be an "American" speaker, as opposed to an English speaker, and what that means for instructional materials. For example business contacts in India assured me that a CAI program that taught in "American" English could not succeed there. The U.S. program under discussion had already been translated into British English for the United Kingdom, but that version didn't work in Australia and was redone a second time for use there. A South African version was also created.

Mike Pellet, who deals with translation in Chapter 6, tells of his experiences with a particular U.S. video. First the video was tried in Britain. It didn't work—too American. Then it was dubbed by British voices. To the surprise of the developers, that didn't work either. It was then clearly "Americans with British voices." In the end it was necessary to entirely reshoot the video using British talent.

When you produce an automated program of any kind, you won't be there to explain what the screen *really* means. It's either right or wrong. It's effective or ineffective. The only way to make it both right and effective for the intended audience is to insure good cultural adaptation.

Here is the key. The need for cultural adaptation, in addition to straight translation, is magnified with automated materials. The most successful original programs incorporate a high degree of creativity. It is the creative element that makes them come alive and succeed. It helps the learner relate to the material. It keeps the programs from becoming boring to the American (or whatever nationality) learner, and leads to project success. Without exception, all the best of today's programs share this characteristic. The problem is that the creative elements are highly culture-specific—to the original culture. The things that "turn on" the American learner most are the same elements that "turn off" the person overseas. This is true of the English-speaking foreign learner as well as those who don't speak English. Solving this problem necessitates careful work and compromises. Let's look the factors essential to doing a good job.

Cultural bias

As you grew up, your family and associates assisted you to thoroughly culturalize in your own culture. We come to embrace a whole system of principles, concepts, and beliefs not obvious to people in other parts of the world. In fact, they may believe the opposite to be true. You may recall the space traveler "Coneheads" segment of the *Saturday Night Live* television show. The father advised his daughter to explain their most bizarre behavior simply by saying, "We are from France." People readily accept the notion that people from other countries are strange.

Clinging to one's own culture is called "ethnocentrism," the fifty-cent word for cultural bias. Ethnocentrism appears to be a very human quality exhibited by members of all groups. The writer H. L. Mencken satirized linguistic ethnocentrism beautifully when he wrote, "If English was good enough for Jesus Christ, it's good enough for me." An international marketplace example of Mencken's ethnocentrism illustration is the failure of U.S. manufacturers to provide foreign-language instructions for the countries to which their products are exported. You must recognize and overcome ethnocentrism's limitations in order to succeed in the international HRD marketplace.

A strong NIH (Not Invented Here) syndrome is in effect for instructional materials used everywhere. Learners want to feel that the people they see and text they read in their instructional materials were developed specifically for them. This may sound petty, but it's certainly true within the U.S. It shows up in other countries as well. Cultural bias in technology-based instruction turns up most frequently in video examples, textual explanations, and narrative material.

The way to spot cultural bias is to use proven formative evaluation techniques when developing the materials. You must try the lessons with *real* members of the target population! This may sound obvious, but it is probably the most commonly violated rule of developing instructional materials for domestic, not to mention foreign, users. Frank Otto is Professor of Linguistics at Brigham Young University, and a founder of the Computer Assisted Language Instruction Consortium. He converted a series of CAI lessons for use by Spanish-speaking U.S. citizens. There were several "situations" that were obviously biased toward the predominant U.S. culture. He wisely surveyed members of the target groups, picked replacement topics, and redeveloped those portions of the lessons. Frank says the extra effort paid off. "I'm glad we did, because the interests shown by the students on the questionnaires were quite different from what we had originally planned."

Even your instructional strategy is not above suspicion. When you adapt existing instruction for a new audience, make a careful check to validate all of the activities included in the lesson. Hal Christensen, of CES Training Corporation, describes how he does this: "We New Yorkers have to be careful how we say things. When I redo an automated package for a new audience in another part of the U.S., I exhaustively reevaluate its entire design and contents. This goes double for packages destined for export." You simply can't be too careful. Caroline Wai-Ying Sin, Personnel and Training Manager of the International Hotel in the New Economic Zone in Shantou, China, provides a warning. She feels that many Chinese view instructional games as bizarre, so they are often not an appropriate strategy for use with Chinese learners. This view has been reinforced by other Chinese colleagues.

Body language can also reveal the material's cultural heritage. So called "spaghetti westerns" made by Italians in the 1960s were obviously linked to their origin. Gestures are especially risky. I recall watching an incident in an international HRD meeting with mixed horror and amusement. A Libyan participant announced to Len Nadler that there was certainly one universally understood gesture. He then proceeded to demonstrate a gesture that he meant to illustrate "all right." His gesture has an obscene meaning in half the world! Make no assumptions about the gestures or actions of the people shown on your video. The final judges of your instructional material's acceptability will be the users in the target country.

Adaptation alerts

As long as you are going to do the job, why not do it right? Attention to the problem areas suggested here will make a remarkable difference:

- Jargon and Clichés
- Acronyms and Initials
- Numbers and Money
- Sports
- Humor
- Sex

Jargon and clichés. Technical or professional terms that are also the jargon of the foreign users are *not* jargon. Petroleum workers in another country probably have already picked up the jargon of that work. It is the other guy's jargon that doesn't communicate; for example, the computer world is filled with universally understood jargon.

To avoid jargon in technology-transfer projects where automated courses are being adapted on a "production" basis, try establishing a dictionary of words that may be used in lessons. Effective courseware can be produced with a surprisingly small dictionary.

Clichés should be avoided in English or any other language anyway. They won't survive the trip abroad. It could take an extra session to explain: "Those guys are coming out of left field. Their managers can't cut the mustard. Our division has its back to the wall. Now is the time to put your ear to the ground and nose to the grindstone."

Acronyms and initials. Initials can have double meanings and carry innuendo. Those that convey a wealth of meaning in one culture may only confuse in another. Initials that seem innocuous may spell an undesirable word in the foreign language or lead to confusion. At a hotel lobby meeting in Abu Dhabi, a client exclaimed loudly and enthusiastically; "I *love* the CIA." He meant CAI, but you should have seen the heads turn! Most of us have difficulty keeping track of our own acronyms. Any courseware importing "foreign" acronyms is in for real trouble.

Numbers and money. Even "unbiased" cultural evidence can be a problem. I read that something cost £ 35 thousand million. I wished the figure were given as $47 billion. Some lessons on math have been exported with examples using "nickels, dimes, and quarters." Lessons just can't get away with showing foreign currency. I suggest you not try such shallow adaptation.

Inappropriate use of numbers can be remarkably distracting for the learner in ways that an American designer might not suspect. It can create what Cheryl Samuels-Campbell, working in the Caribbean, calls "cultural interference." Working with Cheryl on instructional materials for accountants in Barbados, I found out that examples of billion dollar industries not only ran the risk of being boggling for the learner, but also of being dismissed as propaganda—selling the idea that bigger is better.

Sports. People in different countries enjoy different sports. American sports examples or metaphors will often not survive adaptation. What makes something fit congruently into one culture may miss completely in another. American interest in baseball and football is only shared in a few countries. "We have no other choice than to drop back and punt" communicates nothing to most of the people on this planet. Neal Nadler tells of the successful (in the U.S.) consultant who used a snow skiing analogy in a Middle East desert country. Your automated program can't recover from such inappropriate examples, even through good interpersonal skills.

Humor. Humor can be dangerous even within your own culture. Efforts to be humorous often fall flat. I dearly love the zany British humor exemplified by John Cleese's television show *Fawlty Towers*. Other people tell me that it just doesn't work with their American learners.

Humor is culture-related and it is often difficult to translate to another culture. All too often it leaves the foreign learners baffled. Sometimes it leaves them insulted. Well designed courseware generally retains its HRD value in a foreign country even without the jokes.

Sex. Sex roles vary widely in different parts of the world. You must provide native learners a chance to contribute honest input after trial use of automated instruction showing people of either gender. A native development team, free to do what they think right, will not make mistakes in this area.

A scene we consider acceptable may show a person in a role considered inappropriate in the target culture. As with many other aspects of any culture, people in another area are apt to have difficulty relating to text or scenes involving sex roles that they find unreal or—foreign.

Translation

Translation is familiar to almost everyone. Whether you view a gaffe by a translator or interpreter as either funny or horrible depends on its effect on you personally. I can't talk about this without repeating my favorite translation story:

"I'd like one of the singing dogs please!" I never heard anyone say this, but as I rode to work on the train in Japan I often fantasized just such a scene. Every day I saw a large sign on a building along the tracks near Kamakura that proclaimed, "Singing Bird and Dog Sale." Most Americans couldn't read the Japanese characters that had been translated to (hopefully) identify the establishment to foreigners as a pet shop (Reynolds, 1990).

Literal translation is rarely the best approach. A good translation must embody a "sense" of the original. John Eldridge, a computer-based courseware development consultant, says: "The problem is not to translate the words but to convey the ideas across cultures. Employ a writer from the other culture to write your idea in the local language."

Translation subtleties sometimes elude parochial people. For example, in translating a CAI program into Spanish, a problem arose: Which dialect should the final version be in? There are significant differences that could, if incorporated, brand the final product as "Cuban," "Puerto Rican," or "Mexican" rather than the needed "generic Western Hemisphere Spanish." That CAI program only had text. Other automated programs can include audio and video as well.

Translation into Chinese also has difficulties well known to most HRD people. What Chinese? The one spoken in Hong Kong (Cantonese) or the one they speak in Beijing (Mandarin)? This doesn't even address the additional problem that written Chinese characters are not quite the same in Beijing and Taiwan.

Dean Wade, President of Learning Technologies International, stresses the importance of maintaining the translated materials at the designed literacy level. A well-educated native translator ordinarily converts English materials with linguistic and educational pride. You must ensure that the resulting translation does not "upgrade" the material's intended literacy level. Dean says, "It is wise to use a revision matrix to help manage the project. List the factors considered and use it as a checklist before proceeding to actual revision. Depending on the number of different target populations, the matrix may be quite large, but it can be a major aid in ensuring that areas of potential concern have been appropriately addressed."

No local national would make the mistakes an American designer would most likely make. Those suggested here, and many more, have been made by U.S. organizations. You must test *everything* linguistic with the target audience, not only the text and audio. Such verification might have helped General Motors avoid its Nova predicament. The popular Chevrolet Nova was marketed in Latin America under its own name. In Spanish, unfortunately, "no va" means "you don't go." Would you want a car with that name? Simple translation, even when accurate, is rarely enough. Unfortunately, it is common.

Cost

What is the first question your management will ask? If it isn't about cost, you work in a very unusual organization. Technology-based instruction always costs more to develop, compared with instructor-led, but has comparative delivery-cost advantages. They make it attractive in the U.S. and apply to foreign delivery areas as well. There are several different kinds of cost—with radically escalating impact on the project bottom line. The projected costs presented here are a percentage of the original development cost of existing materials. Categories include: creativity, translation, culturalization, and major modification costs. They are presented in ascending order of costliness.

The general and technical considerations (keep it simple, etc.) will not necessarily cost anything. If implemented originally, such standards may even reduce overall costs. However, since all limitations have the potential to curb creativity, they could make the lessons ordinary or boring instead of outstanding. This non-expense is the "creativity cost."

Translation won't be expensive, approximately five percent. But, if you have read this far, you know that such a simple translation won't buy anything but trouble. If the target language uses a non-Roman character set, *translation* cost will be unchanged but implementation will be more expensive. How much more depends on a variety of circumstances, but translations requiring creation of a new character set can have a heavy "front end" cost. Hopefully, it will be amortized over development of many lessons.

Culturalization cost is difficult to generalize. Different instructional materials require various degrees of adaptation. The extent to which foreign use was antici- pated will reduce cost in proportion. Modular design (in anticipation of custom adaptation) will cost more initially, but will speed and improve the instruction. Culture-specific graphics or text could be more costly to adapt, depending on the specific items. Generally, cultural adaptation adds 10 to 25 percent to the cost of development. Specifically eliminating jargon and clichés, acronyms and initials, sports, humor, and inappropriate sex roles will not cost anything extra, since they will be removed in any competent cultural translation. The cost of culturalizing materials with high video content will escalate if the video must be re-shot in another culture. Extra cost could easily run from 50 to 100 percent.

Heavy-duty adaptation includes altering display or text characteristics, or imple- menting changes to the system or application-generated displays. Even with needed technical ability and permission, extensive changes of this type could add 100 percent or more to costs.

Twice-Told Tales?

The principles and techniques listed here are tried and tested. They have been applied to the successful adaptation of learning materials for print and video-based technology transfer efforts for years. They have also been proven in pioneer courseware adaptation efforts for CAI, some of which were described in this chapter. They work.

Once, I started an international presentation with an unusual attention getter. I said, "There is absolutely no difference in designing instruction for delivery to a foreign audience." It led to an animated discussion, because some people did not think about what they heard. What I said is absolutely true. You must consider that a professional job *always* includes identification and consideration of *all relevant differences* in the target population. The instructional design principles remain the same.

The technology-based instruction adaptation business is still new, but we don't have to invent another "wheel." The international HRD wheel was discovered long ago. Today it is considerably refined. There is a tried and true methodology available to those who care to do things right—the first time. If you want automated instruction to succeed, you must apply this methodology.

HRD will succeed when it is well designed and developed. Technology-based materials design must include appropriate adaptation before export in order to be considered well designed and developed. It is figuratively and literally the price of success.

References

Al Romaithy, A., and Reynolds, A. "A New Model for International Training", *Training and Development Journal,* Vol. 35, No. 10, Oct. 1981, pp. 63-69.

Reynolds, A. *Technology Transfer: A Project Guide for International HRD* Boston, MA: International Human Resources Development Corporation, 1984.

Reynolds, A. "Training That Travels Well", *Training and Development Journal,* Vol. 44, No. 9, Sept. 1990, pp. 73-78.

PART TWO

The Global HRD View

The Global HRD View

This part of the book concerns the understanding and application of what we call "the global HRD view." As far as we know, all experienced global HRD practitioners and consultants acknowledge that:

- There is such a view
- That it is different from a satisfactory "domestic view"
- That adopting the global view is necessary to success in a multi-country setting

Each chapter in this part provides ideas, information, and suggestions about how you might approach global HRD. The chapters vary considerably in the positions of the writers. They describe a number of global HRD settings. All of them are generally applicable to any region or country.

Angus Reynolds leads off with Chapter 8 titled "Working With HRD Consultants from Outside Your Country." He takes the position of the HRD manager in a global organization. He provides recommendations and examples for selecting a consultant, establishing a working relationship, and managing the consultant's project activities.

Pierre Casse is a well-known global HRD practitioner. In Chapter 9, "Organizations Are People: The Human Side of Corporate Transformation," he looks at the turmoil that is created as organizations tranform themselves into global entities. He provides suggestions to managers of globalizing organizations to help smooth the process.

In Chapter 10, Mike Marquardt describes "global culture." His chapter, "The Impact of 'the Cultural Environment' on HRD," examines what others in the field have determined. Marquardt's bottom line is that an HRD program cannot succeed if culture is ignored. After providing necessary background, he identifies important cultural factors. He then uses examples from the U.S., Japan, Saudi Arabia, and Mexico to illustrate the factors.

Global joint ventures are the focus of Len and Zeace Nadler's Chapter 11. They address the role human resource development can play in that arena. They examine the difficulties that often arise when the two companies are based in two different countries. After describing the several forms such companies can assume, they consider situations where HRD is a required project component.

Neal Nadler[1] and Jeff Len retell the (HRD version) of the story of Joseph and his coat of many colors, familiar to many readers. The result is Chapter 12, "A Typology of International HRD Consultants." Following the story, they describe several useful classifications for global HRD consultants. They then draw comparisons and suggest implications for HRD people interested in such work.

Is there anyone who has yet to hear the famous saying: "A prophet is without recognition in his own land"? The duo Cheryl Samuels-Campbell and Dunstan Campbell[2] share their experiences in Chapter 13, "The Paradox of the Local Consultant." They work as consultants in the Caribbean. As natives of the area, they face the attitude sometimes seen where snob appeal makes equally or less qualified foreign consultants more prestigious. They describe specific situations and draw conclusions for others who work in their "own land."

In Chapter 14, Mel Schnapper describes HRD tasks that must be achieved by team members who come from different organizational and national cultures. In such situations, conflicts, confusion, tension, and apprehension are frequent. After presenting the general problems, he takes a pragmatic approach to activities designed to bring order and increased comfort. They are designed to produce what he calls multicultural multinational team-building. In this chapter, he describes the implementation of multicultural multinational team-building to one situation

Sandy Mayers-Chen illustrates the application of instructional technology to a global HRD activity. In Chapter 15, she describes the complete process of developing a seminar to heighten American business people's awareness of their own perspective in one specific area. The seminar uses business communications to explore the American concept of time and how it might be altered in global organizations. Her chapter is titled "Training U.S. Business People to be Global Persons."

[1]Neal is not related to Len and Zeace. They simply share the same family name.
[2]Cheryl and Dunstan are related–by marriage.

CHAPTER 8

Working With HRD Consultants from Outside Your Country

Angus Reynolds

If you are an HRD manager, you should be aware that there are both similarities and important differences in using a foreign consultant when compared with using a domestic one. You may be in a global organization, or in a domestic one that will use an external consultant from another country. Consulting is a $2 billion-a-year business. That's the gross income of some 3,500 consulting firms—plus thousands of individual practitioners—in the U.S. and Canada. Big firms usually have expertise in many fields. Smaller firms and solo practitioners tend to be specialists. In either case, expert advice usually doesn't come cheap.

Consultants work with many organizations, and good consultants learn from previous assignments and apply their experience to new assignments. They keep continuously abreast of developments in methods and techniques in the field, including those that emerge from universities. In this way, a consultant can serve as a link between the theory and practice of HRD. Good consultants use their knowledge in the best interest of their client.

Why would you need to call in a consultant in the first place? Consultants are sometimes used when an organization lacks people able to tackle a given problem. It may often involve new techniques and methods in which a consultant has special expertise. Your staff may lack the necessary skills, knowledge, or time to do the project. Some problems might need management attention for long periods of time while the day-to-day running of business leaves little. It is difficult to concentrate on practical and conceptual problems simultaneously. Your internal resources may already be stretched too thinly to dedicate the effort necessary to produce the wanted practical improvements.

Let's look at some benefits that would lead you to seek outside help:

- The consultant acts as a catalyst to get a big job done punctually and well.
- The consultant offers experience or skill called for or needed only temporarily.
- The consultant provides specialized knowledge or technical skills not found in-house.
- The viewpoint of an outsider is needed to give you a fresh approach to a tough problem.

Any of these benefits may be enough to induce you to seek a consultant.

When is a foreign consultant needed? Only when a local consultant is, for whatever reason, not available to achieve the results you need. Don't think you should employ a foreign consultant simply because you think a foreigner is somehow better. You should pick the best person you can find within your budget, regardless of their origin. (We foreigners have to earn your trust, not simply claim it.) Cheryl Samuels-Campbell and Dunstan Campbell describe this situation from the viewpoint of the local consultant in Chapter 13 of this book.

Consultants are problem-solvers and companies usually use them for that purpose. Here are some key recommendations for getting the best return on the money you pay them:

- Define your consultant-related problem clearly.
- Choose the consultant carefully.
- Define your *mutual* obligations.

You can get the best results by working as a team with the consultant. Smart "management" of consultants benefits both you and the consultant. There are many tasks in any project that you can and should do under the consultant's guidance to keep the total costs down.

More importantly, working with a consultant helps strengthen potential programs. No organization wants to become dependent on a consultant. I have always felt that the best service I can provide as a consultant is to leave behind the expertise needed to implement recommendations and let you effectively continue the project without me. If you are an involved client who actively participates in the consulting project, you will be able to intelligently apply the knowledge learned to later in-house programs.

This chapter provides recommendations and examples for choosing a consultant, establishing a working relationship, and managing the consultant's project activities.

How to Hire a Consultant

Whenever the use of consultants is proposed, it is valid to ask whether the work should be contracted out or done in-house. Let's just assume that your boss has decreed that consultants be used. You are your own best defense against hiring unfit and unprofessional consultants. You must be wary from when the proposal is received until the project is finished. It isn't easy, and it may not match your overall style—but it's important.

Hiring a firm

Just who is it that will do this presumably vital work for you? All too often you don't know. You may have been told that the consulting firm to be used is the finest. It has 100 years of impeccable service worldwide and 50,000 satisfied clients. At that moment, remember this: Companies don't do consulting—consultants (people) do. Will you trust an important and costly project to them?

Often, this question isn't asked or, if asked, isn't pursued. You must determine the specific experience of the particular consulting staff members who will be assigned to your work. At one time, I worked for the consulting arm of a huge company. Based on what I saw, I recommend this series of questions that you can insist be fully answered by the consulting firms you're considering:

- What is the specific experience of each person who will work on your project?
- Can you have specific references for each person?
- Will the firm promise that specific people will be assigned to you?
- Who will pay for an unsuitable consultant?
- Can you interview the proposed staff members?

Specific experience. Insist on specifics, not just "five years of increasingly responsible experience." You must know what they *really* did on the projects cited. Not everyone can be in charge of every project. Yet, if you read the standardized consulting firm résumés, you would conclude that everyone was in charge.

Specific references. Do not accept the assurance that you don't need specific references, since the reputation of the firm will protect you. It won't. Even if the firm makes good on its employee's mistakes you will still be left with the disturbance and lost time. Insist on verifiable references, with specific names and telephone numbers. Check them out carefully. Try calling yet other individuals in the referenced companies.

Specific people. I've spent years writing and reviewing proposals. There is a strong tendency to throw everything into proposals. You may see dozens of résumés. The proposal may feature the firm's heavy hitters: the well-known names and published authors. This can be impressive. But when you meet the team that's actually going to work for you, the stars may be strangely absent. Even the so-so hitters may be absent. You can be faced with consultants of obscure pedigree.

Consulting firms won't want to guarantee who will do the work. They will tell you, honestly, that their workload varies. They may correctly point out that you haven't committed to them yet either.

Specific guarantees. Will you have to pay for an unsuitable consultant? The answer, generally, is yes. It's bad enough that the person they sent put your project back a month. They will also bill you at high rates for the wasted time. You should insist on a contract clause where if, in your sole judgment, a consultant proves to be unsuitable within a stated period, the consulting firm will be responsible for supplying a replacement subject to your approval. And, you will not be billed for the time of the unsuitable consultant.

Specific meetings. Ask to interview the proposed staff members. As pointed out, senior consultants and salespeople may be very different from those who do the work. Often, a short interview can warn that you're headed for trouble. Here are three ways to avoid it:

- Prepare tough questions.
- Interview the person privately (with no one from the consulting firm present).
- Ask the person for added references.

Hiring an individual consultant

Where to look. There are several sources for finding global HRD consultants. One is the HRD people in other organizations in your country. You can use the resources of professional associations to identify prospective consultants. You can also make valuable contacts at professional conferences and meetings.

Expertise. First, consider expertise. Obviously, consultants should have top-level skills in the area in which they will serve you. The less obvious expertise—too often overlooked—is human relations. These are interpersonal skills that enable the consultant to work well with your staff, understand your organization, and determine how to make the recommendations work.

Interpersonal Skill. Look for skill in interpersonal relationships even when such relationships are not the focus of the project itself. Good global HRD consultants will be oriented to the people-aspect of problems, and try hard to earn your trust and respect. They will respect the information or points of view expressed by you and your staff. You can expect them to seek your participation in the solution of the problem. They will transfer their knowledge to your personnel.

Communication skills. Again, even when communication is not the subject of the project, a global HRD consultant should have sound communications skills. This includes effective speaking and listening, exploring, and other interviewing. It will be important when the consultant leads the group, conducts meetings, and makes presentations. Also, look for good written communication skills.

Integrity. Look for consultants who will not pursue their own interest at your expense. Find someone that fits in with your style and your need. On the project level, your organization must move to meet the consultant. On the personal level, the consultant should do the moving.

You want an ethical consultant. Consultants should be willing and able to keep information about you confidential and not take advantage of the knowledge they will surely gain on the project. Any consultants who accept a commission from someone else in connection with their work with you are unsavory. They should inform you in advance of any relationships and interests that might influence their judgment. They should also *not* have an interest in any business that is in any way in competition with you—unless they disclose it. They should not hire away any of your employees or suggest alternative employment to them.

I have seen foreign consultants bring "foreign" and potentially incompatible social or political ideas. Perhaps you have, too. When these are not welcome, an ethical consultant will suppress them in the interest of the project. There are plenty of excellent consultants. You should not hire or keep one whose behavior is less than ethical.

Perspective. The company may need a consultant with either a broad or narrow perspective. If all that is needed is an updated performance appraisal system, then hire a consultant with expertise in performance appraisal. However, don't expect that consultant to restructure the organization. A consultant with too narrow a perspective cannot view the broader internal issues that can hinder implementation of a project.

You wouldn't assume the need for a medical specialist without first checking with a general medical practitioner. In HRD, it is often wise to seek the advice of an HRD generalist, who can see your "big picture" and avoid treating only the symptoms. An HRD generalist *may* be able to offer the best overall technical solution and help you understand how to apply it within your organization.

Making a selection
If a consultant who has worked for 20 years in your country, is fluent in your language, and is steeped in your culture is not available, look for one who appreciates your country, your organization and its make-up, and the technical problems. Look for enthusiasm, sincerity, and interest. An organized, enthusiastic, sensitive consultant with a broad perspective can often overcome minor technical deficiencies. Did you understand the proposal on the first reading? It won't become any clearer on the

second. The proposal tells you whether consultants listened to you—or understand you and your specific situation. If they don't before you hire them, they won't later either. (You obviously can't expect them to know internal things that would not be known by outsiders.)

Personal chemistry between you and the consultant can make all the difference on some projects. If it doesn't feel right to you at the beginning, it probably never will. You should not hire that person. Look for someone that you feel comfortable with.

Once you have narrowed your choice, be sure to communicate your situation and the problems clearly. Share the organization chart and even sensitive information. Getting the best person for the job far outweighs the risks. Better informed, the consultant can work out an approach tailored to your needs.

Fees

Be cautious when comparing consulting costs. Hourly rates are not as important as the total cost or project results. Hire the consultant who will do the project most efficiently. One consultant may take half the time allotted but the quality of the results may vary.

In global HRD consulting, many different methods are used to determine fees. There are numerous reasons for this variation in costs. Variables in projects make the consulting field highly individualistic. The larger, more prominent firms and the people with greater experience or unique capabilities can claim higher commissions for their services. Also, the field has not classified skills in a way that could support a standard fee schedule.

Pick the compensation method that best fits your needs. Develop specifications that clearly define the purpose and intent of the project for the benefit of both parties.

Common pitfalls. Failure to include estimates for the following items will bring a project to its knees. Make sure the consultant has included:

- Coordination
- Meetings
- Preparation time
- Project management
- Quality assurance
- Review
- Travel time
- Writing reports

Fee methods. Foreign consultants can work with any payment method that is mandated by your organization. They are accustomed to the following methods:

- Daily fees. Consultants often quote a daily fee if they will spend much time on your site; for example, if they plan a complete large analysis. A daily fee also is good if the consultants must travel on your behalf—it is advantageous for them to charge by the day instead of billing for travel time and expenses. This is the most common method used internationally.
- Flat fees. These involve finite projects, such as analysis of an established job, evaluation of existing facilities or equipment, or routine matters that do not involve meetings, projections, or bidding.
- Hourly fees. These can include anything to do with straightening out instructional errors, interviews with management to define requirements, discussions with vendors after a Request for Proposal (RFP) is issued, contract negotiations when equipment is to be acquired, and system installation and implementation. Hourly fees are uncommon in international work.
- Retainers. These are used in projects that take odds and ends of time over many months, such as projects divided into phases, some of them relatively slow. Retainers are also used to arrange availability for long-range planning on an as-needed basis. A retainer is every consultant's dream, but retainers are rare on domestic and global projects because of the difficulty in administering them.
  Be skeptical of a too-low fee. If a consultant asks for a suspiciously low fee, where will the rest of the money come from? Does the consultant completely misunderstand the project? There may be legitimate reasons for a low fee, but you need to know what they are.

Checklist for hiring a foreign consultant
- Negotiating the consultant's fees and assignment is a reasonable procedure.
- Asking for a lower rate is not always an advantage. If you buy too cheap, you get too cheap.
- Ask your friends and colleagues in the field. This can be important in avoiding paying too much *and* in trying to negotiate lower than the consultant will actually go.
- This is more important when working with a consultant new to your country who is unfamiliar with the latest rules related to your area, such as maximum fees. One sensitive area is taxes, so make it clear whether local taxes must be collected from the consultant's fee. Agree on the currency for payment. Some consultants will prefer payment in their own currency, others may prefer payment in yours. The point is that there should be no surprises about money.
- The more you know before the negotiations, the better prepared you are.
- This will help you to develop a general idea about their projects, financial position, and commitments.
- The consultant may know less of your country and organization than you have supposed. This may be particularly true of the process to finalize a contract, so negotiation may take more time than the consultant expects.

- Establish and keep cordial relations with the consultant and everyone from the consultant's organization.
- A foreign consultant may have a different approach than you expect. Try to understand the way the consultant proposes to work, which may have merit.

How to Work With a Consultant

Working productively with a person from outside your organization and your country should be an exhilarating and totally positive experience. The importance of you and the consultant working as a team to get the best results cannot be overemphasized. If you take part actively in the project, you will reduce the consulting costs. Also, you gain expertise and become equipped to implement future projects alone. You can begin the team approach during the hiring process and build it into the project. You should try to

- Establish a collaborative relationship
- Solve problems in a way that works in your organization
- Ensure that attention is given to both the HRD problems and the relationship

Relationships
The consultant may work in several possible relationships to you and the project. These are self-evident in all projects. Decide which is appropriate in your case and stick with it. The possible relationships are

- Pair of hands
- Expert
- Collaborator

A pair of hands. With this relationship, you will identify the problem, the solution, and how the consultant will implement those decisions. Although this relationship does not take full advantage of the consultant's potential, it is not inherently less desirable than other relationships.

An expert. With this relationship, the consultant identifies the problem and what the solutions should be. The consultant may also implement those solutions; in other cases, the implementation may be left to your staff.

A collaborator. With this relationship, you identify the problem and what the solutions should be jointly with the consultant. The consultant may also implement those solutions, or not, as best suits the project.

Working together

Strong, positive benefits are to be gained from the consultant and client working together as a team. Be sure to choose the approach carefully, making sure it is tailored to your specific situation. Formally or informally make an implementation plan by outlining the tasks, responsibilities, and schedule for completing tasks. Determine how the foreign consultant will work. Possibilities include, but are not limited to, working:

- With you directly
- With your staff
- With the organization (interviewing employees as needed, and discussing ideas as they evolve)
- In isolation (collecting facts, analyzing them and then presenting recommendations)

What should you do?

Establish a project relationship. Help the consultant collect and analyze the data, and discuss recommendations. You should also be actively committed in implementing the recommendations.

Do not wait until the consultant asks for someone to act as an inside-your-organization contact (a sign of a good consultant). Always delegate the best person possible on your own initiative. When the consultant arrives for a working session, hold all calls and prevent interruptions. Remember, their time is your money.

The consultant may work at a faster pace than you are accustomed to. Be sure that your project resources are the best quality, timely, consistent, and continuous (do not pull your person off in mid-project). If you do not live up to your part of the agreement, the consultant may charge more or produce less because of a lack of resources or delays in getting information. This is the biggest frustration to a consultant who wants to do a super job for you. Remember that the consultant wants to please you. Ask yourself, "How can I help the consultant please me?"

Establish a business relationship. Confirm that you and the consultant agree on billing procedures. Something up front? An invoice at the beginning of each month? On completion of project phases? These are all perfectly valid ways of billing and paying.

Agree on how expenses will be handled. The simplest and best way is usually to bill expenses at their actual cost, accompanied by receipts. If your consultant is to bill you for telephone calls, overnight document delivery, etc., you should know at the beginning. Most consultants do bill clients for expenses, but practices vary tremendously between countries. Make sure the consultant understands how this will work before starting.

When the project is finished, meet with the consultant, hopefully to wrap up the successful completion of a complex and challenging project. The consultant will appreciate your honest appraisal of the project's plusses and minuses. The consultant almost certainly will want to work with you again, and if you see that as a possibility, say so. It will be appreciated.

Establish a personal relationship. The consultant may be a stranger in your city, country, or region. Exactly what you can or want to do may vary greatly according to your own social and business customs. Despite how limiting these may be, there are always things you could do to make the consultant's life more comfortable.

A consultant who cares nothing for your culture, customs, architecture, music, food, handicrafts, or anything else is rare—and will ultimately fail anyway. Therefore, you can safely assume the foreigner *is* interested in one or more of these things. The consultant can use a healthy interest in these things to fight culture shock, and you can help. Why not help the consultant to find a copy of the local newspaper, magazine, or embassy cultural sheet that lists local events of interest in the foreigner's own language. If you explore the consultant's interests you can help make arrangements for tours or other activities.

Social events may be a part of the project budget. Beyond that, the cost of entertaining the consultant might be a problem. You should consider simple things. My client in Prague took me to a 400-year-old brewery cellar that was nearly across the street from the project office. The simple luncheon plate was accompanied by a beer brewed right there. The cost was small, the togetherness-building was big.

Listen carefully to what the consultant says. There may be clues to inner feelings and difficulty in coping with culture shock. Ask the consultant about his or her personal interests. Do everything you can think of to help the consultant. Remember the consultant is a human being. Say positive things about the consultant to everyone in your organization.

Checklist for working with a foreign consultant
- Remember that the consultant is a stranger in your land.
- Remember that the consultant will fail without your help and support.
- Remember there is a personal side, as well as a business side, of the relationship.
- Supervise and support the consultant. The consultant is an outsider who represents change, and most organizations react defensively to any change of a time-honored routine.
- Establish evaluation criteria with your consultant, even if they are "unofficial." How will you and your consultant know that the project was successful?

How to manage a consultant

Remember that consultants need to be managed! Even if your consultant is the world's most competent, who can do everything autonomously, the management process will increase your own learning. Insist on frequent, informal project progress meetings. Discuss new ideas as they evolve.

Make the importance of the project clear. Tell the consultant how you will benefit if the project is done well and how your organization will suffer if it is done poorly. Determine how much risk you will take to permit the consultant to complete the project properly. The key is to identify the consequences to the various personnel involved in your organization. This will give the consultant a good idea of how valuable you feel the project will be. Any consultant of value will immediately tune in to this information, and sense that future work depends on success.

Provide needed resources. Determine and agree on how much of your organization's resources you will provide. For example, the numbers and types of people provided for interviewing, material made available, computer time, and any other equipment or reports the consultant may need.

The time you waste is your own. Therefore, don't waste it! Schedule meetings to evaluate project progress and to verify that your needs are addressed. Such meetings ensure that unanticipated elements are dealt with promptly. Long and directionless meetings, lack of communication, and changes in personnel working on the project waste time and boost fees. Try to get everyone involved early so progress will not halt while a newcomer is brought up to date.

A wise consultant will insist in the proposal and contract that if a client's employee causes the consultant a delay, there will be an added charge of so many dollars for each day delayed. Every appointment that your employees postpone or cancel will delay the deadline for the delivery of your products by at least one day.

Will you will benefit from the consulting product coming in on time (or be hurt by its coming in late)? If so, and you have enough influence within your organization, exert it to reduce these kinds of delay.

Identify deliverables. The project "deliverables," or tangible products, should be named clearly at the onset. Deliverables may include presentations, reports, HRD activities, and implementation plans. They may also include specific recommendations such as for enhanced procedures, new instructional materials, or a new HRD system.

Describe end-of-project outputs in specific terms. At the end of the project, refer to these criteria to ensure that the consultant delivered whatever was agreed.

Don't be deceived. Clients often evaluate consultants on how hard they *appear* to work. To improve their evaluation, some consultants work long hours on the client's premises. This is particularly true when clients are naive or are new to the technology involved. Use your list of deliverables and measure progress toward them. Hours spent mean nothing unless they produce results.

Stop potential problems immediately. A wise consultant will *always* listen when you speak. If you see that the consultant is not paying attention to your directions, something is wrong. Have a private meeting and discuss this problem immediately.

A wise consultant will also treat your employees with complete respect. The consultant is there to serve you, and not the other way around. Lack of respect may lead to big problems, in unanticipated ways, later in the project. It may result from a simple misunderstanding, so meet privately with the consultant to discuss it. Also, be alert to the reverse problem, where the consultant for some reason feels mistreated by your people.

Have the consultant compose an invoice. It should itemize and list everything done. Make sure that it includes such things as the name of each person interviewed, travel times and locations, secretarial and production times, telephone calls, and review of your materials. Include anything else that takes the consultant's time.

"Bad projects." Sometimes you may want a consultant to do your "dirty work," such as completing a project that discredits another department, or person or doing a project that is pre-planned to fail. Consultants will try to avoid these kinds of projects because they will kill any hope of future business with the client organization and could taint their reputation.

Measure the results. How can you measure results when there are no clear financial returns on investment? You can devise several yardsticks, including:

- Did you gain fresh and valuable insights into what you should be doing?
- Was the project carried out with the least disruption?
- Were the consultant's cost figures and timetables realistic?
- Would you employ the same consultant again?

Checklist for managing a foreign consultant
1. Remember that the consultant is a consultant.
2. Clearly establish the responsibilities of you and the consultant. Include the details, not just the roles.
3. Make sure the project has the resources it needs to succeed.
4. Don't waste the consultant's project time or let anyone else waste it.
5. Make a schedule. Stick to it!

6. Look for real production. Don't be fooled by smoke and mirrors.
7. Be alert to problems. Detect them early and fix them immediately.
8. Avoid "bad projects."
9. Evaluate the project.

How to get 100 percent from a foreign HRD consultant

A fellow consultant once told me, "Consulting is 90 percent getting along with people and 10 percent knowing the (HRD) technology. But, you'd better know 100 percent of that 10 percent." I've followed that advice ever since. It has made nearly every project a joy, and helped me to get through a few difficult ones.

As a client, you control the whole 100 percent! When you hire the consultant, you can ensure 100 percent of the 10 percent in knowing the HRD technology is there. The key to getting the full 100 percent of the 90 percent is to help the client to get along with people. You can help the consultant succeed by paying as much attention to the personal side of your project as you do to managing the technical side. You'll find that 100 percent of 10 percent plus 100 percent of 90 percent adds up to a successful project.

References

Bell, C., and Nadler, L. *Clients & Consultants: Meeting and Exceeding Expectations* (Second Edition). Houston,TX: Gulf Publishing, 1985, p. 166.

Lippitt, G., and Lippitt, R. *The Consulting Process in Action* (Second Edition). San Diego, CA: University Associates, 1986.

CHAPTER 9

Organizations Are People: The Human Side of Corporate Transformation

Pierre Casse

People change. These life changes and transformations, which everybody experiences, have been analyzed in different contexts and described in various ways by psychologists and psychoanalysts. And, it seems, there are parallels between personal or individual development — called "Individuation" by the well-known Swiss psychologist, C. G. Jung — and corporate growth. Just like people, global organizations can learn from their experiences of growing and expanding. In this sense, organizations are truly like people.

The Unpredictable Corporate World

Company executives who want to gain a competitive advantage must discern the patterns emerging in the corporate world of the 1990s:

- Business is becoming ever more global.
- Corporations are becoming leaner and most corporate strategies now emphasize some type of partnership with the customers, suppliers, distributors and even, God forbid, the competitors
- Executives struggle with a more and more unpredictable environment.

The transformations taking place—sometimes without our will and even more without our awareness—can be difficult and painful. Companies live in a perpetual flux of change. The market place changes continually and requires an ongoing effort by business people to adapt their strategies, structures, and corporate cultures to meet the ever-evolving demands of their customers.

These transformations, which seem to happen on an almost daily basis, raise anxiety among responsible corporate leaders who no longer fully comprehend the scope of what's happening, or who find that the rational and effective controls they have used in the past no longer work. In today's world all global corporations are facing turnaround dilemmas and unprecedented challenges often experienced as incoherent, chaotic, or uninterpretable.

And yet a pattern is out there. It can be recognized and can help corporate people understand the process they are experiencing, prepare themselves for what's going to happen next, avoid problems, and finally, take advantage of the opportunities for transformation.

The Pattern of Transformation

Like individuals, global corporations experience different stages of development and growth, described in Figure 9.1.

Figure 9.1: Individuals vs. Corporations

Individual	Corporation
1. Getting into a stage of inflation	Taking full advantage of business opportunities
2. Going for an inflated act	Taking a risk and going for more
3. Being punished and rejected	Failing and getting into trouble
4. Feeling bad and being in pain	Experiencing confusion and turmoil
5. Looking for easy solutions	Searching for the quick fix
6. Getting serious and analyzing	Taking stock and learning the event
7. Understanding one's own limitations and accepting them	Identifying the company weakness
8. Growing from the experience	Discovering strengths

The process can be visualized as shown in Figure 9.2.

Figure 9.2: The Transformation Life Cycle

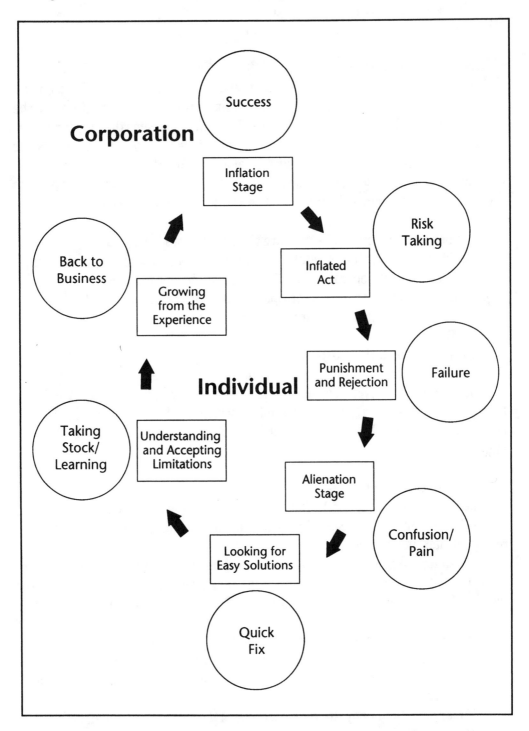

Three phases of the above model can be identified, which can then be used by business people to better understand the Transformation Life Cycle, and to prepare for what's ahead:

- Phase 1: The Euphoria Stage (Aren't we lucky?)
- Phase 2: The Disorientation Stage (Why the pain?)
- Phase 3: The Stage of Learning (Can we get out?)

The Euphoria Stage

There are times in the life of the corporation when everything looks good and promising. Nothing can fail. There is a natural fit between the organization and the environment. All the pieces are falling into place. The sky seems the only limit. This stage can last for quite some time to the great satisfaction of all the key players involved (executives, shareholders, personnel and so forth).

A close analysis of this first phase in the global corporate transformation process reveals several characteristic errors that seem inevitably to be made:

- Experiencing euphoria — "We are the best and we cannot fail!"
- Taking some risk (i.e., stretching corporate resources and people too thin, diversifying into operations far from the core business, investing in marginal activities with no prospect of any sure return on investment)
- Becoming unrealistic and arrogant

Guidelines for global corporate leaders

Leaders of global corporations should take full advantage of this first phase of the Transformation Life Cycle by maximizing benefits through the use of existing business opportunities. The errors characteristic of this phase can be avoided by not getting carried away. Preparation for the surprises of the next phase is critically important.

The Disorientation Stage

The risk-taking attitude of the Euphoria Stage results eventually in one or several failures, whether of unsuccessful ventures or an accumulation of unsatisfactory results. Something is wrong.

Over time, confusion arises as these failures become manifest, but most executives of global corporations remain unwilling to acknowledge either the confusion or the signals that something is definitely wrong. Some typical reactions are:

- To believe that it is only a temporary setback (It will pass.)
- To blame others for what's happening and look for scapegoats (The competitors or the government are responsible...the customers do not understand.)
- To fantasize and deny the very existence of a problem (We are all right, there is no crisis.)

This stage can be subtle, short-lasting, or deep, but seems always in our experience to lead to some pain and turmoil. The suffering of the corporate people depends on three factors:

- The degree of inflation experienced before (the higher the inflation, the more painful the "alienation")
- The capacity of the senior executives to realize that the bonanza period is over and that a new orientation or strategy is needed
- The willingness of the people to mobilize themselves to neutralize the now prevailing trends or, even better, to "go with the new wind"

Guidelines for global corporate leaders

During the Disorientation Stage, leaders of global corporations should scan their environments for advance signals that indicate a turning point has been reached. They must be prepared to learn from their experience and to design a new strategy. The time is up.

The Learning Stage

When one is confronted with the tough reality of a business turndown (profits are going down, the company is losing market share, morale is low, employees are being laid off and so forth), it is common to look for quick fixes. During this stage, global corporations typically restructure without a clear strategy, do more of what's not working, change some key managers, regulate more, or create new policies—all in an attempt to find an easy solution.

Realistically, the only reliable way to move again toward profitability, growth, and development is to take stock and learn from what happened in an objective and impartial way. The company must redefine its mission, vision, and strategies: What business are we in? Where do we want to be in three or five years from now? How shall we get there? Having answered these basic questions, the corporation must then assess its strengths and its weaknesses.

A detailed examination of what happened will enable the corporation to better identify its limitations and define its core business (What do we do well?). This review of critical events gives the perspective needed for learning to take place, and even enables companies to discover new opportunities of which it was previously unaware.

Very few companies understand what this "soul searching" is all about or know how to conduct such an internal "audit." And commonly this exercise is delayed by the CEO or senior management, making the review even more difficult and painful.

Guidelines for global corporate leaders

Understanding the corporate cycle and learning from it are part of the executive's duty. As the global company emerges from the crisis, corporate leaders will benefit from devoting more time to this learning stage of the corporate transformation cycle so that valuable lessons can be identified and used.

Culture and Corporate Transformation

Organizations in different countries cope with the unpredictable world in various fashions, because corporate and national cultures have a strong impact on the leaders' attitudes towards change and transformation. For instance, the ambiguity which always goes with the transformation process described above is defined and handled differently by Western and Eastern cultures.

Ambiguity as a problem

Most U.S. and European corporations still look at ambiguity as something negative which must be controlled. In the Western world uncertainty leads to counter-productive behaviors such as withdrawing or fighting aggressively. Both reactions are commonly defined as unhealthy and sources of trouble as described in Figure 9.3:

Figure 9.3: List of Attributes Attached to Withdrawing and Fighting

• Withdrawing	• Fighting
• Disinterested	• Moody
• Demotivated	• Aggressive
• Uncommitted	• Cynical
• Uninvolved	• Resisting
• Uncooperative	• Conflictual
• Absent-minded	• Confrontational
• Passive	• Destructive

The corporate transformation process must be analyzed, understood, and managed to avoid or at least minimize the negative reactions of the people involved. Leaders of global corporations should try to apply the three following guidelines:

- Inform
- Clarify
- Explain

Ambiguity as an opportunity

Many Eastern organizations have a completely different approach to defining and understanding the same phenomenon. They believe, for instance, that ambiguity can lead to flexibility (more options are available) and innovation (new options are created). Both are opportunities to be seized according to the people's ways of thinking and reacting as described in Figure 9.4:

Figure 9.4: List of Attributes Attached to Flexibility and Innovation

• Flexibility	• Innovation
• Openness	• Creativity
• Willingness to try	• Searching
• Testing out	• Experimenting
• Changing	• Adding up
• Adapting	• Questioning
• Expanding	• Probing
• Switching	• Exploring
• Moving on	• Selling ideas

Leaders of global corporations in this cultural environment will tend to be patient, look for trends, and encourage the trying out of new behaviors. The guidelines in this context are

- Try different things.
- Check what's working and not working.
- Adapt or adjust yourself accordingly.

Consultants working with global organizations must help the corporate leaders learn how to both control and take advantage of the uncertainty which always goes with the transformation life cycle. Consultants can help the corporate leaders to

- Go with the natural flow of the cycle and learn from it as much as possible.
- Invest time and energy to "manage" the cycle so that the painful phases are speeded up and the good ones fully exploited.
- Minimize the risk and the pain, keeping in mind that in any "bad" situation there is always the seed of something good.

Transformation Stages and Cultural Differences

The global consultant should be aware of the variety of cultural reactions of corporate people when they experience the transformation life cycle. Euphoria, disorientation, and learning are perceived and lived differently by people, groups, organizations, and nations. The consultant should keep an eye on three issues:

- What triggers the transformation phase?
- How is it experienced and handled?
- What is the result of the experience for the organization and its members?

The following grid can help the consultant analyze and understand the three-stage transformation process:

Cultural Differences	What triggers the phase?	How is it experienced?	What is its outcome?
1. Euphoria	• economic growth • company image • career opportunities	• people spend more money • people are proud and work more • personal success	• richer people (at least some) • mobilization of people and their talents • promotions and redistribution of power
2. Disorientation	• failures • new challenges • managerial decisions	• fighting/ withdrawing • innovating/ expanding • reviewing/ analyzing	• conflicts and confrontations • change taking stock and trying to understand
3. Learning	• controlling by the organization • imposed by environment • spontaneous from inside	• self examination process • struggling • exchanging/ learning from each other	• accepting limitations/ identifying strengths • restructuration/ rationalization • creation of a learning how-to-learn environment

Conclusion

Individuals certainly experience the periods of euphoria, disorientation and learning described above, and can grow from such experiences. Global corporations, too, can learn. They should follow these rules:

- Know that the pattern exists.
- Remember that in any bad situation, including a crisis, there is always the seed of something good. Look at such situations as opportunities.
- To get a clear picture of its limits and go back to its core business is a healthy process that all companies should undertake from time to time.

Most especially, never lose sight of the fact that global organizations are, indeed, just like people.

About the Author

Pierre Casse is Professor and Director of IMD, the International Institute for Management Development in Lausanne, Switzerland.

CHAPTER 10

The Impact of the Cultural Environment on HRD

Michael Marquardt

Experienced international human resource development professionals firmly believe that understanding the cultural values of the learners is critical in their work. An HRD program cannot succeed if culture is ignored.

Hofstede (1980), who instructed thousands of IBM employees in over 40 countries for 20 years, stated that "national culture explained over 50 percent of the differences in the behavior and attitude of employees. Culture explains more than the differences in professional roles, age, gender, or race." And these differences do not go away if one is employed in a global corporation. Laurant (1983) discovered that the impact of culture was greater in multinational corporations than in domestic-only corporations. As a matter of fact, Laurant adds, because that environment causes "people to cling to their own cultural values."

A Model Showing Cultural Impact on HRD

In HRD, there are generally approved principles as to the sequence and components of HRD design and delivery, the roles of the instructors and learners, and the general administration and environment for HRD. However, the implementation of these HRD principles is significantly affected by the cultural environment in which the activity occurs. Culture is like the filter through which HRD must pass, as shown by Figure 10.1 below.

Figure 10.1: Cultural Impact on HRD

HRD Principles	Cultural Environment	HRD Implementation

a. Roles of Instructors
    and Learners
b. Analysis & Design
c. Development &
    Delivery-
d. Administration &
    Environment
	Factors
	&
	Characteristics
		a. Roles of Instructors
		    and Learners
		b. Analysis & Design
		c. Development &
		    Delivery
		d. Administration &
		    Environment

As Figure 10.1 shows, the factors of culture or cultural environment impact on the
  • Roles of the instructor and learner
  • Analysis and design
  • Development and delivery
  • Administration and environment of the HRD
Before examining the impact of the cultural environment on HRD implementation, let us first define what we mean by culture, its characteristics, and the factors that create the cultural environment.

Culture-definition and characteristics

Culture can be defined in many ways. Barnouw (1963) defines it "as a way of life of a group of people...which is handed down from one generation to the next through the means of language and imitation."

Brown (1976) sees culture as something that
  • Is shared by all or almost all members of some social group
  • Older members of the group pass on to younger members
  • Shapes behavior or structures one's perception of the world

Hofstede (1980) refers to culture as "collectively programming the mind." For him, culture is an interactive aggregate of common characteristics that influences a human group's response to the environment.

For Bierstadt (1963), culture consists of a system of explicit and implicit guidelines for *thinking, doing, and living.* Thinking (ideas) encompass values, beliefs, myths, and folklore. Doing (norms) includes laws, statutes, customs, regulations, ceremonies, fashions, and etiquette. Living (materials) refers to the use of machines, tools, natural resources, food, clothing, etc. Pace (1991) also includes ideology (the combination of ideas and norms), technology (combination of ideas, norms, and materials), and communication and language in his description of culture. Storti (1989) adds sense of self and space, relationships, and work habits and practices to the components of culture and arrives at ten characteristics of every culture:
  • Sense of self (humans are basically good, evil, or combination of both; individual or group-focused).

- Time and time consciousness (past, present, or future oriented; controlled or uncontrolled)
- Norms and values
- Communication and language
- Dress and appearance
- Food and feeding habits
- Relationships
- Beliefs and attitudes
- Mental and learning processes
- Work habits and practices

The cultural environment

The cultural environment is created by nine interacting factors: religion, learning[1], economics, politics, family, class structure, language, history, and natural resources and geography as shown in Figure 10.2.

Figure 10.2: Cultural Environment Factors

Religion	Learning	Economics
Family	HRD	History
Politics		Cultural Environment
Class Structure	Language	Natural Resources & Geography

What distinguishes one culture from another is not the presence or absence of these factors, but rather the pattern and processes within and between them. And each of these factors significantly affects HRD practice, as we will note later in this chapter.

Religion

Religion, the belief in a particular view of the supernatural with accompanying rituals and rules, is probably the single most influential factor in cultural thinking, living, and doing. Religion helps to establish the beliefs and norms, determines whether a people see themselves as basically good or evil, whether they can control or will be controlled by the environment, and what is truly important in life. Many "inspired" religious writings even describe how one should eat, dress, relate to others, and work.

[1]Editors' note: Terminology becomes difficult when mixing discussions of HRD and the formal education system. In general, learning is used here because that is what is meant. Education is used in those cases where reference is to formal education.

Learning

Learning determines a society's means of transmitting the knowledge, skills, and attitudes necessary to live in that society. Learning may be formal (primary, secondary, higher, and vocational), nonformal (structured learning outside the academic system; e.g., workplace learning) and informal (unstructured, such as learning from one's parents).

Some cultures such as the U.S. encourage inductive learning (open-ended, case-by-case) while others are more deductive (general to specific), such as France and Indonesia. Many societies encourage rote learning in an environment with absolute respect and obedience to the instructor while other societies support open, participative learning with a more egalitarian relationship between teacher and student.

Economics

Economics concerns production and distribution. Societies may be
- Free-market, capitalistic
- Centrally planned, government-controlled
- A mixture of the two

Approximately half the world's population lives under a centrally-planned, government-controlled economic system, although recent events in Eastern Europe, Asia, and Africa show a rapid movement toward a more capitalistic economy. Nevertheless, the impact of Marxist economics will influence the cultural behavior of these societies for many years, and the transfer from government responsibility to group/individual responsibility will mean difficult and painful values changes.

Political

The political factor encompasses structures and activities related to the allocation and use of power as well as the regulating of access to resources and opportunities. Political systems may range from totalitarian, with one person in control, to democracy, where the electorate is in control. Political systems may exclude certain groups by ethnic make-up, sex, age, or economic status.

Family

The concept of family in a culture may range from nuclear (immediate parents and children) to extended (including grandparents, cousins, aunts and uncles). The nuclear family has limited interaction outside the immediate family and family members have more freedom to ignore expectations of the extended family or even nuclear family in choosing a marriage partner, profession, home, etc. A member of a nuclear family is more responsible for his personal financial support, and is encouraged to "strike out on one's own" so as not to be a burden on the family. The Anglo-American culture for example, is strongly nuclear family oriented.

In the extended family, the obligation to family members overrides the desires and wishes of the individual. The son, especially, is expected to remain with the family to support it in whatever way he can. Most of Asia, Africa and Latin America place a high emphasis on the extended family structure.

Class structure

Class structure may range from open to closed. In open class structures, individuals have the ability to choose and to move up, down, or laterally in the system without major difficulty. *What you do* is the important criterion.

In a closed society, one's position is determined by *who you are*; that is, by birth rather than by individual achievement. The U.S. has a very open class structure compared with rural India, which is very closed.

Language

Language, according to George Will, is the carrier and conditioner of all cultures. The words and grammar available in a language strongly affect a culture's values, beliefs, relationships, and concepts.

English, for example, is a very direct and active language. To describe one's dropping of an object, in English I would say, "I dropped it," implying my action, control, and responsibility. In Spanish, I would say, "Se caho sobre me" (it dropped on me), implying passivity and lack of control.

Another example: English is an informal language, with only one form of the second person, singular and plural—"you." A more formal, hierarchical culture such as the Vietnamese has numerous words for "you" depending on age, sex, relationship, number, status, etc. Thus it is easy to see how much more natural it is for an American to be informal and egalitarian than for a Vietnamese.

One final example is the availability and many uses of the word "no" in English. The Thai language has no word for "no" since such a term is too rude and direct for the Thai culture.

History

A society's history can significantly impact its culture. China's long, glorious history has created a culture where one's perspective of time is very different than for a newly formed nation in Africa. (A Chinese HRD specialist once told me that China would soon be an economic power—but "soon" for him was 100–200 years.) Colonized countries of Africa and Asia have many values derived from and/or in contradiction to their colonizers. The Arab world identifies with the military successes of Mohammed and his successors. The United States' brief history includes the rugged frontiersman, rapid industrialization and expansion, and pride (arrogance to other cultures?) in being the "last, best hope of mankind."

Natural resources and geography

Obviously, the land in which a society lives influences its culture. The vast space, minerals, forests, and farmlands of the United States helped form a culture imbued with optimism, materialism, and confidence. Societies regularly facing hurricanes, flooding, drought, and having few or no minerals or arable land tend to be more fatalistic and going with the flow of life. The oil and sand of Saudi Arabia certainly affect Arab culture, just as rain and forests affect Liberian culture.

Let us now apply the model discussed earlier in this chapter and examine how the cultural environment affects the implementation of HRD in four distinct and divergent cultures—those of the United States, Japan, Saudi Arabia, and Mexico.

HRD Implementation in the United States

Cultural environment

Religion. The dominating religious influence is Protestantism with its emphasis on individualism, personal salvation, and the work ethic.

Learning. Educational opportunities are universal, with a strong public education system from kindergarten to graduate schools. Emphasis is on learning that is practical, utilitarian, and applicable. The inductive approach of thinking is encouraged. Experiences tend to be evaluated in terms of dichotomies (right/wrong, do/don't, successful/unsuccessful, good/evil, work/play, winner/loser, subjective/objective.

Economics. The U.S. economy is market driven and capitalistic. Competition is considered healthy for economic development.

Politics. The U.S. believes and practices democracy with universal suffrage. Government is to serve the people and not be too powerful. Individual rights are legally protected.

Family. Families are nuclear and children are responsible primarily to themselves for career choices and learning.

Class structure. The U.S. has an open class structure with access for anyone to advance. Initiative is respected and rewarded, and equality of opportunity is the norm.

Language. English is very active, direct, clear, and analytical. Since the United States has a low context culture (i.e., the environment, or context, is low or limited in communicating information), a precise and rich vocabulary is necessary.

History. Compared with the cultures of Asia and Europe, U.S. history is relatively short. The country has generally been economically and militarily successful over the past 200 years.

Natural resources and geography. Farmlands are abundant and fruitful because of arable lands and temperate climates. The U.S. has had vast frontiers and open spaces that encouraged rugged individualism and independence.

Impact on HRD implementation

Each of these nine cultural factors affect the implementation of HRD in the U.S. In the following section we will identify some HRD practices and what cultural factors account for them.

HRD roles. In the United States, there is a far more equal relationship between the instructor and the learner than in any other culture. Instructors can and will be challenged by the learners, so they must prove their competency and credibility. The instructors, however, are able to be informal and casual in working with the learners.

Such regional cultural factors as *class structure*, *politics*, and *language* support these roles and relationships between instructors and learners.

Analysis and design. In determining the objectives of an HRD program, the instructor is expected to analyze the learning needs of the learners in collaboration with the learners and their organization. People are expected to be comfortable in stating their needs. After all, one can always change and improve for the better, and learners in the United States want to achieve success. They are involved in setting objectives since they should have some awareness of what is best for them. If the learners apply themselves, they can reach clear, measurable objectives. *Religion* and *history* encourage this approach to needs analysis and objective-setting.

Development and delivery. HRD programs should be practical and relevant. Behavior can be changed and skills developed. A wide variety of methodologies are encouraged. Both inductive and deductive learning is desired. Appropriate methodologies include analysis, problem solving, learning from fellow learners, and learning by oneself. Lecturing by the instructor is tolerated in small doses.

Cultural factors like *natural resources, learning*, and *economics* push for this type of development and delivery.

Administration and environment. The venue should be comfortable and economical. Fancy ceremonies and speeches from dignitaries are not necessary. Learners are selected based upon the needs of the organization and how the employee's instruction will benefit the organization, not because of family name. *Politics* and *family* cultural factors are behind this preference for administration and environment.

HRD Implementation in Japan

Cultural environment

International HRD professionals who have worked in Japan realize that they must significantly modify their HRD implementation if they wish to be successful. Here are the cultural factors necessitating these changes:

Religion. Buddhism and Shintoism are the dominant religions. Both preach the importance of harmony with nature and one's fellow human beings, of accepting the world as it is, of seeking collaborative means to resolve problems. Humility is a valued virtue.

Learning. The influence of Confucian-based emphasis on learning and respect for the educator permeates the Japanese culture. Although opportunities may be limited, one seeks to learn what one can. In formal education, the teachers are highly respected and teach primarily by lecture while students learn primarily by rote.

Economics. The economy of Japan was historically feudal, but is now very capitalistic. Small family businesses are numerous, with the government providing much support to small and large enterprises. Entrepreneurship and hard work emerges from Confucianism.

Politics. Democracy has emerged, although for many years power was concentrated in the hands of a few feudal lords and the emperor.

Family. The family structure is strongly extended (again the Confucianist influence). One is expected to respect and obey parents and grandparents in the selection of profession, domicile, and spouse. The needs of the extended family and even the village are more important than the individual's needs. Relationships are needed to accomplish results.

Class structure. Class structures have traditionally been very closed and remain so in rural areas. In cities there is a growing opportunity to break away from one's expected position based on birth to opportunity based on achievement and hard work.

Language. The Japanese society is "high context" (i.e., the environment or context can determine more than words as to what is being communicated). The language also has numerous forms of "you" to distinguish the myriad of relationships with others.

History. The Japanese culture and history are thousands of years old, with much past power and glory. Time frames are long term and there is an appreciation of the past.

Natural resources and geography. A large population strains the food and mineral resources of Japan. Numerous floods and earthquakes create an acceptance of nature's power.

Impact on HRD implementation

Because of these cultural factors, the global HRD practitioner should adapt HRD in the following ways:

HRD roles. Learners have the utmost respect for all educators and treat them reverently. They expect the instructor to behave, dress, and relate in a highly professional, formal way. Learners may become uncomfortable with too much informality. They also hope to be treated with respect and sensitivity. The instructor is seen as knowing all and his assignments and expectations should be carried out without question or disagreement. *Religion, learning, politics, family, class structure,* and *language* all contribute to this view of the roles of instructors and learners.

Analysis and design. Since the instructor is omniscient and therefore should know what the learners need to learn, a needs analysis should be unnecessary. And it would be a loss of face or embarrassing for learners to admit weaknesses to an outsider. Questioning of Japanese can cause ritualized behavior, withdrawal, or even resentment of the instructor. Asking for self-analysis may be fine for Americans who value frankness and openness, but it is disastrous in Japan where a much higher value is placed on hiding one's own feelings and thoughts and not prying into the feelings and thoughts of others.

Establishing objectives is also challenging. Rigby (1986) notes that the concept of individual planning and goal-setting is not found to much extent in most East Asian philosophies and religions, which tend to be collective and fatalistic. Therefore, HRD that begins by asking for expectations, needs, and goals is unlikely to meet with comfortable or coherent responses.

Development and delivery. Through their rigid education system, the Japanese are accustomed to lectures, note-taking, and respectfully asking questions of the teacher. Learners attempt to soak up the information like a sponge and feed it back verbatim. They also tend to place a high value on orderliness and conformity and to prefer clear and specific instructions. Therefore HRD materials should be orderly, well-organized, and unambiguous.

Including role-plays and structured experiences in a workplace learning program will be unrewarding because of various cultural factors. First, it is very difficult, as required by role-play, for Japanese to put themselves in someone else's shoes, because of their high respect for others. Role-plays also generally include confrontation and/or innovation, both of which are inappropriate in a culture whose *religion, learning, politics, language,* and *history* value compromise, conformity, clear authority relationships and conflict avoidance. Much better for the instructor to demonstrate what is the best knowledge, skill, and/or attitude.

Mixing learners of different age, sex, or professional rank, and thereby ignoring status differences, may be seen as undermining authority and power in the workplace. Exercises that strip the participants of status tend to cause embarrassment, confusion, and loss of face for all participants at the expense of learning.

Administration and environment. A very high value is placed on visible signs of status and worth. One's authority depends greatly on the location and decor of the HRD professional's office and on how many and what kind of people report to the professional.

The quality of the instruction room, the HRD announcements, and educational resources determine how important the instruction will be perceived and if one will attend. Ceremonies with important dignitaries in attendance, certificates, plaques, and speeches are signs of the meeting's value.

HRD Implementation in Saudi Arabia

Cultural environment

Religion. The Islamic religion permeates the daily life of the region. The five pillars of Islam—the one God (Allah), prayer, charity, holy month of fasting (Ramadan), and pilgrimage to Mecca (Haj)—guide all, whether rich or poor, Egyptian or Iraqi, young or old. The teachings of Mohammed in the Koran—such as the brotherhood of all Muslims, the status of women, the rituals, and the mosques affect deeply the learning, politics, and family life of the Saudi society. Fatalism is so ingrained that the most common phase in this region is "Inshallah" (if God wills) since only God chooses what will occur.

Learning. The key learning for most Saudi Arabs is memorization of the Koran. The education system therefore emphasizes the imitative rather than creative approach to learning. One learns from memorization rather than from independent research and original work. In most places, girls are educated separately from boys.

Economics. Oil has made Saudi Arabia one of the richest countries in the world. Many workers from the poor countries (such as Egypt and Yemen) work in Saudi Arabia, and their remittances back to their families represent a major source of income for their countries. Social relations are as important as getting the job done. Misfortune may be attributed to outside influence, i.e., what God wills.

Politics. Saudi Arabia is an oligarchy run by a benevolent royal family, although democracy is being demanded by more and more people. The mullahs (church leaders) are very powerful and influential among the people. Decisions are made by consensus, by ruling councils, and by families.

Family. The extended family is the central part of Saudi Arab life, and the Koran spells out proper roles and relationships. There are formalized social distances between persons differing in age and sex, i.e., men higher than women, age than youth, married than unmarried. The parent's word is final and great respect for one's elders is expected and given. The family is the primary determinant of individual behavior in such areas as choice of occupation, spouse, living site, and numerous social obligations. Families are paternalistic and male-centered. Many homes will have a special meeting room, a "diwaniah" where neighboring men spend time socializing each evening.

Class structure. Social organization is highly stratified; the division of labor is primarily by class so that social mobility is difficult. Social morality prevails over individual morality, so concepts of right or wrong and reward or shame derive not from an individual's determination of appropriate behavior, but from what society in general dictates as the social norm. People are formal in manner, particularly in initial social relationships.

Language. Arabic, the language of the Koran, is for Saudi Arabs a language to be spoken and heard. They love to listen to Arabic poetry, speeches, and songs for hours.

How one says something becomes almost as important as *what* one says. Saudi Arabs are generally much better at speaking their language (and others) then writing it.

History. Within the first century after the death of Mohammed, the Arabs were masters of an empire extending from the shores of the Atlantic to the Chinese border. While the western world was experiencing the Dark Ages, the Islamic culture was flourishing in the arts and sciences. In more recent history, however, much of Saudi Arabia was colonized by the British, French, and Ottoman (Turkish) empires. Saudi Arabia became independent in 1932.

Natural resources and geography. Much of the region is desert with hot, dry weather. The Bedouin tradition of being very hospitable and generous to people traveling from oasis to oasis remains strong. Elaborate greetings and close physical contact while communicating derive from these times. The main natural resource is the rich deposits of oil that have enriched Saudi Arabia.

Impact on HRD implementation

HRD roles. Mohammed declared that education was the highest profession and therefore, teachers and instructors must be granted high respect by Saudi Arab learners. The learners also will want respect and a friendly relationship with the instructor.

Formality is important, for even casual encounters with a colleague will begin with oft-used and elaborately formal words of greetings.

Males (including instructors) are not to touch (i.e., shake hands with) a female learner. In some areas, men are not even allowed in the same room as women. *Religion*, *family*, and *class structure* are important cultural determinants for HRD roles.

Analysis and design. Identifying needs and weaknesses in an individual or organization is difficult since people must not speak negatively of others even if they dislike them. "God loveth not the speaking ill of anyone" according to the Koran. The frankness of Americans regarding others' faults is regarded as highly improper.

The fatalism of the Arab culture may make learners less motivated to totally achieve learning objectives, since that implies that one can control the future and oneself.

In designing the HRD program, it is important to allow lots of time for socializing and building relationships. Prayer time must also be built in. Things should not be rushed for, as the Koran states, "Haste is of the devil."

Development and delivery. A number of strategies and structures based on cultural factors can enhance the effective delivery of HRD programs in Saudi Arabia:

- Provide ample opportunities for learners to interact with the instructor and with each other (to develop personal relationships and to impress).
- Use more oral than written demonstrations of knowledge acquired.
- Avoid paper exercises and role-playing—they are considered games for school children.

Administration and environment. The Saudi Arabs like flourishes and ceremonies to permeate the learning process. HRD should not be scheduled during Ramadan, the month of fasting. Do not expect quick decisions from one person since the culture is very consultative and time is flexible. (Once I received the definition of "bakra" ["tomorrow"] as being similar to "manana" but *without* the urgency of that Spanish word.)

HRD Implementation in Mexico

Cultural environment

Religion. The Mexican culture is permeated by the Catholic religion, with its historical emphasis on hierarchy, patriarchy, and fatalism. The Spanish missionaries established a highly structured social and economic system. Women are much more active in religion than men.

Learning. The Mexican education system tends to emphasize the theoretical and the humanities, with less emphasis on the practical. Upper classes send children to private schools and universities, most of which are under the auspices of the Catholic Church. Illiteracy is high and limited vocational education is available.

Economics. Free market capitalism is preached, although economic power is primarily in the hands of small number of families in Mexico. Societies are divided between the wealthy and poor, with a small middle class.

Politics. The Spanish tradition of monarchy continued in Mexico until it gained independence from Spain in the early 1800s. Mexico, however, has maintained the tradition of the strong, decisive ruler. The people still elect charismatic, powerful leaders and like their strong individuality ("personalismo").

Family. Mexican culture has an extended family structure and there is high respect for the family. Women are placed on a pedestal and a man's machismo protects and impresses them. Authority is centered in the father and often extended to the "father of the nation," a strong dictator.

Class structure. Mexican culture is primarily a closed class structure in which one is born high or low. There are three distinct classes:
- New corporate leaders and rich families of immigrant descent whose wealth was earned from the land
- Latino workers of mostly mixed Spanish and Indian descent
- Native Indians at the very bottom economically and politically

Language. Spanish is a rich Romance language based upon Latin. It employs the passive voice more frequently than English, thereby showing less active control or responsibility.

History. Like many Latin American countries, Mexico identifies with the long and glorious history of Spain, its colonial ruler for over 300 years. The native Indian population has been nearly decimated.

Natural resources and geography. Many think of Mexico as the land of large cattle ranches and mountains; however, Mexico has become the most urbanized society in the world—in fact, Mexico City is the largest metropolitan area in the world.

Impact on HRD implementation

HRD Roles. As can be surmised from the cultural factors of *politics*, *economics*, *class structure*, and *history*, Mexicans prefer an instructor who is a decisive, clear, and charismatic leader. They like to be identified with a successful instructor and will be loyal to him as a person.

Analysis and design. The macho and personalismo qualities make it difficult to expose weaknesses and faults in a needs analysis. Opportunities for affiliating and socializing are important. Class structure and family factors, however, can cause tensions if Latinos and Indians or men and women are taught together.

Development and delivery. In developing the curriculum, the instructor should be aware of the Mexican *learning* tradition of lectures and more theoretical emphasis than in the U.S. Unlike the East Asian and Arabic cultures, where English is the acceptable language for HRD, Mexicans expect the instruction to be in Spanish.

Administration and environment. The value and importance of HRD is determined to a large extent by venue, which dignitaries are invited for the ceremonies, and the academic affiliation of the instructor. Time is very flexible, so beginning or ending at a certain time is not important. Decisions are often made by a single person at the top of the organization.

Conclusion

This chapter has presented only a few of the ways in which culture impacts HRD. Just as form (i.e., structure) affects function (i.e., operations) in organizations, culture significantly affects how learners learn in a culture and, therefore, how it is best for instructors, too. The analysis, design, development, delivery, evaluation, and administration of HRD programs must be adapted to the culture in which they occur.

References

Barnouw, V. *Culture and Personality*. Homewood, IL: The Dorsey Press, 1963.

Bierstadt, R. *The Social Order: An Introduction to Sociology*. New York, NY: McGraw-Hill, 1963.

Brown, M. "Values—A Necessary but Neglected Ingredient of Motivation on the Job", *Academy of Management Review*, I, 1976, pp.15-22.

Hofstede, G. *Culture's Consequences: International Differences in Work Related Values.* Beverly Hills, CA: Sage Publications.

Laurant, A. "The Cultural Diversity of Western Conceptions of Management". *International Studies of Management and Organization, Vol. XIII*, No. 1-2 Spring-Summer, pp. 75-96 (1983).

Pace, W. *Human Resource Development,* Englewood Cliffs, NJ: Prentice Hall, 1991.

Rigby, J. "Culture and Design of Management Training Programs in Southeast Asia". In *International HRD Annual II.* Alexandria,VA: ASTD Press, 1986.

Storti, C. *The Art of Crossing Cultures*. Yarmouth, ME: Intercultural Press, 1989.

About the Author

Michael Marquardt is Vice President, The World Group, in Reston, Va. Previously, he was Executive Director of the World Center for Development and Training, Vice President of ECI International, and Director of Human Resources at the Overseas Education Fund. He completed his doctoral studies in Human Resource Development at George Washington University. He was named the American Society for Training and Development (ASTD) International HRD Practitioner of the Year and received the President's Award of the U.S. Department of Agriculture Graduate School. He served as President of the Metropolitan Washington D.C. Chapter of ASTD and Director of ASTD's International Professional Practice Area.

CHAPTER 11

Global Joint Ventures and HRD

Leonard Nadler
Zeace Nadler

The globalization of human economic activities has created increased concern about the part that HRD can play in that arena. A joint venture—that is, two companies joining in a common activity—creates complex and debilitating difficulties even when partners are both in the same country. How much more so when the two companies are based in two different countries? In this chapter, we will call such situations "global joint ventures" (GJV).

A GJV can exist in several forms. There are many permutations of the relationship, but the most common ones are: Company A (from country A) joins with Company B (from country B) in a joint venture in

- A's country
- B's country
- Country C

This is just with two countries working in either their own countries or in a selected host country. It can become much more complex if there is also Company C, etc. However, in this chapter we will limit our discussion of the GJV to just two companies.

Given the focus of this book, we will emphasize those GJV's where HRD is a required component. The definitions and distinctions in HRD, as discussed in the first chapter, will be followed throughout this chapter.

Cultural and National Factors Related to HRD

Other chapters in this book have probably made you aware of the need to understand cultural differences. That need becomes even more significant when dealing with a GJV. For example, in many parts of the world culture requires the parties in a business meeting to first share tea or coffee—in essence, "break bread together." To somebody from the U.S. this might seem a minor point, but there have been many times when violating that cultural norm has impeded business discussions and the development of a GJV.

Another example on the cultural/language level is that in some parts of the world it is important to avoid putting the other party in a position where they have to say "no." (Imai, 1981).

Such cultural differences should be recognized, understood, and even accepted by all parties in a GJV. It should not be a question of what is "right or wrong," but rather of what is appropriate. The discussion that follows will indicate some of the areas that should be considered. Keep in mind, however, that these are generalizations and that individuals will differ.

Language

Language can always be expected to cause problems in a GJV, since it involves people from at least two different countries. Even if they all speak some common language, there may still be subtle differences to which all parties need to be alerted.

An obvious language problem occurs in joint ventures where some employees are expected to speak a foreign language. In 1989 we visited China, just about two weeks before the Tiananmen Square incidents. In Guilin we endeavored to cash a traveler's check at the desk in a leading hotel, one that was part of a Chinese-American joint venture. It was virtually impossible to break through the language barrier, even though it was to be expected that a large number of the people staying at the hotel would probably speak English. The physical aspects of the hotel were outstanding, but the parties to the GJV had neglected to provide sufficient English instruction for some of their essential employees.

Time

In some countries, such as the U.S., there tends to be a compulsion about time and doing things "on time." In other countries time may be viewed much differently, so that in Malaysia they speak of "rubber time," meaning that the exact designation on a clock may not be what governs behavior. This becomes important when scheduling HRD learning activities. A program designed by a joint venture member in country A may be completely out of phase with the use of time by a joint venture member in country B.

There are many variations in the time to be allowed for religious observance. It may seem fairly obvious that in a Moslem country, Friday afternoon is not an appropriate time to schedule an HRD experience. Still, it is important for the GJV members to explore this specifically, as there are variations among Moslem countries.

The members of the GJV should also be sensitive to other religious time parameters. In predominantly Catholic countries, Sunday morning should be left open, with no scheduling of meetings or HRD activities. In Israel the celebration of the Sabbath begins at sundown on Friday night and goes to sundown on Saturday night, so it would be inappropriate to schedule HRD activities during that period.

As noted earlier, these are generalizations. There are Moslems, Catholics, and Jews who do not observe those patterns, whether at home or abroad. In each case, it is best to double-check with various counterparts before scheduling any HRD activities during those time periods.

The use of time can also be an organizational culture factor. When working in an oil company in a South American country, we found that we were expected to get to the office at 7:30 A.M. The cultural practice in that organization was that the office staff (professional and clerical) came to the office at 7:30 A.M. Then, they went out to breakfast! They returned to actually start work at 8:30 A.M.. When we asked why the 7:30 A.M. starting time, we were told that in the oil fields work started at 7:30 A.M., so it was expected that the home office people would also start at that time.

So when consulting with this client, we were expected to show up at 7:30 A.M., but not actually start work until 8:30 A.M. For workshops and similar learning experiences, our schedule was expected to show a starting time of 7:30 A.M., though there would be a "coffee break" at 8:00 A.M. We had to recognize these critical realities when we scheduled meetings and learning experiences.

Space

The work of Hall (1966) has helped us to understand the concept of the "space bubble"; the amount of space an individual needs to be effective. As he has shown, this is culturally induced. Looking at space and how it is used can frequently lead to misunderstandings on the part of observers who are not familiar with the culture.

In Japan, for example, few supervisors have their own offices. An HRD person from another country might well infer from this that in the Japanese system the supervisor is not important enough to have a separate office. Such an observation would be totally wrong! Supervisors are very important in Japan, but their importance is indicated by other factors than a separate office, which is a common practice in many other cultures.

There is another concept of space found in various parts of the Asian Pacific area, where there is a practice known as "Feng Shui," which guides the physical placement of a facility, ranging from a single desk to a whole business or industrial complex. There are innumerable stories about HRD failure caused by ignoring Feng Shui. When an HRD program is being conducted in a country where Feng Shui is a factor, the location of the HRD facility may be the single most significant factor related to the success or failure of the effort. This may seem incongruous to a person from a country where Feng Shui is unknown, but to ignore it is to invite disaster.

By no means are these the only cultural factors that must be considered. They are discussed here to highlight the need to look at all the cultures involved when GJV members are considering HRD.

Cultural and National Factors Related to Activity Areas

One frequent mistake is to consider "culture" and "country" to be the same. In most countries of the world, of any size, there are many cultures! The GJV members must identify those cultures and/or cultural groups that they must consider when developing an HRD program.

Let us share some current examples. While recognizing that as quickly as international events occur and make their impact those examples may become dated. Consider Germany and the unification of 1990. The former German Democratic Republic (East Germany) is now united with (West) Germany. However, as we observed when we were there in 1991, the cultural differences between people in those two countries were vast. The former GDR people grew up and lived in a system for over 40 years, and then suddenly with unification that system became obsolete.

That old system emphasized jobs, not work or productivity, so it was customary to have three or four people doing the work that in (West) Germany or other parts of the developed world would have been done by only one person. As a result, the unification brought with it vast unemployment! The concept of work was different in the two Germanys, and that needs to be considered when developing an HRD program involving those from the former GDR.

National and cultural factors are related to the three activity areas of HRD: training, education, development. Here are some examples of what must be considered in those areas by members in a joint venture.

Training

In Japan, most training is organization-specific. That is, a worker on a lathe will usually not be given any general education on lathe work, but only on the particular lathe that is used in the employer's plant. It would usually be considered inappropriate to provide any training on equipment or in ideas that do not currently exist in the organization.

The question may arise, then: How has the Japanese work force become so effective and productive? It has been suggested that the work force can readily learn about new processes or technology because it is usually in an active state of learning readiness. Particularly in large organizations, all employees at all levels are expected to take part in development (non-job related) activities such as flower arranging (ikebana), paper folding (origami), music lessons, or similar activities. Therefore, they are constantly learning and are able to move quickly into training and education programs with less fear of failure in a new learning situation than those who have not been in that learning state.

If the Japanese work force is involved in a GJV, there may be some limits on the kinds of training that can be provided. This problem must be explored by the members of the GJV prior to starting any operations.

In some countries, workers may need some basic skills training to precede any specific job training. This will usually be the case where the work force lacks literacy skills or has had little experience in the general work force. Some years ago we did some work in Zimbabwe for a company that was part of a GJV that was manufacturing furniture. The company's managing director complained about the local work force, who just couldn't seem to get the hinges on correctly. After diagnosing the situation, we were able to point out that the manager was asking his work force to do something for which they could not see the purpose! Where many of his workers came from, the "bush," furniture with hinges was unknown! The skill training for installing the hinges needed to include material on the function of a hinge!

Education

Before providing education, the members of the GJV should determine the policy and culture of the work force to be involved. What kinds of education have they had in the past? An essential of education is deferred gratification: the time lag between learning and utilization. In some countries of the world, this concept is virtually unknown in the workplace, though it may be part of the religious culture.

Even in so-called developed countries, education must be considered in light of the culture and policy. For example, education is generally not an HRD activity in Japan, as the practice in most large Japanese companies is to promote first and then train. Promotion usually results from longevity, seniority, and related factors, rather than job performance. Despite this, one must be cautious. Although it may not be apparent to the outsider, the Japanese work force is in a state of flux. If a GJV requires education, and the activity includes Japanese members, extensive dialogue may be needed to be sure that all parties understand the implication of this HRD activity.

In some other countries, however, education is a significant item, since promotion comes through good job performance. In reality, current job performance alone is not a good measure for predicting future success after promotion. Present performance only tells what the individual can do in the current position, not what that individual might do in a different one. A well-designed education program is one way to determine possible future behavior.

Development

This is not usually part of a GJV-HRD effort, unless it is considered either culturally or nationally appropriate. Both parties must be cautious, however, for nothing is constant in these situations. National priorities, political considerations, and a rapid change in economic conditions can influence how HRD is to be provided. Cultural factors change much more slowly, but they are much more difficult to identify.

Different HRD Practices

The members of a GJV must be unusually sensitive to cultural and national practices. Providing HRD is much more than just having one member translate its material into the language of the other member.

Concept of HRD

In addition to understanding the definition of HRD presented earlier, both parties should understand how each member views HRD. Is it considered a responsibility of the organization or of the individual? Is it customary for private organizations to provide HRD, or is that considered the prerogative of the government in the country where the GJV will be operating?

The following is based on an experience in the Soviet Union, in 1989, but given the subsequent break-up of the Soviet Union, it is presented here only as an example of national policies on HRD. It does not *necessarily* apply to these countries today.

In August 1989, we were told that there were 800 joint ventures with foreign organizations, but we had difficulty in getting specifics on the HRD programs related to those GJV's. The best we could get was that if the GJV involved a Soviet organization of more than 2,000 employees, it could set up its own HRD activities. If, however, the Soviet organization had fewer than 2,000 employees, it would have to work through the appropriate ministry. Nobody could point to a specific document saying this. It only came out during questions and discussion.

Thus, it is important that during the negotiation stage the GJV members carefully explore their assumptions about HRD, their perceptions about appropriate HRD, and which GJV member will have the responsibility of providing HRD.

Providing HRD

In some cases, it may be agreed that each member of the GJV will retain its own HRD operation and be responsible for providing necessary learning to its own people. There may be many reasons for this, including a reluctance to share technology or resources until the members have worked amicably together for awhile and had a mutual success.

If there is no need to share HRD activities, the issue shouldn't be forced. Usually, however, most GJV's identify needs for HRD by the employees of one, if not both members.

When the members agree that *one of them will provide HRD for the GJV*, it is often because one member has entered into the GJV in hopes of upgrading its work force through the HRD efforts of the other member. During the 1980s, this was a major reason that motivated China to invite GJV's. There is, of course, nothing wrong with this if the GJV will still produce other benefits for both members.

In developing the GJV agreement, the unique resources of each member should be considered. For example, the people who need technical training may be in Country A, while the joint venture member in Country B has the HRD capability — so either the HRD resource can be transferred to Country A, or the people from Country A can be transferred temporarily to Country B for training. This can present language problems, of course. Personnel coming from Country A would have to be proficient in the language of Country B, or Country B would have to provide staff with sufficient language capability to instruct those from Country A. An alternative is to rely on interpreters, but that presents other problems that are addressed in Chapter 5.

It is possible that both GJV members lack the HRD capability needed for their venture. If they can't develop that capability themselves, the HRD capability, they may seek a *third party* resource for HRD, either in one of their own countries or in a third world country. This should not be seen as a criticism of either member, but rather as a recognition that both members want to make sure that their people use the best HRD resource possible.

A third party for HRD might also be required when the GJV cannot agree on how to handle it. When this happens, extreme caution should be exercised, for that lack of agreement might well indicate other problems that have nothing to do with HRD but simply surfaced on that issue.

Another possibility is a *combination* of the previously cited alternatives. On the surface, this might seem to be a good compromise, but like many compromises it may carry the seed of future problems. That is not to say that combinations are always negative, but they should be viewed with extreme caution.

Country Goals and Ideas

Although the focus may be on HRD, GJV members should not ignore the variations of country goals and ideas. Indeed, in order to be successful, the agreed-upon HRD program must reflect the political realities of the countries involved. Even where the human resources come from only one country, the parties to the GJV must recognize that there are implications for all of them.

We shall explore the following factors separately, though that is not the reality of international life.

Political and social factors

Each GJV member should recognize the political structure and considerations of the other's country. That does not mean that one member has to endorse the political system of the other's country. A GJV between a U.S. company and a state-owned organization in China does not imply that the U.S. company is endorsing communism any more than it would suggest that the Chinese member is endorsing the U.S. system.

If the political structure of either country presents a serious problem, a GJV is perhaps not the best approach. For example, if a GJV is being considered between South Africa and another country, the members of the GJV must be aware of the fall-out that can result. The non-South African member may contend that it is not endorsing apartheid. However, HRD people in that country may resent being involved in a program that seems to indicate a support of apartheid. This can happen despite the changes that are being made in South Africa at this writing, which indicate that apartheid is being eliminated. Until both members of the GJV agree on a political issue, it might be desirable not to continue, particularly where HRD is involved. Even when the GJV is just on a capital-investment level there can be problems. Consider, then, how much more difficult political situations become when people are involved, as in HRD.

One member may be in a country that has special requirements for some segments of its populations. In Zimbabwe, for example, when a GJV provides HRD for expatriates, it must also do it for the local population. When a company plans to provide HRD for Zimbabweans, it will receive a much more cordial reception than when it ignores the obvious HRD needs of the local population and the political stance of the government.

Politics can also be a factor in determining the language of instruction to be used. In Hong Kong, at least until 1997, it is politically desirable to offer HRD programs in Mandarin, the official language of China, even though the overwhelming bulk of the inhabitants of Hong Kong do not speak Mandarin. A member of a GJV in Hong Kong is well advised, though not specifically directed, to conduct as much of the program in Mandarin as possible.

In Malaysia, the government urges people to use Bahasa Malay rather than English or other foreign languages—so it would be desirable to have the learning materials in that language. In Ethiopia, there are 72 different languages, but the official language is Anharic, though it is the language of only about 25 percent of the population. However, the government has changed, so a GJV will have to find out which of the many languages is desired by the new government.

In Singapore there are four official languages: English, Malayu, Mandarin, and Tamil. That does not mean that all the learning materials must be in all four languages, but GJV members may find it desirable or even necessary at times to provide instruction in more than just English.

In the United States, non-discrimination laws require that HRD be made available to all concerned. This can become a significant concern when another member of the GJV is from a country that requires that priority be given to certain groups, or that certain groups should be excluded.

It can become confusing when special consideration must be given to identified groups. In India, it might be one of the "scheduled castes" that is entitled to special consideration—something of which non-Indian members of the GJV must be aware. In Malaysia, it would have been necessary for the non-Malaysian member of the GJV to give special consideration to Malays under the "bumiputra" program. That was a legislated national program designed to enable Malays to move into the economic activities of the country.

Religious factors should also be considered in some countries. In some Moslem countries, for example, it may not be possible to have males and females in the same learning situation. This varies from one Moslem country to another, but a non-Moslem member of the GJV must be aware of the possibility and explore it before making HRD plans.

Economic factors

A member may enter into the GJV not only for its own objectives, but for the economic return it can bring to its country through improved human resources. For example, several years ago a U.S. electronics company was negotiating with a Malaysian company for a GJV that would involve starting a plant in Malaysia and educating a local work force. The U.S. company was surprised to find that to get government approval it had to agree to also provide education for Malaysians who would *not* be employed in the joint venture! Thus, the Malaysian government was using the GJV to educate a work force that could work for domestic companies.

Some negotiations may also require that the parties provide "scholarships" — that is, funded study — in the home country of the foreign member. As in the previous instance, it is expected that when the students return they will *not* work for the GJV, but will be available to local companies. Of course, these factors must be considered legitimate HRD costs to the GJV and be funded as such.

The GJV members should expect that the *work force* will usually be the result of various political decisions within a country. For example, during the 1970s Singapore had an aggressive family planning policy that was very successful. As a result, by the late 1980s Singapore was faced with labor shortages since its economy had expanded very rapidly. As was the case with some European countries several decades earlier, Singapore increased its reliance on "guest workers," mainly from Thailand, the Philippines, and Malaysia. Therefore, a GJV in Singapore may find that a significant part of the work force is not Singaporean, and that HRD cannot be offered in the same way that it was planned for an educated Singaporean work force.

Funding for HRD

Although there are many different ways to fund the HRD aspect of a GJV, it must first be agreed that funding be provided. Unless specific attention is paid to providing financial resources for HRD, this item can be overlooked.

Funding methods should be related to the various factors discussed earlier. Negotiations on funding should take place after some of the decisions discussed earlier, such as whose HRD resources will be used, culture and national factors related to HRD, culture and national factors related to HRD activity areas, different HRD practices, and country goals and ideas.

Among the funding options is that all HRD expenses will be *paid by one party*. This is usually the case when the financial arrangement specifies that one GJV member will provide most or all of the financial resource. It may be direct payment or it may be "in kind" — that is, one party will provide all the HRD, but will be given financial credit for this, and the other party will provide some financially comparable physical resource.

A common practice is for both parties to *share* the HRD expense. The amount to be paid by each party will, of course, be part of the total financial agreement. A difficulty may arise since it is not always possible to clearly identify all the HRD needs during the negotiation stage. Some learning needs may surface later if there is an unanticipated shortfall in job performance, and it becomes obvious that HRD is the response to that problem. One solution is for both parties to agree to an HRD contingency fund during negotiations.

In some situations, the *government* may be a funding source. This can be expected when the government is a party to the GJV. In some countries, however, even though the government is not a party, it may still have funds available. This can be the case in developed countries as well as developing or newly industrialized countries. If the GJV is contributing to a government goal (e.g., employment of a particular group or in a specified geographical area), there may be government funds available for HRD.

Some countries have a levy system—that is, employers pay a tax based on payroll, and the money goes into a central fund. These funds will be available for HRD projects that can benefit the country, so if the GJV is involved in such a project, it is legitimate to apply for those funds for their HRD programs.

Learning Implications

People learn differently, even when they are in the same country or part of the same culture. Obviously, when a GJV involves people from more than one country, cultural conflicts in learning situations can be anticipated. For example, there is the concept of *andragogy* that originated in Europe, but has become a significant part of adult learning in the U.S. (Knowles, 1984). To date, however, there has not been sufficient research or theory building to determine how these elements apply to other countries and cultures.

Learning is only one part of HRD, as was noted in Chapter 1. A major purpose of HRD is a change in job performance. It is not always possible for a learner to use the results of the HRD activity if there is not sufficient reinforcement, and the forms of such reinforcement will vary from country to country according to cultural factors.

A case in point is the Japan-US foreign aid program in the 1960s, as discussed in another chapter in this book. This was a joint venture involving two countries. One part of the program sent Japanese to the U.S. for training and education. The results of this activity did not make their impact on Japan until a decade later, as it was not until those learners had reached appropriate levels in their companies that they could introduce what they had learned. This suggests that very careful attention must be paid to the learners in relation to the cultural practices in their own countries. They may achieve the learning, but not be able to apply it to the current operations of the GJV.

It is also important to be sure that the learning materials provided can be utilized by the participants in the joint venture. There was the case of a U.S. bank engaged in a joint venture with a bank in Malaysia. The U.S. bank was involved in global operations and was using materials in Malaysia that had been developed by its HRD staff in Manila. There were problems, however, and we were asked to look at the program in Malaysia. We found that the materials had not been modified for Malaysian learners. For example, one case was being used to indicate a domestic transaction. The case started, "Mr. Garcia walked into the bank ...." When we listened to the case discussion, it became obvious that the participants were responding to this as an international transaction, not a domestic one! All that was required was to use a Malaysian name for the customer to indicate that this was a domestic transaction.

HRD providers should also be sure that the learning technology being introduced does not carry an unintended message. In Thailand, for example, it was planned to provide instruction with handouts and worksheets, but no books. Some topics would be presented by hand-held viewers and similar nonprinted material. All this was designed to make the material as pertinent as possible to the local situation. There was, however, a negative reaction by the Thai learners, and the non-Thai member who was providing the HRD could not understand the resistance. After some discussion, the learners said, "When people learn, they get books. Why are we not being given books like other people?" Accordingly, the HRD program was supplemented by books and the learners willingly participated. In the process, however, the GJV lost valuable time on the project.

Conclusion

In this chapter we have tried to encourage HRD people whose company may be part of a GJV to look carefully at their agreement during negotiations, to see what provisions have been made for providing the necessary HRD. As GJV's inevitably increase, so will the need for HRD, and it will be important to do more than just blithely provide learning without considering the various factors discussed here.

Where the GJV already exists, it is still important to carefully examine the HRD components, but it may be more difficult and costly to make needed adjustments as a result of the factors discussed in this chapter. The GJV members should be aware, however, of the costs incurred by not making any adjustments for HRD after the joint venture has begun.

Cultural factors should be examined and used to enhance rather than impede the learning to be achieved through the HRD program. Cultural problems are usually not insurmountable if they are explored before firming up how HRD is to be provided.

Above all, those in the GJV must take the time to define their terms and concepts before they have moved too far into the venture. To rush past that stage is to court disaster when Human Resource Development is to be provided in a global joint venture.

References

Bell, C., and Nadler, L. *Clients & Consultants: Meeting and Exceeding Expectations* (Second Edition). Houston, TX: Gulf Publishing, 1985. p. 166.

Hall, E. T. *The Hidden Dimension: An Anthropologist Examines Man's Use of Space in Public and in Private*. Garden City, NY: Doubleday, 1966.

Imai, M. *16 Ways to Avoid Saying No: An Invitation to Experience Japanese Management From the Inside*. Tokyo: The Nihon Keizai Shimbun, 1981.

Knowles, M. *The Adult Learner: A Neglected Species* (Third Edition). Houston, TX: Gulf Publishing, 1984.

Nadler, L. and Nadler, Z. *Developing Human Resources* (Third Edition). San Francisco, CA: Jossey-Bass Inc., Publishers, 1989.

CHAPTER 12
A Typology of International HRD Consultants

Neal Nadler and Jeff Len

The story of Joseph, as presented in the book of Exodus in the Old Testament, provides an excellent analogy to describe the emergence of the international HRD consultant. The eleventh son of Jacob, Joseph stirred up much animosity among his older brothers. Favored as the only child of Rachel, Jacob's favorite wife, and pampered as the youngest son, he had a special place in the family. Joseph's multicolored robe only reinforced his privileged status and further alienated his brothers with their traditional view that the first-born should inherit a father's love and wealth.

To rid themselves of the problem, the older brothers took the radical step of selling this valuable human jewel to a caravan of traders. Joseph got his first taste of culture shock as a slave in Egypt. Purchased for Potiphar, Captain of the Guard, he became the ideal civil servant as he rose to power to become a key household administrator. The biblical writer stresses divine connection as the cause of his special talents. Apparently, the young foreigner quickly adapted himself to the new culture and became a trusted adviser to those who managed the royal army. However, this new foreign expert soon found himself caught in a difficult situation. Potiphar's wife tried to seduce him, and when rejected she immediately told her husband that Joseph himself had been the unsuccessful suitor. There was no recourse but to imprison him. While he was in prison, the power of Joseph's consultative abilities manifested itself in a new form through the interpretation of the dreams of two other important civil servants of the Court. Whatever these dreams might represent today, they clearly were problematic forecasts of the future that needed interpretation by an expert.

Joseph's fame spread quickly because of his ability to decipher the future, so the Pharaoh released him from prison to interpret his own problematic dreams. Unlike the more mundane nocturnal meanderings of the royal butler and baker, the Pharaoh's dreams reflected key public policy decisions about famine, food, and politics. Again, Joseph showed himself to be a worthy consultant with predictions that saved Egypt from destruction by natural forces. For this, he was promoted to be primary administrator in the Pharaoh's court, even though he was a foreigner.

Joseph as International Consultant: The Field and the Practice

The story of Joseph, though interspersed with both theological reflection and heroic exaggeration, captures the dilemma faced by the international consultant. International consultants are thrown into situations in which they may have little experience or specific knowledge. They must learn quickly how the "helping relationship" so essential to effective consulting manifests itself in the new culture. Just as Joseph had to deal with the seductive lure of power and status, so must the international HRD consultant. The key to success for both Joseph and the consultant is the focus on helping decision makers rather than becoming the decision maker.

A critical juncture in the consulting relationship comes at the point of deciding whether to assume a permanent position of power. The consultant would thereby relinquish the consulting role or maintain the more transitory role of an itinerant consultant offering advice on specific problems. The danger of becoming a permanent fixture is that the foreigner is then viewed as being acculturated and therefore "one of us." For Joseph, this decision point came in the person of Potiphar's wife. She assumed he had become an Egyptian and, therefore, was available for a sexual relationship reserved for men in power. In this interpretation, Joseph's refusal represents the unwillingness of the foreign consultant to abandon personal values, a decision that in his case led to prison. While this is not exactly the plight of most international consultants today, the problems associated with full acculturation are never far below the surface.

Joseph's dream interpretations portray the essential role of the international consultant concisely. Joseph listened carefully to the problem (an early needs assessment) and knew fully the society in which it was occurring. The young Hebrew skillfully clarified the nature of the problem, identified its causes, and worked with his client to determine what should be done. Joseph's approach can be viewed as the essential first phase of any international consulting contract that, if done properly, will usually be the basis for a continued relationship with the client (whether Joseph understood the consulting process is irrelevant). He was justly rewarded for his services by being named the Pharaoh's primary administrator. He helped to prepare the powerful nation for the ensuing famine, thus assisting them through the problem and into years of plenty. This promotion was indeed a great reward, and an example of the strong influences that can cause international consultants, at least for a time, to become part of the system they have helped to build.

This time Joseph handled his permanent managerial position with greater skills that allowed him to preserve both his position and cultural heritage (another lesson for the international consultant). The joyous reunion with his brothers and father after hiding himself from them in the garb of Egyptian royalty is a powerful story about family love. It is also about the continued tension between cultures internalized in a single man. Viewed from the international HRD consultant's perspective, Joseph's story portrays the trials and tribulations with which most international consultants must contend.

Joseph's Colleagues: The International Consultant, Background and Attributes

In this analogy, the special coat given to Joseph with strands of different colored thread can symbolize the rich diversity of international consultants. This diversity extends to skill, knowledge, attitude, and background developed through differing experiences and education. It also manifests itself in the differing strategies each consultant develops for coping with the demands of those in power in a foreign culture. Whether it be offering learning programs for public administrators, presenting workshops to help their participants develop new corporate strategies, training managers in a variety of skills, or helping organizations to cope with the changing environment around them, the approaches are varied both in scope and specificity. The personal views of consultants on their roles in consulting for governmental agencies or corporate offices range across a wide spectrum. The array of international HRD consultants in the infancy of the profession is a collage of colors.

Thus, to try to describe *the* international consultant would be as accurate as speaking of *the* culture of the world; there is no one profile that makes any sense. However, there are certain similarities that we can identify in the areas of background and attributes. In a recent study, successful international HRD consultants were canvassed, and their similarities are shown in Table 12.1.

There are many different interpretations, roles, and activities of the HRD practice in the international sector, ranging from consultants who present learning programs on specific topics like budgeting, finance, management, and agriculture to those who conduct broad organizational change efforts. Because of their diversity, commonality among international consultants becomes difficult to define. There are, however, a few criteria that stand out and tend to differentiate effective from ineffective international HRD consultants.

These criteria are embodied in the analysis of the many roles today's international HRD consultant has to play. The ability to play these roles obviously depends upon the skills, knowledge, attitudes, and experience gained by the consultant over time. Table 12.2 depicts 11 continua that approximate the range of possibilities that contribute to the development of the international HRD consultant. These continua were derived through interviews with practicing international HRD consultants. The effectiveness quotient in this set of criteria is situational in its application, so that success is not necessarily determined at the extremes of the continuum. Success is measured by the consultants' ability to match their profile on the continua with the client's needs and expectations and the environment in which the work will take place.

Table 12.1: International HRD Consultants' Background and Attributes

---

• Usually U.S. Nationals

• Had at least a college degree (disciplines vary)

• Initial international experience was derived from either government-oriented organizations (U.S. AID, military, Peace Corps, UN, or companies working for international agencies, etc) or multinational companies.

• Mostly male

• Average age 40 +

• Most had expertise in adult learning plus one more subject matter expertise

• Self-perception included:
  1. ability to deal with ambiguity
  2. strong desire to work with risk takers
  3. ability to continually experiment and improve their skill and knowledge base

---

You can map any international consulting contract using Table 12.2, as it is about the consultant who ultimately does the work. Here's an example of how these characteristics may affect the international consultant: A contract was developed that called for a consultant with planning expertise to assist the ministries of the country in improving their planning process. The contract required expertise in corporate planning because traditional government planning approaches had been unsuccessful in the past. The international HRD consultant chosen had a content specialty in Corporate Strategic Planning but no experience in the receiving culture. The need in the contract was for substantial process expertise that was also a good "fit" for this consultant's profile. The program might have been enhanced by a native speaker with substantial experience in the country. However, the selected consultant, who had extensive international experience in the Third World, proved to be up to the task.

Each continuum in Table 12.2 depicts a range of possibilities for individuals to rate themselves relative to skill and knowledge, attitude, and experience. It is important to recognize that no one profile (e.g., down the left-hand side of the table) is an indicator for success in the international HRD arena. It does emphasize that these three areas form a range of profiles that predict success in international HRD consulting. Average successful international consultants have at least some work experience with more than two cultures other than their own and approach work in other cultures from a "non-native" perspective. It also includes moderate to extensive content and process expertise equal to the requirements of the contract on which the consultants are working.

Table 12.2: Development of the International HRD Consultant

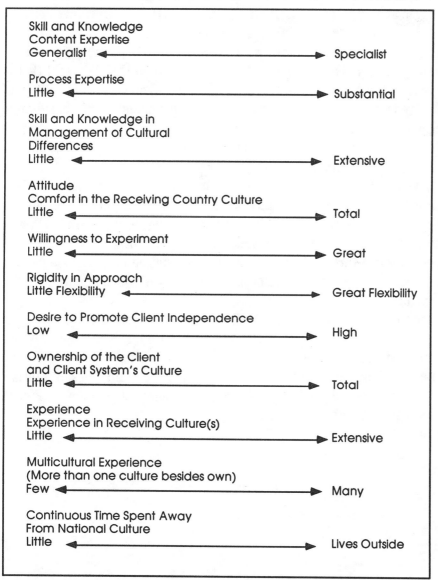

Joseph's Dilemma: The Acculturation Process

Joseph's story exemplifies the dilemma faced by most international HRD consultants. the inevitable question of acculturation. To what extent should a foreign expert adopt the thought and behavior patterns of those who employ them? How does time shape the pressures to become part of the surrounding community rather than stand apart from it? Which values are so ingrained that they defy translation across cultures? How does the technology of learning "fit" with the culture of the client? Which role is best for the international HRD consultant? The spectrum of responses to these questions provides the basis for a typology of international consultants.

There are many stories that have emerged over the past 20 years suggesting that international consulting has regressed to well before Joseph's time. Here are two:

1. A male international HRD consultant working in a poor Third World Islamic country bragged about his "conquests with the ladies" in the nearby village during a class, which was totally inappropriate in an Islamic culture.

2. An international HRD consultant would not entertain the possibility of making changes in his participative management model even when the class said that it would not work in their country. As a result, half of the 12 managers attending the course were fired within the following year for trying to implement the consultant's new management model.

These are examples of consultants lack the appropriate skills, knowledge, attitude, and experience to do a credible job.

There have also been stories of successes; for example, an international HRD consultant implementing a performance appraisal system in an Arabic culture realized the importance of cultural differences. Recognizing the extreme need to save face in the culture, he developed a system that helped workers to achieve the performance objective through ongoing coaching during the performance period. This avoided waiting for the annual performance review where face would be lost for poor performance.

This story portrays an international HRD consultant who has the profiles equal to the tasks required in the consultancy. Above all, it shows one who is aware of the acculturation process and how it affects consultant and learner.

Recent research on this process gives an insight into certain types of international HRD consultants and how they deal with the acculturation dilemma. Figure 12.1 suggests there are four approaches.

Figure 12.1: Dealing With Acculturation

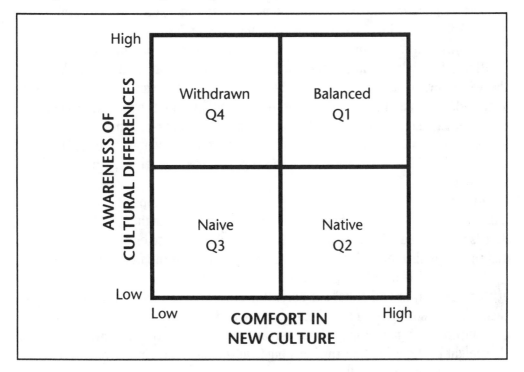

This typology is based on two dynamics that emerged from conducted interviews and from our own personal experiences. These two dynamics form the x and y axes of the model, and both are ever-present in the cross-cultural and international consulting process. These are the awareness of cultural differences and the consultant's comfort in the new culture. Each quadrant represents a response to a new culture predicated on the skills, knowledge, attitude, and experience that the international HRD consultant brings to the consultancy. The typology can be used in two ways. First, it can be used to predict problems in the client-consultant relationship in the international arena. Second, it can be used to describe the response a consultant has to a new culture, given certain levels of skill, knowledge, attitude, and experience.

To use the typology, it is important to understand the two major aspects of any international consulting contract: the consultant and the receiving culture. In both cases, the consultant is viewed as the responder to the dynamics of the new client and new culture. Consultants to whom the typology is being applied must be analyzed to determine their "awareness of cultural differences," which equates to the skill and knowledge portion of Table 12.2 discussed earlier. The consultant must also be viewed from the "comfort in the new culture" perspective that equates to the attitude and experience portions of Table 12.2. Only after profiling the consultant in this manner can the consultant's reaction to the new culture be predicted. We will explain each quadrant by describing the stereotypical responses from a consultant whose primary profiles in that quadrant.

The Withdrawn Consultant: Quadrant 4

The withdrawn consultant tends to panic at the recognition of cultural differences. When practitioners realize that the familiar standards and modes of operation of their own culture are no longer relevant in the new culture, they take a defensive position and withdraw. The profile could be labeled "consultant in trouble." Typically, the withdrawn consultant has lost the perspective necessary to be effective, is confused, has encountered culture-based problems, and is either unwilling or unable to deal with instances of cultural abuse. Whatever the reason, the reaction is the same: The individual perceives the receiving culture as "us" versus "them." "They" do not understand "us." "Our" ways are too sophisticated for "them," therefore "we" shouldn't help.

An example comes from a learning situation in which a participant raised his hand and said, "We are not Americans; nothing you have taught us in the last three days is relevant here." The response of the consultant was to close early for the day and return to his room wondering why he came "here" in the first place.

Withdrawal is usually a process that happens in the following way: First, the attitude of "they are all alike" surfaces. It means that the consultant has ceased to recognize the strengths of the client's culture and has chosen to revert to his or her own culture right (not wrong). If this person has not gone to the extremes of the type, they might be dictating that the learning involved here is to make "you all" operate like people in my home culture.

As the withdrawal continues the consultant passes into the "They'll do it my way or else" phase. This is also characterized by the statement, "I don't remember what is appropriate to do in a different culture and I don't care (about doing it right)."

If the consultant is functioning at all while in this quadrant, the overriding objective is to "get the hell back to where I am safe and comfortable," usually meaning the home culture. The time that a consultant can stay in Quadrant 4 is as short as several hours or it can be permanent. The length really depends on the individual—however, the longer one is in this quadrant the more difficult it is to get out.

The Naive Consultant: Quadrant 3

The consultant who follows this paradigm is low in both cultural awareness and cultural comfort. This practitioner is cut from the same cloth as the tourist or business person who is commonly called the "Ugly American," and believes that there is no difference and people can be treated the same everywhere. Generally, this is an aggressively defensive position developed from an insensitive "because you know me, you know that I am right" point of view. People like these are, without a doubt, the most dangerous. They can do the most damage and never know that it has been done. Generally, this type of consultant is based in ignorance and in a situation where comfort with the client culture causes lapses in judgment and thought. They are people with an egocentric world view.

In Quadrant 3, some consultants say, "People are people wherever they are." What they often do not say is, "Because I know 'people' I know what is right for this group." This aspect of the naive consultants can be seen in two groups. One group is the novice international consultants who have "lucked" into their first assignment. The other is the seasoned consultants who are experiencing cultural confusion caused by exposure to too many cultures, leading to a defensive self-righteous posture. The process is also, at its extremes, justified by the comment, "We are all *my* God's people."

The "Native" Consultant: Quadrant 2

"Native" consultants believe that the best approach is to adopt the culture in which they are working. Usually, this is based on having had an experience in which they have felt a strong sense of alienation from the receiving culture. To compensate, the consultant may over-identify with the next client culture, attempting to gain acceptance from the client or client system by adopting the receiving culture in total. Basically, the "native" consultant has a low awareness of cultural differences and a need to have a high comfort in the receiving culture. This individual's rationale can be categorized into one of three different comments:

"To know them is to love them." After exposure to the culture, some consultants like it so much at the superficial level that they try to adopt it in terms of clothing, customs, and gestures. They lose sight of the fact that they were hired to produce change through integration of the consultant's culture and the receiving culture.

"Their way is better." After looking at the cultural norms underlying the existing process or procedure, some consultants will support that process and procedure. For example, in Pakistan, many organizations in the 1980s had two performance appraisal forms—one shared with the employee and one sent in confidentially on the same performance period. (There appeared to be little commonality in the verbiage or grading of the two forms.) One consultant working with a local firm actually agreed that this was the best approach, given the non-confrontational nature of the Pakistani culture.

"Their way is the only way." When listening to the problems of the client system, the consultant becomes seduced into agreeing that the current way is appropriate given the culture. The consultant then approaches the problem from the same paradigm used by the client and therefore, becomes increasingly less effective.

The Balanced Risk-Taker Consultant: Quadrant 1

The balanced risk-taker consultant is the most effective of the four quadrants in the international HRD consulting arena. This practitioner has a high awareness of cultural differences and a high comfort in the receiving culture. The Quadrant 1 consultant is experienced in the international area and generally has worked in more than one culture as an expatriate. In interviewing balanced risk-taker consultants, we heard the primary philosophy summed up by a professional with extensive experience in the Third World facilitating and consulting with private sector managers and governmental officials. He explained, "I have learned that being effective is based on two ideas that have evolved for me over time. First, there must be a trust that I will not knowingly violate the local cultural norms but that I will make mistakes."

Embodied in this idea is a dual responsibility. The consultant is saying: I must help each person with whom I work to learn. In turn, the participants must help me better understand how that learning can be applied to their culture. This learning is centered on their culture and the applicability of what I bring to that culture. Together we make the learning appropriate.

The consultant explained his second idea this way: "I am going to try new approaches—for them and for me—to see if our learning can be enhanced. In other words, I am a big-risk taker."

Like Joseph, each of the successful consultants who took part in the study recognized the importance of cultural difference and that every culture has its effective and ineffective beliefs and norms. Each consultant operating from Quadrant 1 used this knowledge to build effective working relationships with the client and the client organization.

While it is true that *balanced risk-taker consultants* are the most effective in international consulting, keep in mind that no consultant is entirely in only one quadrant. Because of the diverse nature of the field and the practitioners, every consultant is to some degree present in every quadrant. Effectiveness is reflected by how much of consultant's profile is dominated by one quadrant or the other. Figure 12.2 shows graphically how an effective consultant might look.

Figure 12.2: Comfort in the New Culture

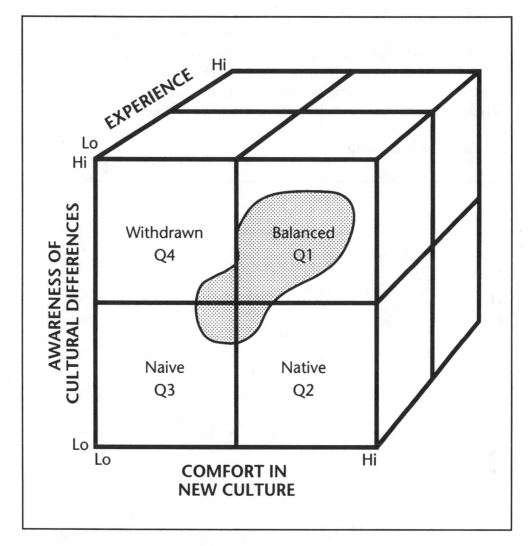

This consultant's profile incorporates part of all four quadrants. It depicts how a consultant, given certain situations, will move from one primary quadrant to another. However, as experience, skill, knowledge, and appropriate attitudes increase, the consultant is likelier to move to a Quadrant 1 style. A new consultant will gravitate toward the withdrawn quadrant rather easily given the first recognition that, "They don't speak the same language" or "I must have done something wrong, but what is it?" The more experienced consultant will anticipate these issues and make appropriate allowances. In practice this is how the characteristics of the international HRD consultant and the typology work. But what about development? What does an individual need to become proficient at helping and learning relationships across cultures?

International HRD Consultant's Development: Joseph's Experience

As with Joseph, who had to recognize there are differences in culture, international HRD consultants must recognize their gaps and develop strategies for filling them. They must continually strive to build the skills, knowledge, attitudes, and experience that make them more effective in the international arena. The benefit of this development can be seen in the Pyramid shown in Figure 12.3.

Figure 12.3: Pyramid

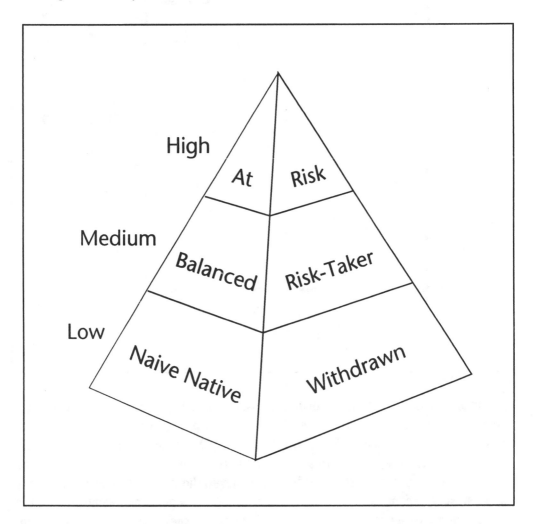

The figure has a three-sided base, each side representing skill and knowledge, attitude, and experience, respectively. Only when these three areas of the international consultant's profile are developed will a practitioner's profile reach the Balanced Risk-taker level. The benefit of this development can plainly be seen in the overhead view of the pyramid shown in Figure 12.4.

**Figure 12.4: International HRD Consultant's Development Pyramid –
Overhead View**

If even one of the three areas is either undeveloped or poorly developed, the
consultant's predominant style will be in Quadrant 2, 3, or 4. Even if these
practitioners have one marginally effective area, they are still extremely vulnerable
to the naive, native and withdrawn reactions to the receiving culture, making them
less effective in the helping relationship they are performing. Development occurs as
they increase their individual skills, knowledge, and experience, and develop appropriate attitudes toward the international HRD consulting tasks. They move from the
bottom line on each of the three sides of the pyramid base into the more effective,
balanced risk-taking level of consulting in the middle part of the pyramid. This is the
level at which the most effective helping relationships between client and consultant
can be developed and the most effective work can be accomplished. The consultant
may occasionally revert to one of the three entry-level profiles, but usually, for only
a short time. As development increases, two potential problems can emerge. Both
are at the center of Figure 12.4. The first is the "At Risk" level where consultants with
extensive experience assume there is no longer a need to explore the cultures in
which they will work. At this level, they also tend to hear only those things that fit their
experience. Ego plays a large part here: "I can't be wrong about this because I have
so much experience."

Without the ability to be flexible, consultants at this level cease to be effective.
They make little or no attempt to learn a new culture. Their self-perceptions and
actions are based on their extensive experience rather than an understanding of the
culture. Their norms and modes of operation are correct by virtue of who they are and
what they have done rather than an extensive study of the receiving culture. They can
only regain their effectiveness by recognizing and addressing this situation.

The second problem at this high level centers around cultural confusion. Cultural confusion happens when experiences in many cultures over the years begin to blur. This problem can affect people who have spent over two years in three or more different cultures without returning to the home culture for an extended period. Here, overconfidence in their experience is not the issue—it is being able to differentiate between cultures. The problem can also be caused by spending short periods (two to six weeks) in different cultures without returning to the home culture. This problem seems to occur frequently during consultancy in the Third World. It is characterized by uncertainty about the appropriate cultural actions and withdrawal. It is still unclear whether once having moved to this level over an extended period, an international HRD consultant can return to the balanced level of consultant development.

Summary: Joseph's Success

Just as Joseph took the risk and interpreted the Pharoah's dream, the most successful consultants are the risk-takers who have a balanced approach to the new culture. As Joseph did, they understand the importance of culture and its implications for success in another country. They are also willing to admit a lack of expertise in the receiving culture and are willing to learn. They are eager not only to test whatever norms and theories have proven effective back home, but also to change them as necessary to "fit" the new culture. They are not adversely affected by ambiguity—in fact, they thrive upon it.

However, balanced risk-takers must continually test themselves to learn whether they are still operating in Quadrant 1 of the model. Often, for various reasons, an effective HRD consultant begins to operate in one of the other three quadrants or at the "At Risk" level. When this happens, the consultant's value in global HRD work is diminished.

As with Joseph, who developed what was necessary to be effective in another country, international HRD consultants must learn to weave their skills, knowledge, attitudes, and experience into their professional coat of many colors. Only when this happens can the HRD consultant truly become effective in the international arena. However, unlike Joseph, who chose to stay with the new culture and become part of it for an extended period, the effective international HRD consultant must become dispensable. The consultancy is directed at giving the client both help and the skills, knowledge, and attitude that the consultant possesses. Once this is done, consultants are free to go to another client, or as Joseph did, back to their home culture.

About the Authors

Neal Nadler is Director of the Corporate Learning Institute of Peabody College of Vanderbilt University in Nashville, TN. Previously, he was the Managing Director of W.O.R.L.D. Associates. His doctorate in Human Resource Development was conferred by George Washington University. He is a member of the American Society for Training and Development.

Jeff Len is Associate Professor and Chair, Department of Strategic Management and Public Policy at George Washington University. Previously, he was Assistant Professor at the University of Connecticut. His doctoral studies were completed at Boston College. He is on the Board of Governors of the Eastern Academy of Management, where he also served as President. He is also a Fellow of the Society for Values in Higher Education.

CHAPTER 13

The Paradox of the Local Consultant

Cheryl Samuels-Campbell
Dunstan Campbell

The dilemma of the local consultant involves a constant struggle for worth. As the saying goes, "A prophet in his own land is without honor." Many forces beyond the characteristic indifference of their own people—the disregard or nonrecognition of the worth of one of their own—conspire against local consultants. The writers' setting is the Eastern Caribbean, specifically the members of the Organization of Eastern Caribbean States as well as Barbados, and Trinidad and Tobago. However, it is likely that forces that conspire against the local consultant in this setting are similar to those at work in other parts of the developing world. This chapter examines some of these forces as they are encountered in typical phases of consulting.

Exposition

As discussed here, the exposition phase of consulting comprises activities that consultants normally undertake to spread the word about their consulting capability in order to get contracts. Such activities include selling, marketing, and networking. Perhaps the most critical obstacle the local consultant in the Eastern Caribbean must overcome during exposition is the image of who is a consultant.

Who is a consultant?

To many Eastern Caribbean minds, the word "consultant" conjures up an image of the foreign expert "brought down" to the region from overseas (primarily from England, the United States, and Canada). The logic is that a consultant is an expert and an expert cannot be local or one of their own, because expertise comes from overseas. Indeed, one way some local consultants try to overcome this image is by basing their practice outside the region, the farther away the better. This image of a consultant is a direct outgrowth of a colonial heritage and has little, if anything, to do with a demand for objective, unbiased (nonlocal) opinions or for the most up-to-date knowledge and skills.

Closed market

The long standing image of a consultant as a foreigner serves to maintain a consulting market that is often closed to locals. The local consultant gains entry based on a reputation or track record for expertise developed in previous or current full-time jobs. Being "known" in relation to a full-time position is critical to gaining entry to the closed consulting market of the Eastern Caribbean. Typically, local consultants fit one of two employment categories. First, as full-time employees of a university department, government, or regional or private organization. They serve in executive level management positions and perform consulting activities related to "known" expertise in their full-time job. Or second, local consultants are retired from full-time senior level positions and have a wide reputation for expertise in their field. It should be noted that the local consultant generally has, from necessity, a source of income other than that from consulting. The status of independent consultant is not widely held or acknowledged in the Eastern Caribbean, as a local resident is seldom able to earn a viable living entirely from consulting.

A similar situation for independent consultants may also exist in other developing countries. For instance, recently in Istanbul, Turkey, a team of five foreign consultants that included three independent consultants presented itself to a group of university professors. One of the professors, himself selected as a local consultant to work with the foreign team, remarked, "In Turkey, it would be impossible to earn a living as an independent consultant. You must be associated with a university or a firm."

Non-receptivity to marketing

A certain degree of conservatism exists in the consulting market of the Eastern Caribbean, making it somewhat unresponsive to standard Western strategies for selling and marketing professional services. This unresponsiveness is also caused by the role that funding agencies play in the market, as will be discussed later. Telephone calls to people in influential positions may seldom, if ever, yield the wanted results. As for direct-mail promotional materials (for example, business cards, one-page résumés, and brochures), retired University of the West Indies Professor Thomas Henderson attests that these are often discarded with a cynical, "There goes another one who thinks he can solve our problems."

In fact, promotional materials are viewed as flashy or as a gimmick. Advertising of professional services is considered overselling, viewed with disdain, and dismissed with remarks such as, "He thinks he knows what we want."

If being "known" can get local consultants inside the door, then having their worth recognized by influential individuals within client organizations serves to seal contracts. It may even be said that in the Eastern Caribbean local consultants do not undertake their own promotion. Rather, promotion is undertaken for them by a handful of influential individuals who reject the image of a consultant as a foreigner.

Slow payoff from networking

Populations of the seven member states of the Eastern Caribbean range from 90,000 to 150,000. Barbados and Trinidad and Tobago have estimated populations of .25 million and 1.25 million respectively. Very small percentages have senior level to executive level full-time jobs. The result is a relatively small professional community where becoming known happens almost automatically as members of the community interact in full-time job functions. If one is not a member of this community, it takes much time to establish linkages, to become known, and to be accepted. And if one is not known, one cannot expect to be accepted as worthy of local consultant status.

Networking in professional circles, as it is practiced in the Western world, would be shunned and viewed with suspicion in the Eastern Caribbean. For instance, on any given workday in Washington, D.C., it is possible for an out-of-work consultant to get leads to consulting opportunities. This is done by telephoning total strangers whose names and job titles were taken from the membership directory of the local chapter of a professional organization. The consultant nurtures the spin-off effect by asking for names of other persons as he or she follows each lead. We know from first-hand experience that these leads, when pursued aggressively, can develop into a series of introductory meetings and interviews. The end result may be not only a desired contract but also a network of professional associates with whom contact can be maintained, further leads obtained, and ultimately contracts sealed.

In the Eastern Caribbean, networking in the small professional "community" tends to be highly personalized. Unwritten codes of social behavior dictate that people do not converse with each other until they have been formally introduced, preferably by a mutual friend or associate. The trend is not for the local consultant to pursue consulting leads but rather for the local consultant to be approached with a contract offer. Sometimes the "offerer" is a friend or associate of the consultant; other times the offerer might have been referred to the consultant by a mutual friend or associate. The offer is made based on the highly valued judgment of the referee. In either case, there would be no formality of an introductory meeting or an interview.

On the surface, this may appear to be a fortunate situation for the local consultant. However, it should be remembered that there are relatively few contracts available to the local consultant, and those are typically matched to a specific local consultant almost from the time of conception. This means a slow payoff for the local consultant who attempts modified networking and seeks to cultivate relationships within a small professional community.

Funding agencies

Opportunities. One grim reality the local consultant faces is that potential client organizations are poor and cannot afford funds for consulting services. Many organizations are in dire need of help but must depend on external funding agencies for assistance. Most consulting opportunities are funded by external (non-Caribbean) funding agencies. Typically, a funding agency assigns consultants to technical assistance projects which it underwrites. These consultants are generally co-nationals of the funding agency. On the rare occasions when the local recipient organization suggests using local consultants, the funding agency reserves the right to assign quotas. Of course, the quota for local consultants is generally lower than that for foreign consultants. Further, a funding agency bundles an ideology with funding and so it wants consultants who support, if not promote, that ideology. Local consultants limit their access to already meager opportunities when it is known that their ideology conflicts with that of a funding agency. They can expect not to receive fair consideration.

Another way in which funding agencies provide consulting opportunities is through periodic (triennial and even biannual) turnover in staff that creates shifting priorities in technical assistance. For example, in the past seven years alone one prominent funding agency serving the Eastern Caribbean has shifted its priority three times—from management training to farming systems to small business enterprise. Undoubtedly, opportunities for the local consultant fluctuate with these shifts.

Bureaucratic approach. As a rule, protocol is observed in approaching a funding agency. This does not discount however, what Dr. P. I. Gomes of Trinidad and Tobago refers to as "a good bit of personal connections at work." Invariably the approach is made from the executive level of the potential recipient organization. A would-be local consultant may be identified but seldom included in initial discussions with a funding agency. Recipient organizations tend to be very cautious in approaching funding agencies. They may downplay the actual need and request only a fraction of the required funds. Consequently, the funding agency may or may not recognize the actual need for assistance and may shift the request to another area of need altogether that more closely matches its current priority. The process from project definition to release of funds takes several months, sometimes years, in the bureaucracies of the client organization and funding agency. This bureaucratic approach serves as a deterrent to the local consultant, particularly one who is not "known" within the professional community and needs a direct line to funding sources.

Client organizations are also reluctant to communicate with funding agencies, even when faced with a need for adjustments in an on-going project. For example, one agency provided six computers and the services of a local consultant at a central location to analyze data collected by field officers in six islands. The consultant taught the six field officers in data entry and analysis, but they are not using this knowledge as the data must be sent to the central location and there is a long wait for returns of the analyses. It is recognized that each field officer needs an on-site computer in each island to perform data input and preliminary analysis. An officer can then ship disks to the central location for review and verification of analysis and preparation of a report on findings. Three computers can remain in the central location, three can be sent to the field, and three more for field use could be supplied by the funding agency.

This reallocation and addition of computers would remove the present bottle-neck in data processing and facilitate timely project completion. However, the client organization is unwilling to approach the funding agency, stating that it is "not worth it," because—given the slow turnaround time in the bureaucracies—the project completion date would be long past by the time the request was processed and a decision is made to supply and deliver the additional computers.

Competition from foreign consultants

Yet another problem that the local consultant faces during exposition is competition from the foreign consultant. This competition is subtle, for, as pointed out earlier, the local consultant functions in a closed consulting market with limited consulting opportunities.

Many consulting contracts offered to the local consultant are short-term, ranging from two weeks to no more than eight or ten weeks. Overseas consulting firms involved in technical assistance for these small projects regard the funding level as low and unattractive, so they tend to dispatch a dispensable, entry-level consultant to get a grounding in preparation for large international projects. The result is that the local consultant is often up against an inexperienced or inferior foreign consultant.

The call to consult

Client organizations tend to hand pick the local consultant and telephone or fax an offer. Seldom is the local consultant chosen from a pool of applicants after a series of interviews and discussions. Again, although it appears that the local consultant gets offers without hunting, he or she actually receives a second best call. Local decision makers generally do not pick a local consultant as their first choice. Not only is the image of a consultant as foreign at work here, but also a real resistance to promoting local expertise. Leaders of the region have been known to reject the suggestion of a local think-tank because politicians would feel threatened by a body of super technocrats.

Resistance to negotiation

More often than not, the local consultant receives an offer with preset terms. The implied message is, "Take it or leave it." Little room is allowed for negotiation on contract duration, schedule, fees, and per diem. It often seems that by the time the local consultant receives the call to consult, the project has run out of funds—so the fee being offered is the highest possible. Also, project scheduling has lapsed—so the tasks must be performed within the stated period. In a few cases, for example, when a local or regional organization is managing a project, the local consultant may be asked to state the required consulting fee. The local consultant knows that this is not necessarily an invitation to bid or negotiate, because the organization expects the consultant to set a low, local fee. Whenever a local consultant states fees more in keeping with those paid foreign consultants, the representatives of the local organizations exclaim in horror that such fees are much too high and that there is no way the organization could afford those rates.

Ironically, the offerer will be influential enough to ensure that the local consultant begins work on the desired date—a conflict in the consultant's work schedule is cleared at the highest level, a standby reservation on an overbooked flight is confirmed, and a room in a full hotel is vacated. Yet, this same offerer suppresses the worth of, and denies any bargaining power to, the local consultant.

Short-term, ad hoc scope of effort

Like professionals everywhere, local consultants find satisfaction in knowing that their tasks are not performed in vain. They want their efforts to make a difference and help to achieve a desired result. On long-term projects involving sustained effort, the local consultant has some opportunity to derive the satisfaction of a worthy contribution. The consultant will be viewed, however reluctantly, as an asset and expected to make a valued contribution.

However, on short-term projects, the norm for the Eastern Caribbean, the local consultant is often hard put to derive such satisfaction. One problem is that funding agencies often include a local consultant for political reasons, to add local flavor or a local point of view. Under these circumstances, the local consultant is not really needed because the important work is done by foreign consultants. Thus, scope of effort assigned to the local consultant tends to be *ad hoc*. In fact, it is not even expected that the local consultant will be able to do what the important effort demands, so instead, on many short-term projects, the local consultant is given limited tasks that will neither help nor hurt the project. This can be humiliating to local consultants, especially when the assigned work does not match their known expertise. For example, a professor of sociology is called upon to instruct population census takers. A curriculum development specialist may be called upon to review a set of manuscripts for the incidence of recognition given to the role of women in agriculture. Of course, the local consultant can refuse such jobs. But, who can afford to refuse when consulting opportunities are limited and word gets around in the small professional community?

Undervalued expertise–lower local fee

As pointed out earlier, the local consultant is generally offered a lower fee, sometimes as much as fifty percent lower, than the foreign consultant. To make matters worse, the foreign consultant is often less qualified to do the given tasks. One argument is that paying the local consultant the same fee as the foreign consultant is out of line with the salary norms of the Eastern Caribbean. Few influential persons in local organizations insist on equal fees for local and foreign consultants. Again, the image of expertise as foreign serves to undervalue local expertise.

In one case where the director of a local client organization insisted on equal consulting fees, the foreign consultant requested more money since he was the designated team leader. The local director questioned the extent of leadership effort needed on a team of two persons of similar qualifications. Finally, he offered the foreign consultant a dollar more per day, adding with a note of finality, "That's more."

No leadership role for locals

Sometimes the local consultant may receive a call to consult alone as in a short-term, one person project. When the local consultant receives a call to consult in a team, the team will invariably include at least one foreign consultant. (On long-term projects, two or more local consultants may work as a team on a subset of tasks, but rarely would they work as a team to complete an entire project.)

On a team with a foreign consultant, the local consultant is seldom designated team leader. One reason is that the funding agency is more comfortable with a home-country (i.e., foreign) consultant representing and promoting its interests. Another reason is that the team leader receives a higher fee than other team members for performing leadership functions, and funding agencies seem to consider it inappropriate to pay a local consultant a higher fee than the home-country consultant.

Briefing

As in most consultancies, the briefing phase informs the consultant on the problems and expectations of the funding and client organizations. When local and foreign consultants work as a team, each consultant can have as many as three briefings, but only two of these will count as "official." The client organization may brief the local consultant alone and then in company with the foreign consultant. Similarly, the funding agency may brief the foreign consultant alone and then in company with the local consultant.

Being perceived as the client's "buddy"

For the local consultant, there is a certain amount of uneasiness during the unofficial briefing from the client organization. At this time, the local consultant is treated more as a buddy than as a competent, nonpartisan professional. The message communicated to the consultant, verbally or nonverbally, is simple and direct: "You have to be on our side."

Perception as "captive" of the funding agency

On the other hand, the local consultant is perceived as a tool of the funding agency. The message communicated in this briefing is, "You're here to perform our will, so act like you're on our side."

Unlike the client organization, the funding agency may do a background check on the local consultant. This check may be done discreetly by the agency's local representative, to confirm that the local consultant can be expected to support rather than threaten the agency's ideology. Depending on the findings of the check, the funding agency may even reveal elements of its hidden agenda to the local consultant. For example, in one case it was found that the local consultant had not only studied and worked for several years in the agency's home country but had acquired citizenship by naturalization. The agency's formal briefing of foreign and local consultants included an off-the-record session on the type of information the agency wanted about the client organization. Of course, the related data gathering and analysis tasks leading to this information were not included in the official scope of work.

When the local and foreign consultants, are task-oriented and experienced in their craft, uphold high professional standards, and have international experience, they are more likely to develop mutual respect quickly and work in harmony to complete the tasks at hand. However, these conditions do not always prevail. Often, as described above, the foreign consultant is at a junior or entry level and arrives in the Eastern Caribbean on his or her first ever overseas assignment. This consultant tends to buy into the perception that the local consultant will side with the local client organization and against the funding agency. A short-term assignment of only a few weeks does not provide enough time for the foreign consultant to cast aside this perception and get on with the task at hand. As a result, the local consultant may bear the brunt of the work for the first few days. Meanwhile, the foreign consultant tries to gain a balanced perception and adjust to the local consultant and the environment.

Contract Performance

The local consultant also strives for adjustment and balance during contract performance. One problem the local consultant faces here is the condescending "big daddy" approach by the foreign consultant. This force can be subtle to overt, depending on the foreign consultant's international experience. The local consultant expects this approach and usually tries to face it with diplomacy instead of antagonism.

An example is the case of the local consultant who was called to consult in a team of four foreign consultants on a mid-term project evaluation. The call came from the regional organization that was managing the local project and had insisted on including a local consultant on the evaluation team. The organization prepared a written scope of effort for the local consultant. But, at the start of work, the foreign team leader declared that the local consultant need not follow the given scope but instead should assume the role of an observer. This role included accompanying the team on site visits but didn't call for participation in team meetings and work sessions. Motivated by financial gain, professional development (yet another call to consult), and a desire to keep faith with the regional organization, the local consultant quietly played the game but endeavored to learn everything possible about the project.

Objectivity

The local consultant must also strive to achieve objectivity, especially considering sensitivity to the local setting. The foreign consultant with a strong professional background and international development experience can help in achieving this objectivity by focusing on a problem situation, identifying critical elements, and drawing logical conclusions.

For example, a two-person team of consultants (one local, one foreign) was assigned to conduct a feasibility study for installing a micro hydroelectric power plant in a small, rural community. A prior study had proposed that the plant could be operated as a cooperative effort by the community. In previous years cooperative ventures had been introduced to the community but none had succeeded. Both consultants identified evidence in the community that would militate against success of the proposed project. The local consultant acknowledged the truth of this evidence but recognized the political fall out that could occur if the study did not recommend the proposed project. The local consultant wanted to give the community the benefit of the doubt and recommend a compromise project so as not to jeopardize his chances for future consulting contracts. But, the foreign consultant was prone to make recommendations based on the evidence as he saw it, without regard to possible socio-political implications. His insistence on performing within the given scope of work helped the local consultant to maintain objectivity in terms of viewing the evidence and making sound recommendations.

Reporting to the client

Part of the deal the client organization is interested in striking during the informal briefing with the local consultant is advance knowledge of "what is coming down"—the findings of the report. Rather than hold secret (unknown to the foreign consultant) meetings with the client, one local consultant responded to this expectation by sharing (with the agreement of the foreign consultant) copies of the first draft of the findings section of the report. Although only ten to fifteen per cent of the findings cast negative light on the client organization, the client representative responded with anger and disappointment. "How could you let this be written? This type of statement is what you were put there to prevent." Clearly, the local consultant was expected to be a buddy even to the point of deception. This client representative could not concede that while it was found that the organization was doing a good job in most areas, there was room for improvement in a few other areas.

Reporting to the funding agency

Local consultants face the reality that the funding agency is not particularly interested in a report from them as might be outlined in the scope of effort. The agency perceives the local consultant as a "captive" who may add some local flavor to the latest information. The message is, "Share some critical information, hint, guidance, something that you know because you're local that I wouldn't know." Sometimes the local consultant is hard put to provide this assistance. There may just not be anything worth sharing. At other times, local consultants may decide not to provide such help because it would be a betrayal of the local client organization.

For example, on one project to review the project management performance of an organization, an unwritten agenda was to identify the controls exerted by the chain of command within the organization and determine the extent of independence given the project management group. The funding agency wanted an autonomous project management group within the local organization. The agency would communicate directly with this group, which would make decisions and implement actions without control from the director and the board. Such in-house group autonomy was a requirement for future funding. But the local consultant knew that the local organization would rather dissociate itself from the funding agency and lose its funding than compromise its organizational structure. The local consultant chose not to discuss this with the funding agency, disclosing only that members of the project management team were not complaining and there were no hints that they were being prevented from functioning as they would like.

Conclusion

We have described several factors that create a dilemma for the local consultant. Despite this dilemma, the local consultant eagerly awaits a call to consult, viewing it as an opportunity to test competencies, advance professional development, and, of course, enhance income.

The foreign consultant who comes to the Eastern Caribbean should try to work in harmony with local consultants. Disregard of the professional status of local consultants, nonrecognition of their competencies, and denial of their input simply aggravate the problems of the local consultant. Ways for a foreign consultant to avoid this include:

- Acknowledge the scope of effort assigned to the local consultant and reach a consensus on proportional responsibility of each team member. If it is necessary to adjust the scope of effort for the local consultant, avoid diminishing the role and denying an appropriate input.
- Communicate with the local consultant as you would with a respected colleague.

- Observe formal social codes of behavior. (Check what these are before departure to the country or ask the local consultant politely if you're unsure.)
- Even if you're the team leader, adopt a management style that does not condescend. Treat the consultant as an equal.
- Don't flaunt your wealth or discuss income levels.
- Devote your energy to completing project tasks rather than dissecting the land, the people, and the local culture. You are unlikely to become an expert on the country on a short-term assignment. The conclusions you voice may not only be overbearing and judgmental, but downright naive.

About the Authors

Dunstan Campbell is an Outreach Lecturer at the University of the West Indies in Castries, St. Lucia. He completed his doctoral studies in Rural Sociology at the University de Paul Valery in Montpellier, France.

Cheryl Samuels-Campbell is an independent consultant in Castries, St. Lucia. Previously, she was Senior Education Specialist at Control Data Corporation in Rockville, MD. She completed her doctoral studies in Educational Technology Media and Instructional Systems at Teachers College, Columbia University. To escape the paradox of the local consultant, she seeks and obtains contracts during the summer and early fall in the metropolitan Washington, D.C. area.

CHAPTER 14

Multicultural / Multinational Teambuilding

Mel Schnapper

This chapter presents an approach to building effective teams where common objectives and tasks must be achieved by team members from different organizational and national cultures.

I will discuss the general problems and conflicts that occur when mergers and acquisitions bring together people whose values, style, beliefs, and reactions may differ radically or just enough to create confusion, tension, and apprehension about the "right" way to get things done. This often occurs when one group imposes its procedures upon the other. The problems are intensified when the companies are from different countries. Intercultural communication and organizational behavior theory explain these situations and possible solutions.

I have developed a pragmatic approach to help resolve these particular conflicts which I call Multicultural/Multinational Teambuilding or "MMT." This chapter describes the implementation, dynamics, and specific outcomes of one application.

The Human Aspect of Mergers and Acquisitions

The last ten years have seen an acceleration of the merging and acquisition of huge corporations on a worldwide scale. In some cases these ventures have been successful and as often they have not been. The reasons for the failures are many: financial and marketing differences, incompatible top management philosophies, and inadequate planning. They will not be described at length here because this chapter focuses on situations where organizational and national cultures have been in conflict. When this has been a critical dimension of incompatibility, MMT has proved itself an effective intervention.

The idea of culture is not new—it has been studied by many behavioral scientists for centuries, and the last several decades of attention to the developing countries has led to an explosion of the field of applied anthropology. There are now many doctoral programs in applied behavioral science for studying and promoting change within organizations, usually called Organization Development (OD) or Organization Behavior (OB).

The accelerated mergers and acquisitions within and between national borders have focused even greater attention on the conscious management of how employees from diverse organizational and national backgrounds can be brought together effectively. MMT brings together the theoretical and pragmatic applications of two disciplines and traditions—the planned macrocultural change at the level of national culture and the planned microcultural change at the organizational level.

National and Organizational Cultures

Many mergers and acquisitions have failed within national borders because of incompatible organizational cultures. Sometimes one organization has norms or dominant behavioral tendencies that have been a "culture shock" to the acquired corporate environment. Since organizational culture reflects many things, incompatibility is likely.

Culture has been defined perhaps thousands of times. This chapter will use the definition given in Chapter 1 of this book. Of equal importance to history is mythology, which, if one believes it to be true, is called one's religion. Corporations also have a religion. It is that collection of stories and "truths" that are seen as non-negotiable, with predictable consequences for nonconformance. The religious aspect is critical because, as with religion, specific data or "proof" need not alter the belief systems. For example, if you confront the president, you'll be fired; if you don't dress a certain way or maintain certain work habits, you have little career opportunity, etc.

When the strength of this corporate culture clashes with a weaker, though equally opposite, set of beliefs and behavioral norms, the more powerful elements will probably triumph, usually after months or even years of wasteful, acrimonious conflict. Vansina (1974) cites many examples of these cultural battles that have exacted extreme costs of energy, productivity, creativity, and emotions.

When corporate cultural differences are combined with national cultural differences, the conflicts are even more exacerbated, with less mutual understanding and chance for resolution. One company may have a cultural norm supporting lifetime employment, and be acquired by a company from a country where employees are "fired at will." The first company will see laying people off—even for legitimate business reasons, such as redundant staff, restructuring, redistribution along different organizing principles, etc.—as ruthless, heartless, and exploitive. The acquiring personnel will think their processes are legitimate and a natural and normal way to conduct business.

These then are the major issues and parameters for utilizing an approach like MMT. It highlights cultural differences and promotes their formal recognition, so that people can understand that the ways to achieve common tasks are myriad.

Before continuing, please refer to the definitions of certain terms in Chapter 1. These terms are *national*, *international*, *multinational*, and *transnational*. With these terms clearly defined, we can now talk about the evolution of a national company that increases its international operations to an extent that merits a modest cultural adaptation. At some point, its international operations may demand greater flexibility and cultural diversity in its management practices so that it is multinational. It may, finally, reach the stage of a transnational company, where its national origin and focus is hardly recognizable, except by some senior historians.

At any stage of this evolutionary process, which is not necessarily predictable, there will be interfaces between procedures, practices, policies, and, ultimately, the personnel who carry them out. When these personnel represent different countries and national cultures, conflict is almost inevitable.

The Traditional Organization Development Solution

A traditional organization-development approach to organizational conflict has been around for several decades. Briefly, OD utilizes various behavioral science techniques which enable the participants in an organizational change effort to take ownership for the data, the problem definition, and, ultimately, the solutions and their implementation (French and Bell, 1973; Bennis, 1969). The focus is on action learning, where every step of the change is evaluated by the actual participants so they can alter the nature of the change and make conscious choices about the norms and culture they are developing.

To give a simple example, participants might recognize that those with the highest status in the work group frequently interrupt those with less status. The OD intervention would be to have the participants formally agree that no one is to interrupt anyone else, regardless of status differences in the group. This will probably require an outsider or facilitator to confront those who continue the old behavior, but ultimately, the facilitator would not be needed as group members assume "ownership" of the responsibility to enforce their own evolving culture.

Cultural assumptions

This OD model assumes an egalitarian culture where conflict is legitimate and public confrontation, is acceptable. It also assumes a culture where people can openly express their feelings and perceptions of each other, and make known up and down status hierarchies and across territorial boundaries what they like and dislike about the "other." These are but some of the cultural assumptions of the democratic and expressive norms of the traditional OD approach (Beckhard, 1969).

Repeated failures

Obviously, these norms present a problem to the many organizational and national cultures where status is highly respected and never challenged, feelings are kept to oneself and expressed only in the most subtle ways, and perceptions of others are never shared for risk of their losing face or being embarrassed. Yet, this traditional model of OD and a specific intervention called "team building" has been used worldwide, often shocking people exposed to it for the first time. This traditional model is inappropriate for several reasons, some of which are

- The trauma of these norms may be so severe that participants never recover the "civility" of their old ways that made corporate life bearable.
- The new norms are not sustainable without the constant presence of the outside facilitator, who, if even an employee/consultant, cannot attend to all that must be managed.
- The degree of stress on some may even constitute "emotional blackmail" as they are subjected to uncomfortable norms dictated to them.

There are real paradoxes here. If a multinational team has agreed to be more confrontational, this agreement may be suspect. Some members whose culture dictates compliance to the will of the majority may have given in to their colleagues and dare not express their disagreement. Such dynamics may have even occurred in the several successful MMT interventions I will describe, although this unique approach should keep them to a minimum.

The frequent failure of the OD approach for a multinational group stems partly from the different definitions of what constitutes cooperation, teamwork and appropriate feedback. From my experiences in teambuilding within my own culture, there is an acknowledgment that the essential beliefs and personal histories of team members constitute a basis for many of the new norms that are introduced by the traditional teambuilding approach. However, my experience with multinational teams when I used these traditional techniques is that almost every nuance of this conventional teambuilding approach is fraught with cultural ethnocentrism.

Specifically, in my early years of using and espousing this approach, I would feel pleased when deeply felt resentment and fear were being expressed across international boundaries. I saw this candid expression of long-held feelings as progress. I also learned, sometimes long after the teambuilding experience, that the team had not improved its performance. In fact, often the opposite was true.

In a few situations I was able to interview the original participants to find out what had happened to original commitments and action plans based on all the other accomplishments of the teambuilding sessions. I learned that those with Western or

North American cultural orientation were baffled by the poor long-term performance of the team. They, like me, had seen dramatic encounters during the sessions with verbal resolution of conflict, role clarification, and negotiations about a whole host of issues.

The non-Western participants and those not oriented to open confrontation, especially across international or status boundaries, were confused and depressed about the total situation. For them, the whole experience had violated all their norms of respect for status and avoidance of public confrontation. They saw these negotiations inflicting incredible duress and intimidation.

So here I saw for the first of many times how the same experience seemed to some to promote group harmony, cooperation, and productivity, while others perceived it in opposite terms. This seemed to depend on national culture of origin, where one's basic conditioning to group life had been inculcated.

Multicultural / Multinational Teambuilding (MMT)

I then decided that the traditional teambuilding approach was not only inappropriate, it was ineffective and would benefit no one in the long term. The bells and whistles of the early interventions and apparent progress were illusory.

Cultural awareness

My initial formulation of the MMT model borrowed heavily from the "intercultural workshop" developed by David Hoopes at the University of Pittsburgh for foreign student orientation to American campus life and culture (Hoopes, 1970). His approach was to use familiar symbols, games, and words to show multicultural/multinational groups of students how culturally sensitive the meanings of all the behaviors in the workshop were.

From this and my other work in multinational organizations, I evolved the MMT model for use with employees of multinational corporations and international organizations where common task accomplishment was non-negotiable (Schnapper, 1973, 1978, 1979, 1985). The student groups had the luxury of walking away from their experience. My teambuilding participants were to live with each other, usually for years after the teambuilding session.

Task orientation of MMT

My challenge was to combine the cultural-awareness techniques of the intercultural workshop with the task orientation of traditional teambuilding. There is a tremendous difference between achieving understanding for its own sake and maintaining it when common tasks must be accomplished. Often, participants will have long-sustained work relationships and even work histories that may go back decades.

Benefits of MMT

MMT is a specialized approach that helps culturally diverse work groups achieve high productivity and cooperation without denying or suppressing the cultural differences. If not understood and managed, these differences can lead to lower productivity, increased waste, and lack of cooperation. MMT can help organizations reduce wasteful time, excessive costs, employee turnover, and labor dissatisfaction that often result from interaction between cultures in collision.

Occasional misunderstandings resulting from cultural differences may have raised levels of antagonism and hostility to unmanageable levels. In attempting to make work groups more productive, many HRD practitioners and OD consultants typically ignore these differences and use traditional approaches which are often inappropriate and ineffective.

MMT helps team members recognize and use cultural differences in productive and creative ways. These cultural differences typically consist of

- Styles of leadership
- Perceptions
- Values
- Problem-solving approaches
- Ways of resolving conflict
- Ways of sharing perceptions
- Means of determining priorities
- Evaluation criteria

These are only a few of the factors that might play out as cultural dynamics evolve in this unique work group. As a task-focused group evolves, these differences must be surfaced, negotiated, and resolved.

MMT focuses on the contexts of various teambuilding issues to an extent that allows team members to share their differences and see them as variables to be recognized, appreciated, and included in all of its procedures. For example, MMT helped a multinational project team appreciate how differently emotions (the context of all behavior) are expressed by North and South Americans, thus clearing up many misunderstandings which resulted from this ignorance.

Quite frequently, multinationals will hire many professionally qualified staff people from different countries and assume that their professional expertise will allow them to facilitate effective teamwork. Too often, their lack of managerial, interpersonal, and intercultural skills minimizes their ability to effectively contribute their expertise. MMT provides these skills.

This is a time of quick start-up project teams handling projects all over the world. Team members need to quickly move into new situations with strangers and begin delivering results that are often urgent and crucial to the success of these international projects. Experts of all sorts are highly mobile, moving in and out of organizational and geographical areas. MMT eases the adjustment process as well as minimizes the ways in which cultural differences and frustrating barriers prevent successful interaction and task accomplishment.

Specific Application: An Example of an MMT Project

The specific example that follows best shows how to apply the theory of intercultural communication, applied anthropology, and organization development techniques of teambuilding to a real work environment with real tasks, objectives, and risks.

The situation

The client is a multinational industrial chemicals company with plants in the U.S., England, and Belgium and a worldwide sales and marketing organization. It evolved as a subsidiary of a consumer products company whose food line produced agricultural waste which was later found to be the source of a valuable chemical. Over the years it had grown into a major profit center for the company and was left alone for as long as it was profitable.

Sales were to the foundry industry worldwide. In the 1930s, all six plants were domestic. When I came there, two plants had been acquired in Europe. They had existed for some 30 years each under British and Belgian ownership, and were just now contending with their new American ownership, which had been pretty much laissez faire. The organization was so loose that even the corporate function of international marketing was not truly international. There were different prices for the same product, depending on the production site, and no worldwide integration of marketing and sales efforts. However, a soft market provoked a corporate move toward a more tightly integrated organization and I was to help integrate the human resource procedures!

I worked with two major sites. One was a factory town north of London, where the dominant British work force felt besieged by a growing East Indian population. I was repeatedly told by my British clients how the only two movie theaters had shown only Indian films for the past several years.

The other town was in Heel, Belgium, with a predominantly Flemish work force, a British plant manager (who was wise enough to learn Flemish, not French) and three other plant managers who were American, South African, and French. They reported to a vice president of European operations—a Hungarian with French citizenship living in Paris, the European headquarters of this company! The mix of cultural variables was vast. And all of this in the context of an American corporate culture that was well-known and respected within many countries.

The task

My task was to install a standard performance appraisal system that would measure and judge individual performance. It would ultimately determine salary increases, promotions, and career mobility on a worldwide basis across a variety of

- Functions
- Levels
- Functional cultures: marketing, manufacturing, sales, research and development
- National cultures: American, British, Belgian, French, German, South African, Italian, etc.

I was to accomplish this after the corporation had failed for decades to develop a formal, logical, or methodical approach within its American headquarters, domestic facilities, or its European operations. Except for annual corporate meetings, occasional trips, and exchange of technical information, there was a great deal of freedom for everything.

The challenge was to please everyone while still being effective. Fortunately, I had already been to Europe and met most of the leadership, who had been exposed to some of the MMT approach. This experience had been very positive since it highlighted, supported, and even gloried in the multiculturalism that each team represented. It was also dramatically different from the host of corporate-imposed policies and procedures that were multiplying during the business downturn. I had already established myself as different from the other corporate people in that I started with their needs and developed programs responsive to them. My headquarters boss may have paid me, but they as a unit were my client.

The workshop design

I will go into some detail about the specific dynamics since that is what is so dramatically different about MMT, but first here are the MMT objectives and purpose.

Purpose. This workshop will enable participants to understand the various cultural and organizational variables that can contribute to more effective teamwork and organizational success.

Objectives. As a result of this session, participants will be able to

- Identify the specific cultural variables that influence decision making, teamwork, task accomplishment, role clarity, and productivity
- Conclude which of these variables contribute and which do not contribute to effective teamwork
- Develop organizationally and culturally appropriate means and alternatives to manage the team culture
- Apply all of the above to developing a performance-appraisal process that meets the needs of the corporation and is culturally appropriate to the facility

To reach these objectives, a specific workshop design was established, as outlined in Table 14.1.

Table 14.1: Time Schedule of MMT Workshop

Day One

8:00 a.m.	**Introduction** to the purpose and objectives
9:00 a.m.	**Culture–National and Organizational**
	This is a formal presentation about these concepts explained earlier in this chapter. Participants are asked to contribute from their own experience.
10:00 a.m.	**Nonverbal Communication**
	A presentation on the cultural basis of human emotion and gesture. Participants share their own perceptions of these concepts and of each other based on these concepts (Schnapper, 1975).
11:00 a.m.	**Case Study: The Coal Corporation**
	A simulation that requires teams to pick an ideal candidate to manage a coal company in Nigeria, followed by a discussion about common tasks, sharing of information, and competition versus cooperation (Nylen, Mitchell, and Stout, 1967).
12:00 noon	Lunch
	(Always 1 1/2 hours in length. That alone wins friends.)
1:30 p.m.	**Organizational Cultures**
	Theirs and Ours. The mirroring technique for sharing perceptions of "self" and "other," done at the level of corporate culture and national culture. Based on Beckhard's (1967) organizational mirroring technique. The data generated are shown in Tables 14.2 and 14.3.
3:00 p.m.	**Cultural Variables–Desirable and Undesirable**
	Discussion of which variables will help and which variables will hinder the accomplishment of the task at hand.
4:00 p.m.	**Feedback and Evaluation**
	An opportunity for the consultant to get feedback and for the group to share its perception of the first day.
5:00 p.m.	**End of Day One**

Day Two

8:00 a.m.	Performance Appraisal – What It is and What It's Supposed to Accomplish.
	A general explanation of the system and how it contributes to professional development, career opportunity, and equity of reward systems.
9:00 a.m.	**How It's Done in Europe** – A freewheeling discussion about Europeans' ways of handling these issues.
10:00 a.m.	**The Corporate System**
	Which parts of it are appropriate and which are inappropriate.
11:00 a.m.	**How to Implement**
	An exploration of what parts of the formal system would be implemented and done in a culturally appropriate way.
12:00 noon	Lunch
1:30 p.m.	**Role – Play**
	A selection of situations that would require feedback, judgment, instruction, and establishing the appropriate reward for that particular performance standard.
4:30 p.m.	Feedback and Evaluation
5:00 p.m.	End of Workshop

Table 14.2: Lists of London Workshop ("How we see them—How we see ourselves")

Chicago Headquarters	Europe
More bureaucracy (rigid)	Entrepreneurial
More specialized	Flexible generalists
No in-depth intercultural experience	Many cultures, languages
Homogeneous	Heterogeneous
Jobs are more money-oriented	Other rewards (friendship, etc.)
Policies accepted	Skepticism, questioning
Centralized	Individualized
What's U.S. is international	Let's see what works here
Hurried/intense	Slower
Robot-type managers	Expressive
Hard/unfeeling	Compassionate
Organization all important	Living
Poor external communication outside U.S.	We talk to each other
One law	Many laws
Performance Planning & Review	Not an incentive is an incentive
Paper work appropriate	Verbal work appropriate
Criticism not ok	Criticism ok
"Right"	"Wrong"
100% perfection, even though done late	Results 75% to have impact
Committee decisions and consensus	Individual responses
Corporate arrogance	Lackey complex

Table 14.3: Lists of Heel, Belgium Workshop ("How we see them—How we see ourselves")

Chicago Headquarters	Europe
Bureaucratic	Entrepreneurial
Accept what's given by top management	Screen utility of objectives
Corporate arrogance	Living with it
It works here, so do as we say	Many ways
Highly specialized jobs	Jack of all trades
Need for high organization	Need for self–starters
More sophisticated management techniques	More common sense
One culture and one language	Several cultures and languages
Facade–building "consensus"	Call it as you see it
Perfectionist	Results–oriented
Criticism unwelcome	Possible
If we want something, we should get it now	If we want something, we may get it
Low risk-taking	Reasonable risk-taking

Table 14.3: Lists of Heel, Belgium Workshop ("How we see them–how we see ourselves") (*concluded*)

Legitimate need for more sophisticated management techniques	More informal approach
Facade–building	Confrontation
Censorship	Frankness
Chicago demands do it now!	Europe: when we get to it
Communication lines poor	Free data showing
Job rotation	Cannot switch around

Developing Cross-Cultural Data

Eventually I led the participants in an exercise to explore the differences between their national and European organizational cultures and that of the corporate headquarters that was imposing this new procedure.

As seen in Tables 14.2 and 14.3, the exercise "organizational mirroring" (Beckhard, 1967) produced the generalized self-perceptions of Europeans ("How we see ourselves") and their perceptions of their American dominated corporate headquarters ("How we see them"). In addition to presenting these different sets of perceptions, which get to the heart of culture, the participants articulated some very real differences in labor/social environments that determined some of these differences in perception. Some of these differences were:

Chicago Headquarters
- Implementation of systems, conformity in salary, promotion, etc.
- Requests to do things with no apparent reason
- Restrictions of local authority—any salary increase at any level, even to change part-time to full-time
- Decisions given—no reason
- Lack of appreciation of local needs and facilities
- One language, conformist, no pay code, unions not so all-powerful, everybody for themselves, expect community work

Europe
- Multilingual individuals
- Government pay codes
- Unions strong and unified
- Social policies protect unfortunate
- Please yourself outside of work

Conclusions of the workshop and follow-up

After the two-day workshop, the European groups concluded that the formal performance-appraisal system was for the most part not relevant to their needs. However, they promised to abide by the requirements for some kind of data that would fulfill corporate expectations. So what the corporation received was the strict "letter of the law" kinds of data. Most of the skills and formal procedures were not adopted.

What did happen, however, is significant. The Europeans readily agreed to a system that met their needs and would give the corporate powers an adequate level of performance data for the new performance-review system.

What would have probably occurred had I not used the MMT approach was reflected during the few years before my arrival. There was constant tension between European and American operations. Europeans dreaded visiting corporate headquarters and the Vice President of European operations was almost fired for being "immature." My perception is that he was emotional and expressive, and thus not compatible with corporate headquarters executive boardroom behavior.

Fortunately, I was able to follow up on events even after my own departure from the company. Several years later, I can report that the basic appraisal format is still used in Europe, even though abandoned in the United States. The level of adaptation was sustainable from the beginning. Because the Europeans had an opportunity to discuss and modify the proposed format, they were committed to, and comfortable with, the final process. The American headquarters personnel, on the other hand, were told to execute a system they had had little part in developing and to sustain a system at a level well beyond their perceived needs.

This is but one of many examples of how the MMT approach can be used to help build teams that are multinational and multicultural. The performance appraisal system was the particular common task in this example. Other foci of the MMT have been long-range planning, reorganizing a marketing function, improving productivity, and goal-setting.

Outlook

This chapter has described the inappropriate use of a widely practiced version of a North American-based behavioral science intervention and how this approach may be counter-productive in a European setting. Additionally, I have described an alternative called Multicultural/Multinational Teambuilding. MMT heightens the awareness of cultural differences in a multicultural task team and allows participants to fully express their differences. This insures that ultimate decision making and problem solving are truly owned by all who must later carry out the various solutions.

My hope is that, in contrast to the assumption by many, we are all heading toward a global corporate culture. There will an additional sensitivity to the powerful force that culture still has in all multinational arenas, even when the newly created company, as a result of mergers and acquisitions, seems to have a unified managerial structure and culture.

The essence of the MMT approach is not the particular model, schedule, or techniques described in this chapter—it is that every situation demands a uniquely sensitive and culturally appropriate approach.

Bibliography

Beckhard, R. "The Confrontation Meeting". *Harvard Business Review,* 1967.

Beckhard, R. *Organization Development: Strategies and Models.* Reading,MA: Addison-Wesley, 1969.

Bennis, W.G. *Organization Development: Its Nature, Origin, and Prospects.* Reading, MA: Addison-Wesley, 1969.

French, W.L., and Bell, C.H. *Organization Development.* Englewood Cliffs, NJ: Prentice-Hall, 1973.

Hoopes, D.
"The Workshop – Pittsburgh Model" *In Readings in Intercultural Communications, Volume 1.* Pittsburgh, PA: Regional Council for International Education, 1970.

Nylen, D., Mitchell, J.R., and Stout, A. *Handbook of Staff Development and Human Relations Training: Materials Developed for Use in Africa.* Washington, DC: National Training Labs, 1967.

Schnapper, M. *Experiential Intercultural Training for International Operations.* Pittsburgh, PA: University of Pittsburgh, Ph.D. Dissertation.

Schnapper, M. "Nonverbal Communication and the Intercultural Encounter". *The Annual Handbook for Group Facilitators,* Jones, J.E., and Pfeiffer, W. (Eds.). La Jolla, CA: University Associates, 1975.

Schnapper, M. "Multinational Training for Multinational Corporations". In *Handbook of Intercultural Communications: Theories and Practice.* Asante, M.K., and Newmark, E. (Eds.). Beverly Hills,CA: Sage Publications, 1978.

Schnapper, M. *Some Multicultural/Multinational Aspects of Organization Development.* Paper presented at the American Society for Training and Development Conference, Washington, DC, 1979.

Schnapper, M. *How to Identify and Resolve Intercultural Conflict.* Paper presented at the Society for Intercultural Education, Training and Research Conference, Washington, DC, 1985.

Vansina, L.S. "Improving International Relations and Effectiveness Within Multinational Organizations". In *New Technologies in Organization Development.* John, A. (Ed.). La Jolla, CA: University Associates, Inc., 1974.

About the Author

Mel Schnapper is President of Melvin Schnapper Associates in Chicago.

CHAPTER 15

Training U.S. Business People to Be Global Persons

Sandy Mayers-Chen

In today's global scene, individuals interact continuously with people of many different cultures. People are constantly being confronted with situations in which their behavior and their every statement may be misunderstood by others. The problem and its ramifications are enormous. For example, a corporate executive who is unaware of how perceptions of behavior are affected by one's own cultural values is less likely to be received positively by representatives of a culturally different organization.

People tend to believe that their own view of the world is the only one that makes sense, and that any intelligent person would see things the same way. Frequently, people are not aware of the wide cultural differences in attitudes toward time, differences that can have major repercussions on daily interactions. A person's orientation to work differs greatly from one culture to another. Generally, people are aware of some of the differences. For example, Americans feel that punctuality and efficiency are very important in some cultures but not so much in others. However, what is missing is the recognition that these differences just reflect U.S. values, which are not absolute, and are certainly not viewed universally as positive attributes.

One can never be completely culture-free. People reflect their own society's deeply held beliefs, which probably differ from those of others. In practical terms, this means that people's best intentions are frequently misunderstood, and consequently end in disaster. Deals fall through, ideas are misconstrued, slights abound, and ill-will proliferates. This major problem obviously justifies an immense learning effort to address it.

As part of that effort, this author designed and conducted a learning activity which focused on examples of written communication that cause a problem by conveying the U.S. perspective on time and activity, thus preventing the development of a global perspective.

The learning activity was designed to enable the participants to uncover such examples and then to identify a global mindset. They then attempted to categorize the component parts and to develop a learning module with practical and measurable objectives. The challenge, however, was to develop a program with wide appeal. This meant that it had to relate to the U.S. value structure in which pragmatism, efficiency, and practicality rule, so that it would be considered useful to the business community. By focusing on the U.S. perspective on time and work, participants could acquire a practical skill, learning by example the way in which an individual's unique perspective can interfere with one's ability to become a highly effective player in the global marketplace.

Perhaps others will be interested in the background and approach to designing a learning activity intended to make U.S. business people aware of their own values. This chapter describes the development considerations for that activity.

Cultural Baggage

Every society develops a culture that meets the needs of the group and solves the problems that are uniquely its own. The values it develops reflect that culture. In the abstract, people are generally comfortable with the knowledge that each culture is unique, designed to address its particular needs. According to Kohls (1984), we need not approve or disapprove of the inherent logic of a given culture to recognize that it "works" for that society.

However, a problem arises when people continually pass judgment on other cultures because of their own deeply held ethnocentrism. People tend to view the values of other cultures as not just different from their own, but inferior to them.

All people are products of their own cultural background, and carry their "cultural baggage" with them wherever they go. Yet, they tend not to realize that their every statement reflects this unique perspective.

Of course, cross-cultural miscommunication is complicated by many factors. Perception is but one. However, this factor is basic to the development of a global perspective. Once people realize that their perceptions are uniquely their own, they will be more open to looking at the way their statements are viewed by others. People assume that perceptual patterns are universal, but Adler (1986) points out that they are neither innate nor absolute. People do not perceive the same things in the same way, even when they are looking at the very same object. Sometimes people see things that do not exist, while at other times they do not see things that do exist. This is quite difficult for people to realize, since few can view themselves objectively. Anthropologist Edward Hall (1976) points out that "what is least known, and therefore the most difficult to be studied, is that which is closest to oneself."

Background of Global Time Perspectives

The assumption that everyone viewing the same thing sees the same thing often leads to serious cross-cultural miscommunication in today's global society. People interact internationally and interculturally on a daily basis; they cannot assume that others see them as they see themselves. This causes misunderstandings, lost opportunities, and failed negotiations which can impact negatively on an organization's bottom line. Therefore, no organization can afford to ignore the danger of failing to acquire a global perspective. If one person's reality is not necessarily another's, then it is easy to see how that seemingly innocuous memo or comment to a cherished client may lead to unintended and possibly irreparable miscommunication.

To minimize this problem, individuals must become aware of the major values that influence their perception and the way they interpret their perceptions. Then, they can learn the ways in which perception differs from culture to culture. The individual who acquires such a global perspective will be better equipped to communicate successfully in an increasingly global society.

Concerned HRD professionals have been seeking ways to meet this learning need for some time. Organizations such as the American Society for Training and Development (ASTD) and the International Society for Intercultural Education, Training and Research (SIETAR), among others, have been addressing these issues in conferences, journals, and workshops.

All international learning is indebted to the earlier works of psychologists, sociologists, and cultural anthropologists, who have explained the ways in which individuals organize and make sense of their world. However, several works by Hall (1959, 1966, 1976, 1983) are seminal. In his basic study (1959), Hall argues that culture is communication and we must be highly sensitive to this "silent language." His subsequent study on how different cultures use space (1966) describes the way people of different cultures react positively or negatively to others depending on their spatial distance from one another.

Convergence or divergence?

Dutch researcher Geert Hofstede (1980) surveyed over 160,000 employees from a U.S. multinational corporation in over 60 countries. After explaining the four dimensions which Hofstede uses to describe the ways in which managers and employees vary from culture to culture, Adler emphasizes a very important point that practitioners must bear in mind: the question of convergence or divergence. Are organizations becoming more similar worldwide or are they maintaining their cultural dissimilarities? According to Adler, studies have shown that there is convergence on a macro level, but divergence on a micro level. In other words, organizational structure and technology is converging, but the behavior of people within organizations is not. If cultural uniqueness is being maintained, then people must be prepared to work with differences in a global context for the long haul.

Time

In Hall's (1976) discussion of the dangers of culturally-based destructive attitudes and behaviors, he refers to M-time (Monochronic time) and P-time (Polychronic time). A later work (1983) relates very closely to the learning experience we are discussing. It explores M-time and P-time in great detail, explaining the perception and use of time across cultures, and the implication for society. A recent joint effort (E. T. Hall and M. R. Hall, 1987) applies Hall's theories to a comparison of Japanese and U.S. cultural differences. It then shows the way in which the two nations' different communication styles impact on their business dealings.

Several HRD practitioners involved in international learning have also written on the subject of time and activity, discussing U.S. values in particular. A few of these works have been particularly helpful in the development of this project.

Discussing organizational behavior in the context of international business, Adler (1986) points out that U.S. business people are quite surprised to discover the way in which non-U.S. people view them. Adler goes on to explain that people can begin to modify their behavior to the extent to which they begin to see themselves clearly through the eyes of foreigners.

Adler also refers to six basic dimensions that describe the cultural orientations of society, designed by Kluckhohn and Strodtbeck (1961), citing management examples for each. These six dimensions include time and work, both of which are relevant to the project described in this chapter. In this way, Adler confirms my belief that teaching business people to understand the basic value orientations across cultures can help prepare them for the increasingly global economy.

Well-known in the international HRD field, Robert Kohls (1984) has been addressing these issues for years. His ability to relate to the international business traveler in a clear, concise, nonacademic style has helped many U.S. people prepare to live and work abroad. In particular, his values categories help to explain the strong American orientation toward action/work and how Americans believe in controlling time. You may wish to refer directly to Robert Kohl's chapter in this book.

Copeland and Griggs (1985) also address individuals interested in the global marketplace. In discussing what they think are the most outstanding differences that separate U.S. people from most of the rest of the world, they focus first on the problems of pace. Citing situations that directly impact on the content of the learning experience being discussed here, they describe the way meetings are conducted across cultures, and some difficulties that arise because of the U.S. attitude toward time and pace. Copeland and Griggs also discuss problems of work attitude, showing how people from the U.S. value working hard, due to their belief that individuals can influence the future and their belief in cause and effect. Needless to say, this causes people from the U.S. to fill their time with carefully programmed activities and continuously watch the clock in a manner that is very off-putting to members of many other cultures.

Stewart (1972) gives a clear description of U.S. cultural patterns, providing the much-needed background for many of these ideas. Stewart discusses in depth the U.S. attitude toward activity and the way in which it affects our work and play, temporal orientation, motivation, and need for measurable achievement. Stewart points out that U.S. people are very focused on doing, and are most uncomfortable with inactivity. He also elaborates on the U.S. perception of the world, explaining in detail the way in which the U.S. concept of time is closely associated with our view toward progress. While Kohls (1984) and others discuss these values and their practical application to the world of business, Stewart creates a framework for applying these ideas.

In the area of cross-cultural research, Hall (1983) explores in detail theories on the hidden walls of time and the way in which time functions as a core system of cultural, social, and personal life. To emphasize the importance of this topic, Hall points out that nothing occurs except in some kind of time frame. Hall believes it is necessary to learn the language of time just as one learns a spoken language.

A particularly helpful work by Brislin, Cushner, Cherrie, and Yong (1986) provides a set of one hundred critical incidents. What makes them invaluable is the way in which they are analyzed and explained. The authors discuss the causes of these misunderstandings both on a situational level and a deeper level. They relate them to a broad framework for understanding these differences, dividing them into three categories: (1) people's intense feelings, (2) knowledge areas, and (3) underlying reasons, for specific differences that are encountered. The authors discuss the concept of time, for example, in the knowledge area, then explain how language is viewed in a cross-cultural context. This was particularly useful as background to the design of the instructional activities for this learning experience that related to vocabulary.

Finally, Bennett (1986) has developed a model which tries to explain how people make sense of differences. The model shows a progression of stages that people pass through when encountering differences and includes strategies to help people move from stage to stage. With this model, a learning specialist can tailor a learning experience to the appropriate learner stage(s), avoiding an atmosphere of anxiety.

Putting Together a Learning Experience Dealing with Time

With the above background in mind, a learning experience was created for corporate people in the United States, focusing on the problem of awareness. The experience was based on the following assumptions:
- U.S. business people need to develop a global perspective.
- An examination of one's own values and assumptions will lead to a broader understanding of the ways in which others view our values and assumptions.

- Doing is the dominant activity in the United States, and concreteness is realized through measurability (Stewart, 1972).
- Learners are adults with at least a high-school education.
- Learners are knowledgeable about some other culture and have interacted with others from culturally different backgrounds.
- Learners are familiar with common U.S. business and professional practices concerning written and oral communication.

Analysis of the Need and Situation

The intention was to develop a learning program to address a dilemma facing U.S. professionals involved in international business who must work with people having widely divergent values and beliefs. But, as a product of U.S. society, the U.S. business person carries unique cultural baggage which strongly influences the way in which the world is perceived. To be effective internationally, the U.S. business person needs a more global perspective.

The goal was to narrow the focus of the learning experience and develop a quantifiable tool, pragmatic in nature and easily grasped by a general business audience. Recognizing the problem of balancing theory and practice, it was felt that the program should have obvious practical applications, yet be built on a solid theoretical foundation relating to the field of cross-cultural communication.

Global communicator job analysis

The "job" task of global communicator was analyzed. The activity described in this chapter only addresses a small section of this composite: that portion that teaches participants to identify the manner in which one's cultural perspective is communicated in writing and behavior. The entire analysis for the global communicator task is shown in Figure 15.1, but this learning experience addresses only items 2.1.1, 2.1.2, 4.1.1, and 4.1.2.

Table 15.1: The Global Communicator Task List

1.0	Communicates effectively (with a global perspective), in body language in a professional setting
2.0	Communicates effectively (with a global perspective), in writing in a professional setting
2.1	Recognizes that the U.S. English vocabulary reflects the U.S. perspective
2.1.1	On time and work pace
2.1.2	On activity, doing
2.1.3	On space
2.2	Identifies target audience (culturally-diverse individuals)
2.3	Assesses appropriateness of content vocabulary and style
2.4	Modifies text as needed
2.5	Originates communications using a global perspective
3.0	Communicates effectively (with a global perspective), in a professional setting, in speaking and listening

Table 15.1: The Global Communicator Task List (*concluded*)

4.0	Communicates effectively (with a global perspective), in a professional setting, in activity
4.1	Recognizes that U.S. behavior reflects the U.S. perspective
4.1.1	On time and work pace
4.1.2	On activity, doing
4.1.3	On space

Target population analysis

All participants were learners whose place of business was in the New York metropolitan area. They were both male and female, mostly middle-aged (40-55) and upper-middle-class. The vast majority were college graduates, some with advanced degrees. All had previously attended a variety of professional workshops, lecture series, and seminars. Further, they all had extensive backgrounds in organizing, conducting, and participating in professional meetings. They were active in community life. The target audience was largely white and U.S. born and had broadened their cultural horizons by traveling abroad and interacting with a variety of people from different cultures, either in their professional or personal lives.

Organizational constraints

Because this learning program was designed as an introductory workshop to which participants came voluntarily, it was held in an informal and relaxed setting. Handouts were used rather than lecture-type overheads, to lend an air of informality and allow for full lighting during discussions (however, an overhead would have been helpful). An opportunity to place the chairs in a variety of configurations eased the learning task.

The greatest constraint concerned time. As the contents of this program attest, people in the U.S. greatly value their time. For this reason, a brief introductory learning program was designed to interest people in considering more in-depth learning later, possibly within their own fields. Therefore, the learning was limited to one hour of actual instruction, preceded by a brief period for socializing and filling out a short questionnaire, and followed by a brief period for the posttest and activity evaluation. Participants were told that the whole learning program would run one and one-half hours.

Therefore, the main constraint was the need to develop a very lean, yet useful, learning program. The facilitator had to be able to move smoothly and efficiently through the steps without appearing harried and without sacrificing learner comprehension. Obviously, a learning program with fewer time constraints would have been easier to design and implement.

Finally, it is important to note that this type of experience would not work in a culture that is not as clock-driven as the U.S. culture. Clearly, this activity was tailored to its audience, and could not be as relentlessly goal-driven if the audience had included individuals from cultures where time to reflect and socialize were necessary for the program to succeed.

Instructional goal

While most U.S. people have a favorite work-related story to share concerning a problem of communication with someone from another culture, the problem is generally attributed to some shortcoming of the other person. Consequently, if anyone needs to learn anything, according to this perspective, it is clearly the other person. While actual performance often indicates many examples of crossed signals, rarely is this attributed to cultural misperception, misinterpretation, and miscommunication. The U.S. business vocabulary is filled with terminology that reflects U.S. values. But the business community often shows little awareness of the connection between its value-laden rhetoric and its problems in communicating across cultural lines.

The long-range desired performance focuses on the ability of learners to link a host of behaviors with the cultural perspective they represent. However, the desired performance referred to here is far narrower. Its implicit objective is to demonstrate to the business community that cross-cultural learning has practical applications and that performance can be measured.

The desired performance for this learning program was to enable learners to identify specific examples of U.S. English that can contribute to cross-cultural misunderstanding, and that permeate such U.S. business communications as letters, memos, and agenda formats. This learning enables individuals to identify texts which might require modification if they were to be sent to individuals without a U.S. perspective on time and activity.

To assure achievement of the desired performance, the business vocabulary to be studied was narrowed down to the expressions and terms associated with communications dealing with a business meeting. This topic was selected because it typifies the behavior of people who are very time-conscious and activity-driven. For example, the belief that meetings should begin on time, have a pre-set time limit (usually short), and be highly goal-driven, is reflected in the vocabulary that is used. The desire to press ahead, sometimes like a steamroller, seriously impacts on the vocabulary that fills our written communications. Needless to say, we may offend many. It was hoped that this program would improve the image of cross-cultural learning in the business community. To do so, the learning activity would have to achieve its desired performance, namely, to enable professionals to pay attention to the way their U.S. values on time and activity permeate their communications and may impact negatively on their organization's "bottom line."

The Goal. Therefore, the instructional goal of the learning program was designed as follows:

Given written samples of business communications addressed to both a U.S. and a non-U.S. audience concerning a joint business meeting, participants will identify text requiring modification, that exemplifies the U.S. cultural perspective on time and activity of doing ("getting things done"), by circling those words and phrases with the potential to cause cross-cultural misunderstanding. Learners will perform with 70 percent accuracy.

Six major tasks were designed to implement this goal. The most difficult aspect in their design was the need to take a very abstract topic and arrive at a series of specific, observable skills that would still retain the implicit goal of the program: increased cross-cultural awareness.

U.S. business reality. Cross-cultural learning was discussed with numerous individuals, including members of the general business and professional community and a variety of learning specialists and consultants working with corporations, government and education. From these discussions, a basic difficulty in designing an instructional goal for today's U.S. business community became clear. It must be very streamlined, and focus on highly practical outcomes rather than on the many abstract concepts that underlie this type of learning.

A variety of ways to solve this dilemma were tried, including critical concepts and abstractions as part of the major tasks. Finally, satisfaction was achieved and the final instructional goal avoided abstractions, yet conveyed the heart and soul of the learning program: to allow members of the business community to link success in an increasingly global economy with increased cross-cultural awareness.

Exceptions. Two exceptions should be noted. Any organization that is already convinced of the benefits of cross-cultural learning might be persuaded to set aside sufficient learning time for a more theoretical basis. Further, many non-U.S. people believe strongly in the importance of building a solid theoretical foundation before proceeding to concrete concepts. These exceptions, of course, do not obviate the rule.

Design of the learning experience

The goal of developing a global *perspective* clearly cannot be achieved in an experience of one or two hours. It is an ongoing task requiring many learning activities, a good deal of outside reading, follow-up, and on-the-job support. The goal of this activity was to design a tool that would address one aspect of the development of a global person.

Domain

A choice had to be made as to the domain of learning to be addressed (Bloom, Krathwohl, & Masia, 1956). While an affective domain would appeal greatly to a designer interested in increasing cross-cultural awareness among learners, it had clear drawbacks relating to measurability. Further, would such a learning program only increase the skepticism of the business community towards cross-cultural learning by seeming too abstract and impractical? Therefore, it was planned to gear the learning toward the cognitive domain (Bloom et al., 1956). This would allow for concrete, quantifiable objectives which could be attached to a practical application.

Learners could become skilled at applying the concepts to be learned (the U.S. perspective on time and activity). Furthermore, by developing an intellectual skill (Gagne, 1985), learners could demonstrate mastery by classifying examples of the concepts learned.

Instructional task analysis

Wasting time. The first task is to identify the "using time well" types of activities that U.S. people view as positive, and "wasting time" activities considered negative. Learners then identify the values behind their choices, and identify the preferred activities as being representative of the dominant U.S. activity—doing—based on the U.S. adherence to monochronic time described by Hall. They complete this task by identifying examples of U.S. behavior which reflect U.S. values on time and activity. This task relates to items 4.1.1 and 4.1.2 in the job task analysis shown in Figure 15.1.

U.S. perspective on time. The second task is to identify the U.S.-English vocabulary words used by learners, and generate a list of words and expressions that reflect the U.S. perspective on time and activity, given its M-time (Monochronic time) culture. This task relates to items 2.1.1 and 2.1.2 in the Figure 15.1 Global Communicator Task List.

Cross-cultural misunderstanding. The third task is to demonstrate a connection between cultural differences and cross-cultural misunderstandings in the global marketplace, focusing on an international business meeting. Learners discriminate between the culturally different behaviors observed that relate to time and activity, and identify those M-time types of behaviors which specifically reflect the U.S. perspective. Learners identify several M-time behaviors which can lead to cross-cultural misunderstanding. This task also relates to items 4.1.1 and 4.1.2 in the task list.

Vocabulary. Finally, the fourth task enables participants to identify specific vocabulary words and phrases that reflect an M-time culture and are frequently used in business communication. They identify instances of U.S.-English business vocabulary which can cause cross-cultural misunderstanding among members of different cultures. This task also relates to items 2.1.1 and 2.1.2 in the Global Communicator Task List.

Through these four instructional tasks, learners will acquire the intellectual skill of classifying rules which relate to culture. The concept to be learned in this instructional module is the U.S. concept of time and activity, represented by the activity of doing, in the U.S. cultural rhythm of M-time.

By acquiring this intellectual skill, learners can choose to use or avoid certain vocabulary. The program's practical application, therefore, is in teaching individuals to identify written examples of the U.S. perspective reflected throughout their business communication. This objective was chosen to address the needs of the U.S. business community, itself a product of M-time, for a very measurable and pragmatic goal. Learners will be able to demonstrate mastery of this skill in an easily observable way by successfully identifying examples of U.S.-English business vocabulary that reflect this perspective and can cause cross-cultural misunderstanding in a global marketplace.

Specifically, participants will

- Identify examples of U.S. behavior that reflect the U.S. perspective on time and activity
- Identify examples of U.S. vocabulary that reflect the U.S. perspective on time and activity
- Identify examples of U.S. business behavior that reflect the U.S. perspective on time and activity
- Identify examples of U.S. business vocabulary that reflect the U.S. perspective on time and activity

Instructional objectives

Reynolds (1991) points out that a written objective should be clear and precise, so that both the learner and the instructor will be able to identify the desired behavior. This requires a clearly stated criterion, so that both instructor and learner can measure classroom success. Reynolds adds that the desired behavior should be the simplest and most direct possible, and the wording of the objective should clearly show how the facilitator will observe the learning.

The following instructional objectives for this learning experience provide a good example of the instructional technologist's approach to cross-cultural learning.

Objective 1. In your own words, identify one positive and one negative behavior that reflect the U.S. perspective on time and activity. Both examples should pertain to leisure-time activities, and should reflect the U.S. M-time culture, with its emphasis on doing.

    1.1　Given an example, recognize that perception is culturally determined.

    1.2　Given an example, recognize that perception is selective.

    1.3　Given an example, recognize that perception is learned.

    1.4　Given an example, recognize that perception tends to remain constant.

    1.5　Given a written sample in U.S.-English, identify an example of U.S. perception.

    1.6　In your own words, identify a positive leisure-time activity.

    1.7　In your own words, identify a negative leisure-time activity.

    1.8　Given a discussion of the positive activities, identify the dominant U.S. activity.

1.9 Given a discussion of the negative activities, identify the dominant activity in contrasting cultures.

1.10 Given a discussion, recognize the characteristics of a culture based on M-time (Monochronic time).

1.11 Given a discussion, recognize the characteristics of a culture based on P-time (Polychronic time).

Objective 2. Given a list of leisure-time activities, identify two positive and two negative U.S.-English vocabulary words or phrases that reflect the U.S. perspective on time and activity. The examples selected should reflect the U.S. M-time culture, with its emphasis on doing.

2.1 Given a discussion, generate a list of time-related vocabulary words that characterize leisure-time activities.

2.2 Given a list of time-related words, identify those words used in connection with positive leisure-time activities.

2.3 Given a list of time-related words, identify those words used in connection with negative leisure-time activities.

2.4 Given a discussion of the lists generated, identify the vocabulary words that reflect the U.S. perspective on doing.

2.5 Given a list of words reflecting the U.S. perspective on doing, identify the vocabulary words that are quantifiable and linear.

Objective 3. Given observation of a simulated cross-cultural business meeting, identify the predominant behavior of each of the three participants as M-time (U.S.) or P-time (contrasting) behavior. In each case, list an example of a misunderstanding that could occur due to the mixing of M- and P-time perspectives, and indicate clearly that U.S. behavior represents an adherence to M-time.

3.1 Given observation of a relevant role play, identify the predominant behavior of each of the three participants.

3.2 Given the predominant behavior of each of the participants, classify each as reflecting an M-time or P-time business perspective .

3.3 Given numerous examples of behavior reflecting an M-time perspective, list one or two behaviors that could create cross-cultural misunderstanding among M-time and P-time colleagues.

3.4 Given a recognition of the difference between M-time and P-time behavior, list one or two ways for an M-time colleague to avoid cross-cultural misunderstandings.

Objective 4. Given examples of U.S. business communication, identify the documents as products of an M-time culture. Indicate one or two misunderstandings that could occur among those not sharing the U.S. perspective on time and activity.

4.1 Given observation of a relevant role play, identify the predominant time-related business vocabulary of each of the three participants.

4.2 Given the predominant time-related business vocabulary of each of the three participants, classify each as reflecting an M-time or P-time perspective.

4.3 Given numerous examples of U.S.-English business vocabulary reflecting an M-time perspective, list one or two phrases that could create cross-cultural misunderstanding among M-time and P-time colleagues.

4.4 Given a recognition of the difference between M-time and P-time business vocabulary, list one or two ways for an M-time colleague to avoid cross-cultural misunderstandings.

Table 15.2 provides a complete listing of all skills and sub-skills.

Table 15.2: Objectives Sequenced and Clustered for a One-Hour Instructional Module

Lesson	Part	Objective	Subskills	Learning Time
1	1	1	1.1-1.11	25 minutes
1	2	2	2.1-2.5	10 minutes
1	3	3	3.1-3.4	15 minutes
1	4	4	4.1-4.4	10 Minutes

This learning experience was designed for a general, professional audience with at least a high-school education. It was assumed that participants had some prior knowledge and interaction with individuals from other cultures. Therefore, this program was designed to begin at Bennett's (1986) third stage of personal development, Minimization. Table 15.3 presents the core of his ideas as adapted for my seminar. At this stage of the intercultural sensitivity continuum, according to Bennett, individuals may minimize cultural differences, believing them to be superficial. They may assume that it is only necessary to be yourself. Further, U.S. people value individuality, openness, and honesty, and believe these traits will suffice in cross-cultural interactions. They do not easily recognize that these ethnocentric beliefs can create problems. Moving from Minimization, with its reliance on simple principles, to an ethnorelative stage where answers are not so pat represents a major conceptual shift. Acceptance is the first step in this more advanced stage.

Table 15.3: Intercultural Sensitivity Continuum

Ethnocentric Stages:

• **Denial.** Does not meet entry behavior requirement. Individuals at this level were not invited to participate. They have few categories in which to notice differences because they have not yet become aware of cultural differences in any meaningful way. They are likely to be very prejudiced, and need some non-threatening cultural awareness activities first.

• **Defense**. Does not meet entry behavior requirement. Individuals at this level feel very threatened by cultural differences and may either denigrate the differences, with negative stereotypes or promote their own superiority. Such individuals are not ready for a learning program which emphasizes that cultures are different, not better or worse.

• **Minimization**. Assumed entry behavior level. At this stage, participants are able to empathize and take another person's perspective.

Ethnorelative Stages:

• **Acceptance.** A most receptive stage at which to participate in in-depth cross-cultural learning. Following a learning program, participants should at least be at the beginning of this stage, if they were not at this level upon entering the learning program. At this stage, learners enjoy recognizing and exploring differences.

• **Adaptation.** Stage at which one becomes a bicultural person—a global communicator

• **Integration.** Stage of a highly bicultural person able to play a role such as mediator.

Learning activities specification

The learning activities are described in Table 15.4, and clearly illustrate the way content, instructional method, and media are used for each activity. Gagne's (1985) nine steps of instruction are referenced here as well, in order to illustrate the functions performed by each instructional event.

Table 15.4: Learning Activities and Instructional Events

Objective	Content	Instructional Method	Instructional Media	Event/ Activity
Objective 1.1-1.5 Activity 1A	Motivator on nature of perception	Handout, supported by discussion and lecture	Printed handout	Gaining attention; informing learner of objective; activating motivation; stimulating recall of prior knowledge

Table 15.4: Learning Activities and Instructional Events *(continued)*

Objective	Content	Instructional Method	Instructional Media	Event/ Activity
Objective 1.6-1.11 Activity 1B	Leisure-time behavior	Handout, supported by discussion and lecture	Fill-in handout	Presenting the stimulus material; providing learning guidance; eliciting performance; providing feedback; assessing performance;
Objective 2.1-2.5 Activity 2	Leisure-time vocabulary	Handout, supported by discussion and lecture	Fill-in handout; large pad and easel	Presenting the stimulus material; providing learning guidance; eliciting performance; providing feedback; assessing performance;
Objective 3.1-3.4 Activity 3	Business behavior	Handout, supported by discussion and role-play	Fill-in handout; sample memo; sample agenda	Presenting the stimulus material; providing learning guidance; eliciting performance; providing feedback; assessing performance.

Table 15.4: Learning Activities and Instructional Events *(concluded)*

Objective	Content	Instructional Method	Instructional Media	Event/ Activity
Objective 4.1-4.4 Activity 4A	Business vocabulary	Handout, supported by discussion and lecture	Fill-in handout; large pad and easel	Presenting the stimulus material; providing learning guidance; eliciting performance; providing feedback; assessing performance

The instructional module encompasses the first eight of Gagne's nine steps of instruction. The eighth step – assessing performance—was also a function of the post-test. The take-home handout provided to learners at the close of the program encompassed the ninth step—enhancing retention and transfer.

Evaluation

Unless a concrete, practical objective could be designed that was measurable, I felt that the seminar's utility would be limited to organizations and individuals who were already convinced of its usefulness. The larger business community would remain unreached, and this module would become one more program that preached to the converted.

The planned evaluation, therefore, involved assessing the learner's ability to classify learned concepts (the U.S. perspective on time and activity) within the context of the program itself. This easily measurable, and practical skill would be demonstrated by classifying examples of business vocabulary—provided to the learners on a sample business memo and meeting agenda—that reflect these concepts.

Pretest considered

This program did not contain a pretest, since time constraints precluded having high-scoring participants removed from the seminar. However, participants were selected only from among those with an average amount of experience in interacting with members of other cultures. This meant that the learners would probably be in the Minimization stage (Bennett, 1986) of development, and training could be geared to that level (see Table 15.3). In addition, the opening questionnaire was given to all participants as they arrived, enabling me to peruse the responses during the brief socializing period preceding training. This data helped me focus my remarks on the learners' particular concerns and interests.

Materials

Upon arrival, the learners received four packets. The first contained the welcoming activities, including a questionnaire designed to assist me in gauging the degree to which participants were within Bennett's Minimization stage. It also enabled me to note the backgrounds and work areas of participants so I could add a degree of personalization to the learning.

The second packet contained the learning activities that served as the embedded test items, specifically Activities 1-4 referred to in Table 15.3.

The third packet contained the closing activities: the posttest and learning evaluation.

Finally, the fourth packet was a take-home handout with some background information on the concepts and topics covered in the program, as well as references to books on the subject which the learners might wish to read.

Posttest

The posttest required the learners to circle those words in the sample business memo and agenda that represent the M-time culture in a way that can lead to cross-cultural misunderstandings. Their responses and comments were incorporated into a quick reference guide that was used for later learners and serves as an on-the-job reinforcement tool.

Of course, the posttest data also assisted in assessing the degree to which the learners were able to apply the skills covered in the instructional module, and helped in assessing the need for instructional modification.

Learning Transfer

There must be an effective learning transfer system—perhaps the most important aspect of any instructional program, since anything worth learning is worth remembering, and applying. According to Broad (1982), transfer of training is the effective on-the-job application of knowledge and skills gained in training. In a complete learning transfer system, the appropriate manager(s), instructor(s), and learner(s) would all be involved in the process, before, during, and after training. However, several factors precluded the development of a complete system for this seminar. First, the participants were engaged in diverse professions, some in large organizations and others self-employed. Further, they had chosen to attend the seminar for their own self-improvement, not as part of a larger organizational HRD plan. Consequently, managers in the participants' own organizations, with the power to effect change were not part of this training loop and could not be included in the transfer process. However, a complete learning transfer system for a global HRD activity would ordinarily include activities on all three levels, such as the following

Role of management

Before training, the client can be involved in the planning process, creating an atmosphere of collaboration between the HRD staff and the client. This elevates the HRD person to the position of consultant or partner. Management can also be encouraged to send motivational letters to prospective participants, validating the relevance of the training to the organization and the importance of having these particular learners attend. During training, immediate supervisors and higher-level management can be invited to a preview session, where a course overview is given, handouts shared, questions answered, and concerns addressed. Following training, management can hold a certificate ceremony to recognize the learners' effort and accomplishments.

More to the point, in a corporate culture where "time is money," management should be prepared to set aside some post-training time for learners to meet and discuss ways of incorporating learning in their own organization's written communications. They can use company memos and agendas to consider whether there is a need for modification. Management can also support transfer by facilitiating the networking process among participants. A list of participants with phone extensions and computer mailboxes can be given to all learners, and they can be encouraged to call upon one another when unsure whether a given text is appropriate.

Management can also periodically set aside time for learners to review various widely circulated documents, such as standard form letters and memos. This on-going review of organizational documents not only reduces cross-cultural misunderstanding, but also serves to reinforce the instructional goal long after the training has ended. Finally, periodical letters of appreciation for their ongoing efforts will further encourage participants to continue to apply learning.

Role of learner

The learner should be brought into the process actively from the outset. Before training, a number of prospective participants can be consulted, creating a sense of inclusion. A questionnaire asking prospective learners to share specific opinions and information can be distributed in advance of the training. This encourages the view that the seminar content will be relevant to their needs. During training, time can be set aside to encourage learners to discuss the training goals in the context of their specific work environment. This allows them to address some of the problems they anticipate in applying learning, and reinforces the idea that transference is a key part of learning. After training, participants can be encouraged to participate in the various activities arranged by management, and can be interviewed at a later date to ascertain some of the problems they have faced while applying learning.

Role of instructor

Finally, the instructor can reach out to learners before during, and after training. Beforehand, the instructor can send out letters, motivating participants to view the upcoming seminar in a positive manner. During training, the instructor can encourage learners to participate in the organizations's network of learners. The instructor can also incorporate some of the specific issues raised by previous learners or in the opening questionnaire. After training, the instructor can follow up with a letter of appreciation, reinforcing the goal of the seminar and providing some pertinent tips or words of encouragement.

Whether or not a given organization can design a complete learning transfer system, the type of system must be planned as part of the HRD activities package. Otherwise, the message to management and learner will be unclear: The instructional goal was not really all that important and need not be remembered or applied on the job.

Getting It All Together

The overall dilemma is that one can never completely lose one's cultural baggage or be completely culture-free. People cannot avoid having values based on their society's deeply held beliefs. Invariably, these values will differ from those of others.

While this is an enormous problem requiring a very large learning effort, the learning activity described in this chapter focused on just one aspect of the problem. It also focused attention on the insidiousness of ethnocentrism, which interferes with effective communication and prevents the development of a more global perspective.

Bibliography

Adler, N. J. *International Dimensions of Organizational Behavior*. Boston, MA: Kent, 1986.

Bennett, M.J. "A Developmental Approach to Training for Intercultural Sensitivity." *International Journal of Intercultural Relations*, 10, 1986, pp. 179-196.

Bloom, B., Krathwohl, D., and Masia, B. *Taxonomy of Educational Objectives. Handbook I: Cognitive Domain*. New York, NY: David McKay, 1956.

Brislin, R. W., Cushner, K., Cherrie, C. and Yong, M. *Intercultural Interactions*. Beverly Hills, CA: Sage, 1986.

Broad, M. "Management Actions to Support Transfer of Training." *Training and Development Journal*, 1982, pp. 42-47.

Copeland, L. and Griggs, L. *Going International*. New York, NY: Random House, 1985.

Gagne, R. *The Conditions of Learning* (Fourth Edition). New York, NY: Holt, Rinehart and Winston, 1985.

Hall, E. T. *The Silent Language*. New York, NY: Doubleday, 1959.

Hall, E. T. *The Hidden Dimension*. New York, NY: Doubleday, 1966.

Hall, E. T. *Beyond Culture*. New York, NY: Anchor/Doubleday, 1976.

Hall, E. T. *The Dance of Life*. New York, NY: Anchor/Doubleday, 1983.

Hall, E. T. and Hall, M. R. *Hidden Differences.* New York: Anchor, 1987.

Hofstede, G. "Motivation, Leadership, and Organizations: Do American Theories Apply Abroad?" *Organizational Dynamics*, Summer 1980, pp. 42-63.

Kluckhohn, F. R. and Strodtbeck, F. L. *Variations in Value Orientation*. New York, NY: Row, Peterson, 1961.

Kohls, L. R. *The Values Americans Live By*. Washington, DC: Meridian House International, 1984.

Reynolds, A. "The Basics: Learning Objectives." *Technical & Skills Training* Feb. – March, p. 15.

Stewart, E. C. *American Cultural Patterns: A Cross-Cultural Perspective*. Yarmouth, ME: Intercultural Press, 1972.

About the Author

Sandy Mayers-Chen is a New York-based instructional systems design consultant specializing in global diversity and workforce 2000. She has a varied background in the private and public sector, and has conducted HRD activities for foreign diplomatic staff. Mayers-Chen has a Bachelor of Arts from the New School for Social Research (Sociology), a Master of Science from New York Institute of Technology (Instructional Technology), and a Certificate in Intercultural Training from Georgetown University. She has been a research assistant at Columbia University Teachers College, an adjunct lecturer at the City University of New York, director of a metropolitan New York training facility, and a designer of interdisciplinary curriculum, emphasizing multiculturalism, and the global perspective. Mayers-Chen is a member of the International Society for Intercultural Education, Training and Research (SIETAR), and the American Society for Training and Development (ASTD).

PART THREE

Working in a Specific Country or Region

Working in A Specific Country or Region

This part illustrates country-specific information and applications. Many of the authors are natives of the country they are writing about. The others are describing specific examples based on their experiences in that country. In a book without any limitation of length, this part would cover every country. That is clearly not practical. However, we have included a coverage of the whole globe. Even so, we live in a dynamic world, and huge changes have transpired or are underway in western Europe, the Soviet Union, the Persian Gulf region, and Africa. This part groups the chapters by region, working generally westward from Asia and ending in North America. In some cases, one chapter follows the logic of another in this book, describing application of a specific case.

Part Three's author's illustrate how one must navigate the global scene. Three of our authors are Chinese: Hui-Chuan Cheng, Florence Ho, and Ng Peck Ho. Each has chosen a different way to represent themselves to English speakers. Hui-Chuan likes to use her Chinese personal name, rather than using a similar English name. Her family name is Cheng. Florence Ho, as with most Hong Kong Chinese, has adopted an English "first" name to ease communications with English speakers. Both Hui-Chuan and Florence put their names in the usual English order, with family name last. Ng Peck Ho prefers to use his name exactly as it was given to him. His family name is Ng. There are parallels to these Chinese examples with many of the other Asian authors, but we will follow this Chinese case. None of these choices will necessarily cause any problem if the English speaker takes care to understand the differences in systems. For example: the official U.S. representative to China during World War II allegedly called Chiang Kai-Shek— "Mr. Shek." This is like calling Len Nadler— "Mr. Len."

In Chapter 16, Leonard Nadler describes his experiences in Japan. The chapter is titled "Using HRD for an Intervention in International Cooperation: A Case Study of the U.S. and Japan." He not only describes the programs that were in effect at that time, he also provides many interesting insights into the Japanese and American-Japanese differences.

Tadashi Amaya provides an in-depth analysis of HRD conditions in Japan. Chapter 17, "Japanese HRD: A Futuristic View" can be read in two ways. His chapter not only provides the information, it illustrates how Japanese themselves collect and analyze HRD information. We think you will perceive a sharp contrast with how most Americans are accustomed to view HRD in their own country.

Masaaki (pronounced Masa-Aki) Imai has succeeded in exporting a Japanese concept to the rest of the world. In Chapter 18, "Adapting a Japanese HRD Idea for Use in Another Country," Imai tells about Kaizen. HRD people in other countries may find it applicable, and then will have to determine the HRD interventions required to make it work.

Chapter 19, "Adapting Technology-Based Instruction for Chinese Users," is an in-depth exploration of the Chinese-specific applications of the global principles Angus Reynolds provided in Chapter 8. The author, Hui-Chuan Cheng, describes specific applications that must be undertaken when adapting courseware for each of the several Chinese markets. Of particular interest are the subtle, and not so subtle, differences between these markets.

Florence Ho grew up in Hong Kong and has worked in the People's Republic of China. She has provided Chapter 20, "HRD in the People's Republic of China—Challenge or Compromise?" It is a look inside the PRC with many valuable suggestions on undertaking an HRD project. Florence provides workable solutions to real problems, as well as fundamental country-specific HRD information.

In Chapter 21, Angus Reynolds follows up on Florence Ho's advice on the PRC. His chapter is called, "Tailoring Events for the People's Republic of China: An Example." Angus explores the specific event needed to establish business ties in the PRC—the key early meeting or visit with a Chinese delegation. After exploring what others have said, he provides his own specific suggestions.

Don Roberts retired from his position in the United States and went to work for the Hong Kong Telephone Company. In Chapter 22, "Management Training Contrasts and Comparisons: U.S. and Hong Kong," he relates his experiences. Don also makes specific observations that are valuable to readers interested in HRD in Hong Kong.

Ng Peck Ho's Chapter 23, "Using a U.S. Model in Another Country: Singapore," has two major purposes. The first is to show how a model, essentially from the United States, was used in the Singaporean context. It is always necessary to make some modifications, and he shows how this was done in a variety of situations in that country. The second purpose is to help those who are interested in working in Singapore. It is important to be able to understand the country one works in, and this understanding is contributed here by a Singaporean who has worked extensively in Singapore as well as in other countries in the Asian-Pacific area.

Chapter 24, "HRD Practices for Multinational Corporation Managers in Malaysia," is based on a study of HRD in that country. Zulaiha Ismail provides in-depth understanding of what is and isn't done, with recommendations for a reader interested in that country. Her chapter includes information about the public and private sectors and various types of organizations that are relevant to HRD there.

Chalintorn Burian and Eduardo Canela provide a broad coverage of HRD conditions in Asian countries, with particular emphasis on Southeast Asia. Their Chapter 25, "HRD Practioner Utilization in Asia," covers the variety of organizations in these countries and provides specific advice about how to succeed in HRD projects there.

Phyliss Cooke, Ralph Bates, and Ronnie Ng present Chapter 26. Its title asks the question: "Generating Team Spirit: Do Western Training Approaches Have Anything to Contribute to Asian Clients?" Their answer is "Yes." They report the results of an adventure-training project with an Asian-based airline. Their straightforward report provides an example of how a "foreign" approach can be implemented.

Chapter 27, "Imperatives for HRD Concepts and Practices in India," is a country-specific analysis. Shyam B. L. Bharadwaj brings his extensive HRD experience to a reasoned analysis of the Indian experience. This information will prove invaluable to anyone considering a project in India.

In Chapter 28, "Staff Development For Multinational HRD Staff," Ali Dialdin relates his experience in managing HRD in the Saudi Aramco Oil Company. Aramco depends on a large multinational staff to deliver a wide variety of HRD activities.

Michael Sandrock relates the HRD situation that has unfolded in the former German Democratic Republic that was unified with Germany in 1990. In Chapter 29, "HRD Consulting in Emerging East Europe," he describes conditions and points the way for the trend that appears to be the natural result of recent history. Although he refers to "East" Germany and "West" Germany, there is today only one Germany. We feel it is important to retain these words to highlight the differences that have existed and, to some degree, will continue to do so for some time.

In Chapter 30, "HRD in the European Community After 1992," Robert Hersowitz has taken on a difficult assignment. We asked him to explore the management and business scenario in which managers and HRD practitioners must operate in Europe after 1992. So he was to write about the future. He provides a brief historical analysis which shows how management trends have developed in different European countries to pinpoint the major HRD issues which have evolved in each country. He describes differences that are rooted in history and culture and examines current practices in dealing with these issues. We feel he provides sound information that is of use to HRD people interested in those countries in this new era.

Ralph Keteku wrote Chapter 31, "HRD in Ghana," an excellent picture of that African country. In less developed countries, the school and the university systems are seen as an integral part of the total national HRD activity. In industrialized countries, that is usually less the case: HRD is seen as essentially the learning that takes place after the individual has left the formal school system. He covers the various organizations and institutions that have shaped HRD in his country, as well as those that will continue to do so.

Alistair Black lived and worked in Southern Rhodesia for many years. When the country's majority population achieved power, it was renamed Zimbabwe. He decided to stay and continue to work to make the country grow. In Chapter 32, "HRD in Zimbabwe," he relates many of the evolutionary changes that have occurred in HRD.

Chapter 33 is an exception. In general we have avoided prominent mention of the author's products and services. Denis Ouimet wrote "Spirit of Quebec." Quebecois are know for their fiercely independent nature and indomitable spirit. He tells us how he was able to sift through U.S.-based management-oriented HRD activities to find those that work in the somewhat unique French-Canadian culture of Quebec.

Serge Ogranovich brings this part to a close with Chapter 34. "Bringing Learners to the Technology-Source Country" tells of his broad experiences doing just that. This is certainly a major alternative in accomplishing technology transfer. He did it successfully, and we think you will enjoy learning some of his methods.

CHAPTER 16

Using HRD for an Intervention in International Cooperation: A Case Study of the U.S. and Japan

Leonard Nadler

Although there are many examples of HRD being used as a strategy to help a country to progress, there is an outstanding one about which too little has been written. During the 1970s and 1980s the world witnessed the fantastic growth of the Japanese economy. Indeed, during that period Japan became one of the major economic powers in the world. Too little has been said, by the Japanese and others, about the significant contribution that enabled the Japanese to move ahead so rapidly and dramatically.

To understand the roots of the effort that contributed to that economic miracle, one must go back to the foreign-aid program of the U.S. with Japan during of the late 1950s and early 1960s. I will limit most of my comments to the period of 1959-1962 when I was stationed in Japan as a Training Officer with the U.S. Agency for International Development (USAID). During that period, we sent 5,000 Japanese to the U.S. for HRD.

Before getting to the specifics of the case study, however, we have to define HRD and present some background material on USAID.

Defining HRD

At the time of this case the term "HRD" was not in use, so I will to use "training" as it was used by USAID. In the final section of this chapter, I will expand on the current definition of HRD and its implications for this type of HRD program.

USAID

The foreign-aid program with Japan started in the middle 1950s, but did not really move into high gear until the end of that decade. A major part of the effort was called "participant training."

Interestingly, the organization that was developed in Japan through the efforts of USAID was named the Japan Productivity Center (JPC). It was established in March 1955 as a central organization to promote the productivity movement in Japan and was part of the AID agreement between Japan and the U.S. Kohei Goshi, long-time Executive Director of JPC, noted that at the beginning of the movement, the word "productivity" sounded too academic and few knew its meaning. But, in a year or so, it became a popular term, and now that the movement has spread throughout the nation, it is a common word today among the people.

The productivity movement was initiated through the U.S. technical-aid program as was a project for observing and studying the industry and economy of the United States, whose productivity has been the highest in the world.

Of course that was written in 1964 and much has happened since then. It is just unfortunate that too many people forget that the U.S. had that position.

The JPC was probably the single most important organization developed in Japan at that time. It is still active today, even arranging for U.S. study teams to go to Japan — a reversal of the original situation. Unfortunately, too many of those U.S. teams appear to focus on what can be adopted.

Here is a description of JPC, as written by one of the Japanese teams: Japan Productivity Center with its five major regional productivity centers is the most active organization in this field. While it has been kept busy absorbing and diffusing newly introduced technical knowledge and experience and promoting productivity awareness, it exists to develop closer cooperation and understanding between management and labor and between industry and universities. It arranged a regular program of seminars and courses on main productivity techniques by utilizing foreign educators and engineers who are invited here mostly from the U.S. and Japanese scholars who are recruited locally.

The Japan Productivity Center also works in close cooperation with ICA Washington, its American counterpart, in implementing various programs of a technical exchange nature. The usual feature of most seminar programs is that they are co-sponsored by both Japan Productivity Center and some other management research organizations to secure widespread support, interest, and participation.

Notice that the Japanese viewed HRD as an essential part of the process, through the study trips and seminars.

The HRD process started with agreement between Japan and the United States on overall program goals. Japan was represented by the Japan Productivity Center (JPC) while the U.S. government was represented by USAID (also called USOM or U.S. Operations Mission at that time).

Once the overall goals were agreed upon, for a year at a time, the next step was to develop a list of areas where the participant HRD program would be used. For the most part, this was done by teams of from 12-14 Japanese who were already themselves involved in the program area or could be expected to be involved. From this list, JPC then developed specific learning objectives for the teams. These were reviewed with USAID officials, essentially the Training Officer (from 1959-1962). The agreed-upon objectives were then sent in a document called the Project Implementation Order/Participants (PIO/P) to AID in Washington.

As necessary, the USAID Training Officer discussed with JPC sources in the United States to help the individual teams meet their objectives. These might include specific companies, individuals, or organizations and associations. The Training Officer would discuss the objectives with each team at a formal meeting. At times, these meetings produced some minor changes and certainly clarification of objectives. This information was forwarded to AID in Washington, where the final decision on the itinerary was made.

After review by AID/Washington, a report was sent to Japan with a tentative itinerary. The people in AID/Washington did a magnificent job! They contacted a wide variety of potential hosts, mainly in the private sector, who would agree to host a group of Japanese for half a day to several days. The U.S. business community cooperated to an extent that has never been fully recognized, all of this without one cent of compensation or reimbursement!

The report from AID/Washington became the basis for another meeting between the Training Officer and each team. In any given week I would have as many as ten such meetings. We would discuss the report and the places and companies they would be visiting as part of the HRD experience. (It also meant that I had to do some studying about companies with which I was not familiar.) If there was any real problem, I could cable AID/Washington, but this seldom happened.

Meanwhile, each team had to develop a report in English about the current state of the focus of their team in Japan. This was a process started before I arrived on the scene. It was continued until I left in 1962, and probably for the few years that followed, until the joint program was phased out. Those reports give a picture, through Japanese eyes, of what the situation was in Japan at that time. It is important to understand how things changed, largely due to the HRD participant program. Those reports will be quoted at various times in this chapter, without any editing.

Before each team left Japan, we had the usual honorific meetings. One was a farewell party hosted by JPC, with all the participants, several USAID officials (they took turns), and any other Japanese who might be involved with the objective of the team. This was followed a day or so later with a farewell coffee hosted by the U.S. ambassador (first MacArthur and then Reischauer) at the U.S. Embassy. I attended all of those, and presented the team leader to the ambassador.

The team members then left for the U.S. and were met by two interpreters at their point of entry. They then followed the prepared itinerary. When they returned home, JPC sponsored debriefing meetings, many of which I attended. They had excellent interpreters—one later became an officer in Japan's largest advertising agency, while another became an official of the Asian Productivity Organization.

Given this framework, we can now look at some specifics of what the Japanese participants learned from the U.S. at that time. We will examine quality, individual-organizational relationships, marketing, managers, supervisors, and the work environment.

Quality

Much has been written about Quality Circles (QC), which presumably started in Japan. Actually, the Japanese combined two practices that they learned in the U.S. —suggestion systems and participative management—and developed what became known worldwide as QC's. These should not be confused with Quality Control Circles (QCC), a different movement that will be described later. To put this into historical perspective, those two concepts, and others that have been added, evolved into the concept of Total Quality Management that became prevalent in the 1990s in the U.S. as well as in Japan.

In pre-WWII days, "quality" was certainly not one of the words associated with Japan. The Japanese side of this was explained to me by a Japanese colleague. He said, in essence: Foreigners came to Japan and showed us products they had manufactured in their countries. Then they would ask us if we could make it cheaper. They did not talk quality, but only price. We made the articles they wanted, and they were cheap and of poor quality. But that is what they had asked for.

Given that experience, it was understandable that the Japanese would have some quality problems. Though they started working on them in the middle 1950s, problems still persisted in the early 1960s. While living in Japan, I bought a hi-fi set from a large and reputable Japanese concern. After it was delivered, it worked for several days and then broke down. I called the Tokoyo store where I had bought it, but they said that all repairs were done by the manufacturer.

I had images of running around with an interpreter and getting nothing but low bows and polite smiles. Instead, within a few hours I was visited by three servicemen from the manufacturing company. They proceeded to spread cloths on the floor and carefully disassemble the set. After a few hours, they had it working and bowed their way out of our house.

Naturally, I was pleased—but after a few short days the set broke down again. This time I called the manufacturer directly, and within a few hours three different servicemen appeared. The process was repeated—spreading cloths, disassembling, testing—and it worked, but again only for a few days.

By this time, I was quite annoyed. When I called the manufacturer I was prepared for lengthy negotiations, referral to higher levels, and everything one expects when trying to return a costly item. Instead, I was told that they were prepared to come out any number of times until the set worked. I told them that this was not satisfactory, so they offered to come and take the set out of my house and refund my entire purchase price—which they did!

My experience was not unique—that was the way the system worked. Few Japanese expected that what they bought would function without on-site repairs. The concept was that quality need not be put into manufacturing as it could be achieved by service after the sale.

Somewhat earlier, there had been attempts at improving quality in Japanese production. Three specialists from the U.S. came to Japan, first brought by our military, and later coming on their own. The man whose name is associated with this effort is W. Edwards Deming. Most people do not realize that he did not come to Japan because he was not recognized in the U.S., which is a common belief. Quite the contrary—he was brought to Japan because of his success with statistical quality control in U.S. organizations.

As a minor digression, there were actually three men in that team, of whom Deming was one. Toward the end of the 1950s, however, a group of Japanese started looking for a way to publicize their new organization, "The Japan Union of Scientists and Engineers." They established an award based on the work of the three men, but named it the Deming Award, for in typical Japanese fashion they chose to honor the oldest man!

Despite that movement in Japan, the emphasis was still on getting production out and making repairs after sale. It did not take long before the Japanese realized that this practice was too costly, and quality control on the line became a prime issue. I recall visiting a Matsushita plant in 1961 and being shown the extensive use of quality control inspectors. Wearing special clothing, they would pounce on items still in production and put them through extensive tests. It was an approach that quickly spread through a good deal of Japanese industry, particularly those related to electronics.

There were other aspects of quality that the Japanese learned from the U.S. In the early 1960s the U.S. aerospace program had a quality approach called "zero defects." The lesson we were teaching then was obvious—build quality into the product. Obviously, the Japanese learned that very well.

The quality concept has certainly been broadened since it was introduced in Japan in the middle 1950s. One can only wonder at what happened to the U.S., the teacher, which seems to have forgotten what the student (Japan) learned.

Individuals and the Organization

Today, people from many countries visit Japan to try to identify the unique relationship of the individual and the organization that has contributed to Japan's growth. But, what was that relationship when the Japanese were learning from the U.S.?

One member of a team that came to the U.S. was the manager of the Yawata Iron and Steel Company. The company was planning to build a new, integrated pig iron plant. Under the conventional Japanese system of plant organization, production and administration were blended into a cumbersome system of industrial togetherness. The Yawata manager and other members of the technical inspection team saw how differently American plants were organized. They asked plenty of questions, such as:

"How do you divide responsibility and authority?"
"To what degree is authority delegated to the plant?"
"How do you coordinate departments within the plant?"
"What are the kinds and the authorities of supervisors?"

Armed with the answers to these, and dozens of other questions, the Japanese steelmen returned and, in the case of Yawata Company, translated them into specific action.

The completely new organization of its Tobata Works was the result. A line and staff formula was adopted and the foreman system introduced. The confusing lines of authority that crisscrossed back and forth between manufacturing and administration were straightened out. Areas of responsibility were laid down in a manner rarely seen before in heavy industry.

Thus, the form of organization prevalent in the U.S. steel industry at that time impressed the Japanese so much that a major company based its reorganization on what it learned in the U.S.

Another team commented that in Japan in the mid-1950s industrial circles tried hard to modernize human relations. They introduced various techniques and systems developed in the United States, such as job evaluation, personnel appraisal systems, and training programs based on the philosophy of better human relations.

Many people have commented on the very humane environment in a Japanese company, such as the concern for the individual. It is interesting to note the status of interpersonal relationships in Japan at the time. In 1958, Heigo Fujii was Executive Director of the Yawata Iron and Steel Company. He came to the United States with a top management specialists team. What interested him, among other things, was the fact that the ability to produce was so highly valued by American firms. This is basic to the entire concept of productivity in the U.S. but not in Japan. There, seniority is all-important. The person who is with the company the longest advances first. He might be what an American personnel supervisor would call "deadwood," but in Japan time with the firm would take precedence over anyone else.

The idea of promoting on the basis of ability to produce actually surprised Mr. Fujii. He made an entry in his notebook: "Personal capacity more valuable than seniority...an important element in the elimination of unsatisfactory elements in the organization."

The U.S. employee welfare programs also impressed the Japanese participants. An example was Jun Kashima, President of the Oval Gear Engineering Co., Ltd. of Tokyo, a small company. He was a part of the small business top management team that came to the U.S. in 1958. When we later visited him as part of the evaluation program, we found that he had come back to Japan convinced that employee welfare was tied directly to the production of quality products. Since his trip, he has designed company policies to reward ability and capacity rather than mere seniority or external connections. Taking a page from the McCormick Company's book, he now also has monthly meetings in which representatives of various departments can raise questions of policy. And Mr. Kashima has gone one step further. There are monthly parties that honor workers who had birthdays that month. He invites small groups of workers each week for a personal dinner at which he can get to know them better. They come to know him as a person rather than a distant company president.

Although some ascribe the individual-organizational relationship in Japan as typically Japanese, it is significant to note what they learned during their U.S. HRD experience that they then adapted into the Japanese culture.

Marketing

Obviously, the Japanese are marketing successfully today, particularly in the international marketplace. This is another significant part of what they learned during their HRD visits to the U.S. One result was that the Japanese steel industry established market research departments—for the first time!

The whole idea of market research was new to Japan. A market research specialists team reported that no other area of industrial management seemed so ill-defined and weak as market research (MR). Production plans for a company were literally a corporate guessing game. Estimates based on vague predictions issued by private and government agencies were about the best an industrial organization had to go on.

Even small companies, however, benefited from improved marketing. Mr. Kashima gives a good description of marketing and production in Japan at that time:

"Japanese manufacturers traditionally made anything and everything in an effort to protect themselves from suffering fluctuations in any one market. Under this system, quality had to be sacrificed. I believe, however, that our companies can do as American firms and emphasize quality by expanding only in the production of closely related items."

Another Japanese executive in a small business commented on the relationship of standardization of output and marketing. Horoshi Kato, President of the Tokai Rika Company Ltd. of Nagoya, recalled how American subcontractors developed components of standard sizes, thus significantly reducing production costs. He presented this rather radical idea to engineers and purchasing agents at his parent company. After considerable study, they tried the plan and it worked. Where feasible, standardization was applied to other divisions and Tokai Rika salesmen were able to open new sales outlets among firms with comparable needs.

Standardization became an important element in Japan where marketing had earlier consisted of producing whatever a parent company or some buyer wanted. It is noteworthy that even supervisors were requesting standardization of products.

The Yawata Iron and Steel Company dramatically changed its market research as a result of experiences in the U.S. Following examples seen there, the company first increased the MR section from 20 to 50 people. It further was made an independent section with a voice in top management. And, for the first time, it was given the responsibility for production forecasting. A systematic study of the company's customers and their needs was also ordered—another innovation.

"Pre-selling" also came into the vocabulary of Japanese steelmen as a direct result of the U.S. study trip. Market development as a responsibility of the MR section was recommended and adopted. Technical Service, formerly a function of plant engineering, was moved to MR to provide continuity between sales and product use — a direct adaptation of the American system which sees pre-sales, sales, and post-sales as an entity rather than as activities of three unrelated departments.

Recognition of the need for market research was not limited to large companies. Mr. Kashima noticed, for example, that almost no American plant was too small to be concerned with market research. In Japan, the idea has always been to sell what you make. True, some months found you with more customers than you could supply, while other times you were overstocked. These expensive ups-and-downs were shrugged off as unavoidable.

In the U.S. things were different. Mr. Kashima discovered the market forecast by which a manufacturer could predict what the market would need and plan its production accordingly. Other changes were the development of customer lists, and in 1959, the development of the first sales training manual in Japan.

Managers

Managers are an essential element of any organization. Much has been written about Japanese management styles, so let's look at Japanese management in the 1960s as seen by the Japanese. At that time, little was done to improve managers. A team made this observation about Japanese middle managers:

When they were young and virile as they first entered the company, they carried tremendous enthusiasm to develop and improve themselves for progress. But now they are promoted to the position of middle management, they begin losing steam to follow through, rely heavily on experience and customary practices, and devote no further thinking to self-development.

Recall the U.S. in the early 1960s. There was a proliferation of HRD for middle managers. The Japanese were impressed by the attention U.S. organizations were giving to keeping their middle managers up-to-date.

The Japanese recognized, at that time, that their managers were out-of-date.

Further development of behavioral sciences and related study is giving rise to the changing patterns of human relations practices in industry. To promote the workers' will to work, motivate them to produce more, to boost morale, and to secure their whole-hearted cooperation in working through the different interests of these people certainly pose quite a problem on the part of the management. To meet this challenge there arises a widespread awareness that the people performing managerial functions must be fully developed and that it definitely pays to do so.

One aspect of Japanese organization admired today is that everybody in the organization appears to have some say in what is going on. But, what was it like in Japan then?

In Japan a company operates essentially in the form of centralized management that results in tighter managerial control at the top level. The decentralized form of management that characterizes the American business is less widespread.

Of course, there are other aspects of today's Japanese management that arise from Japanese experience that are not based on what was learned in the U.S. through the HRD program of USAID. This chapter, however, is focusing only on some of those that *were* the result of that HRD experience.

Supervisors

In Japan, there was a hierarchy among supervisors that sometimes extended to as many as 16 different levels. The Council of Rationalization of the Japanese Ministry of International Trade and Industry (MITI) conducted a study on Japanese supervision. In their report, they listed twenty problems in Japanese supervision, including:

- There is hardly any contact between top management and supervisors below the B class level. ("B class" refers to foreman.)
- There is no adequate contact and coordination between line and staff and among foremen.
- No purposeful education and training is being carried out to equip supervisors with professional ability, production techniques, and human relations skills that are needed to accomplish their present as well as future job responsibilities.
- Supervisors do not have a sufficient role in constructive on-the-job training or other types of training for new employees or the employees already on the job.
- The company policies and practices are not communicated to supervisors as thoroughly as they should be.

- The upward communication is very poor. Ideas, proposals, and suggestions that are based on actual operations of the shop are not reported to top management in such a manner that management can reflect on its own activity and make corrections.

That last item may come as somewhat of a surprise when we read of the QC and similar efforts in Japan today.

In the Council of Rationalization study, we also find data on what Japanese supervisors wanted so they could improve their performance:

- More time should be given to supervising subordinates.
- Management should try harder to understand the position of the supervisors.
- Policies should primarily emphasize human beings.
- Supervisory assistants should be placed with responsibility for small groups.

There was some supervisory training and education in Japan from 1948 on. This was essentially provided first by the U.S. occupation forces and then by organizations such as the Japanese Industrial Training Association (JITA). When I arrived in Japan in 1959, one of my first tasks was to help JITA rewrite the U.S. cases it was using for supervisory and management training to be more compatible with the Japanese culture. Initially, the program with the greatest impact was the Training Within Industry (TWI) program, which was developed in the U.S. first in WWI and greatly expanded in WWII.

In a report on *Supervisory Policies and Practices in the Japanese Factory 1959,* the Plant Supervisory System Specialists Study Team wrote:

The TWI program has certainly given a great impetus upon Japanese supervisors. Supervisory training in the past was always regarded as nothing but a moral lecture or talk that bore no close relationship to the actual job. However, the TWI taught supervisors many skills that they could directly apply back to their own jobs. It helped supervisors foster a humanism concept or democratic type of human relations within factory life, while the general democratization process of Japan since World War II remained superficial and could not penetrate into the heart of the community. Furthermore, it taught supervisors a basic way of thinking about modern industry, that is, the analytical and scientific way of doing things.

Although remnants of that program can still be found in Japan today, their HRD programs have gone far beyond that.

Work Environment

We have long known that the environment in which people work can enhance or hinder their productivity. This includes physical environment as well as the emotional-social environment.

What did a Japanese executive learn on an HRD team visit to the U.S.? Nozomu Matsumoto, President of Fukuin Electric, Ltd., went as part of a Communications Industry Team. After returning, he told an evaluator that he was at one U.S. plant when the noon whistle blew. Surprisingly, the workers didn't open lunch boxes and pull up crates on which to sit besides their machines to eat. Instead, they all disappeared to a clean, well-lighted company lunchroom—an almost unheard of luxury for a small plant in Japan. At another plant there was a fine cafeteria that served hot, low-cost lunches. And in amazement, Matsumoto saw the plant manager joining assembly line workers on the serving line.

Another person who was impressed with the physical environment was Tokai Rika's Horoshi Kato, who came to the United States with a Small Industry Top Management Study Team in 1957. An evaluator reported that Mr. Kato was impressed by the attention that U.S. owners and managers paid to the work environment. A description of what he did in his plant on his return gives us some insight into what small plants then looked like in Japan.

For the first time, the bare, concrete floors of his shop were scrubbed and painted. Guidelines for materials handling carts were drawn and even yellow "danger" circles painted around portable kerosene space heaters. Next, Mr. Kato doubled the illumination in his plant. Customarily, increasing the light in a Japanese shop is achieved by moving a machine nearer a window. Kato, however, invested in banks of overhead fluorescent lights and immediately made his plant the best lit in the area. With more light, the less tidy areas became conspicuous, so more paint was applied—to desks, walls, and machinery. His shop soon become known for its bright "American-style" appearance.

The investment in paint and maintenance soon paid off. The reject rate on his assembly lines was 3 percent before the clean-up campaign; afterward it fell to less than 0.5 percent.

Conclusion

What are the lessons to be learned from this significant HRD experience? There are many, but let me cite just a few here.

Relativity

The plan of using HRD study teams did not originate with the U.S.-Japanese program. It was part of the original Marshall Plan (antecedent of ICA and USAID) in Europe in the late 1940s. It became particularly relevant for Japan because of that country's history. Almost 100 years earlier, in 1868, at the time of the Meiji Restoration, Japan had sent teams of leading Japanese to various foreign countries. The objective was to learn what had happened in the 400 years previously, when Japan had essentially been closed to foreign people and ideas. Using HRD teams coincided with the history and culture of Japan.

Time

One might ask why it took so long for changes to take place in Japan. The answer is that, in general, organizations in any country change slowly. In Japan, some of the participants on the HRD study teams could not begin to make any changes until they had been with the organization many more years and, therefore, could exert influence.

Defining HRD

As noted earlier, there is more to the definition of HRD than presented in the earlier section on defining.

Within HRD, there are three different types of programs, based on where and when the learning is intended to be used:

Training is learning directly related to the *present* job of the learner and intended to be used on that job.

Education is learning offered to prepare an employee for a *future* job—usually one that is defined and specific.

Development is learning that is *not related* to either the present job or a defined future job. In fact, it may be completely unrelated to the organization and offered for the growth of the individual as a person rather than as an employee. However, it can also be concerned with the directions in which the organization is going or jobs that will open up in the distant future.

These distinctions are extremely important, but too many international HRD programs do not make them. Therefore, everyone concerned—the host organizations, the countries, the learners—may lack a focus, making utilization and evaluation almost meaningless.

When countries call all HRD programs "training," the programs often lose the impact that can result when the learning is clearly defined as training, education, or development. In the case study cited here, most of the HRD teams were designed with a training objective. A few of the teams that were not cited here had either education or development as their objective. For those teams, evaluation could not be done the same way as for those where training was the objective.

Too often, both the host country (U.S.) and the participating country (Japan) expected to see immediate results. In most cases, when that does not happen, the HRD program is eliminated before it has had a chance to make any impact. In this case, fortunately, enough time was allowed—resulting in significant success in helping Japan to reach its current stage.

References

This chapter quotes material from the following publications of the Japan Productivity Center, which were prepared by the participants.

Human Relations in Small Business. Small Business Kanto Regional II Team, 1961.

Middle Management Development in Japan 1960. Middle Management Study Team, 1960.

Personnel Management in Japan, 1960. Personnel Management Study Team, 1960.

Personnel Management in Japan, 1961. Personnel Management Study Team, 1961.

Productivity and Wages in Japan, 1959. Wage Determination Specialists Team, 1959.

Supervisory Policies and Practices in the Japanese Factory, 1959. Plant Supervisory System Specialists Study Team, 1959.

The following sources were also used:

Productivity Drive in Japan. Japan Productivity Center, 1964.

Japan's Small Industry Grows Up. A report on American technical cooperation with Japanese small enterprises, 1955-1961.

Two Decades of Progress in Five Years. A report on Japanese-American technical cooperation in the iron and steel industry, 1955-1960.

CHAPTER 17
Japanese HRD: A Futuristic View

Tadashi Amaya

Before describing the present state of the art of HRD in Japan, I would like to outline some current work force conditions and trends in this country.

Changing Management Circumstance

Economic development and manpower shortage. The growth rate of Japan's GNP was 4.6 percent for 1987 and 5.7 percent for 1988, starting from the lower rate of 2.5 percent for 1986. This growth trend of GNP directly influences the labor demand and supply relationship in our labor market.

Figure 17.1 shows the 25-year trend of the Japanese labor situation since 1965 in terms of active ratio of job openings applicants, active job offers, and active applicants. It clearly shows a sharp rise of the ratio in the most recent time frame from 1987 to date, caused by an exactly reverse trend in active applicants for the same period.

Figure 17.1: The Twenty-Five Year Trend of The Japanese Labor Market

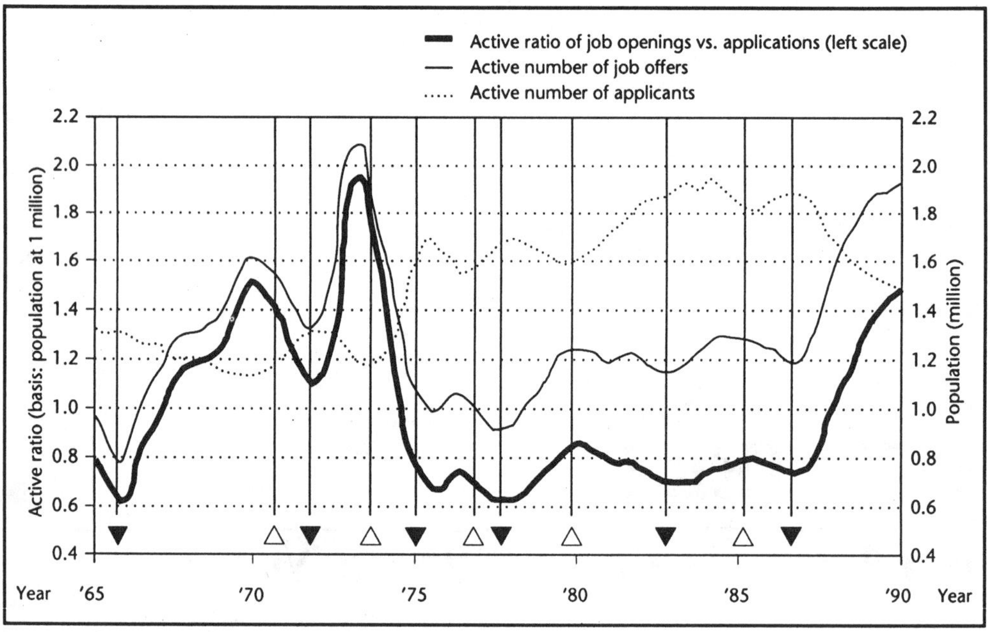

Source: Labor Ministry, Public Employment Service statistics.

Remarks: 1. Number of new college graduates excluded, but number of part-time workers included in the data.

2. The chart is based on the January-March data, each year, from 1965 to 1990.

3. △: when business was brisk, ▲: when business was dull.

This current labor shortage should guide our discussion of HRD in Japan now. A practical question is: How should Japan's HRD meet our needs for (1) facilitating the recruiting task, and (2) stabilizing employees in their jobs?

I expect the labor shortage to last until about the turn of the century. It is caused by the decreasing labor supply (analyzed later in this chapter). However, labor demand could also decrease at a time of economic slowdown that might occur.

Aging manpower trend. Figure 17.2 shows a curve of the Japanese male working population as projected to 2015, starting from 1985. It shows that the population under age 64 and the younger generation from 15 to 24 would start decreasing sharply around 1991. On the contrary, the elder population from 55 to 64 would keep rising to a projected peak in 2005, with minor fluctuations. The principal working population of 25 to 54, meanwhile, would keep rising moderately to a projected peak in 2000.

Figure 17.2: The Trend Forecast of the Male Working Population by Age Group Up to 2015 A.D.

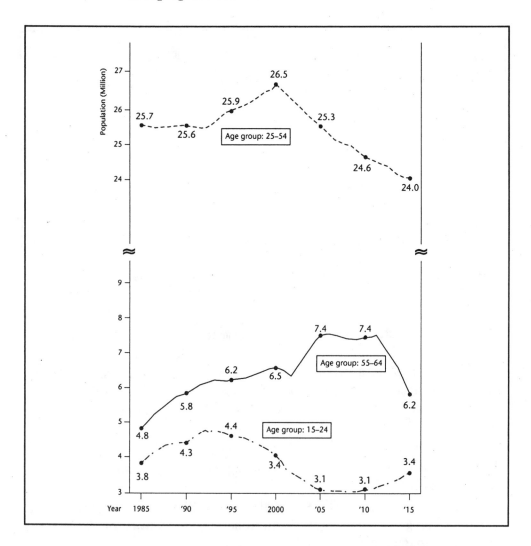

Source: Economic Planning Agency, "Technology Innovation and Employment," April 1986

Next, Figure 17.3 represents the situation for the Japanese female working population. An aging phenomenon is apparent during the last half of the 1990s. The working population between 25 to 39 will keep going down whereas that in the 40s and the 50s will go up. From 2000 to 2005, the population from 25 to 39 will increase, while the older working population from 40 to 54 (or older) will decrease, by infusion of younger replacements. After the year 2010 and on, the younger generation would again go down and the middle-aged generation would increase, resulting in an aging trend of the female working population.

Figure 17.3: The Trend Forecast of the Female Working Population by Age Groups Up to 2015 A.D.

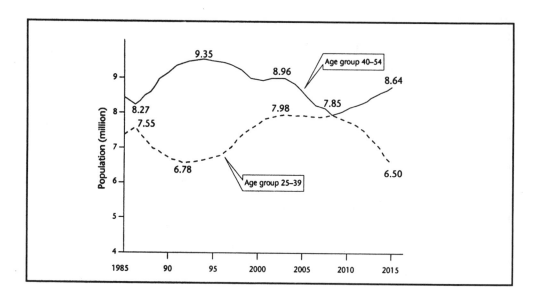

Source: Economic Planning Agency, "Technology Innovation and Employment," April 1986

Generally, for Japan's working population as a whole, there is a sharp sign of a decreasing younger working population. There is also a growth trend in the older working population, pulling up the average age of the working population toward the year 2000.

One of the currently felt needs is for extending worker retention to around 65. It is linked with the governmental policy of sliding the annuity-granting age from the now stipulated 60 to 65.[1]

Such being the case, one of the essential issues in HRD should be to question what kinds of HRD programs would most effectively help those older workers to be able to keep working to the age of 65.

Changing phenomena in industrial and business structures. Table 17.1 shows the changing trend in the working population by types of industries. It tells us that the population of tertiary industry exceeded 50 percent of the total working population. It also forecasts a rise to 65 percent in the year 2000. Meanwhile, the population of primary industry is sharply decreasing and that of secondary industry slightly decreasing (perhaps because of labor-saving investments).

[1]Currently, the annuity-granting age varies by the type of official, industrial, social and other pension systems. However, the most widely committed pension system as authorized by the Welfare Ministry allows pensioners to start receiving pensions at the age of 60.

Table 17.1: Change of Working Population Among Industries

Year	Primary	Secondary	Tertiary	Total
		Industry		
1970	17.4	35.2	47.3	100.0
1980	10.4	34.8	54.5	100.0
2000	4.9	30.1	65.0	100.0

Source: Economic Planning Agency: "Technology Innovation and Employment"

Along with this overall change in industries, restructuring of individual corporations is taking place.

Table 17.2 reflects the three-year trend of how corporations are diversifying their business areas. Each of the companies surveyed is placed in the table under the category of its "core business." Their actual business shares, however, often indicate that sales from "new business" exceed sales from the core business.

Table 17.2: Sales Shares of Core Business Areas

	1979	1984	1986
Foods	96.1	96.8	97.0
Textiles *	66.3	60.3	57.1
Wood and wooden products *	86.1	77.3	68.8
Pulp and paper	86.1	93.0	92.5
Publishing and printing	99.9	100.0	88.3
Chemicals	88.4	88.7	84.6
Oil and Coal products	99.2	99.7	99.2
Rubber products	90.0	89.6	88.5
Ceramics	75.6	76.4	71.4
Iron and steel	85.8	81.8	78.6
Non-ferrous metals*	89.1	67.7	60.8
Metal products	91.5	90.9	90.0
General machinery	75.9	77.9	73.1
Electric machinery	93.3	95.3	83.6
Transportation machinery	79.4	77.0	79.0
Precision machinery *	59.1	45.1	37.6
Other manufacturing *	71.0	69.7	67.4
Average	86.7	84.5	80.2

Source: Fair Trade Commission Survey   * Core business share is particularly low.

Outstanding in Table 17.2 are Textiles at 40.2 percent, non-ferrous metals at 47.4 percent, precision machinery at 32.0 percent, etc., each showing low shares by core businesses. Such industrial restructuring will seriously affect Human Resource Management in Japan.

The main principle of Human Resource Management, widely practiced by Japanese corporations has been life-time employment combined with the seniority system. Under this rule, employees are recruited fresh from their college graduation and retained under a seniority-based framework which guarantees employment until the stipulated retirement age. However, with the current industrial restructuring trend, Japanese companies would be less able to assure full employment of necessary human resources if they keep depending on the instruction of the retained personnel only. Therefore, Japanese companies are now doing what they have been least familiar with: hiring "mid-career" human resources.

Evidently, the big question here is how the salaries and other treatment of the newly hired mid-career personnel should best be balanced with the "built-up" treatment of their colleagues who have been retained since their graduation. The fact that such mid-career new faces have been hired because they are valuable in launching new business lines would require "better" treatment to tie them to their new posts. This could easily cause an unbalance of salary and wages for longer-retained "regular personnel." Both types of personnel should be equally appraised under the same evaluation criteria of evaluation, or in terms of the individual's job-performing capability. Also, the long retained personnel should be subject to more frequent conversions from old jobs to new jobs. This is a big issue in Human Resource Management.

Diversification of values. Values of younger Japanese are now notably changing. Such trends are reflected in Figures 17.4, 17.5, and 17.6, showing the result of a questionnaire survey.

Figure 17.4 shows a 5-year trend in replies to the question "What is your purpose of working?" Apparently, the society-oriented purposes—to be highly regarded in the society and to serve the society—are least chosen, while the self-centered purposes —to live a life of affluence, to enjoy life, and to live a competence-testing life—are more often chosen. However, the category of living a competence-testing life is gradually decreasing, while the two others seem to stay on the 30 percent level.

Figure 17.4: The Purpose of Working – "What is your major purpose of working?"

	To live a life of economic affluence.	To enjoy life.	To be highly regarded in the society.	To live a life of testing and proving my own competence.	To serve the society.	Other causes.
1989	33		35	1	22	3	7
1986	35		30	2	25	4	6
1983	33		32	3	22	4	8
1980	34		27	2	28	2	6
1977	30		28	1	28	3	11
1974	21		25	2	36	5	11

Source: Japan Productivity Center/ Junior Executive Council of Japan "A Survey Report on Working Consciousness" N=1.165 (1989)

Figure 17.5 reflects respondents' choice of either work-orientation or life-orientation. As seen in the 1989 result, it is noteworthy that the answer that *work and life are equally important* is dominant at 69 percent, followed by *life at home is above all* at 25 percent, and *work is above all* at only 6 percent. The data also show an increasing trend in life at home is above all, and a decreasing trend in *work is above all*.

Figure 17.5: The Work-and-Life Relationship – "Are you work-oriented or life-oriented?"

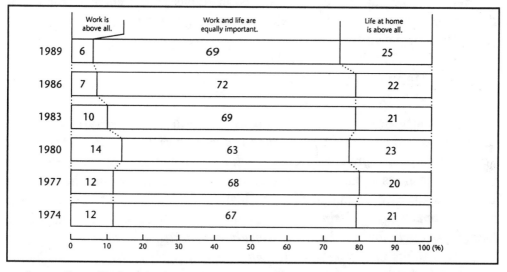

Source: Japan Productivity Center/Junion Executive Council of Japan "A Survey Report on Working Consciousness" N=1.165 (1989)

Figure 17.6 deals with motivation factors among Japanese workers. The general tendency is that 50 percent are satisfied with average output and 30 percent like to work harder than others. In six years up to 1989, the dominant "Satisfied" group is slightly on the increase, and the workaholic group seems to be constant.

Figure 17.6: Individual Work Motivation – "Are you motivated to work harder than others or just satisfied?"

	Like to work harder than others.	Satisfied with the average level.	It all depends.
1989	30	54	17
1986	31	51	18
1983	34	48	17
1980	31	51	18
1977	33	48	19
1974	34	44	22

Source: Japan Productivity Center/Junion Executive Council of Japan "A Survey Report on Working Consciuosness" N=1.165 (1989)

As seen in the trends shown in Figures 17.4, 17.5, and 17.6, one of the imminent issues in HRD is how Japanese young people should best be linked with their working life.

HRD Strategies Adapting to Changing Management Environment (Current and Five Years Later)

Here are the author's comparative observations of the current trends and five-year projections of HRD strategies for adapting to the changing management environment in Japan.

Business Management Strategies

Referring to the current graphs in Figure 17.7, high percentages are for *improving employees' competence, expanding sales structure and sales power, developing new products*, and *upgrading existing products*. Common to these categories is the goal of optimally using the various resources already available within the company. Looking at the Five Years Later graphs, high percentages are for *exploring new business and changing business lines* (for more diversified businesses), *acquiring human resources for new business, globalizing (multinationalizing) corporate businesses, reinforcing group business management*, and *selecting and developing "elite" staff*. The characteristics in this situation are two-fold:
- Focusing on issues of changing business structures
- Recognizing need for developing human resources capable of undertaking such changes

Figure 17.7: Current Business Management Strategy: Current and Five Years Later

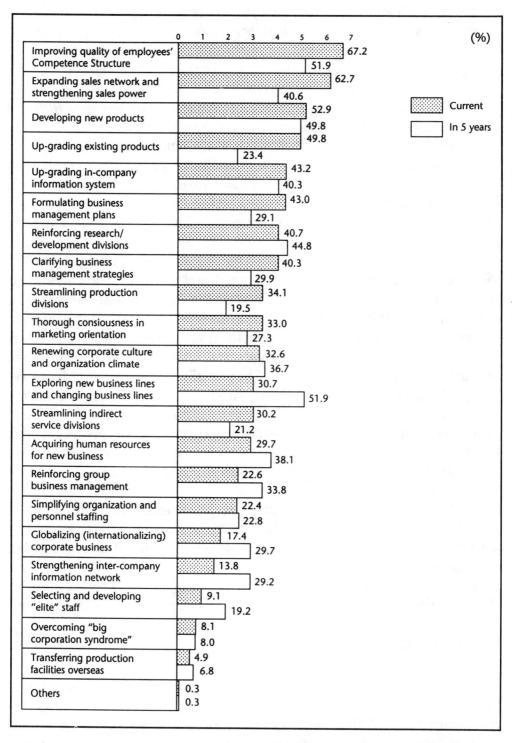

Source: Survey of Industrial Training Programs in FY 1990, Japan Federation of Employer's Association/Japan Industrial & Vocational Training Association

Issues in Human Resource Development.

As shown in Figure 17.8, currently emphasized issues are *reforming managerial consciousness*, *taking measures on the labor shortage*, and *thoroughly implementing employee learning*. With labor shortages being the most critical situation in HRD, *taking measures on the labor shortage* should be the most important action item. This calls not only for filling the shortage, but also upgrading the quality of the individual worker. Such issues as *thoroughly implementing employee HRD* and *reforming managerial consciousness* should also be emphasized.

Because of *acquiring human resources* as an item in Business Management Strategy, *placement of human resources to new businesses* becomes an important issue in Five Years Later. Similarly, *globalizing corporate business* as an item in Business Management Strategy means that *meeting the need for business globalization* and *using multinational personnel* are important items in "Five Years Later."

Another characteristic observed here is the establishment of a specialist staffing system and using older workers to meet the problem of the aging trend of the working population in this country. The traditional belief in Japanese society is that older persons are best treated by their sticking to a career path to reach a high managerial post under the same employment. However, the growing population of older workers is increasingly "closing the door" to many of them. Not all such persons are promised an eventual post in higher management. The specialist staffing system in Japan was initially designed for laying a new career path for older workers in parallel with the traditional but increasingly crowded "managerial career ladder".

Not many Japanese companies have been able to make such a specialist staffing system function well. Further, there are clear indications that we must be more seriously committed to utilizing the capabilities of older workers in Five Years Later. They will be an important issue from now on.

Next, we must face the issue of the utilization/promotion of female workers. When the nation's economy must proceed with a chronic manpower shortage, it is important for us to more effectively utilize and promote not only qualified male workers, but also competent female workers.

Lastly, the item *selecting and developing "elite" staff* as a Business Management Strategy is also carried over as an important issue in Human Resource Management.

Issues and Target Groups in HRD

In the current graphs in Figure 17.9, *HRD for section-level managers* and *HRD for division-level (higher) managers* reflect the HRD issue of reforming managerial consciousness. Next, *HRD for the sales work force* becomes a priority issue, considering the current Business Management Strategy.

Figure 17.8: Issues in Personnel Management: Current and Five Years Later (Multiple Answers)

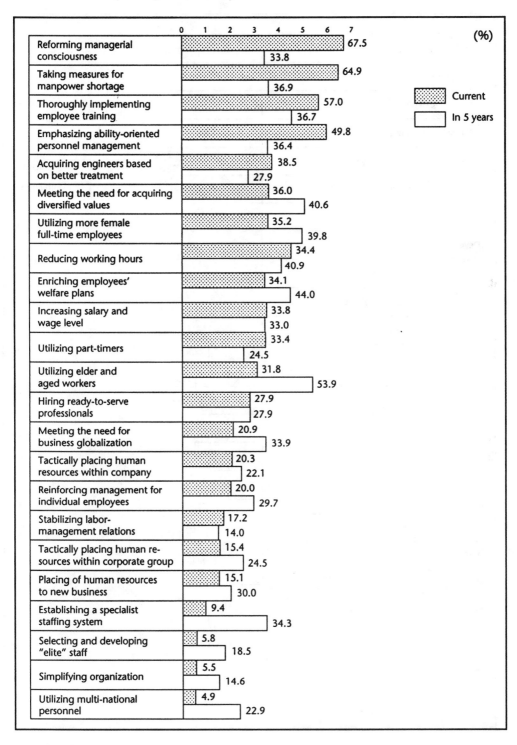

Source: Survey of Industrial Training Programs in FY 1990, Japan Federation of Employer's Association/Japan Industrial & Vocational Training Association

Figure 17.9: Issues and Target Groups in Human Resource Management: Now and Five Years Later (Multiple Answers)

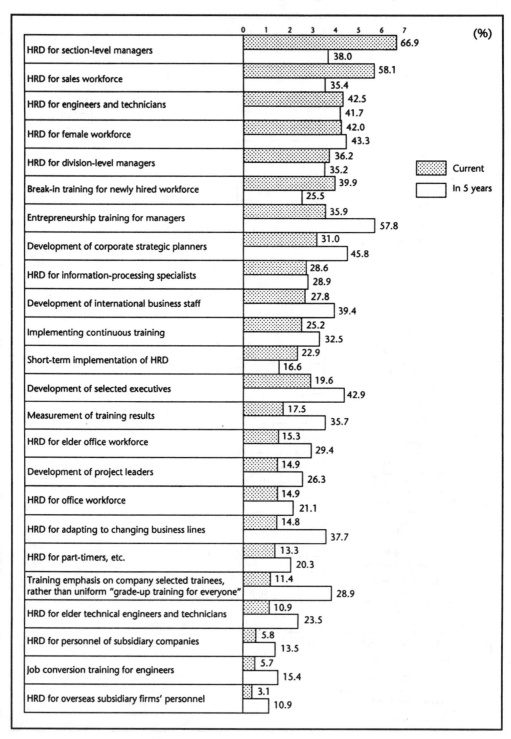

Source: Survey of Industrial Training Programs in FY 1990, Japan Federation of Employer's Association/Japan Industrial & Vocational Training Association

The most important issue in Five Years Later is *measurement of HRD results*. This is followed by *HRD for the older work force*, reflecting the issue of the aging work force in Human Resource Management. *Placement of human resources to new businesses* leads to such items as *HRD adapting to changing business lines*, *entrepreneurship instruction for managers*, and *development of corporate strategic planners*. Lastly, the issue *selecting and developing "elite" staff* is reflected here in such items as *development of selected executives* and *training emphasis on company-selected trainees*.

General Trend of HRD

In the Current graphs of Figure 17.10, *short-term accomplishment of high competence* through *HRD with carefully organized curriculums* and *more classroom instruction within working hours are notable*. In the Five Years Later picture, *every employee selects HRD opportunities* and *more emphasis on self-development* are listed, reflecting a shift of emphasis to every worker's willingness. Nonetheless, *more HRD for company-selected employees* is notable, although this is a company-initiated action. Lastly, the HRD issue of *measurement of results* is reflected here as *in-company HRD staff being reinforced*.

Figure 17.10: General Trend of Human Resources Development: Current and Five Years Later (Multiple Answers)

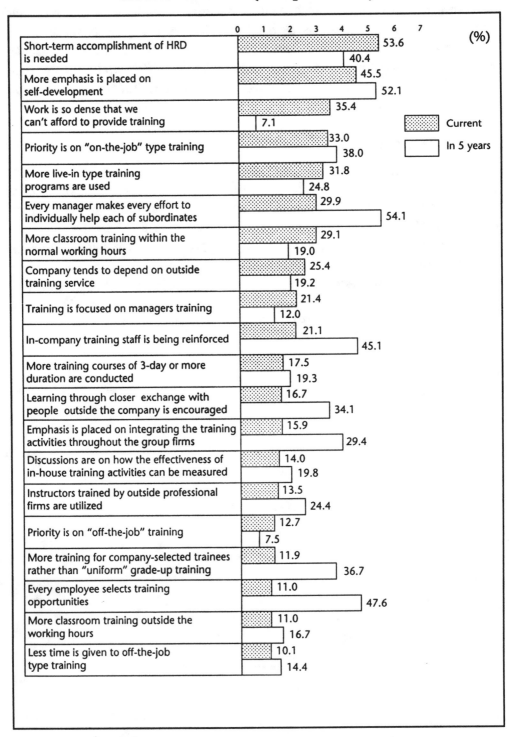

Source: Survey of Industrial Training Programs in FY 1990, Japan Federation of Employer's Association/Japan Industrial & Vocational Training Association

New Directions of HRD in Japan

I would like to describe HRD movements in this country in three different types of human resources: executives/managers group, young workers, and female workers.

Executives and managers

Table 17.3 shows changing trends in HRD policies in the three different groups, based on the percentage data of 1990 with plus/minus percentages five years before and after 1990.

Table 17.3: Changing Trend in HRD Policies – 1989/1990 as Basis/1995

	Executives			Division Managers			Section Managers		
Self-development	−14.5	41.2	−5.8	−7.5	51.0	−7.5	+3.1	60.2	−5.8
Direct guidance from the top management		50.0	−11.5		39.4	−7.4		18.0	−3.1
In-company training	−13.1	11.9	−0.7	−11.8	32.1	−3.4	−14.3	59.4	−11.7
Training courses/seminars sponsored by outside training houses	−40.5	45.3	−2.9	−27.3	54.5	−2.1	−15.9	52.9	−4.0
Excessive job assignments		4.7	−0.3		7.1	−0.9		10.4	−1.1
Training programs by correspondence	−0.2	2.9	−0.6	+3.2	9.3	−0.7	+10.7	28.6	−5.4
Cultivating job atmosphere toward self-development		7.5	−0.5		10.9	+0.1		18.8	−0.1
Providing support to the study group consisting of top executives and managers		0.3	+0.9		10.4	+2.1		17.2	+3.2
Supporting managers in their OJT efforts	−1.2	1.9	+0.9	−1.4	3.1	+2.6	+0.7	10.1	+5.6
Utilizing a lean number of capable staff by reducing personnel size		4.4	+1.1		5.8	+2.8		6.7	+3.7
Job-rotation	−0.5	7.3	+1.6	−0.8	16.7	+3.6	+3.2	28.1	+8.4
Long-term "schooling" or "internship" in other companies	−0.9	1.0	+2.1	−0.9	1.1	+3.9	+0.6	2.8	+6.8
Overseas college schooling	−5.5	2.9	+2.8	−3.5	2.1	+4.4	+0.1	3.4	+7.2
Overseas business assignments		3.4	+4.2		6.0	+7.0		10.2	+9.2
Increase/decrease at 5-year intervals	±from 1985	1990 data	±toward 1995	±from 1985	1990 data	±toward 1995	±from 1985	1990 data	±toward 1995

Source: Survey of Industrial Training Programs in FY 1990, Japan Federation of Employer's Association/Japan Industrial & Vocational Training Association

General trends. I observed changing HRD policies in the following three categories:

1. Employees participating in the company-designed HRD programs.
2. The company supporting and subsidizing what the employees initiated as their HRD programs.
3. Providing HRD opportunities of longer duration, such as job-experience-based HRD (job rotations, internships in other companies, and job assignments away from the company), assignments for college studies (domestic and/or overseas), etc.

A decreasing trend under category 1 can be observed. Policies under categories 2 and 3 seem to be on the increase, particularly Category 3, with *job rotation* highest.

Trends as seen from a hierarchical perspective. The above indicate trends that the lower the hierarchical echelons are, the higher the changing percentages become, especially under Category 3. Assignments to overseas college studies as a notable trend is expected to keep increasing, especially at the level of section-level or junior managers.

Currently, a personnel management system that can support the above mentioned HRD directions for the executive/manager group is being highlighted.

The HRD-support system for the executive/manager group. Thus far, Japanese personnel appraisal has been largely based on "demerit-counting." Under that system, a new employee is given a full score, from which points are subtracted for each "fault" of the person. These points can never be restored with any merit points, even though the same person has done something meritorious. Under the system, employees tend to be afraid of making mistakes, avoid risky jobs, and simply concentrate on safe and easy jobs.

However, as we are going into a period of business restructuring and finding new business opportunities, jobs will be highly risky. Enterprises strive to develop executives and managers who are entrepreneurial and willing to confront risks. Managers' attitudes, however, will not change as long as they are still subject to personnel appraisal on a demerit-counting basis.

A notable trend in recent years is toward a "merit counting" appraisal system, which is being adopted in many advanced corporations, particularly focused on division-level managers. The system is designed to encourage division managers to seek new business and innovation. Should they make any mistakes, no "fault points" are subtracted in the appraisal. Only people who haven't sought any new opportunities or taken any risks (by sticking to their familiar jobs) get "demerit-counted" or subtracted to a lower score. One corporation has adopted a system in which such "demerit data" is eliminated from a division-level manager's personnel file after three years.

Younger workers

As was previously stated in *Diversification of Values*, there is a trend, particularly among younger Japanese, toward preferring life to work (*life at home is above all*). However, *work and life are equally important* is dominant (Figure 17.5). In working style, *satisfied with average* is on the increase (Figure 17.6). Now, how do our young people consider their work itself?

How working life is viewed. Table 17.4 shows the results of a survey of young Japanese workers on their working life. There are two phenomena apparent: the "challenge orientation" and the "short-time-working orientation." The latter can be linked to the notion that work and life are equally important. That is, Japanese young people don't mind working hard as long as the required working hours are short so that their life as a whole can be more enriched.

Now, I would like to analyze their "challenge orientation," as more young workers tend to start thinking about changing their jobs when they don't feel satisfied with their working life even right after their employment. The results of a survey of young workers' reasons for quitting are summarized in Table 17.5. Largely, they were concerned about three factors: (1) Top management (business policies, future prospective, etc.), (2) salaries and other working conditions, and (3) the work itself (no challenging work, finding a more suitable job, challenging a completely fresh working situation, and wanting to expand personal experiences). It can be concluded from these indications that people could find a challenging and suitable job only after experiencing various jobs (say, through job rotation, etc.).

Table 17.4: How Do Japanese Youth Consider Working Life?

	%
However hard the work is, I like to be committed to a challenging work.	70.8
I like to work with ease even though the work may not be so challenging.	28.9
I don't mind working hard as long as the required hours are short.	66.7
I don't mind working long as long as I can be on the job with ease.	33.0

Source: A Summary Report on the Survey of New College Graduates' Awareness about Working Life and Leisure, August 1989, Labor Ministry-Labor Standard Bureau/All-Japan Federation of Social Insurance Consultants (N-5,600)

Table 17.5: Businessmen's Reasons for Job Conversion

Reason	%
Salary and promotion opportunities were narrow.	43.2
Couldn't believe in top management's (superior's) management policies.	35.6
Couldn't feel challenge in work.	33.9
Labor conditions (in terms of working hours, annual leaves, etc.) were poor.	29.8
Wanted to find a job more suitable to myself.	28.3
Wanted to try my capability under a completely fresh circumstance (i.e., in a new world).	26.2
Was concerned about the future situation of the company as well as the industry.	25.3
Wanted to freely expand my personal experiences.	22.3

Source: A Survey of Job Conversion by 10,000 Businessmen, October 1989, Recruit Research Co.

Systems to assist employees' career building. The basic rule of Japanese HRD for younger workers is "To assist the young work force in their HRD by helping them find more suitable and challenging job opportunities." Here are some of such career-facilitating systems used among Japanese industries.

- *Self-Assessment System*: Under this system, employees are each asked about their preferred careerpath and choice of HRD opportunities they think would help them toward career goals.
- *Interview System*: Based on the result of self-assessment, interviews are conducted between the employee and his or her superior or a personnel counsellor to discuss how such preferred opportunities can be realized.
- *Management by Objectives (MBO)*: MBO is often introduced in Japan as a device to improve individual competence. Employees are each asked to develop a MBO plan. They write down their preferred area and necessary method of HRD to help their own career development, submit it to the superior, and try to accomplish the plan themselves.
- *Planned Job Rotation or Career Development Plan (CDP)*: An attainable career path is preset for each employee, and efforts are made to systematically develop the employee.
- *In-Company Vacancy-Filling Publicity System*: Although it is not yet widely adopted, this in-house procedure disseminates information of vacant posts throughout the company for application by interested persons. The system is attracting wider attention as more Japanese firms undergo restructuring. When new business lines are being explored, the system would simplify finding interested talents within the company. Recently, many large corporations have adopted this approach.

The idea common to these approaches to young workers is to make them think themselves about ways to select their desired career paths and determine the methods to realize them. This is something new and completely different from the traditional Japanese notion that employees' careers are what the employer "gives" them. With the nation's labor shortage, stabilizing the younger working population is one of the critical issues. An important key to solving this issue is to provide job opportunities according to individual options selected through these approaches.

Female workers

Figure 17.11 represents a comparison of the working potential of female workers in 1979 and 1989. In the ten-year period, all age groups except the 15-18 group somewhat increased their potential.

Table 17.11: Working Potential of Female Workers

Source: Labor Force Survey, Prime Minister's Office – Stastics Bureau

Issues of female working population in general. Recently highlighted in career development for female workers is a system named "Employment Management by Career Courses." This is a combination of career courses differentiated by (1) "main line" operations and "supplementary or helper" operations, and (2) "non-relocatable" posts and "relocatable" posts (as would require moving one's home). Each of the combinations adopts a different style of employment management. Today, almost half of the female workers in the generalist category are those who have completed the courses, with some 40 percent of them over 30 years old. This proves that the system is achieving remarkable results, and many companies plan to expand this system. Because most of the generalist posts are assumed to require relocation, a new system of establishing "intermediate posts "(Chukan-Shoku)" is rapidly spreading. This type of post is in the "main line" category, just like a generalist, but does not require any relocation.

The Current and Future (five years) policies of HRD for the Japanese female working population are analyzed in Table 17.6. Whereas *in-company HRD*, *self-development* and *education by correspondence* seem to remain high in both time frames, these three policies are declining annually. Such policies as *supporting employees' study group activities* and *job rotations* are on the increase.

Table 17.6: HRD Policies for Female Workers

Policy	Current		Future		±
	Rank	Points	Rank	Points	
In-company training	1	64.3	1	57.1	−7.2
Self-development	2	56.3	2	51.8	−4.5
Education by correspondence	3	39.6	3	34.6	−5.0
Cultivating job atmosphere toward self-development	4	28.2	4	28.2	0.0
Training courses sponsored by outside training houses	5	23.9	5	23.4	−0.5
Supporting employees' study group activities	6	17.7	6	22.4	+4.7
Job rotations	7	16.9	7	23.2	+6.3

Source: Survey of Industrial Training Programs in FY 1990, Japan Federation of Employers' Association/Japan Industrial & Vocational Training Association

Table 17.7 reflects the five-year trend of corporate-sponsored classroom learning activities for female workers. Main themes in both Current and Future are *work ethics and business manners* (high at top), *building motivation and right work attitudes*, *learning about QA and expanding computer knowledge*, *expanding job/ industry knowledge*, etc.

Table 17.7: Changing Trend of the Themes of Class-room Training for Female Workers

Theme	Current	Future	±
Developing creative power	10.9	16.4	+5.5
Improving foreign language capability	8.9	14.4	+5.5
Developing problem-formulating/solving capability	11.0	13.0	+2.0
Improving interpersonal competence	17.5	18.3	+0.8
Reactivating the organization and work-team	13.8	14.3	+0.5
Learning finance/accounting knowledge	12.2	12.2	0.0
Learning sales and marketing skills	12.0	11.5	−0.5
Cultivating self-motivated role behaviors	30.2	29.4	−0.8
Building motivation and right work-attitude	42.7	41.1	−1.6
Expanding the knowledge about jobs and the industry	32.1	28.6	−3.5
Learning about office automation and expanding computer knowledge	35.4	31.7	−3.7
Learning about total quality control programs	16.4	12.7	−3.7
Work ethics and business manners	70.5	53.4	−17.1

Source: Survey of Industrial Training Programs in FY 1990, Japan Federation of Employer's Association/Japan Industrial & Vocational Training Association

These themes are focused on personnel instruction for improving skills in dealing with routine jobs. However, these "routine area" themes tend to be on the decrease in the five-year period. Such competence-boosting themes as *developing creative power, improving foreign language fluency, developing problem-formulating/solving capability*, etc., are increasing. Higher expectation for the upgraded competence of female workers is widely evident.

Part-time workers. The ratio of female part-time workers to the total female working population has kept increasing in the recent five years: 22.0 percent in 1985, 22.7 percent in 1986, 23.1% in 1987, 23.6 percent in 1988 and 25.2 percent in 1989. The average tenure of these part-timers in the same period is also increasing, but slightly: 3.9 years in 1985, 4.0 in 1986, 4.2 in 1987, 4.1 in 1988 and 4.3 in 1989.

The three most notable sectors of industry using female part-time workers are: 35.6 percent of *wholesale-retail-restaurant* sectors, 28.2 percent for *other services* sector, and 21.8 percent for *manufacturing* sector. Altogether, 85.6 percent of the part-timers work in these three sectors.

Evidently, female part-time workers occupy an important piece of the Japanese labor market. Companies that positively promote HRD for part-time employees emphasize such areas as "manualizing work procedures" and "reinforcing their pre-placement training." However, many other companies admit that "HRD for female part-timers of our company is not yet organized."

In five years, we anticipate many more companies will be active in this area. Particularly considering the importance of human resources in the wholesale-retail-restaurant and other services sectors, higher human competence should be a big HRD prerequisite. Moreover, advancing innovations and changing consumer awareness in these sectors keep renewing worker requirements. All research seems to promise that these HRD needs will keep rising higher. Even current HRD implementation in these areas is only in its infancy.

References

Amaya, T. *Recent Trends in Human Resource Development*. Tokyo: The Japan Institute of Labor, 1990.

About the Author

Tadashi Amaya is Professor, Department of Management Information Teikyo Institute of Technology in Ichihara, Chiba, Japan. Previously, he was Director of Human Resource Development for Oki Electric Industry Company, Ltd. He is a graduate of Tokyo University and is active in the Japan Society for Personnel and Labor Research, Japan Society for Study of Business Administration, Japanese Society for the Study of Career Guidance, and the Japanese Society of Industrial-Organizational Psychology. He published "Human Resource Development in Industry" in the Japanese Industrial Relations Series and "Recent Trends in Human Resource Development," published by the Japan Institute of Labor.

CHAPTER 18

Adapting a Japanese HRD Idea for Use in Another Country

Masaaki Imai

This chapter explains some aspects of Japanese HRD, with particular emphasis on Kaizen and quality improvement. Kaizen is a Japanese word for improvement. Further, it means improvement involving everybody in the organization, and without spending much money. The English word "improvement" tends to mean improving the physical properties of products, equipment, and systems at a great cost. On the other hand, Kaizen is usually directed to people's continual efforts to bring about a change to the status quo. In my opinion, the Kaizen concept has been the key to Japan's competitive success.

First, Kaizen is a state of mind which never accepts the status quo. Kaizen always starts with the premise that there must be a better way. One looks for problems surrounding one's own work and constantly tries to find solutions to such problems. Problems are welcome in Kaizen-minded companies, and a corporate culture is fostered where everybody is free to discuss problems without inhibition and fear of punishment.

The second key premise of Kaizen is that it is an action-oriented approach, based on common sense. In Kaizen, the only thing that matters is practice, and not much emphasis is placed on the knowledge itself.

Quality is the rage of the day. Companies that do not have a system to realize quality are destined to fail. What is quality, then? In my opinion, quality is anything that can be improved to satisfy the customer.

Traditionally, quality has meant conformance to specifications. Kaizen emphasizes improvement of all aspects of activities in developing, designing, manufacturing, and marketing products. The unique feature of the Japanese approach to quality has been to stress the improvement of existing systems, procedures and activities, wherever and whenever appropriate.

Let's look at the implications of action-oriented Kaizen for quality improvement and examine why most of these problems can be solved without sophisticated knowledge and problem-solving tools.

Japanese Approach to HRD

Managers often believe that sophisticated tools must be employed in order to solve problems and improve quality, which is why they keep searching for the latest scientific tools, theories, and formulas. There is no doubt that sophisticated approaches—such as statistical quality control, design of experiments, and computer applications—are needed to solve some quality problems. However, today's managers have more than enough expertise to solve *most* of their problems. What they need to do today is *not* to gain more sophisticated and state-of-the-art knowledge, but to simply put common sense and wisdom into practice.

There are two basic requirements for maintaining and improving quality: variability control and prevention of recurrences. To control variability, standards must be introduced and key processes must be confined within specified parameters. To prevent recurrences, data must be collected, causes of problems analyzed, and corrective measures sought out and standardized.

To do the above, sophisticated tools are not necessary most of the time. There are several axioms which have been used in Japan in the context of human resources development and have proved to be extremely useful in addressing quality problems. Some of them are introduced in the following section.

Axioms for Japanese HRD

Don't get it, don't make it, don't send it
There are three dimensions of quality: namely, the incoming quality, the value-adding quality, and the outgoing quality. First, this axiom means that, one should not receive defects from the previous process. Second, one should be determined not to make defects in his or her own process — and to do this, standards must be followed, and every time variability occurs the existing standards must be reviewed. Third, one should not send defects to the next process, which means that each person must inspect their own work before sending it to the next process.

This axiom is based on the premise that quality is everybody's job throughout the entire range of processes. This is in sharp contrast to the conventional approach, where quality is assured by a third party: namely, inspectors. When everybody lives up to this principle, a good system of quality assurance is at work.

Speak with data

Whenever a problem (or a variability) occurs, management's job is to study it, identify the root causes, and take actions on these causes. Then, new measures to prevent recurrence must be established and followed.

When a problem occurs, one can usually find enough data. In one machinery company for instance, management had decided to collect data every time malfunctions were observed. From such a data base, they prepared a checklist to be carried out by the operators before work on the daily, weekly and monthly data bases.

By simply following this checklist, they were not only successful in greatly reducing the machine downtime, but also the reject rate. This episode supports my belief that quality is something which most managers can do by collecting data and analyzing them.

Collecting data is the starting point of quality improvement. Quality starts with *quantification* of data. Once data are collected, analysis should follow. Then, analysis should lead to decision making and then to actions.

Ask "Why?" five times

Where there is a problem, there is always a root cause. Problem solving means to keep asking "Why?" five times (or as many times as necessary) until a root cause is identified. Otherwise, people tend to address a symptom, mistaking it for a root cause.

An example of this is throwing sawdust between machines. Sawdust is needed because the floor is slippery. The floor is slippery because there is oil. The oil is there because the machines leak. Thus, the root cause is the leakage from the machine and unless that is stopped, the problem will never be solved. However, in reality, how often do we see people throwing sawdust every day?

Go to Gemba

Gemba is a Japanese word for the shop floor, where value-adding actions take place. Managers are urged to go to Gemba at once whenever variabilities occur.

When the manager sits behind the desk and awaits for the quality report to arrive after a few hours (or days!), the conditions that have contributed to variabilities are lost, and it will be too late to take proper actions. Hence, go to Gemba at once, and ask "Why?" five times.

In Gemba, what one sees is data. Usually, no lengthy report of data is needed in Gemba, since one can take actions right on the spot. In my opinion, better than 90 percent of quality problems in Gemba can be solved with common sense by simply going to Gemba at once and asking "Why?" until the root causes have been identified.

Kaizen—The Rules

Finally, I will introduce the 10 basic rules for practicing Kaizen, used in encouraging people to practice Kaizen in Japan. They are shown in Figure 18.1.

Figure 18.1: 10 Basic Rules for Practicing Kaizen

1. Discard conventional fixed ideas.

2. Think of how to do it, and not why it cannot be done.

3. Do not make excuses. Start by questioning current practices.

4. Do not seek perfection. Do it right away even if for only 50 percent of target.

5. Correct mistakes at once.

6. Do not spend money for Kaizen.

7. Wisdom is brought out when one is faced with hardship.

8. Ask "Why?" five times and seek root causes.

9. Seek the wisdom of ten people rather than the knowledge of one.

10. Kaizen ideas are infinite.

What Is Kaizen?

People may say that what I have described above is nothing but common sense. Then, the question is "Why is common sense not a common practice?" The companies that have been successful in quality management have done it.

To sum up, this is a Japanese style of problem identification, always challenging people to work for improvement, placing much value in action taking rather than gaining knowledge. We have also found that it is possible to make improvement by simply putting common sense to practice.

About the Author

Masaaki Imai is Chairman, The Cambridge Corporation and President, Kaizen Institute.

CHAPTER 19

Adapting Technology-Based Instruction For Chinese Users

Hui-Chuan Cheng

This chapter examines adapting technology for a specific country, following the same format as Angus Reynolds' chapter on the problems of adapting technology. The specific considerations are for use where Chinese language and culture prevail.

Automated instructional packages include print, video, audio self-study packages, computer-assisted instruction (CAI), and interactive video. This courseware obviously lacks the local Chinese to provide key on-the-spot cultural adaptation. However, Taiwan has high technological capabilities, and local subsidiaries or customers probably have or can obtain the technical capability to adapt technology-based software to fit in with their own circumstances. In the People's Republic of China (PRC), the capability may or may not exist, and there is a question whether they can obtain it.

Adaptation before export is possible, as is adaptation "in the field." This chapter will examine various aspects of adapting automated materials for Chinese audiences, and is applicable to the People's Republic of China, Taiwan, Hong Kong, Singapore, and any other location where a Chinese population must be specifically addressed. I will present the information needed to appreciate the scope of the Chinese adaptation problem, without attempting a full-scale Chinese technology education.

General Considerations

"Keep it simple" and "Insure clarity" are advice as appropriate to Chinese delivery as any other. However, these terms apply more to an original than its adaptation.

Technical Considerations

To understand the problems with Chinese, we must set forth some basic information about user input and the related hardware and software considerations. Then we can view the resulting design considerations.

User input. We will talk about the language later in this chapter. For now, remember characters are different in the PRC and Taiwan, and slightly different characters are used in Hong Kong.

The Chinese learner's keyboard will look just like yours. You might expect it to be covered with Chinese characters, but it isn't. Now, ask yourself, how would you go about using that keyboard to display your name in Chinese on the screen?

Chinese computer input is different from European languages. The Chinese character is not a built-in function in the computer itself, and users cannot find Chinese characters on the keyboard. For example, when you type the English *I* (meaning myself), you need only one keystroke. To type *woo* (see Figure 19.1) in Chinese on a computer keyboard takes at least three keystrokes (using 倚天 E Tien, Chinese word processing software).

Figure 19.1: Woo

There are several systems of inputting from a keyboard. For example, if I were using the E Tien word processor at this moment, I would type *x*, *o*, and *3*. The *woo* character shown in Figure 19.1 would be displayed. This is based on pronunciation. Users of another software program might type *p*, *i*, *o*, and *u*, based on the character itself.

You need not be concerned about me. Think of the poor learner. Will your learner have a knowledge of this type of keyboard input? If not, it may not be practical to expect any character input from the learner. The lesson may have to be restricted to selecting keys that are related to things on the screen. For example, the learner can be directed to press *1* if a certain condition is true, etc.

Hardware

Because of computer hardware and software limitations, it is more difficult to convert technology-based instruction into Chinese than into French, Spanish, or other alphabetic languages.

Memory size. We can use one byte of memory to present English characters, but we need at least two bytes to present Chinese characters. In the case of *I,* one byte is needed. In the case of *woo*, at least two are needed.

In English, no matter whether the word is from English prefixes, suffixes, or roots, it is not necessary to reserve computer memory for new English words. The user can easily create any combination in the keyboard. In Chinese, it is necessary to reserve a big computer memory space (data base) for storing Chinese characters. Basic literacy requires about 5,000 characters. However, a minimum word-processing data base will need space for 5,401 most often used words, 7,652 less often used words, and 441 symbols.

Special hardware and software. You can begin to see that making Chinese happen on a computer is an entirely different problem than Russian, for example. Keep this in mind when you convert computer-based training (CBT) courseware into Chinese. These problems suggest that you will need a larger hard disc for running special Chinese word-processing software to generate Chinese characters for screen display.

Software

There are three methods used to create CBT:

- Authoring language
- Authoring system
- General-purpose language

An authoring language is specifically designed for writing instructional software. Most authoring languages require at least a rudimentary knowledge of programming—for example, TUTOR, TenCORE, or Coursewriter.

An authoring system, such as SUMMIT or Authorware, already has most of the programming done. The programmer is responsible for providing the display details and some of the branching logic. When using an authoring system, the programmer only has to fill in the menu blanks provided by the system. It provides an easy way to implement lessons.

General-purpose languages—such as BASIC, Pascal or C—require the programmer to specify every detail of what the computer will do. Nothing can be left out. Every aspect of answer judging has to be programmed, every variable or counter updated correctly, the sequencing of displays managed, and the collection of data ensured.

Authoring systems are used most commonly in today's CBT marketplace. You may want to convert an English CBT lesson, originally created with an authoring system, into Chinese. Either you must use a compatible Chinese version of the original authoring system or an English authoring system. If an English authoring system, the Chinese characters can be displayed as "graphics." You can use Chinese word-processing to generate Chinese character sets or hire someone to generate Chinese sets by hand. These will be more work for you, and considerably more space will be required than for the English version, but it is possible.

If you are lucky enough to find a Chinese authoring system (there is no prominent Chinese authoring system on the market at this moment), you will not need to change the original interaction format. The learner can input responses in words and even sentences.

Even if you use the original English authoring system to convert the software, you must still consider culture, translation, and screen text display space (to be discussed more fully in the following sections). Your *big* concern will be the interaction input format. English authoring systems cannot recognize Chinese characters. Therefore, I strongly recommend multiple choice, object matching, and true/false questions, which only ask the learner to select the number of the correct answer. This input is much simpler than demanding that the learner input a Chinese character.

If the CBT software was written in general-purpose programming language, there are fewer conversion problems than in the previous two situations. For example, in BASIC you use the following statements to display character *I* (myself) on the screen. Therefore, the developer need only worry about how to generate Chinese character sets from the keyboard, not about how to change the interaction input format.

PRINT *I* (in English)   PRINT *xo3* (in Chinese)

The information-presentation part of tutorial software is easy to convert into Chinese. You don't need to change the user input, you need only the text display format. Traditional Chinese writing proceeds vertically in columns from top to bottom, while the columns proceed from right to left (see Figure 19.2). However, Chinese can also be written on horizontal lines from left to right, proceeding downward, exactly like English (see Figure 19.2). Learners can read either way, so it will not matter if your software is not capable of displaying the characters in the traditional way.

Figure 19.2: Vertical/Horizontal

百
戰
百
勝

知
己
知
彼

Vertically

知己知彼
百戰百勝

Horizontally

Design Considerations

There are two possibilities for converting lessons:

- Keeping graphics apart, changing the text into Chinese
- Using the original paper-based design as the draft to convert

Anticipate Chinese use. If you think there may be Chinese marketing opportunities for your courseware, standardization can help to avoid difficulty. You should already have courseware development format standards, and you should establish additional Chinese-specific standards. One standard might specify that graphics (for example, equipment views) have numbered labels instead of English labels. English labels will brand the course as foreign. The numbers permit a common referencing in any language. Also consider consistently including metric measurements. This will give your courseware a "global" appearance even before any export. Avoid U.S. coins, dollar signs, and famous U.S. landmarks. Avoid "typical" culture-bound examples and humor. Chinese learners enjoy humor as much as Americans. But, like people anywhere, they may not understand foreign humor.

Although there are large companies, many companies are medium size or smaller. Generic instruction will be appropriate to a wider market—probably a good idea in this marketplace (you may allow customized features in your software).

Space. There are two types of text screen display in Chinese, 16 x 15 and 24 x 24, while in English 8 x 15 and 12 x 24 are enough (see Figure 19.3). Chinese text requires at least 100 percent more space than English. Reserving 50 percent of every display is an extreme design limitation. Nevertheless, the designer should make the best use of this forewarning. Without allowances for more space, a conversion could ruin the entire design.

Figure 19.3: Space Consideration

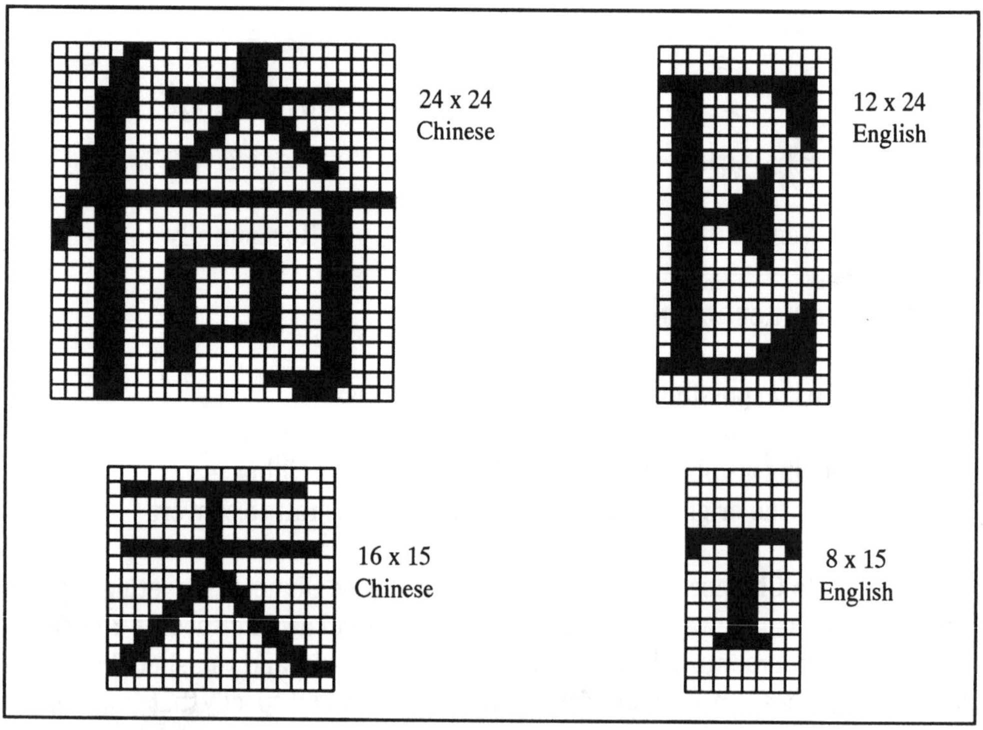

24 x 24
Chinese

12 x 24
English

16 x 15
Chinese

8 x 15
English

Anticipate display format. Translation of English material into Chinese will normally not create a format problem. Using the horizontal, left-to-right display of text will appear natural. Only the total space used must be considered. Figure 19.4 shows an example of the screen.

Consider text characteristics. This is a basic difference. Figure 19.3 illustrates the differences in text display requirements for character-based languages. This chapter has covered the difficulties in learner input that character-based languages impose.

Development involving special character sets always takes foreign developers relatively longer because of multiple-step text entry. This is not true of Chinese data-entry people. Their familiarity with the input system makes them quick and since they can also read what they are typing, they make fewer errors.

Deal with system- and application- generated messages. As mentioned earlier in this chapter, Chinese organizations may have the know-how to alter system- and application-generated displays. Typically, you will not own the code for the programs used to develop and deliver your automated instructional materials, but you may be able to obtain access to change the automatic displays.

Figure 19.4: Computer Screen Example/Horizontal

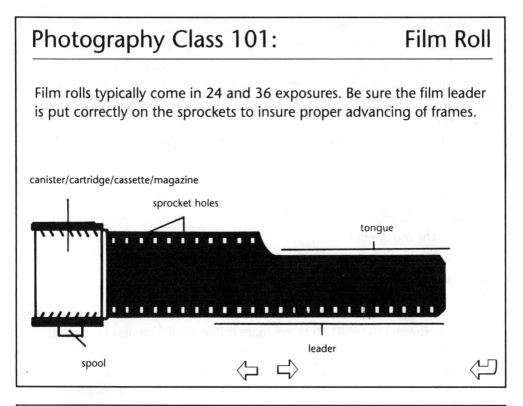

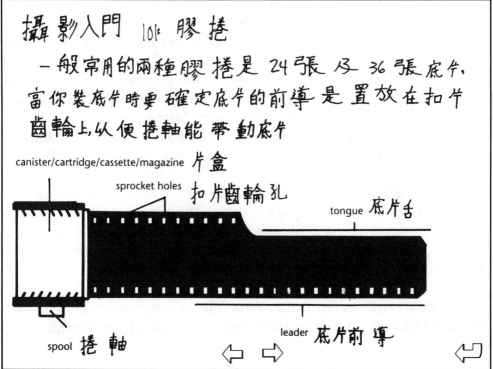

Culturalization

Be sensitive to Chinese culture rather than imposing your own. Experienced "China hands" understand the need to consider cultural as well as linguistic differences when translating an HRD program into another language. Angus Reynolds pointed out that there are 273 potentially different sets of conditions that obtain for individuals in technology transfer projects. Competent culturalization is needed for all of them.

The Chinese do not represent a single culture. Traditionally, there are five groups:

Han - the largest ethnic group of the Chinese race
Man - the Manchus (near Korea)
Meng - the Mongolians
Hwei - the Muslims (near Russia)
Tsang - the Tibetans

So, even if you were only considering the PRC, there are obviously cultural differences. Beyond the PRC there are more differences. You may be considering a particular interactive video program for translation into Chinese for Taipei. That version will not work in Beijing. It should be redone a second time for use there. Why?

1. The accent of Mandarin is different. Either audience will understand the other, but perceive it as the "other" version.

2. More subtle aspects of appearance will cause either audience to consider actors to be of the "other" group. An analogy is that a well-done presentation for use in rural Texas would not have a "Madison Avenue New Yorker" as the narrator.

3. The social environment in the two locations is different. Refer to Burian and Canela's chapter on HRD in Asia for more detail. References and subtle differences will be readily noticed by learners from the "other" group.

You must be careful in preparing computer displays and the video in many areas. Consider color, symbols used, gender, body language, and politics.

Symbols. One picture is worth more than one thousand words, but when you misuse it, you mislead the readers. Be cautious about using symbols. If the symbol is necessary, it should be universally recognized. For example, the religious cross is a universally recognized symbol. Whenever you cannot make sure whether a symbol is universally recognized, you should avoid using it.

Spoken vs. written word. In the case of Chinese, spoken interaction is easier to implement than written. This is an important consideration for multimedia instruction.

Gender. Unlike Japanese women, Chinese women are completely integrated into situations likely to be depicted in instruction. Therefore, it may be helpful to balance depictions of people in roles by gender as would be appropriate in the United States.

Body language. The Chinese are less physically expressive than Americans. For example, they do not make a show of kissing when greeting. But do not be afraid to show scenes of such behavior when foreigners are depicted. The Chinese are accustomed to seeing it and are not offended.

Politics. Avoid symbols specifically associated with either Taiwan or the PRC. Mainland China's five-star flag and " 毛澤東 " Mao Tse Tung should not be used

in a Taipei-bound version of your HRD program.

Learner reaction. There are significant differences between Chinese and Western learners. Joyce Tuck shared her experience with a Japanese client with me. Her learners did not get involved in her HRD program as Americans do, asking questions and sharing their feedback during the program. At the beginning, she was afraid they did not understand. Then she realized it was a cultural difference. It is the same with Chinese learners. They are used to learning in the conventional instructional environment, so you must use an effective instructional strategy to motivate them to get involved in learning activities. Ordinarily, Chinese do not appear to be active learners in class, yet interactive instruction requires an active learner. This does not mean that instructional games cannot be used in technology-based Chinese HRD activities. In fact, if games are well integrated into the instruction, you will succeed better with Chinese learners. But if you do not have a good strategy to motivate the learners to change from passive to active, your computer-based lesson is unlikely to succeed.

Chinese Adaptation Alerts

Jargon and clichés. Dealing with jargon and clichés is essentially universal, so the Chinese learners may already know the needed technical or professional terms. In Taipei, learners probably know the needed computer jargon. Establish a standard dictionary of words that may be used in your Chinese lessons, or support "Glossary" features in CBT lessons.

Acronyms and initials. You may not be aware that MIT stands for "Made in Taiwan" to people there. There are undoubtedly other acronyms and initials with potential for misunderstanding. If these appear in the original lesson, you can prepare for future adaptation by always including a side-by-side, spelled-out version.

Measurement. Establish a standard to always use metric measures in the original development. This will ease adaptation for Chinese learners since they all know metric measures.

Sports. People in Taiwan know baseball very well. Those in Hong Kong may know cricket. Learners in the PRC are unlikely to know either. The danger of making sports-related references to a Chinese audience are obvious.

Humor. Everyone enjoys laughing, but humor is often related to its original culture and social environment. You may find it difficult to translate for Chinese learners. If you insist on using humor, take care to avoid culturally and environmentally specific humor.

Always verify materials with a native. For example, ask the translator for a cultural review of the materials. Of course, some translators may be totally faithful to your original text, so you must make it clear that you specifically want a translation of culture as well as words.

Translation

According to modern scientific linguistics, differences between one language and another (Chinese and English, in this case,) are not limited only to the obvious ones in speech sounds, word forms, or word connotations; nor are they limited to word-order or syntax. The most important differences lie in linguistic ways of thinking and of expression. It is no easy task to put English—even a phrase or a single word—into correct and idiomatic Chinese. Good translation puts more emphasis on translating the meaning of the original and interpreting the mind of the writer. Many translators consider word-by-word translation the best method for observing the so-called "principle of faithfulness in translation." Thus, only the outward meaning of the original version would be preserved, sapping the translated version of its vitality. More harm is done if a work is thus translated than would be done by leaving it untranslated. Text translated in this way tends not only to be less readable and less understandable, but misleading, stylistically dead, and even causing linguistic pollution in the translated language.

Principles for translation to and from Chinese
There are three principles in the art of translation:

- Be scrupulously faithful to the original text.
- Fully convey the meanings expressed in the original.
- Render the style of the original appropriately.

In other words, a sentence, a term or even a single word translated from one language to another should be faithful to the original, readable and reflect the original style. Style, however, is relative. If the style of a well-written original is either classic or vernacular, the translated version should be the same. As for an originally bad style, you must overcome the reluctance of your translator to make it a better style.

In translation, it is more important to fully convey the original meanings or readability of the translated materials than to be literally faithful to the original words or the style. Of the above mentioned translation principles, the second is of paramount importance. Actually, a version rendered incorrectly on account of adhering to literal faithfulness of the original text may be misleading or even of less use than leaving the original untranslated.

Philosophy

The supreme philosophy of translation is to render the *sense* rather than the *sentence*. The greatest differences between Chinese and English lie in the linguistic ways of thinking and expression. For instance, the Chinese equivalent of the English *northeast* is　東北　(*tung pie*) or *east-north*, while *hot and cold* in English

is　冷熱　(*leng je*) or *cold-hot* in Chinese. Another example of opposite word order is that Chinese name a person from family name to first name. At home, I wouldn't be called Hui-Chuan Cheng, I would be Chen, Hui-Chuan. Chinese put a title after the name. For example, Americans say President Bush. In Chinese he is called Bush, President. One of the best English equivalents to the Chinese idiomatic phrase

物以類聚 (*wu yi ley jiu*) is *birds of a feather flock together*.

These simple examples show the great differences between two languages caused by the respective linguistic ways of thinking and of expression. No matter which language is used as a medium of translation, the translated version must mirror, as much as possible, the native language of the learners. That is to say, the Chinese should be Chinese-like, and not the Chinese expressed in English word order or thought patterns.

As we have just pointed out, equivalent terms found in two languages are sometimes entirely different due to different linguistic ways of thinking and of expression. In addition, the connotations of the same terms in these two languages may also be entirely different because of dissimilar cultural backgrounds. Due to ignorance of the connotations of Chinese, some Americans can make unconscious conceptual mistakes in translation.   Take, for example, the English words *beer, wine, liquor, alcohol,* or *booze*. They can be translated into the same Chinese word, 　酒　(*chiu*), because according to Chinese, *chiu* includes all alcoholic beverages, whether strong or weak, fermented or distilled.

An opposite confusion occurs in translating family relatives into Chinese. For example, *aunt* in English can be either the father's or mother's sisters, but in Chinese, you need to figure out which. Is she your father's sister 姑 (*gu*) or your mother's sister 姨 (*yi*)? From the above two examples it can be seen that a good translation of Chinese and English terms, which will not mislead readers, goes beyond a superficial conversion from one language to another. For accuracy in linguistic concepts, the cultural backgrounds must be understood.

Dialect

The need for translation is obvious. Yet, there are still subtleties that sometimes elude parochial Americans. For example, in translating a video program into Chinese, a problem arose. Which dialect should the final version be in? There are at least 10 popular Chinese dialects in the world. For example, Singapore uses Fukien dialect (Hokkienese), Hong Kong uses Cantonese, Taiwan uses either Mandarin or Fukien. There are significant differences that could, if incorporated, brand the final product as "Hong Kong," "Singapore," "PRC" or "Taiwan" rather than the desired generic Chinese. This doesn't even address the additional problem that written Chinese characters are not quite the same in Beijing and Taipei. So "Translation into Chinese" leaves an unanswered question: What Chinese? The characters used in Taipei

(繁骨豐字 (*farn tii tzyh*) or the one used in Beijing,

(簡骨豐字 (*jean tii tzyh*)? Some different forms of social address

in Taipei and Beijing make translation more complex. For example, in Taipei the English *wife*, is translated into 太太 (*tai tai*). In Beijing it is translated into 愛人 (*ay ren*), but in Taipei, *ay ren* means lover, not official spouse. This is only one example that illustrates the importance of identifying and using the right terms in your program.

In professional or technical translation, key words should be in the universally accepted term. It does not need to be translated into a Chinese word. For example, the English *computer* does not need to be translated into the Chinese 電腦 (*diann nao*). You can use English and Chinese side by side, like

computer (電腦) for the first appearance in the text, then use English only for subsequent appearances. Chinese everywhere are looking for internationalized technology and universally accepted key words that are helpful for them.

Foreign Sounds

Additionally, foreign words can take on new meaning when given a representative Chinese character to help locals pronounce them, so you should consider meaning and pronunciation. A classic Chinese translation is Coca-Cola,可口可樂. It carries the original English pronunciation well and means "delicious and make you happy" in Chinese.

Your Chinese System

Richard Hall is a program manager in the Education and Development Division at Exxon Central Services. He was in charge of a project to instruct Saudi Arabian engineers on site. He likes to tell how the project manager, designer, developer, evaluator, and instructor were a good instructional team. You can consider the Chinese-specific things related to a typical systematic approach to instruction. Here are some suggestions, phase-by-phase.

Analysis. Your needs assessment will identify appropriate courseware for Chinese adaptation. You must always know your target population. In this case, you will determine the particular characteristics of your Chinese audience.

Design. In the case of conversion, the layout is there. You will have to identify the changes needed because of differences in space requirements. You will build in the appropriate cultural specifics.

Development. You may become involved with special software, character sets, graphics, and other technological considerations. Formative evaluation must include a tryout of your courseware by members of the targeted Chinese population. Second-generation Chinese in America are different from the Chinese in their home country.

Implementation. In the case of technology-based instruction, the delivery may not involve instructors. Still you must provide for customer service, learner help, and local technical support. These are always important, but even more so because Chinese learners will be at a distance from your support base. Your efforts will be appreciated.

Evaluation. The most important evaluation will be results. Is the return on your HRD investment satisfactory? Customer satisfaction will be measured in marketplace success.

Your Chinese Courseware Team

We task-organize for any special project. Why would automated instruction be any different? In addition to previous teammates, augment your development team with the following players for Chinese projects:

- A local Chinese to advise you about cultural considerations
- A competent translator
- Technically competent people to handle software and hardware considerations

In Sun Tzu's *The Art of War*, he said: "...knowing one's situation and that of the enemy guarantees victory in every battle...." Your client is certainly not your enemy, but I think that we can use the thought in a constructive way. I would say: "Knowing your situation and that of the client guarantees victory in every project. Do you agree?"

References

Reynolds, A. "Training That Travels Well." *Training and Development Journal*, Sept. 1990, pp. 73-78.

Reynolds, A. "Adapting Courseware for Technology Transfer." In *Technology Transfer: A Project Guide for International HRD*,Reynolds, A. (Ed.). Boston, MA: International Human Resources Development Corporation, 1984.

About the Author

Hui-Chuan Cheng is a Partner in Princeton Software in Kearny, NJ. She is an instructional courseware developer active in the areas of distance learning, hypermedia, and computer-based learning. Previously, she was Assistant Professor of Instructional Technology at New York Institute of Technology. She is a graduate of National Ching-Hsing University in Taiwan and completed her doctoral studies at Purdue University, where she was also a Research Assistant and Instructor for undergraduate and graduate courses in the School of Education. She serves on the American Society for Training and Development Instructional Technology Professional Practice Area Executive Committee. She is a presenter at international conferences and her work appears frequently in books and articles.

CHAPTER 20

HRD in the People's Republic of China – Challenge or Compromise?

Florence H. C. Ho

It is gratifying that texts and articles on helping businesses working in an international environment or managing a diverse work force have tripled in the past two years. The phenomenon is largely a result of business becoming more international. Forty percent of respondents in a recent ASTD National HRD Executive survey said that today international business is a significant part of their overall business. Sixty percent reported that international business will increase over the next three years. Another attributing factor is the gradual disappearance of a homogeneous work force. Its replacement by a multicultural work force has caused increased management challenges.

However, the same proliferation does not exist in literature for HRD practitioners working internationally, especially those involved in HRD projects in the People's Republic of China (PRC). This chapter will try to help HRD practitioners to work effectively in the PRC.

Following its adoption of the "Open Door" policy, China, once called "the sleeping giant," became the focus of attention. As a result of eagerness to win her as a trading partner, foreign investments flooded in. China seemed to be undergoing another Industrial Revolution. State-owned and joint venture enterprises boomed. The days of rationing had passed. I still recall our monthly food parcels to lessen the plight of relatives in China during the 1950s and 1960s. Even staple foods such as rice were scarce. Cooking oil was unheard of. The annual allowance of three meters of fabric to a household member was hardly enough.

The price to rebuild the war-torn country was high. Personal sacrifices were immaterial and Mao's doctrines advocating a classless system and total self-sufficiency became the sole ideological backbone. The world cheered when China's political outlook softened in the 1970s and became more attuned to a free enterprise economy. However, the hope that China was heading for liberal reforms was shattered by the Tienanmen massacre. China's atrocities shocked the world, and the bloodshed left an indelible scar. China suffers for her inhumane way of crushing the student movement and again caution, if not dismay and suspicion, is apparent.

Caught in the emotional turmoil, I was torn between professional commitment and moral justification. I was then working with Coopers and Lybrand and had been negotiating for two years to undertake an HRD project in China. The Chinese Society of Accountants and Ministry of Finance initiated the project, which was funded by the World Bank. But because of the June 4th massacre, the World Bank put a freeze on all projects in China. It took six months to lift the freeze and resume negotiations in January, 1990.

To Coopers and Lybrand, whether we should go ahead with the project was more than a business decision. We felt that we were treading on thin ice. On one hand, to honor our professional commitment we should remain impartial and carry on. On the other, we could not obliterate our apprehension about, and sheer disappointment in, China's retrogression and violation of human rights.

After a series of debates and self-questioning, we made our major decision to go ahead with the project. What better opportunity than this would arise to show there are other, more effective ways of doing things? It was not a mere HRD assignment but a tremendous opportunity to practice HRD skills in a cross cultural environment, and most important of all, to affect China's development. We accepted the challenge. But, we were not ready to compromise on the ideological differences.

Both Angus Reynolds and Len Nadler have given me tremendous encouragement and insights. They were especially helpful when I emigrated from Hong Kong to set foot in a new country. The transition was probably the most turbulent I have ever experienced. I wish to dedicate this chapter to my parents, and my brother and his family, with confidence in our ultimate reunion.

Background Information on the Project

Over the years, I have been involved in many projects in China, ranging from training to organizational development. In the process, I established close ties with the sponsoring bodies. I have always wanted to share my experience with fellow HRD practitioners and the invitation to contribute to this book is an excellent opportunity. The chapter is primarily based on my own experience.

The Chinese Society of Accountants and Ministry of Finance arranged the World Bank project, which was to design and deliver a course on management consulting. Participants were accounting professionals, either working in the government administration—such as various bureaus within the Ministry of Finance and state-owned enterprises—or joint-venture enterprises. Both China and the World Bank had a long-term goal. They wanted more indigenous professionals involved in future management consulting projects, whether undertaking such projects independently or working together with their foreign counterparts on a joint-venture basis. The stipulation was enforced.

The Negotiation Process

To begin, let's examine the negotiation process that is such a critical part in a contractual relationship with clients.

Negotiators' status

To show respect, Chinese expect the other side's representatives to bear the same status as their Chinese counterparts.

Sensitivity to cultural norms

· We tend to assume that our host country will do things the same way we do and have the same business practices. However, in reality, there are basic differences of style and communication. Failure to acknowledge and understand the differences will doom or endanger many endeavors.

Observing the protocol details

These will include such logistic arrangements as meeting time, duration of the meeting, choice of venue, setting of the room, seating arrangements, and exchange of business cards. For instance, arranging a meeting at the crack of dawn would not be a good idea, nor would a breakfast meeting. Business does start as early as 9:00 A.M. the morning, but unlike their Western counterparts, Chinese—especially at the senior level—use the first hour or so of the day for getting ready. Chinese consider breakfast meetings too disruptive and not sufficiently businesslike. I remember my American colleague's almost disasterous experience of inviting his Chinese business associates to the Great Wall Sheraton for a breakfast meeting. There was a buffet table with food galore: hot and cold cereal; poached, sunny-side up, boiled and scrambled eggs; a whole array of fancy cold-cuts and cooked meat; pastries and exotic fruits. Despite this exquisite ambiance, his guests listened to his business proposal with a frowning look. They did not show displeasure, but puzzlement at the breakfast ritual. They felt it resembled a three-ring circus—spectacular but distracting. However, we have found informal occasions like lunch and dinner (very often a reciprocal gesture) a good opportunity to cultivate a working relationship. Chinese always appreciate consultants using chopsticks and having an in-depth knowledge of the local customs.

The invisible agenda

Meetings generally have a formal atmosphere. In the Western culture, meetings provide the opportunity to discuss and resolve problems. We cannot expect the same candidness and directness in China, especially in the first phase of negotiation, which is usually preceded by much probing and clarifications. Chinese regard it as discourteous to "rush and ramble." To handle the situation, you need to demonstrate exceptional patience and sensitivity. I have seen cases where both parties came to a deadlock situation—the Western counterparts were regarded as overbearing and representatives from the host country as lacking sincerity and commitment.

We learned from experience to set an agenda before the meeting. It not only showed our preparedness, but we could also set the pace of the meeting and achieve our goal without too much "meandering." Getting prior agreement to the agenda can further hasten the progress. However, you should always have a contingent plan should the agenda be rejected.

Watch out for the atmosphere and for the comfort level of the representatives on both sides of the negotiation table. You must be sure to build rapport with your counterparts, and get on the same wavelength. On the one hand, we have to be flexible. On the other, we need to know where we stand, and the total cost or profit we aim to achieve.

The essence of sincerity

Coming to an agreement and getting into a win-win situation calls for "give and take" instead of abusing the goodwill of the other party.

I must emphasize the need to remain objective at this early stage. Being judgmental and trapped in good-bad comparisons impedes our objectivity. We must clearly identify points of convergence and divergence, and be aware of the diverse ways to obtain common ends.

I would like to use the Chinese character (誠) to illustrate the analogy. (誠) means sincerity. It has two parts. The left side means "a dialogue." The right means "success" and "fulfillment." In short, the success of any negotiation lies in the desire of both parties to reach agreement.

The Workplace, Hierarchical Structures, and Business Environment

This chapter will examine how cultural differences affect learning. Before getting into more detail, let us examine the individual in the workplace, the influence of the hierarchical structures, and the business environment.

There is a general perception that having the latest technologies is synonymous with progress and prosperity. There is nothing wrong with the notion—if the technologies are properly applied, managed, and serviced. However, that has not been the case.

I recall visiting a university in one of the Special Economic Zones. Its nearness to Hong Kong has enabled the university to get considerable funding from owners of the neighboring joint-venture enterprises. The vice-principal wished to prove how well-equipped the university was. He told me that they had more than 100 IBM PC computers installed two years ago. At the invitation of the vendor, they took a study trip to Hong Kong and visited one or two similar institutions. He was proud that not only were they computerized like their Hong Kong counterparts, but theirs were superior, later models.

I asked if they had any problem in time scheduling, a common problem faced by consultants and practitioners all trying to use the resources simultaneously. He replied, "No." Thinking that he might have a superior scheduling system that perhaps we could model, I asked my question again. To my amazement, I found out that the computers were never put into use. They did not even have the necessary software. It would be purchased later—provided funding was available. He assured me that it was more important to have the hardware first.

Chinese acceptance of technological change is almost automatic. In other areas, change is not viewed as favorably. A classic example is the absence of productivity measurement and performance-based pay systems. China bases pay scales on seniority rather than productivity and performance. Without any performance indicator, there is no incentive to work hard, especially for employees of a state-owned enterprise. Another example is that in the West we reward people for initiative, enterprise, and performance. The Chinese place priority on acquiring status and preserving respect.

The same attitude applies to issues such as quality control. Quality awareness is zero. That explains why in some joint-venture enterprises neither the supervisors nor the workers "buy into" the concept of quality. Quality management tools and techniques may be in place. Management, however, remains oblivious to the expectations of markets and product and service users. So, unless there are conscious efforts to arouse the general awareness of quality and to reinforce quality-improvement behavior, all quality-improvement methods will be futile.

Unfortunately, the rigidity of the organizational hierarchy and societal structure makes a breakthrough almost impossible. The line of authority is clearly delineated. Communication is top-down. Decisions made by superiors cannot be repudiated and superiors rarely give feedback to their subordinates.

The majority will readily conform to the hierarchical order and succumb to the paternalistic and patriarchal restraint. The ambitious ones will try to align with their superiors, adopting a more conciliatory approach rather than one of defiance or ridicule. Winning an ally in one's superior is a definite leverage. In the Chinese society, there is great emphasis on relationship. Relationship comes before the task, and it is widely known that the ones who do well are usually those who are well-connected. Business people active in China trade believe there are three ingredients most important for success: communication, relation, and corruption. Perhaps it is too blatant to admit using back-door influence, but having the right connection really matters in China.

In the workplace, getting the work done is the prime concern. On-the-job training and application are done simultaneously. Emphasis is on sitting-by-Nellie type of training and hands-on practice. Formal and organized HRD is more often knowledge-based. An off-site HRD course will often contain elements of ideological reinforcement. During Mao's heyday, a factory hand trying to fix his worn-out machine would be reminded to read Mao's book, as if it were some kind of repair manual. How Mao's doctrines could remedy the mechanical malfunction remains a puzzle. Perhaps his wisdom shed some light and provided the eternal solution.

Now, we shall examine the issues arising from a learning situation between a learner and the HRD practitioner.

The Learning Situation

Positive traits for intercultural effectiveness
Figure 20.1 shows the attributes HRD practitioners will need.

Figure 20.1: Attributes for HRD Practitioners in China

1. Technical Competence, Functional Expertise
2. Personal Characteristics—Flexibility
3. Language Skills
4. Knowledge of the Host Culture
5. Cross-Cultural Skills

Let's examine each of these attributes.

Technical Competence, Functional Expertise
First, what can we contribute to the host country?

Personal Characteristics–flexibility
- Adaptability
- Tolerance of ambiguity
- Empathy, a negotiating instead of controlling style of conflict resolution
- High self-esteem and good interpersonal skills (liking to meet and be with people, interest in communicating)
- Interest in the assignment
- Eagerness to learn about another culture

Recognizing cultural differences—in value systems, thought processes and behavioral patterns—is vital. For instance, Chinese are more circumspect, whereas Westerners are direct in expressing what they want.

Language Skills

Language skills are useful but not an absolute must. Putonghua is the official spoken language. Most people in China can speak one or more other dialects, depending on the region they come from. The written language situation is less confusing.

Knowledge of the Host Culture

This means an understanding of the host country's:
- Legal and educational systems
- Political structure
- Economics
- Heritage
- Social structure and business practices

Cross-Cultural Skills

Cross-cultural skills include sensitivity to differences of style and communication and the ability to understand the unwritten or unexpressed rules of another culture. It includes nonverbal communication, like body language and eye contact. Some might take these "soft skills" lightly, but failure to use appropriate and courteous behavior in another culture will put us at a disadvantage.

Our prior learning is crucial to the success of an international assignment. It helps us adjust to the new situation in the host country and improve our project performance. We can use a variety of methods, described here on a continuum from least to most vigorous:
- Factual (area briefing, lectures, books)
- Analytical (classroom language training, case studies, culture assimilators)
- Experiential (interactive language training, role-plays, field trips, simulations, working with someone who has relevant experience, absorbing experience in the host country)

Selection of Learners

Consultants and practitioners working in China do not have the luxury of screening the participants for their HRD programs. Group size is normally an issue beyond their control. From an originally agreed number of 35, we had to cater to 60 in our management consulting course. Participants had varied education, work experience, and exposure to operations in a business environment other than state-owned enterprises.

Instruction is most effective if the participants are fully aware of its objectives. Unfortunately, the Chinese often base the selection of participants on very skimpy criteria. Furthermore, the organization's goals are never too explicit. The belief that the pursuit of knowledge is divine precludes any need to look at its pragmatic values—what can be achieved through HRD?

We observed that many of our participants had no sense of ownership. They saw hardly any profit in transferring their skills to their own workplace. They could not relate their learning to their future career goals and development needs. Moreover, participants are not chosen through any performance- and competence-based assessment. The acquisition of knowledge does not automatically guarantee the ability to apply it effectively.

Although we cannot have participants who will fully match our expectations, there are ways to remedy this situation. We can
- Describe the goals of the program
- Set up a demographic profile of the participants
- Send them (directly or through the coordinating body) detailed pre-course information
- Have them fill in a questionnaire to get a feel for perception and expectation of the program

Availability of Resources

HRD practitioners, used to easy access to all sorts of instructional aids and technologies, must prepare for the worst state of deprivation when working in China. You have to be more accommodating about facilities and availability of resources. It is prudent to draft a checklist of the items you need and another list for contingencies. Prior preparation can allow time for your sponsor or client to get items ready. This could include customs clearance if you need to bring such items as a computer or audiovisual and printed materials into the country.

A visit to the HRD venue is always helpful to avoid any last minute panic. You can also familiarize yourself with the environment and make the best of what is available. For instance, instead of a flip chart stand, I once used a wooden newspaper clip, each end tied to a piece of string, and hung it on the wall. I even recycled transparencies. You have to use your ingenuity to come up with practical solutions.

Allow ample time for translation of instructional materials. Proofread and check them. If possible, have someone who is conversant in both written and spoken Chinese read over the materials. Someone Chinese-born but raised overseas might not be able to read Chinese although they can speak in a Chinese dialect. Even professional translators might not know HRD-related terminology and jargon.

You should also make sure that the host's printer strictly follows the original layout. I had a disastrous experience when I discovered, much too late and beyond any remedy, that to save production costs all the page and paragraph spacing was eliminated. The handouts looked muddled and cramped, and my presentation was riddled with intermittent clarifications and cross-referencing.

In China, adult learners are accustomed to programmed instruction. One often finds them flipping back and forth through pages of the text.

If you need to work through an interpreter, good suggestions can be found in Chapter 5 by Zeace Nadler. There are a few particular points to remember about China. Get to know your interpreter. Examine the text together. Orient the interpreter to its content. Some terms might be foreign to the interpreter, especially terms where it was difficult to find an analogy or an equivalent for illustration. It is no easier even for fellow Chinese from Hong Kong and Taiwan. Vocabularies, especially technical and scientific vocabularies used in Taiwan, PRC, and Hong Kong, may have different literal expressions, even though they refer to the same object or element.

Try to use short sentences when making a presentation. A colleague of mine, in trying to pace his speech, paused every two seconds for his interpreter to repeat the part in Putonghua. However, because of the different grammatical structure the sentence lost its meaning when dissected into pieces. You should speak clearly, in a well-modulated, well-paced voice, and be sure that the participant materials are translated and culturally adapted.

Presentation Style

One of the things I enjoyed most in attending the ASTD annual conference, apart from catching up with old friends, was bringing home loads of new ideas, anecdotes, and little gimmicks. I have a weakness for games—just love them! However, although it is always tempting to try them out in our own presentations, you should carefully consider their relevance in a different cultural context. I was greatly impressed by a presenter from one of the sessions I attended recently. On each table we found a slice of bread, and the message he was trying to get across was: "Training Is the Bread of Life." It gave me a great idea for my Chinese audience. I made the statement shown in Figure 20.2, and I suggest that you consider it when you work in China.

Figure 20.2: Suggested Comparison of Learning and a Rice Bowl

> "Learning to life is like rice to a bowl. It gives us the vitality and essence of life. When it's empty, we need to fill it up again."

These are words of wisdom, teachings from philosophers that we can readily use. Try them on your Chinese friends—they can always tell you if they are appropriate or not.

Cultural differences have a major effect on learning, and the last thing we want is to become victims of our own cultural myopia.

Instructional Design and Delivery

In the West, we dedicate many efforts to learner-centered and directed program design. This is not so true in China, where there is almost total reliance on printed resources. As a result, learning is slow and restrictive, with learners accustomed to reading in a sequential linear manner. They expect to encounter information in a logical order determined in advance. Thoughts and ideas are confined by the constraints of the printed words. Text limits the reader's ability to forge logical and creative connections between old and new ideas and to synthesize them into conclusions.

However, we should readily apply the adult learning principles and practices in our program design and delivery. We should make it more learner-centered and participative. Adult learners think critically about themselves and their personal and organizational contexts. They are more inclusive and discriminating in their integration of experience.

You may find that in China the participants have difficulty accepting their "new" roles. It's not easy for them to become empowered learners and take an active role in the decision-making process. They find it is inappropriate to take direct action and initiative — instead, they expect to follow the authority of the instructor. This is especially trying for instructors with a Western orientation. They prefer to see learners as partners in the learning process. They encourage equality rather than control, directness instead of obliqueness.

I recall one time my American colleague told me that he did not know what to do with his class. I asked if they had walked out. He quickly said, "Oh, No! They are so quiet and they keep their heads down." My colleague is not the only one who has been baffled by the lack of eye contact from a Chinese class. It is not a sign of disrespect nor a lack of interest. Chinese consider it imprudent to look directly at their instructor. Likewise, the avoidance of confrontation and indication of agreement or disagreement will create unnecessary confusion if we are not aware of them.

Here are a few suggestions for optimizing the learning situation.

Learning climate

Try to provide a supportive environment that is responsive and conducive to personal risk-taking and change. Involve participants in decision-making exercises so they can learn how to consider options and reach higher levels of discrimination and integration.

Immediate application

Relate program content to the participant's personal and professional problems and needs.

Content Learning (Knowledge) vs. Process Learning (Experience) vs. Thinking

There is a general perception that learning is knowledge-based rather than competency-based. Everything is right or wrong. Knowledge is a collection of facts to memorize; authority figures (such as instructors) have all the answers. Rather than a learning experience, instruction is a series of education events.

However, learning is not simply amassing information, but acquiring new information and high-level thinking skills. There can be a variety of opinions and viewpoints on an issue. We can test different perspectives through our cognitive, problem-solving, and reasoning skills.

I recall teaching the subject of creative thinking. My class got more out of the exercises than the theoretical aspects, and they readily applied them during the course. It was amazing. Once they realized they could unlock themselves and jump out from their old mindsets, they had a better chance of dealing with and solving problems.

Instructional Methods

You can use a variety of methods, but with all of them you must encourage participants to take personal responsibility for their own learning.

The conventional model in China is classroom instruction, with emphasis on theoretical aspects. Typically, an instructor will enter the classroom and immediately address the topic. This is appropriate for dealing with technical subject matter. But conceptual learning calls for a different approach. To start with, devote some time to building rapport. You will find this a worthwhile investment of time.

Plenary sessions and small group discussions

You can balance large plenary sessions with small group discussions and project teams. Engage them in

- Intensive discussion, critical analysis, problem posing, reflection and alternative scenario assessment of the action plan
- Rotating membership (group relationships foster reciprocal learning)
- Experiential exercises (group projects, situation simulations, case studies, role plays)

Team instruction

You should also consider team instruction in program delivery, especially when the course lasts more than one week. Intellectual stimulation that accompanies sharing with, and playing off, each other can generate more energy. It introduces occasional light touches (useful if a presenter gets too intense) and helps to break down barriers to learning. Colleagues can often supplement, emphasize, redirect, clarify, or enrich the contributions made by the "up-front" team member, either during a pause or as a graceful interruption.

Preparation is crucial to the success of the team. Allow plenty of time for preparation in
- Producing materials
- Marshalling resources
- Making organizational and other decisions
- Agreeing on individual and joint responsibilities
- Sharing information about intended relationships between perceived needs and the planned activities

When two or more people work together in presenting and managing an HRD session, the frequent transfer of responsibility for up-front tasks must be done in a natural, fluid, and graceful manner. This includes speaking and leading discussions.

A Unified Approach

Figure 20.3 highlights the differences between the Western and host cultures, comparing their effect on the mode of adult learning, designing learning programs, instructing, instructional strategies, and evaluation.

Figure 20.3: Comparison of HRD Characteristics in China and the West

	Characteristics of Western Culture	Characteristics of Chinese Culture
Adult Learning Orientation	Life centered, holistic approach.	Task-centered, problem-centered.
Climate	Essential to establish a climate conducive to learning. Mutual respect. Collaborativeness supportiveness, trust. Instructor as facilitator or helper. Active inquiry.	Classroom setting; formal relationships with instructor. Control. Competitiveness. Authority figure, the ultimate problem solver. passive reception.
Instructional Strategies	Openness. Use variety of learning methodologies, both experimental and experiential.	High Anxiety, defensiveness. Mostly lectures, modeling.

Figure 20.3: Comparison of HRD Characteristics in China and the West
                (concluded)

Evaluation	Jointly by instructor and participants. Qualitative (such as participant observation, in-depth interviews, analysis of performance changes etc.).	Solely by instructor. Content-based (e.g. written test).

Recognize differences in cultures and adapt your instructional techniques to them. To achieve desired results, HRD consultants and practitioners operating internationally need to

- Identify the dominant characteristics so as to understand the why of many practices of the host country which otherwise may be confusing or seem arbitrary
- Recognize the diversity of ways to obtain common ends
- Remain objective; refrain from being judgmental and trapped in comparisons of your own and host countries
- Find the means to integrate
- Balance enthusiasm with realism

About the Author

Florence H. C. Ho is Human Resources Officer at Cariboo College in Kamloops, British Columbia, Canada. Having spent most of her life in Hong Kong, she moved to Canada just before writing this chapter. Previously, she was Training and Development Manager, Coopers & Lybrand in Hong Kong. Earlier, she was Staff Development Officer at the Hong Kong Productivity Council. She has presented papers at various regional and international conferences and has also lectured at the Copenhagen School of Economics and the University of Lund in Sweden.

CHAPTER 21

Tailoring Events for the People's Republic of China: An Example

Angus Reynolds

This chapter presents a specific example of the general problems involved in working cross-culturally and internationally. It explores the question: How should a meeting be conducted with Chinese? It provides a limited extension of Florence Ho's ideas and examples in Chapter 20 of this book. It proposes to help readers in preparing for business relationships with Chinese.

The People's Republic of China (PRC) was essentially closed to the west during the 28-year period from 1949 until 1977. Current business, social, economic, and political situations in China continue to evolve but are utterly unlike those before 1949. Despite the changes since 1977, relatively few U.S. persons have experience in business dealings with Chinese from China.

Business experience with Chinese from other locations, although valuable in its own right, is of limited value in China. The form of government and economy in China since 1949 is unique, and its political and social institutions remain unlike those encountered anywhere else that ethnic Chinese do business.

Multinational corporations vary greatly in the preparation that they give for international contact. Cultural preparation is important for employees, even those who are only going to another country on a temporary assignment or will be meeting and working with persons visiting from another country. The lack of significant preparation for these situations is a paradox. The cost, in any terms, is little, while the potential for great harm to a business relationship is substantial.

Cross-Cultural Business Encounters With Chinese

China is a large developing country. People from the United States consider it a "difficult" country, meaning that it is very different from their country and unfamiliar to most of them. But the potential importance of the China market for products and services is enormous, particularly in some business areas. The competition is keen, and the need by any company for the best representation is high. The entire industrialized world is competing for a share of this business. Failure to complete successful business negotiations and unsatisfactory operation of projects can have costly results.

The discovery that the China trade was a new and different market reflected in contemporary accounts. There is some sign that business in China may differ importantly from projects in other countries. U.S. business people find that dealing with the Chinese is different from dealing with other nationals, such as Mexicans or Canadians. Seligman (1983) reported that many Westerners are uncomfortable around Chinese officials because they are uncertain about the proper protocol for dealing with them. This chapter will explore that subject.

Robert Kohls said that the culture-blindness of U.S. companies shows itself. We expect the foreign national to do all the bending. The president of one company doing business in China said: "We're asking our Chinese partners' people to significantly change their habits and the way they run the business."

Good advice

Many more firms have negotiated with the Chinese than have actually secured business. Perhaps for that reason, there have been many suggestions for negotiating with the Chinese. Since negotiation is a prelude to business, it would be wise to consider them. Based on the advice offered by business people who have negotiated with the Chinese, Rosalie Tung (1982) derived the "golden rules" for such negotiations. She dubs these the PRC's of doing business with China, as shown in Figure 21.1.

Figure 21.1: Golden Rules

Patience	Research	Competence
Preparation	Respect	Cost
Persistence	Rested	Consistency

These are expanded nicely by Jane Ren (1980), who suggests 10 principles for negotiating and doing business with the Chinese:

- Patience
- Perseverance
- Persistence (stamina)
- Flexibility

- Friendliness (sincerity)
- Firmness (at the right time)
- Frankness (honesty)
- Detailed knowledge of the product (technical staffing required)
- Tact (including sense of humor)
- Communications (clear, concise language)

Sandy Fowler worked with Chinese while representing the U.S. Navy. She approached dealing with Chinese from their cultural viewpoint. The important points she identified for understanding the Chinese are

- Danwei—the work group
- Quan-xi—network of obligations rules of etiquette
- Mianzi—"face"
- Renao—hot and noisy (Fowler, 1984)

A set of guidelines for negotiations presented by Wilson in 1974 are still worthy of consideration today. He recommends the following:

- Make preparations for negotiations with the Chinese. Assemble at least 12 complete sets of the following items, two sets of which should be air-mailed as far in advance as possible to the Chinese and ten sets of which should be carried with your negotiating team:

  1. Corporate annual statement for the current and five previous years.
  2. Brochure or pamphlet containing pictures and text generally introducing the company.
  3. All business brochures, pamphlets, catalogs, and like items, illustrating your facilities, products, and achievements.
  4. Copies of "House Paper" or corporate magazine for the past year, if available (read to ensure that it does not include discourteous materials).
  5. Newspaper stories or releases that show effective uses of your product or constructive social values.

- Choose a negotiator or negotiating team as early as possible. Include a vice-president or equivalent. Team members should be sensitive people, preferably with warmth and quiet dignity, able to communicate well and to persuade in English.

- Negotiating team members should read at least the following books[1] and articles:
  1. Edgar Snow, *Red Star Over China*
  2. Edgar Snow, *Red China Today*
  3. Barbara W. Tuchman, *Stilwell and the American Experience in China, 1911-45*
  4. John King Fairbank, *The United States and China*
  5. Ross Terrill, *800,000,000 – The Real China*
  6. Chang Hsin-hai, *America and China*
  7. Francis L. K. Hsu, *Americans and Chinese*
  8. Boarman and Mugar, Eds., *Trade With China*

- Show a color slide presentation or a motion picture with a professional commentary in English introducing the company, its facilities, its history, its product (shown in production and in operation), and other relevant aspects of favorable import.

- Have special training in round-table sessions conducted by experts in Chinese attitudes, procedures, manners, and customs.

- Technical or similar staff should prepare specific presentations for negotiators.

Meeting With a Delegation of Chinese

A first step in trying to secure business in China is to host a delegation of Chinese. Preparation should include preparing a corporate briefing paper, a China briefing, and meeting planning. I have planned or participated in several business meetings with Chinese. In addition, I conducted a study to learn the practices of U.S. Fortune 500 companies who were active or interested in business with China. Information gathered in that study (Reynolds, 1986) is discussed here.

Corporate Briefing Paper
Corporate briefing papers are a potential tool for orienting employees for a meeting with Chinese. A briefing paper on China should contain at least the following contents:
  - Recent China events
  - China trade
  - Chinese topics specific to the organization's business
  - PRC key organizations
  - Protocol

[1]Many good books have been written since these recommendations were given. Supplement these classics with some more recent titles.

My study found that, of the companies surveyed, only mine had a China briefing paper. It is unlikely that employees who will only meet once or twice with the Chinese will receive instructor-led training.[2] Yet, they should be prepared. This is the "professional" way to get ready for a visit.

China briefing

I asked, "Do you include a China briefing paper?" Based on some responses, it appeared that some organizations that supplied briefings in session format answered with the information about those briefings. Therefore, the information collected refers to a briefing in either paper or session format.

This activity received more and generally stronger positive responses than any other. All the industry groups except petroleum showed 50 percent or greater "yes" responses.

I compared the largest 100 and next 400 companies, and companies of all sizes said that they use a China briefing.

There was no strong relationship between industry category and use of a China briefing paper except for the petroleum and motor vehicles industries. The tendencies of these two groups were in opposite directions. The petroleum industry group tended not to use a China briefing, while in the motor vehicles industry group all companies did.

Among study participants, those with a "sale completed" had a much larger "yes" response to this training activity, compared with the "no sale" group.

National Council briefing

The National Council for U.S. China Trade prepares corporate staff about to be sent to China. The content of their China-specific briefing is organized as shown below:

- Practical aspects of living in China
- Overview of the political and economic organization of Chinese industry including the decision-making process
- Cultural differences
- Protocol, customs and etiquette
- Chinese language

---

[2]I did not have this experience with a Chinese group when I worked for a Fortune 500 company. However, in meetings with Saudi Arabs, the behavior of one of our group members was so far from what could be tolerated that the Saudis asked that he "no longer meet." This particular project did not materialize. Was it related to the poor impression created by an individual? How many other groups have been offended, but did not complain?

OPTIONAL:
- Practical aspects of opening an office in China.
- Regulations concerning registration, customs, visas, taxes and local labor. Preparing a budget for a China representative office.

Another briefing
The content of the China program conducted by another group provides insight into history and politics, analysis of social and cultural difference, and language training.

Conduct of China-specific cross-cultural programs
I also asked whether companies provide China-specific cross-cultural programs. Slightly more than one-fourth of the companies indicated that they did.

The strongest use of these programs was in the aerospace industry. Sixty-seven percent of the aerospace organizations reported that they use such programs. The petroleum, electronics, and appliance industries tended not to conduct them.

A marked relationship existed between whether a company had completed a sale and practices of conducting China specific cross-cultural programs. Also, the difference between these business-success related groups was greatest for this practice. Companies that have completed a sale are more likely to provide these programs.

The length of the programs ranged from one-half day to seven days. The specific lengths were one-half, two, three, five, and seven.

There was no difference between the largest 100 and next 400 companies in conduct of China-specific cross-cultural programs. The organizations reported that from one to 20 employees take part in their programs.

Conduct of general cross-cultural programs
As a comparison between getting ready for business with China and other countries, I asked about general cross-cultural programs. Slightly over one-fourth said that they do conduct general programs. There was no significant relationship between company size and conducting a program.

Again, a relationship existed between whether a participating company completed a sale and whether it conducted a general cross-cultural program. Responding companies that have completed a sale are more likely to conduct a general cross-cultural program than those that have not.

Amplified comments on the programs
I asked these business people for added information about their programs. There was substantial amplification. Here are a few of the comments they supplied; each comment represents a different company:

- "Although through our 14 Divisions we have established initial business in China, we haven't done it properly (or nearly as effectively) as we could have with better training."
- "Preparation is not really *formal* training—more a sharing of experience by employees who have had some with the Chinese."
- "...conducts in-house training programs on an 'as required basis' for a specific assignment. We also utilize the experience of other employees who have recently lived and/or traveled in China."
- "Employees include native-born Chinese with language capability. Non-Chinese employees have done extensive reading to familiarize themselves on culture and business practices."
- "All done informally. None done in a classroom setting."
- "Past programs have been informal, in-house programs based on personal experience during previous visits to China or negotiations with Chinese. No language training was involved...."
- "For employees resident in the PRC, we select Chinese-Americans with appropriate technical/business experience. We rely also on employees of Chinese descent in our divisions' regional offices in Singapore. Employees who come into contact with visiting Chinese in the U.S. are briefed on protocol with regard to cultural difference and usual business practices in the PRC."
- "At present we do have a ...China company that is staffed by both local national and...employees on international assignment. Many of these assignees speak Mandarin and are therefore able to converse with our customers in their native language. This negates the need to provide special language training. All of our assignees receive a briefing before they go on an international assignment and an additive briefing on working and living in China when they arrive. The on-site briefing is conducted by the...China personnel staff and is standard procedure for our assignees throughout the world."
- "We do prepare our employees for work in China. The degree to which we prepare the employees depends on the nature of their work, the length of their stay in China, the lead time we have, and the training resources we have in each particular case. In principle, employees being sent to China for a project are given an oral briefing and reading materials by the PRC program staff. Employees assigned to permanent positions in China are sent to (name of consultant company deleted) for country familiarity training, except for those who are already familiar with the country's social and cultural environment.
- "Although a formal training program for employees assigned to work in China is generally desirable, we have found that the pressure of doing business does not allow this luxury. In addition, we found that since we do have many Chinese-origin employees involved in our China business, it is relatively easy to provide the subject employees with informal, but nevertheless very useful, country-specific indoctrination."

- "We feel that the most critical part of a China familiarization program is the psychological preparation of the employee to not only anticipate the inconvenient living conditions in China, but also to appreciate the fact that the Chinese people have made much recent progress towards improving such conditions and are proud of their achievements."

Why Conduct any program at all?

Perhaps the most telling information was provided by those companies who do not conduct any program. Many comments were collected that bear on the situation. The following comments were among the most interesting provided to explain their rationale:

- "We are satisfied that we know how to work the China Market."
- "...has no formal human resources development program for employees that either work, live, or visit the People's Republic of China."
- "We don't see the need of language program due to transient assignment and the Chinese provide translators on the project."
- "Our office provides individual briefings and training on the specific circumstances likely to be encountered by company traders going to China. As the corporate structure among our 36 divisions is relatively loose, each division generally develops its own China Plan, usually with the assistance of this office, which is provided as a corporate resource funded by...overhead. There is a need for more detailed cultural training, but people who have worked in China for the past 10-12 years in our divisions are generally disdainful of so-called China experts who claim to offer advice and training based on relatively thin experience here." (Received from the Beijing office of one responding company.)
- "Training for China has involved meeting a large number of people who have experience in business and/or government relations in the PRC. A network of contacts has been set up, which continues to be a source of information. Selection of people with Chinese responsibilities has been limited to individuals with extensive international experience and, consequently, generalized programs were not indicated."
- "Personnel employed to handle business and marketing in China are Chinese with Chinese culture background. Therefore we do not have language, culture, and business graces training programs for them other than our own management educational training program for our international worldwide business."

- "We do not provide...for the following reasons:
    1. The number of staff does not justify an effort.
    2. The turnover among these employees is low and does not justify
       an effort.
    3. Cross-cultural experience level—especially with Asian cultures—
       is extremely high among current staff.
    4. The professional ability level of current staff is high."

The survey asked about training for U.S. national employees. The confidence of
the companies not providing training is especially interesting in light of the limited
success they enjoy.

Recommendations for Meeting With Chinese

The decision process in China is complicated and expensive. The final judgment
is seldom made by one person but is the consensus of a great number of involved
people. Remember that the Chinese government is a participant, and any conclusion
must fit into government directives.

With consideration of the ideas of Nicholas Ludlow (1978), Herbert Azif (1981),
and Florence Ho, here are my recommendations for planning a meeting with PRC
representatives.

Before the visit

- Appoint a visit coordinator.
- Gather information on the delegation: composition (will decision-
  makers be present?), industry represented, other sponsoring groups.
- Establish the purpose of the group.
- Understand and accept the need for lengthy negotiations.
- Make a schedule.
- Select sites to be visited—suit the schedule to the delegation.
- Arrange transportation.
- Use your own interpreter only if qualified—otherwise use the Chinese
  interpreter.
- For longer stays identify appropriate sources of food.
- Arrange press coverage.
- Carefully select the members of your meeting team.
- If you have ethnic Chinese employees in relevant positions, include
  them in the meeting.

- Prepare a China briefing paper for everyone involved, including:
    1. Game plan for the encounter
    2. Protocol
    3. Sensitiveness
    4. Topics for discussion
- Plan, carefully prepare, verify, and rehearse your presentation.

During the visit

- Regard the Chinese as complete equals.
- Establish an informal and pleasant atmosphere.
- Be modest and avoid excessive flattery.
- Do not try to force or make any threats or conditions.
- Making an impression of being reliable and trustworthy is more important in the long run than achieving a signed contract.
- Deliver a presentation on your organization.
- Conduct plant, laboratory, or other tours.
- Host social occasion:
    1. Provide seating arrangement
    2. Make prepared toast
    3. Avoid talking business unless the Chinese raise the subject
- Present a small gift to each member of the visiting delegation.

After the visit

- Follow-up.
- An invitation should always be accepted.

A relationship may exist between training and success in the China trade. For-profit organizations can hardly afford to ignore this possibility. Based on the relatively small cost of providing training compared with the substantial rewards of business success, China-related preparatory training can be recommended. Major private-sector organizations should more aggressively use HRD activities related to the employee's work in China or with Chinese.

References

Azif, H. *China Trade: A Guide to Doing Business With the People's Republic of China*. Coral Springs, FL: Intraworld Trade News, 1981, p. 49.

Fowler, S. *The Chinese Culture: Really Getting It*. Address at Metropolitan Washington, DC Chapter, American Society for Training and Development meeting, Nov. 14, 1984.

Ludlow, N. *Hosting a Delegation From the PRC*. Washington, DC: National Council for U.S.-China Trade, 1978.

Ren, J. *Doing Business in Today's China*. Published for the American Chamber of Commerce Hong Kong by the South China Morning Post, 1980, p. 44.

Reynolds, A. *Intercultural Training Programs Conducted for U.S. Multinational Corporation Employees Doing Business With the People's Republic of China*. (doctoral dissertation, George Washington University). Ann Arbor, MI: University Microfilms International, 1986.

Seligman, S. "The Shirt-Sleeves Guide to Chinese Corporate Etiquette". *The China Business Review*, Jan.- Feb. 1983, p. 9.

Tung, A. *Expatriate Selection for Overseas Assignment*. Paper presented at the Annual Meeting of the Academy of International Business, Las Vegas, NV, June 1979.

CHAPTER 22

Management Training Contrasts and Comparisons: U.S. and Hong Kong

Don Roberts

"Nobody ever asked me that question before!" So spoke the Managing Director of Hong Kong Telephone when asked why he wanted management training established. He had just completed his eighth year in the job, and had led the company from the edge of bankruptcy to winning the award for the best utility service in Southeast Asia. It was financially sound and led all telecommunication companies in the world in the use of new technology. So the question— "Why do you need management training? You seem to have managed very well." —was to the point.

After looking out the window for about two minutes (it seemed much longer at the time), he turned back and a very productive discussion followed. What had started out to be a short get-acquainted meeting became a serious discussion of the current and future problems faced by the company. We discussed how management training might contribute to their solution.

This chapter describes the training strategy that evolved to respond to the problems identified in that initial discussion. It describes the differences in how a U.S. telecommunications company (C&P Telephone) and Hong Kong Telephone introduced a behavior-modeling approach. It includes the cultural adaptations used for program design, the selection and preparation of trainers, program implementation, and program maintenance. Current issues and future considerations are discussed in closing.

Background

To better understand the chapter, you should know a little about the author. Also, let's review the events that brought Hong Kong Telephone to the point of needing a systematic approach to the training and development of its managers.

First, a few words about my background. I worked for C&P Telephone for 34 years before taking early retirement in January, 1982. I spent the first 15 of those years in a number of management jobs, progressing through the ranks to become a senior field manager. Senior staff jobs at the corporate headquarters followed. Then, I moved to Personnel and served as the corporate college recruiter before being reassigned to take a fresh look at management training for C&P—then a company with about 43,000 employees. My title evolved over time until it became Director of Management Training and Organization Development. The years that followed included several short-term assignments at AT&T, the most important of which was as an assessor on the landmark Management Progress Study staff during the 1960s. I also participated in the introduction of behavior-modeling-based Supervisory Relationships Training (SRT) during 1974 and 1975. To keep up with the rapidly changing management training field, I returned to school in 1976, receiving my Masters in Human Resource Development from George Washington University in 1978.

In June of 1981, I participated in a study tour to the Peoples Republic of China (PRC). After a productive five weeks, we stopped in Hong Kong before returning to the United States. While in Hong Kong, I visited Hong Kong Telephone (HKT) and met their new General Manager of Administration. He had recently joined HKT and was charged with modernizing the personnel system, establishing the management training function, and creating both strategic and manpower planning capabilities. By January of 1982, I had taken early retirement from C&P Telephone and was back in Hong Kong as the first manager of HKT's newly created Management Development Division (MDD).

As mentioned earlier, Hong Kong Telephone had weathered a service and financial crisis in the mid-1970s. As a result of improved service, the company had grown very quickly—from about 7,000 employees in 1977 to just over 12,000 by the summer of 1981. The increase in management and supervisory jobs (called Senior Staff) had been even more dramatic, from 380 persons in 1977 to 852 by mid-1981. The company had an active policy of localizing the management and supervisory staff. All the additions (more than doubling the size of the Senior Staff) had been local Hong Kong Cantonese. Everyone with any supervisory or management experience had been promoted at least once—many several times.

The result was a large, new group facing the challenges of middle management for the first time. They were directing the efforts of first line managers, most of whom were brand new to their jobs. "It was the best of times; it was the worst of times. . . ."

With continued growth expected, it was clear that the company had to find a way to accelerate the development of managers at all levels, to assure a steady supply of persons qualified to fill management and supervisory jobs in the future. My new boss and I had corresponded during the Fall of 1981 and had agreed that a behavior-modeling-based course would be an excellent way to begin the work of our new division. When I arrived in January, negotiations were well under way to obtain a course from Development Dimensions International (DDI). The course was Interaction Management (IM) and was quite similar to the SRT course that had been so successful in C&P Telephone.

Hong Kong Telephone had a policy and a set of procedures for introducing expatriate managers to the company. Called "Assimilation," it consisted of visits and discussions with senior and middle managers in all parts of the company. The number and depth of these discussions were tailored to meet the needs of each of the expatriates to enable them better to carry out their responsibilities. This was particularly advantageous to me and gave me an opportunity to conduct an in-depth management and supervisory needs analysis.

From almost the first day, it was clear to me that "a telephone company was a telephone company." The needs of HKT managers and supervisors were quite similar to those that I had worked with for years. It was equally clear that the forces that had stimulated the development of SRT in the U.S. were also at work in Hong Kong. In the early 1970s the Bell System, like every other U.S. company, was concerned about the need for better work quality, improved productivity, better employee morale, and other work-related improvements. Supervisors were not effective in dealing with the "new work force." At that time in the U.S. telecommunications industry, many persons were moving into what were, for them, nontraditional jobs. Women moved into technical and craft jobs, while black and Spanish-surname Americans moved into positions previously not open to them. Also, those entering the work force were younger, better-educated, and had attitudes and values about work quite different from those of their predecessors. To add to the confusion, there were rapid changes in the basic technology of the industry.

Many of these same issues arose as I listened to managers and supervisors tell me about the problems in Hong Kong Telephone. For example, improving quality had become a key priority and increasing productivity was increasingly critical to survival. The growth of the company and the high cost of expatriate managers made it imperative to use local Chinese managers and supervisors in ever-increasing numbers. These new managers and supervisors were younger, better educated, and certainly had different attitudes toward work, and the basic technology of telecommunications was in the midst of another leap forward. So, an SRT-like approach to improving management and supervisory skills to meet these kinds of problems was appropriate, and the first training course offered was Interaction Management (IM).

Program Design

Before beginning to design any program, it is good policy to carefully examine the environment in which the program will run. In the U.S., C&P Telephone had a well-developed, established management training and development function which included a family of courses in the traditional subjects. There was also a separate support group to provide process consultation services to line and staff managers throughout the company at senior and middle management levels. Therefore, a "culture" already existed that accepted and practiced the values and style advocated by behavior-modeling theory. In this situation we could introduce SRT as a "stand alone" course supported by the larger curriculum of the established management training function.

The situation at Hong Kong Telephone was quite different. HKT had never had in-house management or supervisory training. There was a substantial technical training school that used the lecture method. There was also a half-day, lecture-based orientation course, the Assimilation program, and a one-day course for new supervisors about management theories.

HKT was a British-owned and-managed company, with a traditional, autocratic, bureaucratic management style quite different from C&P Telephone. This style is not well suited to coping with rapid and constant change. So, the question was how to install a behavior-modeling-based training program—which is quite at home in a participative management setting—in an autocratic setting.

This question was paramount in my mind as I systematically moved through the company during my three-month assimilation program. As I listened to managers and supervisors describe their workplaces, staff, problems, and concerns, a set of principles and processes emerged that became a framework for building our new Division and guiding the design and introduction of a new approach to training. The principles were

- Technical training is primary.
- The Management Development Division provides support.
- There should be a balanced focus on company and employee goals.
- Individuals are responsible for their own learning.
- Adults learn best when four conditions prevail.
- Learning is natural and continuous through life.

Principles

Technical training is primary. In a rapidly changing high-technology business, people have to be trained and then continually retrained to keep up with the technical aspects of their jobs. HKT was proud that it had the largest technical training school in Southeast Asia.

The Management Development Division provides support. "Real" management training takes place on the job with a good boss. The best you can hope for in the five to ten days of off-the-job training an employee gets is to accelerate the development of carefully selected skills needed to improve performance on the job. Therefore, bosses must participate in selecting the training required and be able to support the transfer of learning from the classroom to the workplace.

Balanced focus on company and employee goals. When we clearly express a company goal, employees have the opportunity to achieve their personal objectives within that goal context. This enhances motivation and increases productivity.

Individuals are responsible for their own learning. While trainers are responsible for the effective design and delivery of training courses (the teaching), individuals are *always* in control of what they learn.

Adults learn best when four conditions prevail. These are when
- They participate actively in the learning process
- What they learn is directly applicable to their work
- What they learn enables them to perform better
- What they learn is reinforced on the job

Learning is natural and continuous through life. The changes affecting the workplace *will* continue, so we need to keep searching for ways to be more effective in learning how to adapt and cope.

Processes
With these principles serving as strategy, the following processes became the tactics for implementation:

Focus on local senior staff. Since a large number of senior staff people were added between 1977 and 1982, the average length of service on the job was about two years. Incumbents in these jobs were approaching full technical competence. Therefore, training to facilitate their managerial effectiveness was important and timely.

Continuous needs analysis. Every class in every course would complete a specifically designed needs analysis form covering all management and supervisory skills. This data would provide a current view of what the participating supervisors and managers believed to be their training needs. The data could be summarized by department, and department bosses could then validate it. The result would be an always available total picture of the training programs needed, by department, to focus on improving job performance.

Training support system. This procedure would provide a method for clearly understanding what the trainees and their bosses believe is necessary for improved job performance. We could then provide that training, and follow up with the trainee and the boss to see if what was learned really helped improve job performance. Then, we could make any specific revisions required.

Extended delivery system (EDS). This was a new concept for HKT and it was only applicable to selected courses. Carefully chosen line managers would participate in the delivery of training courses. We would select line managers with outstanding performance ratings who had performed well in the training course they were going to teach from the organization level above the level of the trainees. There would be five steps in the process to equip these line managers with the skills needed to be effective:

- A trainer skills workshop
- Observation of the training
- Co-training the group with an experienced trainer
- Conducting the course under supervision
- Conducting the course on their own

The line managers selected would be available to conduct training ten days per year. (After the first year of implementing EDS, the managers' bosses were pleased with the increased confidence and presentation skills acquired by the managers and supervisors who participated. There was always a competition for the part-time trainer slots available.)

Integrated curriculum. This meant building a common language of management terms into all the courses across levels of management. Also, at each level from a person's first appointment as a supervisor through successive promotions to a senior management position, they would complete the appropriate skill training.

Action learning in small groups. Acquiring skills for use on the job does require practicing them in class. Therefore, it is imperative that class sizes are small—from six to ten students in most courses.

Modular design. We obviously didn't want to require all supervisors and managers to attend all courses. We built the curriculum of skill modules. People would take only those modules that they and their boss felt necessary for their current job or for their next assignment. These modules would be one, two, or three days in length. This would minimize time away from the job and encourage practicing the skills soon after training. We planned to offer the IM course one day per week for six weeks. This would allow participants plenty of time to practice each set of skills learned.

Management and interpersonal skills. Clearly, supervisory effectiveness requires both technical competence and interpersonal skill. Technical competence includes the generic management skills of planning, organizing, leading, and controlling. In addition to separate interpersonal skill courses, all management skill courses would have the interpersonal skills needed for implementation built in as reinforcement.

Information and records systems. To complete the cycle, every successful training division must have four processes in place. They are for
- Obtaining information from its host organization about needs
- Communicating back to the organization about the programs developed to respond to those needs
- Specifying when the programs will be conducted
- Keeping appropriate records of the training experienced

All were essential to establish and maintain the new Management Development Division.

Given these principles and processes, we constructed the framework shown in Figure 22.1. It illustrates the flow of management-skills-training opportunities between the boundaries of technical training and on-the-job coaching, counseling, and appraisal. This became a key part of the meeting introducing our new Division to the organization and helped us cope with the political issues, especially since it focused only on the future. The IM design matched our needs, principles, and processes very well. Later I will explain how we introduced it to senior management.

One further strategy was to start all of our training courses as high in the organization as possible. Then managers initially trained would be able to coach their subordinates when they received training later. We used this strategy of "cascading" new training down the organization in introducing every course, beginning with our first IM.

Selection and Preparation of Trainers

The strategy adopted by AT&T and C&P Telephone, given the managerial environment, was to begin with experienced management trainers, who were certified as senior trainers. They developed and certified a network of line managers to function as the on-going training delivery team. Since the value system for management training was well-developed throughout the company, this was a reasonable strategy that worked well. Of course, those line managers who participated part-time in delivering SRT there were periodically observed in the classroom and given an annual skills updating workshop.

Figure 22.1: Management Development Plan

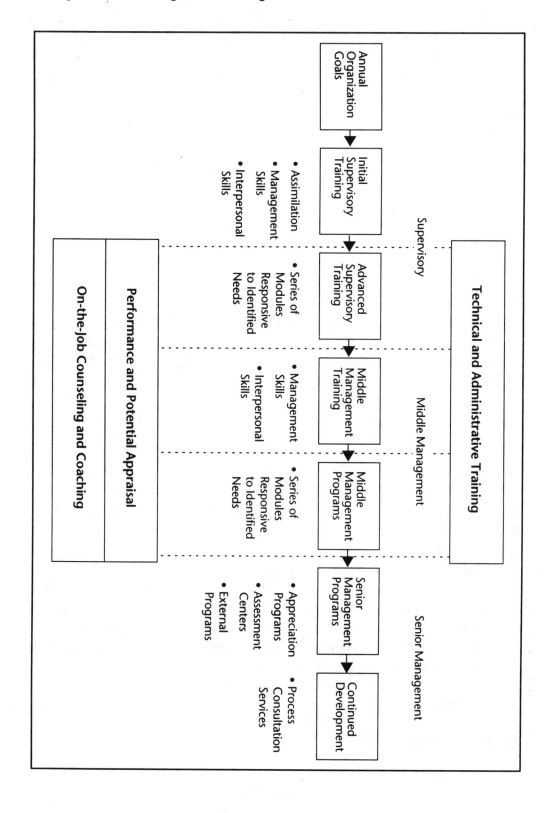

The Hong Kong Telephone plan had to be quite different. DDI provided HKT with a senior consultant, experienced in the ways of Southeast Asia, to train and certify our first behavior-modeling trainers. We began IM by using the Technical Training School (TTS) staff who were conducting the existing introductory and supervisory courses. The head of the TTS, who was well respected by his Engineering colleagues, supported the IM approach and even agreed to attend the training and serve as the first IM Program Director. This sent strong signals throughout Hong Kong Telephone, and since the Engineering Branch employed 80 percent of the company's staff, was critical for making the transition as smooth as possible. This was a key political event in establishing a new direction in training. It equipped the TTS head with the background needed to personally convince the Managing Director and his Engineering Branch colleagues to proceed.

Two Assistant Managers recruited for the new Management Development Division (MDD) from outside the company also attended the certification training, which was conducted off-site. Some participants achieved certification and some received provisional certification. Using English proved to be a stumbling block for some new IM trainers, so we dubbed Cantonese on the videos and presented lectures in Cantonese in the on-going classes. We used this approach in other courses and found that presenting new concepts in the learner's first language speeds up the process of understanding. As soon as the new IM program was up and running (about three months), we transferred the trainers and the program to MDD. One of the new Assistant Managers took over as Program Manager to complete the transition.

We had to consider differences in the participant populations. At C&P and AT&T, the managers and supervisors to be trained lived in a semi-participative environment. OD consulting was familiar to senior managers, so reinforcement of the SRT/IM principles was natural. The management was also well-ordered, with spans of control ranging from four to ten employees per supervisor. To use a farm analogy, the ground had been plowed and fertilized. It was ready for good seed which *would* be watered and tended as it grew.

Again, the situation at Hong Kong Telephone was quite different. There was a fundamental need for good communications, especially due to the rapid growth and increased complexity of the organization, but there was suspicion rather than acceptance of management training. There was no tradition of the values needed to sustain a behavior-modeling-based program like IM. In addition, the rapid growth had not allowed time to sort out a rational, stable organization structure. Spans of control were erratic, with a number of one-to-one reporting relationships and some as high as fifty staff members to one supervisor. A large number of new jobs had been created, including computer programmers, sales persons, and number of highly skilled electronic specialists.

All this made the identification and selection of participants for the initial stages of the IM program of special importance. We built the IM program on the assumption that a supervisor should have at least four direct reporting subordinates to provide enough opportunities week-to-week to practice the newly acquired skills. However, it was difficult to find this situation at the first line of management across the organization, so a new set of tactics was required.

We decided to begin by enhancing the skills of the second level of management, where the number of direct reporting subordinates was sufficient. Then we would train the first-level supervisors, who interacted directly with technicians and clerks. The theory was that by the time this second stage got underway, some reorganization would have taken place. What is more important, we would have a built-in reinforcement system for the first-line supervisors. This would be the initial step in beginning to move the organization culture away from its autocratic roots toward a more participative management approach. As we completed our course materials we decided to strengthen the communication linkage between the boss and subordinates involved in the IM process. We wanted to build a foundation for the development of skill in participative managing.

Our plan consisted of informing bosses, during the briefing on their role in IM, that their subordinates were to meet with them to review what they had learned after each of the six sessions. This established a series of regular, work-related discussions between the participants and their bosses. Since this made it "OK" for subordinates to brief their bosses, we had established the first step of improving communications.

Program Implementation

At C&P and AT&T the management/supervisor team was reasonably mature. The plan was to do the needs analysis to identify the most needed specific subjects or modules. Based on this needs analysis, we would select the materials from the large library of videos developed by Development Dimensions International and conduct the training. We would schedule the training for one day per week over five weeks, at the rate of two modules each week. The use of line managers was an important consideration since C&P was spread over a large geographical area, and most of the work sites were from 50 to 400 miles from the central training center. Training and certifying line managers enabled us to conduct SRT near the workplace of participants, which made attendance cheaper for the company and less burdensome for participants.

At Hong Kong Telephone, travel to the training center was not a problem, because Hong Kong is geographically small by comparison. All the potential participants worked within 15 miles of the Technical Training School (TTS) and had attended courses there often, so that is where we established the offices of the Management Development Division and our training rooms. As the program grew, we moved to the nearby Operations Building to have more space. A well-equipped training room was dedicated to the delivery of IM, with permanently mounted plasticized wall charts, a large screen TV, and all the other things needed to support the program. Due to the language issues, and the newness of the participative approach, we decided to conduct the course for one day per week over six weeks. We limited the number of modules to one per week. We selected the Operations Branch for the first phase, and we divided it into four geographic areas, each divided into the same four departments. Each of the departmental populations was large enough to support a course on its own if the needs justified it.

We translated the needs analysis questionnaire into Cantonese and collected data face-to-face in small groups of ten to twelve persons. The summary indicated that the four departments had the same needs for four of the modules, but each had a different need for the fifth and sixth modules. Students were drawn from the four geographic areas to minimize the number of persons off the job in any one locale. In this way we did not unduly disrupt work flow at any work site and did not generate unnecessary opposition.

IM has a clear focus on the workplace and the modules are designed to address solving the problems most supervisors encounter. For example, our four common modules dealt with solving problems of low work quality, low work quantity, goal setting, and discipline.

The fifth module responded to department-specific problems and the sixth module taught the process skills of developing a solution approach to any other problem encountered. Each module stemmed from a common set of key principles and included a list of steps to reach a solution. We used video models to demonstrate these steps, and required each participant to practice them in class to develop skill before returning to their workplace to apply them on the job. From module two on, each module started with a review of the experiences of class members in attempting to apply the skills of the previous module.

The methods and materials of SRT and IM were quite similar. However, the SRT videotapes were much more realistic for the U.S. participants than the IM videotapes were for the Hong Kong participants. Both sets of videotapes used American role models and the U.S. work settings depicted were not comparable to those experienced by the Hong Kong Telephone employees. To compensate, we increased the number of "behavior rehearsals" (role-plays), dubbed Cantonese onto the videotapes, and translated the written course materials to facilitate mastery of the concepts. This was particularly important as we moved to lower levels in the organization, where the language problems were more pronounced. As time passed, we videotaped enough classroom activity to develop our own localized videotapes for use as role models.

The program was introduced to senior management. The problem was introducing a program that was familiar in a participative management setting to an organization with an autocratic history. It was critical for the first steps to be on firm ground, because the full support of senior management was essential to success. The steps in the approach used in Hong Kong were similar to those used in the U.S. except that we moved more slowly and with greater care in Hong Kong. First, we presented the idea of IM to the senior management group, with the DDI representative as the primary presenter. He used videotapes and samples of the program to illustrate what to do and provided case studies from companies in Southeast Asia to demonstrate the benefits. The presentation and discussion took about two hours and resulted in a decision to proceed. A written proposal then laid out the steps involved in implementation. It was formally approved and transmitted to the heads of all divisions to advise them of the decision and the role they were expected to play. The steps were

- Management Preparation Meetings
- Needs Analysis
- Report to Senior Management
- Initial Course

Management Preparation Meetings

The first step was to schedule briefing meetings, which we held for the Division Managers (two hours), the Department Heads (two hours, in groups of ten to twelve), and the bosses of the proposed participants for the first class (four hours for this group of six). This step would be taken for each group of bosses as we scheduled their subordinates for training. The boss training included experiencing part of the first module and receiving specific instruction on how to provide the reinforcement to their subordinates, which would help facilitate the transfer of skills from the classroom to the job. The bosses reviewed a binder that included the reinforcement steps they were to take after the training each week. These steps were practiced to provide bosses with the "feel" of the behavior modeling their subordinates would be receiving.

Needs Analysis

Since the Operations Branch was to be the starting point, the second step was to identify the managers and supervisors in all four departments with four or more direct reporting subordinates. Then they were invited, through their bosses, to attend one of the sessions at which the needs analysis questionnaires would be completed. The document asked them to identify the specific modules of training that would be most useful.

Report to Senior Management

After the needs analysis was complete and the data summarized, the third step was to prepare a report to senior management and the Division Heads, identifying the modules that had emerged as most needed and setting the dates for the next steps.

The Initial Course

The first course served as a pilot to identify any problems with mechanics, equipment, or training space. Only minor problems emerged, and after making adjustments we established a full schedule beginning the following week. Given the population to be covered, a full schedule meant classes for six weeks held every day except Wednesday, with Group A on Monday, Group B on Tuesday, Group C on Thursday and Group D on Friday. This meant that we could accommodate 24 students for an entire course and start a new group every six weeks.

To determine if the training was effectively transferred from the classroom to the job, we scheduled a two-week gap immediately following the training for the first group of 24. During these two weeks the trainers visited the job site of every participant and conducted evaluation interviews with the participant and her/his boss. The evaluation confirmed that the training was effective. After this first group, the evaluation plan was modified. Only a sample of participants/bosses were interviewed and we sent questionnaires to the rest. As our training staff became fully experienced, we found that with an adjustment in design we could double the number of students in each class while maintaining the quality of instruction.

The participant-boss linkage described earlier worked very well, and it became an important first step in moving the company from an autocratic toward a participative management style. We did find that providing the participant with a second set of the classroom handouts each week helped make the discussion with the boss go more smoothly. We also took another step: When we sent a boss a letter scheduling a subordinate for training, we included a reminder to refer to the binder describing the steps for reinforcement with the subordinate.

The training had good acceptance from the beginning. The only concern occurred when participants developed enough skill and understanding to recognize when managers at higher levels were not using IM concepts in their interactions with subordinates. This became an important input for the design of the senior manager courses that started about four months after the first IM course.

We published our evaluation reports in the new monthly MDD newsletter along with the course schedules for IM and other courses. As you can see, we took exceptional care to see that our "flagship course" got off to a good start. It established the pattern for all future courses and incorporated the concepts needed to move toward a more participative management style.

Program Maintenance and Support

All organizations experience turnover and ours was no exception. After nine months, one of our trainers was transferred to the TTS. At the same time we received approval to enlarge the IM staff by one and decided to obtain certification for the other two Assistant Managers. This not only provided flexibility but enhanced their understanding of IM concepts. Reinforcement of these concepts could be built into other courses in our management curriculum during development, so we arranged for training of the persons new to IM. We also had the trainer stay an extra day to do an updated workshop for the existing training staff.

By this time we had developed and introduced our second course — Performance Goals and Standards (PGS) — to middle management. As with all of our courses, PGS employed adult-learning principles. The content was similar to that in courses on management-by-objectives. However, it also included a four-hour module at the end to equip the trainee to discuss the implementation of PGS with a key subordinate. This module was constructed just like an IM module—using the IM key principles, discussion steps, and behavior rehearsal. Since these middle managers had either participated in IM, or had trained subordinates, a better understanding of the concepts resulted. They obtained additional experience with the application of the concepts, which worked extremely well in getting the skills learned in class applied on the job. As a result, we built a similar module at the end of all future courses. This tactic systematically strengthened the skills of the managers and supervisors receiving training in participative management.

Another way we maintained the focus on developing skills to improve job performance was to do continuous needs analysis and evaluation. At the end of every class each participant completed our standard needs-analysis form and an evaluation instrument. Since we had limited resources to spend in developing new courses, the needs-analysis information was essential to be sure that we had our priorities straight. An evaluation instrument was administered at the end of every class to obtain the reaction of students to the course. In addition, a sample of the trainees' bosses was either interviewed or asked to complete a questionnaire to determine if the skills taught were in use to improve performance.

This approach was well received by managers throughout the organization and their positive evaluations enabled us to get the budget approvals needed to

- Enlarge our program offerings
- Modernize our training equipment
- Obtain the additional staff to develop and deliver all the courses in our growing curriculum
- Get approval for our own training center
- Keep the organization being served currently informed is critical to maintaining a successful program. We did this by
  1. Publishing our own monthly Management Development Newsletter
  2. Establishing a corporate Training Advisory Committee
  3. Putting regular publicity in the company magazine
  4. Providing input for a section in the Annual Report
  5. Providing monthly reports to the General Manager to whom we reported
  6. Doing an annual review with top management

Cultural Considerations

The most critical strategic principle that we adopted for our new MDD was that any organization anywhere trying to survive in the midst of constant change must be managed in a participative way. We realized from the beginning that we were embarking on a five- to seven-year plan. This put our task into perspective and enabled us to start on the right foot, building on the strengths that existed within HKT while helping managers and supervisors gradually acquire the skills necessary to improve performance.

We had some concerns from the beginning about whether the IM and behavior-modeling concepts would transfer successfully to the Asian environment. That is why we paid such close attention to language—translating needs analysis instruments and written course materials into Cantonese and dubbing Cantonese onto the sound tracks of films and videos. The problem-solving approach that we adopted appealed to the pragmatic nature of our technically oriented and mostly Cantonese trainees. The IM principles stressed problem solving, open communications, and maintaining self-esteem, and were a good match for the young Cantonese managers. Research conducted with young managers in Hong Kong using the Intercultural Value Inventory developed by Dr. L. Robert Kohls confirmed that they held values very similar to those of their counterparts in Western countries. One hypothesis that might explain this is that there may be a common set of values that arise when a society moves from a cottage industry and rural economy stage into an industrial stage. In any event, the management concepts embodied in IM were consistent with these values, and the training was effective in helping trainees improve their performance.

However, the past educational experience of the trainees was rote learning in an authoritarian environment. Their initial attempts to apply the training they had received to their workplace often were just the rigid application of the steps in the IM process. This is where the coaching provided for the bosses of the trainees paid off. Trainees were supported in their attempts, not ridiculed or ignored. We spread the training over six weeks and other MDD courses reinforced the concepts. This provided ample opportunity for trainees to practice their new skills in a supportive environment until they became the "regular" way to manage day-to-day.

This chapter has described how the Hong Kong Telephone Company established the management development function. It also compared the introduction of a behavior-modeling-based training course at C&P Telephone with that at Hong Kong Telephone. It explained the adaptations made for program design, the selection and preparation of trainers, program implementation, and program maintenance.

References

Beckhard, R. and Harris, R. T. *Organization Transitions: Managing Complex Change.* Reading, MA: Addison-Wesley, 1977.

Casse, P. *Training for the Multicultural Mind.* Washington, DC: SIETAR, 1981.
Goldstein, A.P., and Sorcher, M. *Changing Supervisor Behavior.* New York, NY: Pergamon Press, 1974.

Kohls, L. R. *Developing Intercultural Awareness.* Washington, DC: SIETAR, 1981.

Nadler, L. *Corporate Human Resource Development.* New York, NY: Van Nostrand Reinhold Company, 1980.

Redding, S. G. *Cultural Clues to Success* (Leadership and Change Series, #33). Hong Kong: The Chinese University of Hong Kong, 1983.

Roberts, D.G. *Establishing a Management Development Programme: A Case Study From Hong Kong.* Euro-Asia Business Review, 1985.

Roberts, D.G. *Values and Beliefs of Young Managers in Hong Kong.* Hong Kong: Performance, 1984.

About the Author

Don Roberts is Associate Professor in the School of Education & Human Services at Marymount University in Arlington, VA . Previously, he was Management Development Manager at Hong Kong Telephone and had been Director of Management and Organization Development at Chesapeake and Potomac Telephone. He completed his doctoral studies in Human Resource Development at George Washington University. He is active in the American Society for Training and Development and the OD Network. He is a former Brookings Fellow and has served on various Federal, State, and local government commissions, including the National Manpower Advisory Commission. He is a regular contributor to U.S and U.K. publications.

CHAPTER 23

Using a U.S. Model in Another Country: Singapore

Ng Peck Ho

As a major American vendor and consultant for HRD systems for business organizations, we are blessed with a very creative, competent group of research and development learning specialists who develop "learning systems that solve business problems." Change affecting the workplace is constant, and business needs are ever evolving. Add societal and organizational cultural issues and we have very complex relationships to deal with when we talk about "learning systems that solve business problems."

This chapter will share our experiences and insights gained in responding to the HRD needs of business units in Singapore. Our HRD practices and experiences are vast and diverse. At one end of the range is a simple sale of an American generic learning product such as "Supervisory Skills." At the other is using learning as one of the major interventions bringing about future-oriented, strategic organizational change.

I will focus on "Designing and Implementing a Learning Solution," and hope to show how Singapore HRD practitioners provide a culturally appropriate design and implementation of a learning solution.

Singapore

Singapore is an Asian city-state on an island located right on the equator and at one degree north latitude. It is about 228 square miles in size. It is tropical, with an average temperature of 28 degrees Centigrade and a humidity of 88 percent. Culturally Singapore is a cosmopolitan melting pot. The population was 3,002,800, as of 1990 with the ethnic composition shown in Figure 23.1.

Figure 23.1: Ethnic Composition of Singapore

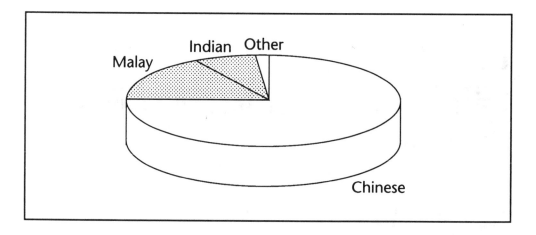

The official languages are Mandarin, English, Tamil and Bahasa Melayu. There are four official New Year's, and TV programs are in each of the four official languages. We also have four official newspapers and four main religions, Buddhism, Hinduism, Islam, and Christianity. Each of the four official languages is a compulsory second language in school. The main language of instruction is English.

Economically, Singapore is known as one of the four "Dragons," the others being Hong Kong, South Korea, and Taiwan. "Dragon" is a nickname given to these four states to describe their economic aggressiveness and virility for growth.

Singapore is also within the "growth triangle"—an area covering Singapore, Malaysia, Indonesia, and Thailand that is expected to grow economically at a phenomenal rate within the next decades. An average of 8-10 percent growth per year for these North and South East Asian Countries based on the past five years' performance is quite normal and expected.

What is HRD to the Singaporean practitioners?

The definitions of HRD are varied and loosely used to mean management development, adult education, or training, or education, or learning, or a combination of these terms.

What are the other background factors in the "design & implementation" focus of this chapter?

One major background factor is that the business issues within Singapore's business organizations are varied—the results of these organizations' endeavors to grow and be profitable in a world of competition and change.

The lack of organizational homogeneity is another background factor. In Singapore this goes beyond organizational growth differences. The lack of homogeneity is a result of Singapore's multicultural settings, stemming both from Singapore's multi-racial make-up and the diverse international investments Singapore has received from almost all over the world. Organizational cultures are driven by multiracial societal values and norms, by expatriates, by the headquarters management style of multinational corporations (MNC's), or by a combination of these. In Singapore these cultural forces are often at work simultaneously in an organization.

Governmental investment in business units is another major background factor. It started as a series of national efforts to industrialize Singapore and to grow economically in the early 1960s. It has left the Singaporean business world with a legacy of major government-owned business units that exert powerful influence.

Government involvement in HRD is unique and requires special mention here. The National Productivity Board (NPB) is the HRD arm of the government. Its activities include providing HRD consultancy services to organizations in both the public and private sectors. It also develops and designs HRD programs and implements them for client organizations. One division within NPB is the Skills Development Fund (SDF). SDF was set up in 1979 to encourage employers to upgrade their employees' skills and knowledge so as to increase the productivity and technological skills of the average Singaporean worker. Companies are required by law to contribute a sum equivalent to one percent of the salaries of all employees drawing S$750 (U.S. $249) or below to the SDF. The money is kept aside by the Government and used to reimburse companies that send their employees (salaries S$750 and below) for HRD. The amount of reimbursement is decided along guidelines established by the Skills Development Fund Board. The NPB is thus a major driving force that influences HRD practices.

Against this background we can broadly group Singapore's business organizations into the following categories:

- Multinational Companies (MNC's). Examples are Hitachi, SGS-Thomson, Hewlett-Packard, IBM, DuPont.
- Large Local Companies (LLC's) listed in the local Stock Exchange. Examples are United Overseas Bank, Singapore Airlines.
- Government Statutory Bodies (GSB's) and Government Business Organizations (GBO's). Examples are Singapore Telecom, the National Productivity Board, Public Utilities Board, Temasek Holdings.
- Small-Medium Enterprises (SME's) which include the rest of Singapore's business organizations.

Each of these four types can be found in industries such as banking, insurance, computer sales, ship building, manufacturing, hotels, etc. Each group has its fairly distinctive HRD practices and culture, with variations according to the industry they are in.

Multinational Companies (MNC's)

The multinational companies in Singapore are major economic players, mainly from the United States, Japan, United Kingdom, France, and Germany. Other smaller Asian and European MNC's are also present.

The American MNC's use "American English" as the main language of communication, while "British English" prevails in British MNC's. Singaporeans who work in these MNC's communicate in the respective English versions as best as they can.

With the Japanese, French, German, and other European or Asian MNC's, the main languages of communication among the expatriates are their native languages. They often use Singapore's English (Singlish) when communicating with Singaporeans. Between themselves, the Singaporeans working in these MNC's often use Mandarin or local dialects, such as Hokkien, Cantonese, or Hainanese. This is unique to Singapore, where English is one of the official languages.

Corporate culture and management style among the MNC's clearly distinguishes them from each other, with the American and the Japanese MNC's exerting the most influence. Most American Fortune 200 MNC's are theory Y in culture and style. Some are inbetween theory X and Y, while a minority fall into the area of theory Z. In Singapore, Japanese MNC's are very much more theory X in culture and style than their operations in Japan. Other MNC's are generally X or between X and Y.

Like most Asians, Singaporeans have unique cultural norms and values. Behaviorally they are more structured and dependent, quieter, appear less assertive and less expressive, and yet are more relationship-based. Depending on what MNC's they work with, Singaporeans adapt to the different organizational cultures. Obviously they need to adapt more to the American MNC's that cultivate values like transparency, less structuredness, more creativity, more assertiveness, and more interdependence. Singaporeans bring with them their own societal cultures that vary depending on dialect and background, but generally reflect the acceptance of paternalistic and hierarchical authority and a sense of communal relationship.

There is in a sense a kind of osmosis taking place between the Singaporean and the MNC culture. We shall see the implications of this in the critical events of HRD designing.

One other observation is that Singaporeans who work in MNC's are generally better educated, better skilled, and better paid than most Singaporeans.

Large Local Companies (LLC's)

These are Singapore's own conglomerates, and like the MNC's are very major players in the economy.

The languages used in this group are English, Singapore English (Singlish), and Mandarin. At supervisory and staff level, the main Singapore dialect, Hokkien, is frequently used with a mixture of Singlish. Corporate culture tends to be theory X, and management style tends to be bureaucratic and hierarchical. Singaporeans who work in these organizations are more "Asian" than their counterparts in American MNC's. There is an even greater tendency for them to be more structured, quieter, less assertive, less expressive, and less transparent.

Government Statutory Bodies (GSB's) and Government Business Organizations (GBO's)

The GSB's and GBO's are tied into the government national building efforts and are often part of a bigger game plan for national strategic, long-term, and political implementations. The organizational needs tend to be very focused on total cost or profit and productivity.

GSB's are significant organizations in Singapore for HRD work, as the Singapore Government is one of the major driving forces for HRD. All GSB's are expected to operate without being subsidized—therefore they operate very much like a business organization despite their national-interest role.

English, Mandarin, Tamil, and Bahasa Melayu are the four official languages used —mainly English and Mandarin. Dialect speaking is not encouraged.The organizational culture tends to be theory X, and management style is bureaucratic, hierarchical, and structured.

GBO's as business units are very much the same as LLC's.

The Small-Medium Enterprises (SME's)

SME's are the up-and- coming Singapore business units, the entrepreneurial hub of Singapore business. They are mainly owned by Singaporeans and the main language of communication is Singlish and Mandarin with some Bahasa Melayu. The main dialects used are Hokkien and Cantonese. The organizational culture tends to be theory X, authoritarian and paternalistic.

From all this it is easy to see that HRD work in Singapore is culturally complex. Almost every HRD intervention must relate not only to the needs of a given situation but to the organizational culture as well. The rest of the chapter will share what I have learned, applied, and modified over the years, using examples of HRD design and implementation practices.

The Critical Events Model

The Critical Events Model (CEM) has helped us to do some of our best learning design and implementation work for clients. The steps in the model are shown in Table 23.1

Table 23.1: Steps in The CEM

- Identify Needs of the Organization
- Specify Job Performance
- Identify Learner Needs
- Determine Objectives
- Build Curriculum
- Select Instructional Strategies
- Obtain Instructional Resources
- Conduct Training
- Evaluation and Feedback (after each step)

Our designing proceeds from "Identify the Needs of the Organization" to "Select Instructional Strategies." Implementation proceeds from "Conduct Training" to "Meet the Needs of the Organization." Implied is transfer of learning back to the job.

I will not touch on the details of the technical process of each critical event, but will focus on how we used each event in a culturally appropriate manner working with Singapore HRD practitioners in the background described.

Identify the Needs of the Organization

For the learning specialist, identifying the needs of the organization is crucial to setting the context of the learning design and its implementation. For example, a major need of our banking client in Singapore was to change from an order-taking culture to a culture of aggressive marketing and selling. The issue was that their managers saw themselves as staid bankers not as businesspeople. The context for the learning design in this case was "change," "mindset shift," and "cutting a business deal."

Earlier we mentioned that the context of HRD work is crucial to help us understand HRD practices. This critical event, "Identify the Needs of the Organization" tends to set the parameters for each of the other critical events and ultimately determines the working processes and the final learning deliverables and implementations.

From our experience, each of the five types of business units described earlier has interesting organizational needs behaviors. We see a general pattern in each type. For the MNC's, the organizational needs are generally driven by global competition. The changes tend to be strategic for future refocusing and on going improvements. The exercises tend to cover both the technical and human behavioral aspects of the business. This is shown by the example we will refer to throughout this chapter. It involves an MNC client that in order to acquire a global competitive edge had a major organizational need to change from a product, technologically driven company to a market, customer-driven company. The impact of this refocusing was major: It involved not only streamlining the production system and equipment to be more responsive to market and customer needs, but also getting all employees to change their attitudes and behaviors towards the customer and market needs. Behavior turnaround is considered the only evidence of a successful change before profit measurements.

For LLC's and GBO's, the organizational need tends to be primarily driven by local and intra-regional competitions. The focus of change tends to be on technical areas like structure, work flow, instruments, and equipment, with secondary emphasis on qualitative behavioral areas such as customer service and leadership. One of our LLC clients has much of its HRD budget in technical-skills training and a smaller portion in behavioral customer-servicing skills. This group of companies tends to be "technical." For example, one company's customer-service focus was on convenient locations, enough car parks, lighting, timeliness, and accuracy of statements.

For GSB's the organizational focus is on national interests, which means that technical needs take precedence. For example, the vast and on-going infrastructural improvements for Singapore call for extensive technical training. For the SME's the focus is bottom-line profits and costs. Organizational needs tend to be reactive and concern productivity, cost, and profit management.

Other than business-issue needs for these types of organizations, there are differences in the cultural needs, which are also a major part of the organizational needs for the Singapore HRD practitioners.

The organizational needs described here are general to each organizational type, but each organization will also have its own unique needs depending on its industry and its development stage. But the HRD practitioners in Singapore need to understand the general context of these organizational needs, so that as they work with each critical event, there will be no surprises.

Specify Job Performance

This critical event has to do with "the performance expected of a person who is doing a designated job" (Nadler,1985). Continuing with our MNC example, job performance is now driven by two major desired goals:

- Production System Change and Upgrade
- Customer Sensitivity and Customer-Focused Behavior

The first is a technical-learning design and the second is a qualitative or behavioral-learning design. For most MNC's, these two types of job performance are relatively balanced as priorities. However, the shift towards technical job performance as a priority is seen with the other types of Singapore's business organizations. Our HRD experience is that in Singapore practitioners find it:

- Easier to arrive at for specific job performance, it is technical, specific and measurable
- Tends to be behavioral and to involve setting up behavioral criterion that are observable and measurable

This is where the learning designer will have to consider the Singaporean culture and that of the organization in a major way and where the organizational culture begins to drive the design.

In our particular example, the new behavioral job-performance requirements lead to behavioral needs such as "working as a team for the customer," "exhibiting problem solving," and "making customers feel good." By themselves, such behavioral needs can be accepted as "solutions" to an organizational need, but the behavioral "style" that it takes can determine the success or failure of the learning design. We have often heard clients remark: "This is too American. We are not like that!" "It is too artificial!" "Too professional!" or "That is too Japanese. We do not bow. We show more warmth!" The learners' need for the right style of qualitative behavior applies to all the types of business organizations in Singapore, particularly when the designer works with HRD practitioners from LLC's, GSB's, GBO's, and SME's. The job-performance area is only the form. The learner's needs on the deliberateness of these desired qualitative behaviors in the right style become a culturalized learner's needs issue.

Identify Learner Needs

The focus now switches from the job to the person doing the job. It is a critical event "to identify the learning needs of those who are doing the designated job" (Nadler, 1985). Besides job performance both in the technical and behavioral areas, the learners' conception of right style is a key factor at this stage of the learning design. For example, Singaporeans and Asians in general are less up front, less direct, more subtle in expression, and take more time to warm up. So in the behavioral areas the design should not call for too expressive, outgoing, or up-front kind of behavioral skills. This will impact in a major way, as we shall see in the critical event of instructional strategies.

"How would learners want to learn?" This is another key question for a Singaporean learning designer. Many Singaporeans had their primary, secondary, and initial tertiary education in Singapore. Generally, their comfort zones of learning are content, structuredness, and learning by modelling. They are generally good in symbolic analytical skills. In the American MNC's, the learning environment is one of "Think, Think, Think" or "Be Creative." Structuredness or content orientation is not the norm. The Singaporean learner in these MNC's tends to be pressured into a style of creative, unstructured, process-based learning. A good designer will provide in this environment a design that, for example, will help learners learn how to learn in an American MNC's culture. In Japanese or other MNC's, the Singaporean style of learning is more in sync with the MNC's leaning culture. Here the learning designer tries less to help the Singaporean learners learn how to learn, but instead provides a more content-oriented and structured design to meet learners' needs.

The Singaporean learners' style finds its full expression in the culture of LLC's, GSB's, and GBO's. The structured learning style and the structured culture are in sync. The learning designer should provide for this in building curriculum and instructional strategies.

Another related learner's needs area is language. Singaporeans learn better in American English in American MNC's, and in British English in other MNC's, LLC's, GSB's, and GBO's. A significant number in SME's and some in LLC's learn better in Singlish or Mandarin.

Determine Objectives

This critical event requires the designer to "list the specific program objectives and learning objectives related to the design under consideration" (Nadler, 1985). Program objective is used here to mean the learning experience to be designed, while the learning objective is the desired outcome to indicate the performance of the learner at the end of the learning experience.

The job performance needs related to "Production System Change and Upgrade" and "Customer Sensitivity and Customer-Focused Behavior," as in our earlier example, will drive the program objectives and the curriculum content, while the "Right Cultural and Language Style" will drive the main body of instructional design.

Program objectives may be in the areas of skills, knowledge, and attitude. In the MNC's, skills and knowledge are main program objectives for technical needs, as in our example "Production System Change and Upgrade." In the American MNC's there seems to be an added dimensional stress on skills and attitude program objectives for "qualitative needs" as in our example "Customer Sensitivity and Customer-Focused Behavior." One reason is that the American MNC's desire more than just technical competencies in their employees.

HRD practitioners in Singapore should be aware that the average Singaporean learner is more comfortable with the development of task or technical objectives than of qualitative behavioral objectives. This is particularly so in LLC's, GSB's, GBO's, and SME's.

Build Curriculum

This critical event requires the designer to "develop a specific list of the items to be learned to meet the previously determined objectives" (Nadler, 1985). It answers the question: "What is to be learned?" Continuing with our example, there will be two curricula areas: one for "Production System Change and Upgrade" and the other for "Customer Sensitivity and Customer-Focused Behavior."

In building curricula, MNC's tend to fall back on "HQ materials" from their home offices. This has often proved quite successful in technical training. In qualitative behavioral training, it has not, due mainly to cultural and language issues, which often call for major redesign.

"Customization" has become a buzzword for MNC HRD practitioners for building behavioral curricula based on subject matter from HQ's. The content is rewritten in a culturally acceptable manner to reflect local needs, situations, examples, and issues. In our example of "Customer Sensitivity and Customer-Focused Behavior," many behaviors of U.S. customers need to be rewritten to reflect local customer behavior; many U.S. case studies or examples need to be redesigned and rewritten to reflect local needs; specific local business issues need to be part of the design context to create local "buy in" from participants; many simulation or video scripts need to be rephrased to reflect local conversational style and so on.

Sometimes MNC's purchase outside behavioral products from vendors, and if these products are Japanese or American or from another country, they also must be customized.

Singapore's local companies—the LLC's, GSB's, GBO's, and SME's—do not have HQ's to fall back on, but they do have the Singapore Government's National Productivity Board (NPB). The NPB has designed many generic technical HRD programs ranging from "safety measures" to "computer literacy" and has commissioned many trade bodies—for example, the Singapore Retail Merchant Association—to develop industry-related HRD programs. Partnerships or associations have also been formed with such MNC's as IBM, Motorola, and Philips to tap into technical learning technology. Partnerships have also been formed with large local companies such as Singapore Airlines, to do specialized training in customer-service areas. The Management Guidance Centre of NPB consults, customizes, and designs for many local companies and some MNC's.

It is important for Singapore HRD practitioners to consider the "level" of the curriculum content. It should be related to the level of the learners' ability to learn. The Singaporean HRD practitioner must decide during curriculum building what target population and type of business organization the learning design is for. This is particularly important in Singapore because of the level of education and the cultural settings.

For local companies in Singapore, the subject-matter expert is frequently also the curriculum designer, and this tends to produce technical-content presentation without much learning technology. The problem is due mainly to the existing level of design expertise and failure to see the difference between the two roles.

Select Instructional Strategies

This critical event requires the designer to "select instructional strategies that are appropriate for the curriculum, the learner, the instructor and the organization." (Nadler, 1985). For the HRD designer in Singapore, this is an extremely critical closing link to all the threads spawned in earlier critical events, because of both organizational and societal cultural differences. This is where the designer's creativity and understanding of Singapore's culture can make a big difference to the learning design.

For each organizational type, certain instructional strategies work better than others. However, there is an existing pattern to be discerned in Singapore, starting with the learning model itself as a fundamental instructional strategy.

In figure 23.2, we have tried to put this Singapore pattern into a matrix based on our observations and experiences (adapted from Knowles, 1984).

Figure 23.2: Singapore Matrix

Organizational Levels	MNCs		LLCs		GBOs		GSBs		SMEs	
	Technical Training	Qualitative Behavioral Training	Technical Training	Qualitative Behavioral Training	Technical Training	Qualitative Behavioral Training	Technical Training	Qualitative Behavioral Training	Technical Training	Qualitative Behavioral Training
Senior Executives	Cognitive	Adult Learning Process	Cognitive	Adult Learning Cognitive	Cognitive	Adult Learning Cognitive	Cognitive Behavior Modelling	Cognitive Behavior Modelling	Cognitive Behavior Modelling	Cognitive Behavioral Training
Middle Managers	Cognitive	Adult Learning Process	Cognitive	Cognitive Behavior Modelling	Cognitive	Cognitive Behavior Modelling	Cognitive Behavior Modelling	Cognitive Behavior Modelling	Cognitive Behavior Modelling	Cognitive Behavior Modelling
Supervisory	Cognitive Behavior Modelling	Adult Learning Cognitive Behavior Modelling	Cognitive Behavior Modelling	Cognitive Behavior Modelling	Cognitive Behavior Modelling	Cognitive Behavior Modelling	Cognitive Behavior Modelling	Cognitive Behavior Modelling	Behavior Modelling	Behavior Modelling
Staff	Cognitive Behavior Modelling	Cognitive Behavior Modelling	Behavior Modelling	Behavior Modelling	Behavior Modelling	Behavior Modelling	Behavior Modelling	Behavior Modelling	Behavior Modelling	Behavior Modelling

Complexity of Learning Task: High ← → Low

Level of Learning Ability

"Adult Education" refers to the andragogical approach. Process follows from the andragogical approach and has reference to nonstructured content, skills or attitudinal learning. Cognitive has a reference to structured content and knowledge, and is more pedagogical. Lastly, behavior modelling refers to learning a set of doing skills.

The Matrix assumes complexity of task and level of learning ability to be correlated to organizational level. We find this correlation relevant in Singapore. This matrix may be a "rule of the thumb" guide to help the Singapore HRD practitioners to feel for the general learning models that are being used in Singapore. The LLC's and GBO's seem to have a "common" learning model, a reflection of their homogeneity, while SME's, MNC's, and GSB's seem different from each other and from the rest.

We can also see distinct patterns in the use of learning models between technical and qualitative behavioral training in MNC's and to some extent LLC's. For example, cognitive and behavioral modelling are fundamentals for technical training, while adult learning and process are fundamentals for qualitative behavorial learning. However, cognitive and behavioral modelling are used frequently in qualitative behavioral training by LLC's, GBO's, GSB's and SME's. This reflects the structured organizational culture, learners' learning style, level of content, learners' level of learning, and instructor skills. Adult Education, especially with process design, is not very common for these groups, although there are many who have embarked on it successfully.

For technical HRD, the different types of business organizations generally use cognitive and behavior modelling models, which traditionally suit technical HRD. In fact, it is the prevalence of technical training that has largely contributed to the use of cognitive and behavioral modelling for *qualitative* training. However, Singapore is at that stage of HRD growth where we are shifting more and more to qualitative behavioral training, and we anticipate that adult learning with process design will be used more and more, with the MNC's setting the pace.

I am not judging the "rightness" or the "wrongness" of the learning models used frequently among Singapore HRD practitioners. The cognitive model historically derives from the educational system and behavior modelling derives from technical training, while adult learning practice and process learning are derived from the MNC's in Singapore. For cognitive learning in technical training, some common instructional strategies are use of overhead projectors, flip charts, whiteboards, lectures, demonstrations, videos, some basic practice, and handouts. For behavior modelling in technical training, overhead projectors, videos, simulations, and repetitive hands-on practice are the norms.

For adult cognitive learning in qualitative behavioral programs, some common instructional strategies are the use of overhead projectors, videos, flip charts, lecturettes, facilitation, work groups, case studies, structured content, and handouts.

For adult-process learning for qualitative behavioral programs, some common instructional strategies are flip charts, facilitation, work groups, "real" case studies, process content, handouts, indoor and outdoor experiential games, role-plays, and simulations. For behavior modelling in qualitative training some common instructional strategies are overhead projectors, videos, simulated role-plays, tracks, and practice sessions.

Obtain Instructional Resources

The MNC's generally have well-developed instructional resources, either as a geographical regional center, or as an independent HRD in-house unit either independent or within HRM. As mentioned, many MNC's use instructional resources from HQ's.

The local companies are fast developing and prioritizing their instructional resources. HRD is usually within HRM. Much of the HRD budgets and instructional resources allocated are driven by the government skill development fund subsidies. The fund's current policy is to subsidize as high as 70 percent of an "approve in principle" program and as low as 50 percent. In-house program subsidy is S$2.00 (U.S. $1.15) an hour per learner. The HRD efforts of many LLC's, GBO's, GSB's, SME's and some MNC's are driven by these fundings, which exert tremendous influence on instructional resources.

Conduct Training

Instructor is a term commonly used in Singapore for a technical training program and is associated with a pedagogical approach. *Facilitator* is not a common term in Singapore and is used in an andragogical adult-learning design to mean a session leader. Good instructors are not easy to come by and good facilitators are even more scarce. This is an area where Singapore HRD practitioners will need to develop more.

Evaluation and Feedback–Transfer of Learning

The major link between conducting training and meeting organizational needs is transfer of learning. In Singapore, this is a major area for HRD practitioners to develop—or to try to have developed, as it is really the job of the line function. In most MNC's, learning reinforcement is the responsibility of supervisors and managers. However, in LLC's, GBO's, GSB's, and SME's, many supervisors and managers do not see learning reinforcement as their role, and this has often hindered behavior change, particularly in the qualitative behavioral areas.

Current Issues

Role of the government in HRD

As pointed out earlier, the National Productivity Board and its division, the Skills Development Fund, powerfully influence HRD in Singapore as providers of organizational learning and subsidizers of HRD work within "acceptable guidelines." The Singapore government's role in HRD has been very successful in "waking up" business organizations to the need for HRD and in implementing and providing HRD in various key areas to increase productivity and competitive edge for Singapore business organizations. The Business Environment Risk Intelligence (BERI) ratings drive a major part of the competitive-edge context. The subsidy criteria and guidelines are used to shape HRD focus strategically based on national interest. (Figure 23.3 shows Singapore's position in terms of BERI's Quality of Work force Index.)

Figure 23.3: The Top Five – BERI's Quality of Work force Index

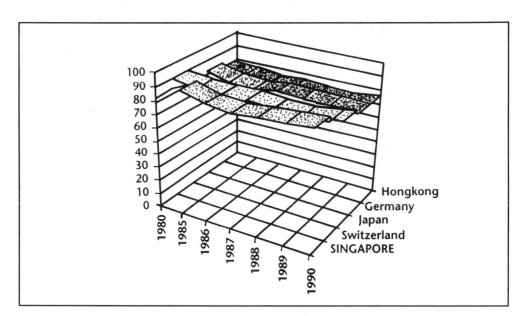

For example, at one stage Singapore's HRD efforts were directed almost totally to the managerial level. This was necessary and rightly so. However, when economic evidence became available showing that it was critical for Singapore's future success to focus on non-managerial employees —particularly those with less than nine years' education—the subsidy criteria and guidelines were changed to steer HRD focus to this group of employees. It is anticipated that as business issues become increasingly complex and competitive, and change quickens, the subsidy criteria and guidelines will need to keep pace. It is also expected that the time will come when an organization in a certain stage of maturity facing increasingly complex change and diversities may have to give up SDF subsidies for the freedom to develop on its own. This trend is already beginning to happen with some companies.

The quality of HRD work

The HRD profession is one of the newest in Singapore. With Singapore's rapid economic growth and NPB's thrust for a national HRD effort, qualified HRD professionals are not easy to come by. There has been a proliferation of "consultants" as many less qualified people have jumped on the bandwagon. There is an urgent need for the quality of HRD work to be improved, particularly in delivery skills and designing skills. It is encouraging that the NPB has joined with Motorola to teach

Singapore practitioners basic learning design. The NPB will also soon be launching delivery-skills training for instructors/facilitators.

HRD role of managers and supervisors

Traditionally the HRD role has been almost the exclusive domain of HRD practitioners. As transfer of learning back to the job takes on increasing critical importance, the HRD role of managers and supervisors is becoming more and more of an issue in Singapore. Most managers and supervisors do not see HRD function as a line responsibility. However,there is increasing pressure for managers and supervisors to take on HRD responsibilities—essentially in reinforcing learning and managing nonlearning areas—as support to successful organizational change.

HRD maturity

What has probably taken the United States 15 years to achieve in HRD progress has been achieved in Singapore in seven years. Much credit must be given to the Singapore Government for its HRD initiatives. HRD development in Singapore has passed the stage of start-up explorations and basic patterns, and is at the stage of refining, improving, and consolidating HRD practices. HRD efforts have now achieved an ongoing momentum, particularly in technical training.

The issues for HRD in the 90s will be important for Singapore to determine, for this is when the foundation of future growth must be laid. Several areas for further maturation may be seen in the following:

A holistic approach. Much HRD work today is relatively reactive and therefore confined to a particular need or work unit. The organizational needs I have discussed are frequently not the area of initial focus. This has resulted in many learning designs lacking a relevant context. A consequence of this is that many nonlearning interventions to support the desired outcome are either not implemented or not brought into alignment. I believe this to be one major foundational block to HRD development for the 1990s.

Training of HRD practitioners. If Singapore is to succeed in making HRD a strategy tool for desired organizational behavior outcomes, the quality of HRD practitioners as internal consultants, learning specialists, and managers of HRD needs much improvement.

Commitment and involvement of management. Generally, management in Singapore is committed to HRD, being driven by both issue needs and government initiatives. However, the third foundational block for HRD maturity that Singapore needs for the 1990s goes beyond commitment to actual involvement. HRD ultimately must have to be a management responsibility, not that of HRD people alone. This involvement is critical to enable business organizations to achieve their strategic intents.

The Future

The HRD scenario in Singapore is one of continuous growth and change. HRD is getting to be more and more of a dynamic intervention to produce organizational change and desired outcomes, both technical and qualitative. Intra-regional competition, particularly between the newly industrialized economies,—Singapore, Hong Kong, South Korea, and Taiwan—is getting more intense. Business issues are related more and more to global change and competition. Singapore's main resource is its people, and the development of this resource is critical to Singapore's future success. National issues such as productivity growth, the skills level of Singapore workers, or the number of days of absenteeism and other BERI ratings are sensitive issues in Singapore.

Figure 23.4 shows Singapore's position in terms of productivity. Although Singapore's growth compares favorably with that of other countries, the government, through the National Productivity Council, has charted out three new areas of focus for the 1990s to spur further improvement. The three priorities are

- To improve workers' skills and attitudes so as to develop even more of a world-class quality work force
- To more effectively deploy manpower resources
- To upgrade small-and medium-size enterprises(SME's)

It is anticipated that for HRD to play a more significant and strategic role for Singapore's business organizations in the 1990's, several HRD areas will be developed.

Alternative HRD delivery systems

Increasingly, hi-tech learning technologies will be introduced into Singapore. This will be due, in part, to the increasing need for more technical HRD programs as well as for having participants learn outside of formal classroom situations. There will be more interactive video, computer-based learning, and other technological advances in delivering learning.

Electronic assessments of skills and attitudes for selecting candidates for a job as well as for identifying skills, knowledge, and attitudes training needs for a particular job will also be significant.

Figure 23.4: Average Productivity Growth – Percent (1981-1990)

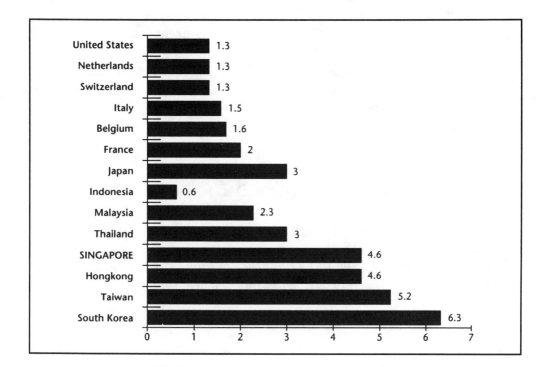

HRD for qualitative areas

As part of the maturing process for Singapore's business needs, it is envisioned that more and more organizational needs will cover qualitative behavior areas. There will be relative balance between technical training and qualitative training. Signs of this are already seen, with the government putting much greater emphasis on customer services.

Asianization of HRD products

This will to be a major development for HRD products in Singapore and other Asian countries. Many HRD learning systems are of American, British, and Japanese origin. Many of the videos, examples, and workbooks reflect those origins. It is anticipated that if HRD is really to play its role, many current HRD products will have to be Asianized.

Government role

The government's role in HRD is expected to continue, with the NPB and the SDF as major national HRD builders. The NPB will probably be empowered to form joint ventures and strategic alliances to increase their strengths in HRD technology.

Regional

At this stage of HRD growth—especially with the wealth of experience, resources, and expertise from the NPB—Singapore may soon be in a position to be a regional player for Asia and Pacific countries. It is likely that Singapore's HRD technologies would be one item for future export.

The future of HRD in Singapore is indeed exciting. It is an area that will gather more interest and more growth momentum—and it will be increasingly relied upon as a tool to move Singapore's economic development to the year 2000.

Bibliography

Knowles, M. *The Adult Learner: A Neglected Species.* Houston, TX: Gulf Publishing Company, 1984.

Nadler, L. *Designing Training Programs: The Critical Events Model.* Reading, MA: Addison-Wesley, 1985.

Nadler, L., and Nadler, Z.(Eds.). *The Handbook of Human Resource Development* (Second Edition). New York, NY: Wiley-Interscience, 1984.

About the Author

Ng Peck Ho is President, Central Asia of Wilson Learning Asia PTE Ltd. in Singapore. He is responsible for the overall business and professional performance of Wilson Learning from South Korea to India. Previously, he was Managing Director of Qualitative Management PTE Ltd. Managing Director of Gromark PTE Ltd. and Credit Marketing Officer of the Bank of America. He completed his M.A. degree in HRD. He is a member of the American Society for Training and Development, and has been involved as a learning specialist, facilitating and designing roles for business issues with major Fortune 200 companies.

CHAPTER 24

HRD Practices for Multinational Corporation Managers in Malaysia

Zulaiha Ismail

Malaysia has long recognized the need to nurture the human resource capability to develop and enhance managerial, professional, and technical competencies. By the turn of the century, Malaysia could join the ranks of the other prominent, newly industrialized countries, of the Pacific Rim. Foreign investments have increased significantly, with the accompanying influx of multinational or foreign corporations. The role of management in national development is undoubtedly far reaching. Effective utilization of human and nonhuman resources depends on planning, organizing, directing, and control activities carried out by managers. As is the case elsewhere (Eurich, 1985; ASTD, 1986), management learning is the most prominent area of HRD in Malaysian business and industry.

In 1987, I conducted a study of HRD practices for managers in selected public, local, and foreign corporations. It aimed at explaining HRD philosophies and policies, objectives, activity areas, and management support actions,. It also addressed design, implementation, and evaluation of management programs (Ismail, 1988).

In the foreign-controlled category, the ten organizations picked for the study were from a spectrum of industries, ranging from the manufacture and sale of industrial goods to consumer and edible products. Included also was a leading life insurance corporation. Of the foreign corporations, three originated from Great

Britain, four from the U.S. and one each from Japan, Sweden, and Switzerland. Because of the small sample, I did not attempt to compare HRD practices according to national origin. Numbers of employees ranged from 573 to 3,500. As a group, the foreign companies employed 17,695 people, of which 14 percent were managers. The foreign companies reported that 74 percent of their managers attended some form of organized HRD activity during the year. The analysis of the study and the discussion that follows attempts to describe the HRD "state of affairs" for managers in multinational corporations.

Senior Leadership Philosophies on HRD

The foreign-controlled or multinational corporations were forthright in stating their philosophies on HRD. The philosophical assumptions that emerged from the group were

- Valuing human resources as the most important corporate asset
- Developing human potential
- In-house learning as the HRD vehicle
- HRD contributing to productivity and the bottom line
- HRD facilitating career progression
- Demonstrating corporate citizenship by contributing to the professional development of Malaysians

Eight companies explicitly stated their commitment to developing human potential, and said they value human resources as the most important corporate asset. Although the other two companies were less explicit, they nevertheless valued the importance of HRD. One company said that it had not made any overt attempt to control and coordinate HRD, but it preferred instead to give the individual employee the responsibility and authority to pursue learning at his or her own pace. Another company stated, "A management which upholds consensus and collective decision making would obviously value the human resource. In valuing the human resource, we seek to develop our people."

All the foreign companies, mindful of the different organization cultures they possessed, preferred learning to be in-house. Three companies believed that on-the-job training (OJT) was the most important means of providing HRD for managers. They added that line managers had a responsibility to instruct and coach their subordinates. Four companies looked upon HRD as an organizational strategy to improve overall productivity and profitability. One of them tied HRD to Human Resource Utilization, and another integrated it with Organization Development (OD). The idea that HRD should be effectively combined with career progression was voiced by five companies. They also emphasized the need to develop local managers to take over from expatriate managers. Three foreign companies consciously showed a commitment to contribute to the development of the people of Malaysia, by offering scholarships to Malaysians for locally conducted degree programs.

Policies and Guidelines on HRD

All except one foreign company documented their policies on HRD. Eight had specific guidelines on how management programs should be carried out and centralized their learning activities for managers.

Most companies stated that HRD for managers was not a "one-shot" learning experience, but a long-term development process that was needs-based and practice-oriented. Six companies were explicit regarding formal learning that managers had to experience. Programs had titles such as Management Development Program, Graduate Development Program, and Personnel Integrated System. The effort and expense that went into implementing these programs showed the organizational commitment to management programs.

About half the corporations placed a premium on identifying and developing managers with high potential. They incorporated HRD with personnel and career development strategies, so that the chosen managers could become both generalists and functional specialists. The need to instruct local managers so they could take over from expatriates was documented in the guidelines of three organizations. Two others incorporated the training and education of Bumiputra (ethnic "sons of the soil") executives into their HRD guidelines in recognition of national manpower policies.

Three foreign companies stipulated that all managers had to attend at least one HRD program a year. Two companies did not provide any written guidelines on how HRD for managers should be carried out. Instead, they conducted management programs dictated by upper management on an ad hoc basis. Both these corporations valued technical skills for managers and saw OJT as the prime means of developing people.

Objectives of Management Programs

Most of the multinational organizations said that the main aim of HRD for managers was to upgrade existing skills and competencies. The objective of developing managers to fulfill career progression and management needs was also clear in five organizations, who saw HRD as a tool for developing professional managers.

The three organizations that practiced selective tracking of high-potential managers said that developing them was a major objective. Another two aimed at enhancing the personal development of individual managers.

Developing the needed specialization to meet existing and future challenges was also an expressed goal of two foreign companies. Two other companies offered HRD programs that supplied broadening experiences and exposure for senior managers. Another company saw a need to help new graduates settle efficiently into their jobs and to help them in developing their skills, knowledge, and expertise.

Activity Areas for Management Programs

HRD objectives for managers appeared to reflect different approaches to the three main activity areas. However, the foreign companies did not make conscious distinctions between training, education, and development. One corporation preferred to use the term training to refer to any form of organizational learning. Two others referred to the Nadler model and claimed that it helped them in program design and implementation. Even then, one focused only on training and education. The other concentrated just on training and development as seen in its graduate development programs, which were five-year learning endeavors. However, another two corporations felt that management development applied only to those with potential who were capable of further personal growth.

The other five companies saw development as an encompassing term for all learning activities specifically suited to management learning. This explains the frequent use of the terms "management development" and "supervisory development." They also saw management development as an activity area that used training and other tools, including the assessment center method, career management, and management succession planning to achieve the goal of an effective management corps.

Education played a minimal role in most of the foreign companies, and more often than not they did not provide or conduct educational programs. Instead, they preferred to consider education the prerogative of external institutions of learning. They occasionally sponsored or subsidized their employees' attendance at such institutions for personal growth.

Levels of HRD for Managers

Nearly all the foreign companies organized HRD activities for managers at three levels—supervisory, middle, and senior. However, the bulk of HRD programs was directed at middle management, with a few companies reporting that two-thirds of their management program budgets were reserved for middle management learning.

Supervisors were also provided with a fair amount of HRD activities. However, altogether they did not receive the attention, planning, and organization that middle management received. HRD programs for senior and top managers were done on an ad hoc basis. HRD units or departments had little control over the nomination of participants and choice of programs. For two multinational companies, HRD for expatriate officers, senior, and top managers was dealt with separately by the chief executive and had separate budgets.

Management Support Actions

The foreign companies attributed much of their success in implementing management programs to the undivided support they received from line managers from the chief executive down to middle management.

Actions reported

Commitment. Nine companies stated that had it not been for the commitment and involvement of the chief executives, programs for managers would have been less developed. In addition to the more ritualistic attendance of chief executives at top management programs, a few chief executives and general managers personally conducted closure sessions. One organization made it a practice of having the managing director or the general manager (at branch levels) conduct "Learning Points Reviews" at the end of programs. Chief executives of two companies personally examined the HRD needs of managers.

Budget. Eight foreign corporations said a generous budget showed management support for HRD. A few reported that added funding was feasible should they overrun their annual budgets. One organization said, "HRD needs determined our HRD budget."

Involvement of line managers. The active involvement of line managers in the HRD design process was another significant behavior in eight foreign companies. Line managers have been involved in HRD needs analysis, objective-setting, choice of curriculum content, and methodology. One company asserted, "Our general managers are committed to the idea of internal resourcing."

Line managers as instructors. Five companies regularly utilized line managers as instructors for in-house HRD programs, and the recognition of such services enhanced the image of the manager-instructor. These companies claimed to be highly supportive in releasing managers for HRD programs.

Line managers in evaluation. Four companies asserted that their managers were actively involved in follow-up evaluation, and monitored and supported the action plans to which participants were committed. The quarterly business-review meetings in one company gave the HRD units an opportunity to ensure that HRD was on target. This company also confirmed that line managers were working on follow-up evaluation.

Special project teams. Several companies formed special project teams or committees to help their HRD units implement activities for managers. "High powered" management development committees, training committees, and the like were said to have been instrumental in giving HRD units the necessary clout.

Other indicators. There were other important management-support indicators:

- Line managers in two companies attended reinforcement programs briefing them on proposed programs for subordinate managers. This was to ensure that managers were aware of the content of HRD programs.
- In one company, each department had an HRD contact person to handle the HRD activities of the department.
- Management by Objectives (MBO) was used by managers in one company as a tool to back up HRD.
- Line responsibility for OJT was another prevalent support behavior in one company.
- Divisional heads in one organization, to link HRD strategically to its organizational plans, used HRD programs as avenues of feedback from subordinate managers.

Funding of Management Programs

The question of how HRD was funded elicited more complicated responses. All except one company quoted figures for HRD that ranged from MR$150,000 to MR$1.3 million. However, they were quick to add that their budgets were not all-inclusive—expenses for activities such as training at regional centers, specialized training for various divisions, and educational grants were often listed separately.

Actual costs for management programs ranged from 30 to 70 percent of total budgets. While some companies complained that the economic recession had resulted in reduced HRD budgets, a few others claimed that only cost control measures were enforced. Commitment to HRD was best summed up by one corporation's stand: "If training is costly, try ignorance."

Records of HRD for Managers

All the HRD units kept files on managers' attendance records at HRD programs. There was also provision for the sharing of such information with the personnel and line divisions. However, while three companies recorded the integration of HRD files with personnel files, the other companies found little use for such integration. Neither did they find line managers having a use for such records. Two multinational companies kept "nonthreatening" evaluation records on participant performance at management programs. Still another recorded expenditures incurred in sponsoring individual managers for HRD programs.

Design of Management Programs

From the analysis of HRD needs of managers and the figures projected, HRD personnel in all foreign companies followed these procedures:

- Prioritized programs for managers, first for company needs and second for individual needs
- Developed objectives, content, and methodology, using input from line management
- Selected resource people from the HRD unit, line management, or external sources
- Prepared the proposed HRD calendars for the coming year, with synopses of topics, times, dates, and program venues. Then the division heads reviewed and reconfirmed the tentative calendars. Only one foreign company did not produce an annual calendar

Besides using input from line managers, two companies used the expertise of external consultants to help design programs for managers. Some also bought packaged instructional programs for managers and supervisors. HRD personnel were trained and then licensed by an overseas vendor to conduct the programs. For one company that conducted specialized in-house programs, program design was carried out by the relevant heads of departments, with the HRD unit only coordinating the program delivery.

Needs Assessment Procedures

The foreign corporations recognized the importance of assessing learning needs of managers before planning specific programs for them. They usually used a formalized instrument, such as the performance appraisal process used by nine foreign companies, as a major means of obtaining needs assessment data.

Six foreign companies also used other procedures. These included HRD-needs inventory questionnaires and assessment centers to augment the data derived from performance appraisal. Formal discussions held by line managers with training committees, training assessment groups, and management-development committees also helped to define and verify data regarding the HRD needs of managers. In two organizations, the Managing Director and the General Manager, Personnel, played the role of internal consultants with line managers to define and determine programs of action.

Mode of Conducting Management Programs

All the foreign companies conducted in-house and OJT programs, and in addition sponsored their managers for public, local, and overseas programs. Middle and senior managers were also often required to attend programs at their HRD centers abroad.

A third of the companies reported conducting internship programs for newly-recruited managers. A further third stated that their internship programs were temporarily shelved because of the recession. Several multinationals sponsored their junior and middle managers for public programs conducted by local management institutions. They also sent participants to public programs in Hong Kong, Singapore, the United States, Britain, and Switzerland.

Dominant Management Topics for In-House Programs

The foreign companies conducted a wide variety of management programs, with the ten most popular topics being

- Management processes and skills
- Problem solving and decision making
- Performance-appraisal processes
- Leadership and human relations
- Finance for non-finance managers
- Presentation skills and report writing
- Time management
- Communication in management
- Quality control circles
- Team building

Selection of Participants

Nomination by superiors, based on information derived from the needs assessment, was the major method by which participants for management programs were selected. Three organizations further catered, where possible, to personal requests to attend programs if superiors supported such applications. In one company, all fresh graduates had to undergo a Graduate Development Program that was staggered over five years.

A few companies nominated senior managers to attend specific programs that were mainly conducted abroad. However, most senior managers relied on chief executives or governing boards to approve their applications for attendance at advanced management programs. A few HRD personnel voiced their resentment of this practice, one remarking that many of these programs were " in actuality, holidays disguised as training."

In one multinational company, selected in-house programs were opened to managers from a public company, based on the provisions of a long-standing contract between the two organizations. This transfer of managerial know-how was considered an integral part of the overall transfer of technology.

Instructional Methods and Materials

Lecture supplemented by group discussion was the major instructional technique for managers' programs in the 10 foreign companies. Companies also used other techniques—such as case studies, role-plays, demonstrations, and simulations—from time to time to supplement the lecture method. Audiovisual aids included overhead projectors, filmstrips, films, and video.

Selection of Instructors and Facilitators

Line managers were the major source of instructors for in-house management programs in the foreign companies. Four companies officially regarded the role of instructor as a job duty. The foreign companies also preferred internal resources for their in-house programs, with one being explicit about not using any external consultants or instructors. Seven companies also used HRD personnel for their in-house programs.

At least four companies conducted formal train-the-trainer sessions for would-be instructors. This was separate from the specialized training that licensed instructors had to undergo before conducting purchased package programs. Still another company relied on visiting expatriates from its Head Office to conduct HRD programs for its managers.

Evaluation of Management Programs

Reaction forms completed by participants at the close of in-house sessions were the most popular source of evaluation of management programs. One company additionally provided for both formative and summative evaluations for the duration of its training programs.

Several companies felt the "reaction level" evaluation to be inadequate and relied more on feedback from line management to assess the effectiveness of the training programs. Of this group, two companies required that action plans be completed by participants. Their superiors were expected to monitor the progress of the action plans. A few companies formally followed up evaluation with post-instructional questionnaires to be completed by superiors from three to six months after the HRD activity.

When programs were conducted externally, formal evaluation was not feasible, so companies called for participants to submit reports summarizing program content and learning points to their superiors. Occasionally, HRD units were given copies of such feedback reports. Senior managers were excused from fulfilling the feedback requirement.

Conclusion

Obviously, any organization operating across national boundaries introduces a plethora of complications to the question of how HRD should be planned, organized, and run. At one extreme it can opt for a centralized HRD system and subject each employee to a unique program at some central location. At the other extreme, it can decide to delegate the HRD function to the management of the subsidiary, wherever it happens to be. A third approach is to structure HRD around a cluster of activities or regions — for example, a training center for agrochemical marketing or a training center for the ASEAN subsidiaries of a petroleum corporation.

The study revealed a diversity of approaches in HRD activities for managers in the foreign subsidiaries based in Malaysia. These approaches reflected different philosophies, content, and levels of programs. Often, the administrative setup for HRD divisions of multinationals prevented the function from getting the necessary visibility and strategic thrust.

Comparisons

The Malaysian study shows that multinational corporations displayed higher and more sophisticated levels of HRD activities for managers when compared with local and government corporations. Yet, in no way did they measure up to the real world of HRD at their corporate headquarters. The foreign companies' long-term perspectives in management development showed overt sensitivity and commitment to national policies. After all, it makes good business sense to display corporate citizenship. The question of eventual management control will inevitably surface, so it is not premature for foreign companies to take a long-term view and invest heavily in the development of local management capabilities.

The study indicated a correlation between equity control and the implementation of the HRD function. Where there was local equity involvement and accompanying host-country influence, the HRD function often displayed a balance between parent company guidelines and local aspirations.

The foreign companies usually had head-office support plus an international network of external resources to fall back on in their HRD efforts. However, there have been instances of parent companies imposing HRD activities on their Malaysian subsidiaries with insufficient regard to relevance, application, and cultural appropriateness. A few organizations often presented highly visible "one of a kind" sessions with expatriate management gurus—a practice which has caught on in the local scene.

While local managers were often groomed to manage local operations, their exposure to the rest of the organization was limited to what they had to know to succeed locally. The practical, operational, and technical slant was evident in the content of their HRD programs, compared with the more strategic, visionary, and creative flavor of programs for parent-company managers.

More recently some multinational enterprises have recruited graduating Malaysian students in overseas higher institutions for potential placement in Malaysian subsidiaries. The basic assumption was that such candidates would have the "right" academic and cultural orientation, besides the privilege of attending parent-company orientation programs.

Technology transfer

The clarion call for technology transfer—incorporating the managerial learning element—by multinational enterprises was based on the need to make clear the meaning of the "technology packages" —that is, the ability to absorb, understand, and use the transferred technologies. As early as 1974 Robinson wrote:

"Rather the question is whether corporations operate in ways which enhance the country's total and particularly internal capability for further growth, for if they do not, we have merely transplanted organisms which may well generate the antibodies leading to their ultimate rejection" (p. 47).

Perhaps it would be inappropriate to generalize from earlier studies that multinationals in both Malaysia and Singapore did not contribute as much to local technological development when compared with local organizations (Lim, 1978; Saravanamuthu, 1985). Provision for greater technological self-reliance would be a key factor in future multinational-host country relations.

As was true with the other Malaysian enterprises, the multinational corporations focused their HRD investment at middle-management levels. Moreover, their programs were mainly geared to helping managers function at current operational instead of future or strategic levels. Limited attention was paid to supervisory levels, although the supervisor's position on the front line of management demanded specialized capabilities and skills. This is very pertinent for Malaysia, where most supervisors do not have the benefit of formalized management programs before they begin their work life.

Cross-cultural issues

The growing concern with cross-cultural issues in management on the international front has made itself felt on the local scene. Companies have become increasingly concerned with the appropriateness of transferring of managerial concepts, theories, and techniques from a Western cultural context to a Malaysian one. Japanese management theories have been less questioned, because there are more cultural similarities!

Cross-cultural issue is further compounded by the fact that Malaysia is a pluralistic society comprising three distinct ethnic groups. In dealing with this diversity, both foreigners and locals alike resort to ethnic stereotyping, and negative connotations surface. Practical answers on how best to transmit culturally appropriate management know-how in a culturally appropriate manner are still not forthcoming. Meanwhile, it may be well to adopt de Bettignies' positive stance on this issue. He argued that "local cultures and indigenous values can probably be used more as assets around which appropriate learning systems are designed, rather than perceived as liabilities that must be eliminated through an imported learning system." (1983, p. 35) After all, most chief executives and senior managers of multinational enterprises in Malaysia have learned the cultural appropriateness of making ritualistic appearances and speeches at the opening and closing of HRD programs!

Multinational enterprises in Malaysia are also becoming increasingly sensitive to appropriate teaching and learning styles and techniques for their HRD programs. Basic commonalities in Asian culture suggest that Malaysians prefer learning situations more didactic and teacher centered, with instructors playing the role of providers of knowledge (Kirkbride et al, 1989). This is further substantiated by Hofstede's research on the cultural dimensions of work behavior that rated Malaysia as having the highest "power distance" ranking in the international sample. Power distance is seen as the extent to which members of a society accept unequal distribution of power in organizations (1980). In extending this model to the HRD situation, Hofstede (1986) deduced that when there is high power distance, practitioners would be regarded as authority figures who should not be challenged.

Toward a Malaysian management system

All of these cross-cultural issues present program planning dilemmas to HRD personnel in multinational organizations. To stereotype Malaysians as exhibiting the learning style described above would obviously be too simplistic. At the same time, if they are thrown into the deep end of the experiential learning continuum, with unstructured and spontaneous activities, the charge of being culturally insensitive could surface.

The evolution of a distinct Malaysian management system on which multinationals could base their HRD programs still appears to be elusive and remote. Even so, it is said that Malaysian managers tend to be caught up with a grand search for identity. They appear to be torn between developing a distinctly indigenous management system and importing management models. This attempt to be eclectic against a backdrop of Islamization is no mean challenge!

References

Agthe, K. E., and Pendegast, K. J. "Bhurniputra: What Is It? And Why Do I Need It?" *Business Horizons* Nov. - Dec. 1983, pp. 60-68.

American Society for Training and Development. *Serving the New Corporation.* Alexandria, VA: author, 1986

de Bettignies, H. C. "Management Development: The International Perspective." *Malaysian Management Review* X (2),1975, p. 3846.

de Bettignies, H. C. "The Challenge of Management Training in Asia". *Euro-Asian Business Review,* II (4), 1983, pp. 34-39.

Dyrnsza, W. A. "The Education and Development of Managers for Future Decades." *Journal of International Business Studies,* Winter 1982, pp. 9-18.

Everett, J. E., Krishnan, A. R., and Stening, B. W. *South-East Asian Managers.* Singapore: Eastern Universities Press, 1984.

Eurich, N. *Corporate Classrooms: The Learning Business.* (A Carnegie Foundation special report). Princeton, NJ: Princeton University Press, 1985.

Forrester, P. "Developing Professional Managers." In *The Future of Management Education,* A. Kakabadse and S. Mukhi (Eds.). New York, NY: Nichols Publishing Co., 1984, pp. 193-202.

Hamid, A. A., Md. Salleh, A. M., Muhammad, J. and Ismail, Z. "Management Education in Malaysia." *Malaysian Management Review* XII, 1985, pp. 478-93.

Hofstede, G. *Culture's Consequences: International Differences in Work Related Values.* Beverly Hills, CA: Sage Publications, 1980.

Hofstede, G. "Cultural Differences in Teaching and Learning." *International Journal of Intercultural Relations,* 10, 1986, pp. 301-320.

Ismail, Z. M. HRD "Practices for Managers in Selected Malaysian Corporations."(Doctoral dissertation, George Washington University). Ann Arbor, MI: University Microfilms International, 1988.

Kirkbride, P. S., Tang, S. F. Y., and Shae, W. C. "The Transferability of Management Training and Development: The Case of Hong Kong." *Asia Pacific Human Resource Management,* Feb. 1989, pp. 7-19.

Lee, J. A. "The Dangers in Importing Human Resource Management Theories." *Berita Personnel,* 1983, pp. 15-23.

Lim, L. Y. "Multinational Firms and Manufacturing for Export in Less Developed Societies: The Case of Electronics Industry in Malaysia and Singapore." (Doctoral dissertation, University of Michigan). *Dissertation Abstracts International,* XXXIX / 10A, 1978, p. 6236.

Nadler, L. *Corporate Human Resource Development: A Management Tool.* New York, NY: Van Nostrand Reinhold, 1980.

Nadler, L. "Management Education in an Independent World." In *The Future of Management Education,* A. Kakabadse and S. Mukhi (Eds.). New York, NY: Nichols,1984, pp. 344-359.

Nadler, L. "High Stakes HRD: Working Internationally" *Training and Development Journal,* 39, Oct. 1985, p. 25.

Pillai, P. "Benefits From Training of Malaysian Staff in Japan." *New Straits Times,* Oct. 15, 1986, p. 8.

Robinson, H. "The Challenge of National Development to Multinational Corporate Management." *Malaysian Management Review,* IX, 1974, pp. 42-52.

Saravanamuthu, J. "The Look East Policy and Japanese Economic Penetration in Malaysia." In *The Sun Also Sets: Lessons in Looking East.* K. S. Jomo (Ed., Second Edition). Kuala Lumpur: INSAN, 1985, pp. 312-316.

Smith, W. "A Japanese Factory in Malaysia: Ethnicity as a Management Ideology". *The Sun Also Sets: Lessons in Looking East,* K. S. Jomo (Ed., Second Edition). Kuala Lumpur: INSAN, 1985, pp. 278-304.

About the Author

Zulaiha Ismail is Head of the Resource Center for Teaching and Learning at the Institut Teknologi Mara in Malaysia. Previously, she was Senior Lecturer in the School of Business and Management at the Institut Teknologi Mara. She is a founder and a committee member of the Women for Women Association of Malaysia, and a member of the American Society for Training and Development and the Malaysian Institute of Management. She completed her doctoral studies in Human Resource Development at George Washington University.

CHAPTER 25

HRD Practitioner Utilization in Asia

Chalintorn Burian
Eduardo Q. Canela

Asia has come a long way in the past decade! Gradually, it is moving from a chiefly agricultural region to one that is increasingly industrial. Its populations are changing from landholders to industrial entrepreneurs; from mere raw materials suppliers to industrial processors of finished goods. Its industries are changing from being labor intensive with rudimentary technologies to those that apply advanced technologies.

What are the implications for Human Resource Development? How are these changes reshaping HRD practice in Asian countries? What are the implications for foreign HRD practitioners? We will address these and other questions in this chapter.

For the past decade, the development of most Asian countries has been remarkable. For example, Japan is now a major global-development aid donor. So are Taiwan and Singapore. Asia started its hard drive for rapid industrialization in the early 1980s. In 1990, it created an economic uproar by spawning industrial "dragons" (Newly Industrializing Countries, NIC's): South Korea, Taiwan, Hong Kong, and Singapore. Resilient despite many global odds, Asia will continue to create ever more economic "tigers" as it rushes into the twenty-first century: Thailand and Malaysia, and soon Indonesia and the Philippines. And these comprise merely the tip of the iceberg—China and the entire subcontinent led by India have the necessary human resources and potential markets to sustain long periods of growth. This is also true of Cambodia, Laos, Vietnam, and Burma, most of which are trying to restructure at least parts of their economies with "free" markets.

Some Asians are turning from being international employees to global employers. Japanese, Taiwanese, South Korean, and Singaporean companies have begun to sprout in the European and North and South American continents. A few Bangladesh-based companies have established joint ventures in the West. Such companies are employing people from their host environments.

These changes are happening because of Asia's geopolitical advantages. The continent has an expanding population that is still relatively young and vigorous. It is not only a source of cheap labor but also will remain the most influential market for the next century.

Asia has a dark side, too. Except for a handful of countries, most of Asia is still beset with crippling poverty, occasional natural calamities, periodic political upheavals, stalled economic progress, unemployment and low labor productivity, inadequate physical infrastructure, and persistently inequitable income and opportunities distribution. Today, many Asians are no better off than they were twenty years ago.

These two faces of Asia will continue to baffle even the brightest development economists. Some countries have yet to explore many relevant economic and non-economic factors. They are still being debated in academic circles and development forums. Most are beyond the scope of this chapter, but while these factors exist, they will continue irreversibly to reshape Asia.

Exploding Needs for HRD Services

There are several factors determining the exploding needs for HRD services in Asia. There is a persistent mismatch between the qualifications of the graduates of the existing educational systems and specific needs of the economic machinery. These are experienced in the industrial, agricultural, and service sectors. They cause shortages of needed technical and skilled labor. Rapid technological changes further exacerbate the earlier mentioned "education-to-economy" mismatch, while Asia continues to benefit from the current globalization and "multinationalization" of industrial activities. Meanwhile, the need intensifies for employees to learn new knowledge and skills and to gain new experiences . Some global events add to the pressure, for example, the 1990-1991 Gulf crisis. Millions of Asian workers in Middle Eastern countries faced the grim prospect of having to go back to their respective countries. Many had to be trained or retrained.

However, even this side of Asia is not altogether dark. As in past decades, Asia will continue to attract capital development funds from various sources. At the same time, there is an emerging consensus toward self-sustainable initiatives. Questions like "How can we maintain the services with little or no external supports?" have surfaced. This type of question demands that the transfer of knowledge and skills should be fast and effective.

The national five-year development plans (in some cases, a sectoral manpower plan also exists) usually quantify the HRD needs for many Asian countries. Therefore, it is essential to conduct HRD needs assessment before undertaking any HRD-based interventions in those countries.

Qualitatively, however, most Asian countries agree that they must meet their HRD needs effectively in the coming century. These HRD needs will vary from country to country. They will include at least the following:

- Technical knowledge and skills (preferably in high technology areas)
- Development management
- Organizational skills development
- Management skills for small and medium size businesses
- Indigenous entrepreneurship
- Quality control
- Human resource development skills
- Human resource management skills
- Management of change
- Safety and loss control management
- Environmental management (including pollution control and industrial waste management)
- Cross-cultural and cross-disciplinary communications
- Use of computer, telecommunication, and information technologies

To meet these HRD needs effectively, professional inputs from HRD practitioners become essential

The Asian HRD Scene: The "Players" and the "Game Plan"

This section deals with issues concerning HRD "players" in Asian countries. We will examine how needs for HRD practitioners are triggered, how HRD practitioners are chosen, and how HRD is managed. As suggested in the chapter title, we will emphasize foreign HRD practitioners, especially external ones.

The HRD players

There are several ways to classify HRD players. We will classify them into three HRD-related groups: decision-makers, practitioners, and beneficiaries.

The HRD decision-makers. These are the people responsible for human-resource development schemes. To complete their missions, they sometimes employ HRD practitioners to carry out assignments. The Asian HRD decision-makers are usually in the government, the private sector, and the many nongovernmental organizations (NGO's). HRD decision-makers —also called "HRD clients"—are usually responsible for HRD results.

In Asia, the HRD decision-makers in the government have many titles. They are development project director, training manager, project officer, and a host of other titles. They are either hired for a fixed term or as permanent civil servants, and they perform many technical and administrative functions. Decision-makers in the private sector also have many titles, including corporate HRD manager, training manager, HRD vice president, or management support services manager. With the NGO's, the titles include chief operating officer, project manager, or training manager.

Usually, the HRD decision-makers have been exposed only to traditional lecture training methods. They also often think of the HRD field as equal to "training," and they usually have neither the time nor means to learn about holistic and systematic HRD approaches. Neither do they really wish to shop around for appropriate HRD practitioners or packages. Instead, they rely on their friends or constituencies for information on what worked and what didn't. "Good reputation of HRD practitioner," "package efficacy," and "relevant track record" passed via word-of-mouth are still the best ways to reach them.

But HRD decision-makers are intelligent, experienced, and dedicated to their work in many Asian countries like Thailand, Singapore, Malaysia, and Hong Kong. They understand systematic, holistic HRD approaches and strategies, and the long-term benefits these approaches and strategies will provide. They often quickly become the most valuable advocates for the HRD profession. This usually is when a holistic HRD endeavor starts to take root. In practice, to get to this stage, you must help HRD decision-makers to understand HRD.

Who are HRD practitioners? Although Nadler and Nadler's model of HRD roles and subroles is derived from research carried out in the United States, the model has proven applicable in Asian countries. It is fair to say that on the Asian HRD scene, local, Asian-based, and foreign HRD practitioners are given an equal opportunity to prove their worth. Contrary to the past, today's HRD decision-makers usually do not sacrifice quality of work for racial sentiment or "connections." Unsatisfactory outcomes of an HRD intervention could mean losing face and credibility, which have an immense impact in Asian societies.

While still a recent development, more Asian decision-makers prefer practitioners who are willing to learn about Asia. They prefer ones who are willing to help in Asia's transformation. A Filipino legislator once remarked: "Without adequate in-country exposure, foreign consultants (most especially those with significant HRD content in their job descriptions) intending to work in the Philippines cannot properly contextualize the constantly evolving changes in the country."

In Asia, such changes are creating numerous opportunities for foreign HRD practitioners with the needed HRD know-how.

HRD beneficiaries. HRD beneficiaries are people who directly or indirectly gain knowledge and skill through HRD interventions. Some project documents call beneficiaries "target groups."

How needs for external HRD practitioners are triggered

In the government sector, organizations try to meet HRD needs outlined in each country's national five-year development or sectoral manpower plan in-house. Still, they often engage external HRD practitioners in areas where there is no in-house staff with the needed HRD knowledge and skills. Sometimes, bilateral or multilateral negotiations for development aid trigger the need for external HRD services. Usually, the Project Document and the Plan of Operations for projects specify the job description of the needed external foreign HRD practitioners, and the HRD practitioners are selected from the donor's country. However, HRD is relatively a new profession, and many donors have become more aware of the lack of needed HRD practitioners from their own country and will allow selection of HRD practitioners from other countries. While donors still have a say in the choice, Asian governments increasingly prefer joint selection processes. Eventually, selection decisions will be made less by the donors and more by the host countries.

Private enterprises usually feel the need for HRD practitioners in response to the newness of the technologies they are using, multicultural eccentricities, and labor intensity. In most cases that involve joint ventures and technology licensing agreements, the technology donors (especially the Japanese, Taiwanese, and Europeans) prefer to use technology experts from their own organization's system.

The success of technology transfer depends largely on the inputs from HRD practitioners. Qualified practitioners are usually not available internally, and the immense risk of not having staff properly prepared for new changes and efficient technology transfer often encourages management to hire external, foreign HRD practitioners. They hope this will ensure the success of the technology transfer. The numerous Asian NGO's—whether local or international—have a significant demand for HRD practitioners. In the Philippines, estimates claim there are more than 15,000 NGO's, in Indonesia 2000, in Malaysia more than 200, and about 200 in Thailand. More than 300 each operate in Sri Lanka, Bangladesh, and Nepal. Most NGO's provide their target groups with knowledge and skills in

- Income generating
- Small business management
- Entrepreneurship skills
- Family planning, health care
- Appropriate technology

The need is growing for HRD learning specialists to design learning programs with subject-matter experts in these areas. NGO's often call on HRD practitioners to design and implement a "train-the-trainers" program for their personnel.

Hiring of local or foreign HRD practitioners is usually done by the NGO's themselves. Their decisions on recruitment and hiring normally derive from close consultation with their associates in various formal and informal NGO networks. However, to ensure the quality of the HRD done in NGO's, donors sometimes hire their own HRD practitioners to evaluate it.

Besides hiring external (especially foreign) HRD practitioners for their specialized expertise, there are other reasons for using them. Sometimes in-house staff have no time to do the tasks themselves. The decision-makers may also need objectivity from outsiders or, in certain situations, it's more politically advantageous to use external HRD practitioners.

How external HRD practitioners are chosen

A general set of selection criteria for an HRD Practitioner is usually a part of "Terms of Reference" (TOR). These criteria are sometimes combined with other specific requirements, such as cultural sensitivity, language capability, etc. Usually, organizations consider expertise, experience, competency, approach, working relationship, and professionalism. The discussion that follows will cover how they evaluate these criteria and balance them against other factors in the selection process.

Working relationship between HRD decision-makers or counterparts and HRD practitioners. In many organizations, decision-makers also become counterparts of HRD practitioners. As a result of the complicated Asian organizational hierarchy and bureaucracy, organizations often assign an individual or group of people as counterparts of HRD practitioners. Whether also the decision-maker or not, a counterpart is an HRD client and plays an important role in ensuring that the HRD engagement is on the right track to complete the agreed objectives on time and with maximum benefit. We discuss the practitioner-counterpart relationships, which usually determine the success of the engagement, later in this chapter.

Formerly, Asians viewed external expertise with great respect. Those supplying the expertise used titles that indicated a superior role, such as "advisers," and "experts." That has all changed. Today, the HRD practitioner should not expect to become a "supervisor," but an equal partner with the Asian counterparts. Gone are the days of the adviser-advisee relationship. Partnership has replaced it. Decision-makers are looking for effective practitioners who cherish relationships more than paper results. They seek those who will be able to relate to their counterparts more easily than those who either don't care to do so or simply cannot.

Expertise, experience and competency according to job description. Obviously, an HRD practitioner needs expertise compatible with required tasks. Experience, especially Asian experience, serves as a measure of how well an HRD practitioner can assimilate and work well within the culture. What is possible and plausible?

What is definitely impossible? It would be extremely difficult now to penetrate the HRD market without solid Asian experience.

Besides HRD know-how and appropriate experience shown by a proven track record, sponsors consider other qualifications, the most notable being the ability to transfer practical experiences to one's counterpart. Such practical experiences usually include the capacity of the practitioners themselves to unlearn, and then learn the host country's preferred behavior and style of working.

Ever more human relations skills are required from HRD practitioners. We can simply describe such competency as "facilitator plus." The "plus" part would normally include relationship building, empathy with counterparts, clarity in all transactions, and mediating skills.

A résumé or *curriculum vitae* cannot totally reflect most of these types of knowledge, experience, and competency. The interviews that HRD decision-makers hold with the HRD practitioners themselves identified them. Recommendations of their references and past clients, as well as other observations, are also important.

Approach. Previously, the approach was normally a transfer from the West to the East. Now the approach should definitely be a combination of what is Eastern and what is Western. Unfortunately, because the HRD field is very new in Asia, not much HRD research is based on Asian countries. Therefore, most strategies and techniques in use remain influenced by research findings from the West. For example, European and North American research is the basis for the approach to adult learning.

Practitioner's professionalism. Whether an HRD practitioner is working as a learning specialist, manager of HRD, or consultant in HRD matters, clients expect the practitioner to handle the job professionally in all aspects of the engagement. Decision-makers and counterparts recognize the professionalism through the way the practitioner handles

- Negotiations
- Contracting, and diagnosis of situation and problems at hand
- Approaches used to solve problems
- Techniques (and tactics) in securing assistance and getting needed data and information
- The work plan and time management
- Measures in securing continuing commitment
- Involvement and feedback from decision-makers and concerned parties
- Techniques in helping clients (decision-makers and HRD counterparts), beneficiaries, and others in the supporting system to help themselves and to maximize the benefits from the intervention
- Developing and maintaining relationships with clients
- Recording and reporting
- Techniques in closing the engagement

Implications for Foreign HRD Practitioners: The Client's Perspective

We gathered the following comments, suggestions, and recommendations from interviews with processors and users of foreign HRD practitioners. We also drew on observations of HRD practitioners at work in various engagements in some Asian countries.

Selling of services

Usually, Asians—especially government decision-makers—prefer nonselling techniques. Word of mouth is still prevalent despite advances in telecommunications. If you intend to work in Asia, you must have already tested and proven your methodologies elsewhere, preferably in countries economically and socially comparable with the client's country. Direct selling through advertisements is normally regulated by the professional public relations businesses and has little effect in getting the users to consider one's HRD services. More effective is a referral by decision-makers' or counterparts' trusted individuals or organizations. A referral from another HRD practitioner who has proved his or her worth and gained trust from decision-makers and counterparts is also most useful. The importance of a courtesy call resulting from these referrals should not be overlooked, because it often leads to engagements or other employment possibilities. Valuable leads can also come from local HRD associations and societies.

Handling contracts and agreements

Clarity and accountability concerning what and how much is to be accomplished through the engagement are important considerations. Discuss and agree upon fees at an early stage—Asians usually enjoy bargaining in all sorts of negotiations. Some HRD practitioners offer some significant "extras," such as an additional few days free of charge to prepare their clients to work with them. Clients consider this a plus.

HRD know-what and know-how

As with the 1980s, the HRD needs for the 1990s are focused on the "how" instead of simply the "what." HRD "whats" and "hows" are still quite unfamiliar in the Asian experience. A need for HRD practitioners who can provide the HRD "know-what" and "know-how" will rise in Asian countries during the next decade.

Cultural and cross-cultural skills have also become essential in HRD services. An interesting recent phenomenon is that Asian HRD decision-makers are becoming more aware of their own traditions and cultural heritage. They have developed a healthy questioning attitude. For example: "Is this concept appropriate in our context, culture, diversity and uniqueness?" They also now know of the inherent strengths of "Eastern ways," and they try hard to preserve them, as well as to benefit best from them.

Relationship with clients

It is wise to involve one's clients actively in decisions about the project throughout its life. If one has counterparts who are also HRD practitioners, or at least understand the HRD concept and philosophy, one is very fortunate. Most counterparts still do not understand HRD, and it is essential for external practitioners to help them understand the HRD field and its contribution as early as possible in the project. "Teaching someone how to fish, rather than giving them a fish" still works as the best concept in practitioner-client relationships. We asked Asian counterparts to name one most important point they remember about their liaisons with HRD practitioners. Many agree that they are most impressed by the effort certain HRD practitioners take to prepare them as capable counterparts. A Thai counterpart explained it as follows: "He helps me to understand what I should expect and demand from him through contract development and evaluative measures. In the end, not only have we accomplished all the tasks, but I also could prove to others that I was capable of handling both the engagement and the external practitioner. In fact, now I think I can handle other engagements and HRD practitioners with even better efficiency."

Relationship with donors

HRD practitioners usually do not have to deal with donors at all, but sometimes they are secured for clients by donor agencies themselves. In this situation, HRD practitioners need to deal cautiously with both donor and client. Donors often use the same HRD practitioners repeatedly in various situations, so having a good relationship with donors is always helpful.

Relationship with other HRD practitioners

Sometimes a situation calls for two or more HRD practitioners to work together on an assignment. How one HRD practitioner deals with other practitioners reflects on his or her professionalism. Never "put down" others with your clients, as this tends to backfire. Cooperation should rise above competition. If there are too many conflicts to provide a win-win situation, stay away from one another. Clients should not have to play referee or take sides. It is wise never to force them into this undesirable role.

Relationship with subject matter and technology experts

Often, organizations call on HRD practitioners to work with subject matter experts. For example, these include petroleum engineers, marketing experts, computer specialists, and organization development consultants. However, most subject matter and technology experts do not understand HRD, so the relationship can be tense and tiring at times. Human relations skills and professionalism can help to reduce tension and bring about a successful closure of an engagement.

Some reasons HRD practitioners are not called back

HRD decision-makers and counterparts often describe their working experience with some foreign HRD practitioners as "trying to squeeze orange juice from an apple." When HRD practitioners lack the needed skills, it shows. This is a major reason for not using those HRD practitioners again. Other reasons we also hear include cultural differences and different working styles and habits. Most interesting, however, is when it looks as though everyone is developing a splendid relationship. Then the practitioner is not called back for another assignment because of "playing too much internal politics" or "knows too much about our organizational politics." It is important that you know where the line is drawn. Then you will not cause the host discomfort.

Current HRD Issues

Establishing an acceptance of HRD practitioners

One of the most important issues both local and foreign HRD practitioners must deal with in Asia is the need to establish acceptance of HRD practitioners and their contributions. HRD is a familiar term to many of Asia's policy makers. Many have even included HRD statements in their National Development plans. Yet, most people still do not understand HRD and its real contributions. Because of their naiveté, they simply equate HRD with "training," and claim that through their "training," HRD has always been a major concern of their government for their constituencies.

Left with no specific HRD guidelines, many newly industrialized countries still approach HRD needs on a piecemeal basis. They employ a hit-and-run approach. They focus more on content of knowledge and skill to be learned, than on confirming that learning does happen and that problems get solved.

Many Asian countries have become more affluent, so money is available to fund learning experiences for their work force. They really cannot afford to waste time and energy by not handling their HRD endeavors the "right" way through competent HRD practitioners. There are several ways to establish acceptance of HRD philosophy and the roles of the HRD practitioner.

Promotion of the HRD concept and philosophy. HRD is a set of concepts and philosophies calling for immediate and large-scale application. It is the HRD practitioner's responsibility to help establish the knowledge and understanding of HRD. This can be done by providing workshops and seminars on HRD philosophy, strategy, and techniques and making appropriate HRD literature available. Most of all, practitioners themselves must demonstrate their capability and integrity.

The process of gaining acceptance is slow. In Thailand, for example, the term "HRD" has appeared in the Five-Year National Economic and Social Development plans since the early 1980s. Still, not many people, policymakers included, can clearly define the meaning of HRD. In 1986, a seminar on "Human Resource Development for

Thailand's Industrialization: Policy, Strategy, and Techniques" was held by the Petroleum Institute of Thailand. Only then did participants from the public, academic, and private sectors begin to understand HRD. It has taken quite some time from the stage of "understanding" to "implementation." All sectors expressed an urgent need to establish an HRD degree program at selected universities in Thailand at the 1986 seminar, but it was not given serious consideration until 1990. The same pattern in handling HRD issues exists in the Philippines, Singapore, and Malaysia. Unless the HRD field is well understood and established, HRD practitioners will always risk not receiving the right kind of credibility and acceptance from users.

Helping people to understand how to maximize inputs from HRD practitioners. Part of the problem is the difficulty of helping Asians reap the benefits of HRD, irrespective of whether the inputs come from locals or foreigners. There are signs that times are gradually changing. There are ever more HRD practitioners contracted to work alongside subject-matter or technology experts in achieving learning, management, and consulting goals. Many development cooperation projects fail in Thailand and the Philippines. Attempts have been made to introduce methodologies in which project success is measured by whether problems are solved or not. This is instead of whether activities (training, consulting, etc.) are carried out or not, as in the past. Helping people understand how to measure an HRD practitioner's competency is a constructive task that every practitioner should undertake.

Establishing HRD networks and societies. There is certainly a dearth of HRD networks and societies in Asian countries, except some on the subcontinent. However, most Asian countries, particularly those in ASEAN, have national societies for training and development. There is a need for foreign practitioners to help these professional societies go in the right HRD direction. In February 1990, Dr. Leonard Nadler gave a dinner speech on "How Managers Can Benefit from HRD Societies" to members and nonmembers of the Thailand Society for Training and Development. A certain rapport was established among the audience because they gained better understanding and appreciation of HRD as a profession and the HRD practitioner's role.

Standardizing HRD practitioners and services. HRD is unlike recognized professions such as management consultants, engineers, accountants, medical doctors, and nurses. HRD practitioners still need to be established as professionals in many Asian countries. This will require much time. We must separate what is HRD from what is not, through initial qualification requirements, certification methods, enforcement of certification standards, and professional grading systems. Some HRD professional societies in Singapore, Malaysia, Thailand, and the Philippines are looking into measures to provide certification standards in the field.

Establishing HRD critical mass

A critical mass of initial supporters of HRD is needed in Asia. The few who understand the practice are not able to disseminate and promote the work required. Indeed, a truly Asian HRD institution has yet to evolve, whether on a specific country or a regional basis.

Formal HRD degree programs. There is no highly acclaimed HRD degree program in Asia. Most HRD practitioners have backgrounds in public administration, business management, organizational development, higher education, or applied industrial psychology, with some training in HRD. Many local HRD practitioners have learned in the "hard knocks" school. Also, many educational programs would not qualify as HRD because they lack depth or breadth. However, there have been some attempts to establish HRD degree programs in several countries. In the Philippines, for example, a master's program in HRD has been established by the University of the Philippines Institute of Industrial Relations. Although Malaysia and Singapore do not have in-country HRD degree programs, both have collaborated with George Washington University in the U.S. They arranged for students from those countries to do some course work in their own country. Some went to the U.S. to receive a graduate degree from George Washington University. Also, there are a few colleges throughout Asia that offer courses emphasizing training methodologies. Although these are still small efforts to create a critical mass of HRD practitioners, they represent a significant improvement compared with the past decade.

Training HRD practitioners. While we wait for HRD practitioners to graduate from degree programs, there is also an urgent broad-based demand for other training of HRD practitioners. To help those who are responsible for HRD services to do their tasks better, many Asian countries have sponsored a series of intensive training programs for HRD practitioners. This type of program goes beyond the train-the-trainers module. It is designed to provide participants with knowledge and some specific practical skills in performing HRD roles: learning specialist, manager of HRD, and consultant. In 1990, thirty-six HRD practitioners graduated from this program in Thailand. Similar programs are also available in Singapore, Malaysia, and Japan.

Helping management executives to understand HRD. To facilitate the implementation of HRD schemes and the work of HRD practitioners, efforts have also been made to help management executives understand the HRD concept. Intensive one-day seminars and workshops on HRD can provide executives with the right frame of mind about HRD and its contributions as a management tool. For political reasons, the presentation should be conducted by external (and foreign) HRD practitioners, as long as they are very competent in delivering such presentations.

Future Trends

The preceding section is not intended to suggest ways and means to replace HRD practitioners in Asia with local ones. There is no threat to the employment of foreign HRD practitioners in Asia in the foreseeable future. However, the expertise needed from foreign HRD practitioners will be different than in the past. As the HRD field grows, needs will certainly be modified. Some trends for providing HRD services include the following:

Research in HRD

As the HRD field in Asia matures, research in HRD will be more in demand. Issues like how Asian adults learn, who should provide learning programs for HRD practitioners, and where the HRD system fits best into an organizational structure must be answered.

HRD Management Information System

As in other parts of the world, HRD activities in Asia accumulate considerable data and information. Learning how to manage an HRD Management Information System (HRD-MIS) will become crucial.

Laws and regulations concerning HRD

Except in Singapore, there are presently no specific laws and regulations about HRD in Asian countries. But soon Asian countries will have to deal with this issue, especially when facing problems on work force migration.

Cooperation among HRD organizations at the national, regional, and international levels

Some cooperation is already taking place. For example, there are the Asian Regional Training and Development Organization (ARTDO), and the Asian Productivity Organization (APO). More cooperation of this type can be expected soon.

Developing local HRD practitioners to work in other Asian countries

Vietnam, Laos, Burma, Cambodia, and China are opening their societies. More HRD practitioners, especially those of Asian origin, will be needed by those countries. Many Asian HRD practitioners are already tuning and sharpening their knowledge and skills for these possibilities.

Conclusion

Through contributions from foreign HRD practitioners, HRD in Asia has advanced rapidly. It still has a long way to go. A part of growing up is becoming independent and self-reliant. That means "cutting the umbilical cord." When local HRD practitioners are finally capable of meeting HRD needs in their country, the need for foreign HRD practitioners will decrease. Many foreign HRD practitioners are aware of this eventuality. Many have claimed they are doing their best to move themselves out of business. When that goal is achieved, it will demonstrate the debt owed to the skills of foreign HRD practitioners who are currently helping people to learn "how to fish." And that is commendable.

References

Block, P. *Flawless Consultants*. La Jolla, CA: University Associates, 1981.

Bell, C., and Nadler, L. *Clients & Consultants*. Houston, TX: Gulf Publishing, 1986.

Hofstede, G. *Culture's Consequences*. New York, NY: Cultural Press USA, 1988.

Nadler, L., and Nadler, Z. *Developing Human Resources*. La Jolla, CA: Jossey-Bass Inc. Publishers, 1989.

Nadler, L., and Nadler, Z. *Corporate Human Resources Development*. Alexandria, VA: American Society for Training and Development, 1980.

Nadler, L., and Nadler, Z. *The Handbook of Human Resource Development* (Second Edition). New York, NY: Wiley, 1990.

About the Authors

Chalintorn N. Burian is a doctoral candidate in Human Organization Development at the Fielding Institute. Until recently, she was Human Resource Development Director of the Petroleum Institute of Thailand. Previously, she was President TED (Training, Education, and Development) Systems, Inc. in Hawaii, HRD consultant to Coopers & Lybrand in Thailand, and training consultant to the Provincial Waterworks Authority of Thailand. She was the Vice President of the Thailand Society for Training and Development. She is a member of the American Society for Training and Development, East-West Center Association Executive Board, and Bangkok Woman Forum.

Eduardo Q. Canela is Managing Director of the Foundation for Entrepreneurship and Appropriate Technology (FEAT) in Manila, The Philippines. Formerly, he was with the German Agency for Technical Cooperation, the World Bank, the International Labor Organization, and Technonet Asia. He holds a B.S. in Electrical Engineering and an M.B.A.

CHAPTER 26

Generating Team Spirit: Do Western Training Approaches Have Anything to Contribute to Asian Clients?

Phyliss Cooke, Ralph Bates, and Ronnie Ng

Much has been written about the need for increased cultural sensitivity as consultants and trainers attempt to adapt and transfer their theories, materials, and techniques to the expanding global training markets. Indeed, skilled and experienced professionals have discovered, to their surprise, that while they may have worked successfully with a wide range of culturally sensitive issues in the U.S., if they are to work successfully with Asian groups and clients they still have much to learn.

If you asked a group of American consultants or training professionals who have worked with a variety of Asian clients to list their distinguishing characteristics, the factors that affect how one works with them, and their issues, no doubt the list would include

- An emphasis on "saving face"
- Avoidance of conflict or disagreement
- Reluctance to take risks or to voice personal opinions
- A hesitancy to question ideas, especially those presented by the leaders or experts
- Reliance on the direction provided by others, usually the formal leaders

- General acceptance of unusually long working hours (more than 10 hours per day at the workplace, plus commuting time)
- Dislike for participating in open dialogue with the leader or expert in a group setting

Are these differences in attitudes, preferences, or expectations? Are they really that significant? Are there significant cultural differences in these areas between U.S. and Asian participants in training? If so, do Western concepts and approaches to training have anything to offer to Asian client groups?

A Training Intervention

Our answers to these questions follow in what might best be described as a case study of a training intervention. The primary objectives of the intervention were

- To implement a training program based on experiential learning concepts and techniques within an Asian client system
- To incorporate laboratory education components in the design
- To provide an intensive laboratory education experience for trainees who had not previously participated in such training design in order to assess the validity of commonly held assumptions about Asian learners
- To introduce experienced supervisory personnel to specific personal and group issues thought to affect attitudes and performance in current job responsibilities, such as how to generate team spirit, the importance of personal accountability, self-initiated leadership on group performance, and the effects of group support on individual motivation and risk-taking behavior

Before describing the client system and the training intervention in more detail, we will describe the more traditional educational (and previous training) experience of the Asian learners involved in this project.

Traditional Approaches to Education and Training

Learning needs

The teacher, trainer, or expert is responsible for determining learning needs and directing interests. What is important, relevant, and accurate is determined by others than the learner, who is responsible for comprehending the prescribed content and acquiring and mastering the skills as they have been demonstrated.

Instructional process

- Learners move through three predictable stages: acquisition, practice and perfecting, and application.
- Objective is to close the gap between the learner's entering behavior and the desired terminal behavior.
- Instructor's role is to develop a sequence of learning experiences that shape the learner's behavior in ways determined during the needs analysis phase.
- Learners are shown how to apply the knowledge and skills so that the desired behavioral sets (habits of thought or action) are developed.
- Learners (or trainees) are guided through observation and practice, especially of a detailed, logically sequenced series of steps or a model of the desired outcome.

Evaluation of the learning/training outcomes

Since the desired outcomes have been determined for the learners, the primary responsibility for their achievement of the outcomes lies with the persons guiding and assessing the process.

Adult Learning Theory and Experiential Approaches to HRD

Learning needs

Learning needs are determined by the individual, based on his or her perceived needs, interests, or on objectives mutually agreed to by the individual and those who are to be resources to them in this process.

Mature learners have a pragmatic view of learning—a high need for relevance. New facts, skills, and concepts must fit the existing patterns of thought or behavior if they are to be readily accepted.

When new learning conflicts with existing patterns of thought or behavior, mature learners try to integrate or adapt the new content to existing patterns, based on its relevance, anticipated rewards or consequences, or other factors with the capacity to motivate this process.

Instructional process

Learning occurs when individuals engage in some activity, reflect on what they have experienced and observed, abstract some useful insights from their analysis, and use the results of this analysis to make changes in their thinking or behavior that enable them to achieve their goals more effectively. This is assumed to be a natural process experienced by everyone during their daily existence. Thus, learning opportunities do not have to be "structured" by others.

Emphasis is placed on inductive reasoning, proceeding from personal observation to conclusions and applications, rather than on deductive reasoning processes which emphasize what has been previously established as meaningful by others.

Teachers, trainers, peers, or other experts can, however, share in this process when and if their experience is seen as relevant and their advice is desired.

Highly participative "discovery" methodologies which call upon the learners' previous experiences to illustrate points are emphasized, along with the use of analogy, experiments, and examples drawn from everyday life. The teacher, trainer, or expert is at best an external catalyst to the learning process, an arranger of the learning environment rather than a director of the content to be learned or the behaviors to be acquired.

Evaluation of the learning outcomes

Since the learners are primarily responsible for determining their learning needs, as well as for integrating new concepts and skills into their existing patterns, attainment of the learning outcomes becomes a mutually shared responsibility between the learners and the external resources who are involved in this undertaking.

In the author's view, the Asian learners—like Asian learners in general—involved in this project are primarily oriented to traditional learning assumptions and strategies. Several assumptions about Asian learners (compared with Western learners) to be explored during this training intervention are as follows:

- Asian learners are more likely to participate actively and be more satisfied with a non-traditional training event if they have volunteered to attend it.
- Asian learners are less inclined to search for deep psychological or philosophical meaning in their personal experiences, habits of thought, or behaviors, due to a predominant belief in fate and destiny. (There is less perceived value in exploring more complex ways to interpret and understand oneself when simpler organizing principles satisfy and seem to work.)
- Asian learners are less inclined to be reflective or negatively judgmental about their previous traditional learning or training experiences, even when their experiences during a nontraditional training event are highly rewarding.
- Creating a safe learning environment, where learners feel comfortable experimenting with new behavior, is as important when working with Asian learners as it is when working with Western learners.
- Symbolic rewards, ceremony, and celebration would be effective in bridging the cultural gap between the traditional training our Asian learners are familiar with and the experiential approaches to training this program would emphasize.

It is important to note that this is not a research study. The authors and the client system were and are primarily interested in the goals of the training intervention. However, since assumptions about Asian learners and the effects of cultural differences on training practices could be readily explored during this project, we included this as one of our objectives.

Background and Rationale for the Training Intervention

Our client, Cathay Pacific Airways Ltd. (CPA), is undergoing tremendous changes. Until recent years it has been a small, relatively stable airline, wholly owned by John Swire & Sons Ltd., London, England. CPA is based in Hong Kong, where the economical and political climate has grown increasingly complex, and the airline industry is continuously changing routes, partners/affiliates, technology, pricing, etc.

The accelerated changes at CPA include a wider global outreach, the culturally diverse makeup of the rapidly growing employee population, expansion of the number of port offices, and decentralization of the technical training and management of the port offices. These changes have combined to shift CPA from an informal, friendly place to work to a more formal, less friendly, and unfamiliar workplace. This has placed enormous stress on the system and on the willingness and ability of CPA's employees to cope with the burdens these changes place on them.

The so-called "brain drain" in Hong Kong is a very real phenomenon, and active recruitment from within the pool of skilled, local workers is one of the problems that affects every organization. However, CPA is still considered by many to be a "preferred employer" in Hong Kong, and employees tend to want to stay even though other organizations try to tempt them to leave. While acknowledging that they pay well below the going rate for their skilled workers in all categories except management, CPA remains committed to maintaining their "preferred employer" status through a combination of strategies designed to increase morale and reinforce employee commitment. These strategies include well-publicized praise and recognition ceremonies, discounted travel privleges, longevity awards, and innovative HRD/OD programs.

Our involvement in this project began when a high impact program was desired that would both increase CPA visibility in the community as a preferred employer and prepare supervisory employees to function more independently and effectively under pressure.

The most difficult aspect in the early phases of program development was to clarify the priorities of the parties involved. Prior to designing the new training program, the two Western consultants, working with the internal Malaysian Project Director (our direct client), reviewed the designs and content of CPA's existing supervisory training programs. We found that they provided traditional didactic training in basic concepts and skills—no surprise to us, but no "high impact" potential either. There was nothing in these training programs to help supervisors understand the differences between their level's and the next level's responsibilities, such as management practices and organizational functioning. Similarly, there was no specific program or training emphasis on motivation, or on the effects of informal leadership on performance or attitudes. And yet, supervisors were increasingly being asked to demonstrate initiative in risk-taking and decision-making situations. No attempt was made, either during or after training sessions, to bring supervisory employees together in order to strengthen relationships or to exchange views on organizational issues.

In a system as culturally diverse as CPA's, where open communication between and within ports is vital, we believe that these issues are extremely important to the long-term viability of any training effort. Hence, these were the themes that we decided to emphasize in the new training intervention.

Our new program was designed to serve as a high visibility, model program for the entire CPA system. It was intended to showcase a nontraditional approach to training (highly participative, experiential learning) in an area not previously emphasized in supervisory training though thought to be increasingly relevant to supervisory performance: the impact of one's personal attitudes and informal leadership ability on group motivation.

Though the program was sponsored by the Hong Kong-based Staff Development Training Center, participation was open to all CPA supervisory personnel throughout the system, and "outport" candidates were especially encouraged to apply for the sessions scheduled for the first year in order to enhance the system-wide visibility of the program.

Program size was targeted at sixty to seventy persons per session, with three sessions per year scheduled for the first two years of the intervention. The ideal candidate was an employee who had already completed his or her supervisory skills training and who had sufficient on-the-job experience in that role to be able to relate to the broader contexts of fellow CPA trainees. Thus, we sought trainees who would be mature enough personally and organizationally to benefit from sharing their experiences with counterparts from across the system.

Transfer of Learning from Outdoor, Physically Challenging Activities to the Workplace

The development of the final design of the program was greatly influenced by a growing awareness within training circles that "Outward Bound"-type programs offered unique strategies for enhancing team effectiveness. Our internal client had a strong background in this area, and CPA had a history of sending selected employees to the Hong Kong Outward Bound School for personal development. Early in the project planning phase, it was thought that existing programs might be adapted to suit our purpose. However, as Outward Bound-type programs operating in Hong Kong and other parts of the world were reviewed, it became apparent that to achieve the desired outcomes of our training intervention we would need not only to design an original program, but to staff it with instructors who could process the type of indoor activities we had in mind. It was our opinion that the training design and delivery problems that most vendors had not successfully addressed lay in their overemphasis upon conquering personal fears related to physical risks during the outdoor "adventure" activities and their relatively light emphasis on helping trainees utilize insights and relate their experiences more directly to business concerns and to the everyday challenges on their jobs.

Also, we knew that our program would combine outdoor activities with indoor planning and strategy tasks, and that our instructors would be guiding our Asian trainees in sharing not only their personal reactions, but in exploring the organizational implications of their attitudes toward leadership, group membership, competitiveness, team spirit, etc.

For this, we did not need instructors who projected the "macho" outdoor adventure role models characteristic of the staff members who lead typical outdoor programs. Instead, we needed instructors who would be perceived as credible, wearing business attire, leading and processing the indoor activities, and focusing trainees on group dynamics and traditional business issues, such as employee motivation and performance management.

Overview and Highlights of the 3C's Program: Courage, Commitment, and Change

The 3C's program was designed to focus learning at several levels: learning about one's personal strengths, learnings about group membership and the dynamics that affect a person's attitudes and behavior when working collaboratively to achieve a group goal, and learning about how these personal choices impact the organization through one's daily performance on the job.

Several specific objectives and topical themes were identified in these different areas: Self-Awareness, Group, and Back-to-Work Applications.

Self-awareness
- To gain an understanding of the elements of leadership and one's potential for leadership
- To become more aware of one's personal orientation to taking risks and initiative
- To explore the motivational effects of "can-do" attitudes and their application to everyday challenges

Group
- To encourage the behaviors of cooperation and risk taking
- To create team spirit, trust, and support among supervisors

Back to work applications

- To prepare for and create a positive attitude toward the changes occurring at Cathay Pacific Airways
- To provide an opportunity to strengthen personal commitment to Cathay Pacific Airways
- To identify ways to "work smarter" rather than harder, and to understand the consequences of one's attitudes and actions
- To increase a sense of personal and professional accountability
- To provide an opportunity for discussing the application of group members' learnings to everyday situations encountered on the job

The design of the 3C's program features a unique blend of outdoor, physically challenging activities and carefully structured indoor training activities which highlight the negative consequences of thinking and actions characterized by timidity rather than courage, disinterest rather than commitment, and resistance rather than appropriate flexibility when faced with the need for change.

The outdoor activities emphasize personal awareness, risk taking, and team support. The indoor activities reinforce those themes and emphasize setting outcome targets, strategy, teamwork, and competition as it affects the whole group as well as the working unit. The importance of the manager's (or task leader's) role, and the impacts of informal leadership on group performance are underlying themes in all of the indoor activities.

Figure 26.1 is an example of the content presented in the participant's manual to help supplement the presentation on this theory.

Figure 26.1: The Experiential Learning Cycle

The Experiential Learning Cycle

The distinctive design of the 3C's program, compared to more familiar, traditional training designs, is based on a theory of adult learning depicted in the model and described in the following five phase cycle:

1. Activity Phase: the outdoor "ropes course" activities, and the structured indoor games and events

2. Publishing/Reactions/Sharing Phase: talking about the significance of the experience, what happened and what was observed

3. Processing Phase: reflecting on how what one has experienced relates to specific theme(s) and objective(s) of the module or training event

4. Generalizing Phase: exploring the implications of the learning and relating them to broader contexts (patterns, themes, past experiences, etc)

5. Applying Phase: relating the training experiences directly to one's personal life or work situation, and planning meaningful applications of what has been experienced or learned

---

Project Status: Assumptions Revisited One Year Later

To date over 350 trainees—including Chinese, Malaysian, Singaporean, Korean, Taiwanese, Indonesian, Japanese, and a few Caucasians—have participated in the 3C's program, enough for us to draw some conclusions about the success of this intervention and about the cultural appropriateness of experiential training for predominant Asian audiences.

We believe that *Asian learners do differ* from Western trainees in their expectations, initial preferences or comfort, and in their lack of familiarity with highly participative training approaches. However, these differences do not appear to have affected the outcomes of our training, nor did they affect the quality of participation during the event. Cultural differences were in fact recognized as the foundation of CPA's success in the marketplace and celebrated during the sessions.

The more common "team spirit" training offered by outside training program vendors in Japan and other Asian countries emphasizes the importance of the formal leader as catalyst or director, and control over external rather than internal factors. What we have demonstrated to our client's and our learners' satisfaction is that it is each individual's attitudes, choices, and level of personal commitment that ultimately generate and sustain team spirit and motivation to achieve, and that every individual has the potential to affect these factors in others. The participant satisfaction ratings have been consistently high (5.2 on a 6-point scale) for each of the five sessions that have been held to date, over the course of a year.

Comments and testimonials, during the training and on evaluation forms completed at the end of the program, and in follow-up interviews, support our conclusions that this type of training works! Cultural differences are not significant when individuals decide that they are not. They do not in and of themselves affect the quality or type of participation that occurs in the training.

The *South China Morning Post*, the region's largest daily newspaper, sent a reporter to participate in and write about the event. The innovative design of the program has also been reported in *Asia Magazine,* and at an international conference of Outward Bound school instructors in Melbourne, Australia. A number of leading Hong Kong organizations, such as Inchcape, Hong Kong Bank, John Swire & Sons, and Jardines, have sent trainers to the program to see what we were doing and how we were doing it, so that they could begin to incorporate our ideas into their own training. Other interested professionals, including Outward Bound directors, came to the program site in Macau to see for themselves how we combined the outdoor and indoor activities so as to achieve our results.

While this attention has been flattering and has helped CPA achieve one of their objectives—sponsoring a highly visible, innovative training program—we believe that the more important achievement has been to provide support for the notion that Asian learners share with their Western counterparts an ability to learn through highly experiential training strategies, in spite of previous traditional educational backgrounds or cultural differences.

We believe that the success of the 3C's program is not due to its design, to the staff, or to the uniqueness of the CPA trainees. Rather, the credit belongs to the universal correctness of applying adult learning theory and experiential techniques to training design, regardless of the nationality of the trainees.

Revisions to the 3C's program

The current design of the 3C's program reflects changes made between August, 1990 and June, 1991. All of the design modifications were made in response to the issues/factors that we believe to be "culturally based preferences" rather than adaptations based on more significant "cultural differences."

For example, in order to "jump start" the process of informal interacting and to set the tone for the Monday outdoor physical activities, the opening session on Sunday was changed from a more traditional, didactic evening start-up, to an afternoon start-up which begins with a series of highly interactive outdoor "Ice Breaking" activities and closes with an informal group dinner.

This change helped to prepare the trainees for informal interaction with the instructors and with each other, something quite unusual and unexpected. The original, more traditional approach set a "stiff" tone for Monday's session, and the instructors had to work hard to get the trainees to interact freely with them and with each other. By changing the opening Sunday session we could show the staff members in action in a way that made their roles in leading Monday morning's activities easier for the participants to anticipate and to accept.

As a result of this one design change, the time allocated to establishing the desired context on Monday morning needed to be modified only slightly, while it allowed us to quickly highlight the nontraditional nature of what was to follow during the week, and to set the desired climate for the highly interactive, physical tone needed for Monday's outdoor activities.

While this particular design change was based on a "cultural" factor, we believe it is an improvement regardless of the nationality of the target audience.

A second design modification illustrates what we decided to do about something that many consultants and trainers have encountered, the relative lack of familiarity or comfort that Asian learners have with identifying, focusing on, or discussing their personal feelings and opinions. They seem to be unfamiliar with even the most basic concepts of personal awareness that HRD professionals rely upon to help trainees explore issues related to their personal development. Typical comments are "I don't know what I am feeling," and "I am feeling very emotional, but I don't know why, or what to do about it."

While this condition may be true for many Western trainees as well, among Asian trainees there appears to be a very clear "culturally" based challenge to the appropriateness of discussing inner experiences. In a program designed to achieve awareness objectives, we were committed to dealing with this issue head on. Our solution was to provide more informal time needed to allow trainees to experience their feelings more fully. However, early attempts to guide this process more formally, by using highly structured, interactive group processing techniques, resulted in escalating the effect rather than in helping trainees to integrate their experiences.

Now, we have fewer learning activities, establish support partners, debrief in cross-group trios, and spend less time in structured sessions. This has resulted in more informal processing.

A third "culturally" influenced design change was to discontinue the Mid-Course Review session on Wednesday afternoon. In the U.S., we could safely assume that trainees attending a week-long, highly experiential event would expect, or at least be receptive to, a structured way to participate in reviewing and modifying the training event to improve it and/or bring it into closer alignment with their expectations. But this apparently was too radical an idea for our 3C's design. Not only did our trainees not like this module, they challenged the idea that their suggestions regarding modifications were valued by the staff, and were unwilling to accept the responsibility for testing them out while the event was in progress. They were, however, more willing to offer a few minor suggestions and general constructive criticisms on their evaluation forms at the close of the event.

We have now substituted a Mini-University in this time slot. This provides trainees with an opportunity for engaging in self-directed, interest-based learning, a somewhat related objective. With Western client groups we would probably stay with the Mid-Course Review strategy to increase the sense of shared ownership of the session and the outcomes. However, the lack of familiarity with this concept so distracted our Asian trainees from the intended emphasis that we felt our design change was warranted.

Our final design change was to drop the Thursday morning module on the Myers-Briggs Type Indicators. Although this change meant that we had to sacrifice one of the few conceptual links that the 3C's program had with other departmental training programs, we gained valuable time for reviewing the insights from Wednesday evening's Tai Pan Game.

From the start, the Myers-Briggs input had proven to be difficult to incorporate into the design. We felt that the concepts were too abstract to be included early in the event. While an understanding of personality types is desirable in personal awareness training, we wanted to emphasize other themes and physical challenges in this program.

By mid-week the intended program emphasis was on group dynamics, planning and strategy, and competition, also not a good fit with Myers-Briggs concepts unless considerable time was devoted to didactic input so that trainees could see the relationships between personality types and behaviors in groups.

Our decision to drop this content freed up time for better integrating the learnings we had generated so far, and relieved our trainees of the struggle imposed by an ill-timed, too brief introduction to potentially useful but complex, unfamiliar information.

Program Evaluation. We helped the organization determine an appropriate strategy for evaluating the effects of this type of motivational, non technical- and non skills-based training.

Since this program is still in the initial stages of implementation, we are not yet able to conduct a useful audit of its impact. However, anecdotal information and testimonials from the participants are systematically collected and reviewed. They provide self-report data to support the conclusion that the awareness and attitude objectives have been achieved. The usefulness of the experience and the experiential approach to training has been established to the satisfaction of both the client and the consultants involved in this project.

While there was never an intent, and there has not been an attempt to establish a direct connection between the trainees' behavior on the job and their participation in the 3C's program, indicators of the positive effects of this training are expected to emerge in the work environment. Supervisors who have attended the event will be trying out their new courage and commitment to change, and their attitudes toward fellow workers and ability to communicate more freely with their fellow supervisors is expected to improve.

The time, resources, and effort needed to design and carry out a sophisticated comparative research study to evaluate the effects of this training and to establish the causal relationships involved seem unwarranted. However, ongoing efforts will include a follow-up survey to be sent to all participants to obtain comparative data on the perceived usefulness of satisfaction with the training.

A more rigorous evaluation study could compare data from supervisors who attend more traditional "Outward Bound" training with data from participants in the 3C's program. Perceived usefulness and satisfaction with the experience could then be compared in order to support the conclusion regarding the appropriateness and efficacy of the experiential approach in training design.

Unfortunately, in a study this ambitious there would be too many methodological problems in controlling for the factors that affect the comparability of the two study groups. For example, the results that could be attributed to the differences in the mix of activities in the two different programs (outdoor versus combined outdoor/indoor), to the differences in site and facilities (spartan camp versus luxury resort hotel), or to the typical group size involved (twenty versus seventy), and so on.

Such an attempt to structure a useful comparative study in order to measure differences and outcome benefits of the 3C's program (other than simple self-report) was clearly beyond the interests and the available resources of our client. Our recommendation was that at the very least anecdotal data be collected on site and that a long-term plan be established for analyzing trend data and post-training comparative data.

At the present time, the department is working with consultants engaged in what is described as a "systematic evaluation" of training program "results." Their study compares numerical data collected and collated from the trainees in all of the department's programs. The data consist of ratings and rankings on a wide range of items, including satisfaction with the food, perceived usefulness of the training concepts, and satisfaction with the trainer's performance ratings. In our opinion, this hardly constitutes a sophisticated analysis of training effects. There has been no attempt to control for any of the factors that affect the comparability of data sources, and there is no clarity about how results will be used, or even how they will be interpreted. Moreover, while such evaluation efforts generate huge quantities of potentially impressive, visually profiled data, they cost the system in terms of both the resources committed to them and by creating the illusion that useful evaluation procedures are in place. They simply do not serve the same purpose that data from a methodologically sound evaluation strategy could.

In the future, it is our hope that this training intervention will lead the department to consider their decisions about program evaluation strategies more carefully, and determine how they can best link those strategies more formally and more effectively to other department performance indicators. As always, it is the client who ultimately determines how to invest its resources in evaluation projects. However, we believe that it is our responsibility as consultants to educate our clients about this process.

Using a Pilot Program to Influence Strategic HRD Planning and Training Program Design

When the designers and the client are clear on the broader goals of the intervention, are committed to the same theoretical orientation, and bring rich, varied backgrounds to the task of designing, the creative process of program design can be fun, pure, and simple!

The final design of the 3C's program reflects the theoretical orientations and the creative capabilities of both the external consulting resources contracted for the project and the CPA Staff Development Training Department Project Officer who assumed responsibility for bringing the program on line.

From its inception, this training intervention was designed to accomplish more that just to create a new training event. We made sure that all of our objectives were spelled out and supported by the department's senior management at each step.

Steps in the creation of the 3C's pilot program
- Establishing objectives and evaluation criteria
- Establishing criteria for assessing existing programs
- Sourcing possible vendors, external resources, and programs
- Field-testing high-potential vendor's programs and resources
- Continuous progress meetings with CPA Staff Development Training Center managers in order to renew commitment
- Soliciting proposals from selected vendors

- Reviewing proposals and starting of contracting negotiations with potential program resources
- Final negotiations on site, construction materials, contracting for the services of the delivery staff, scheduling of the first sessions in the department's training catalogue, and numerous other factors involved in the successful creation and launch of a new program of this scope
- Start-up of the design team's work, preparation of the training aids and participant manuals
- Construction of the outdoor activities structures
- Administrative procedures involved in participant nominations, staff travel and lodging, arrangements for the participants' on-site room assignments and travel to and from the training site in Macau, shipment of the training aids to the site, etc.
- Start-up of the pilot session, design review, and modification

To succeed in attaining two of the departments' longer term objectives (reducing dependence on external, non-Asian consultants and enhancing of the skills of the Project Officers), this training intervention was designed from the start to develop internal or local resource people who could eventually make up the delivery staff. After attending the 3C's event as participants, interested candidates develop their design and implementation skills through a series of training courses and personal coaching in the technical aspects of leading the outdoor activities, resulting in certification as 3C's program instructors. This "certification" process was designed to be entirely under the control of the department and its Project Officer, though expert consultant resources would be involved initially if the department's management decided that they were needed.

During the second year, the process of preparing CPA in-house and local (Asian) staffing resources for lead trainer roles was undertaken, and at present only one of the original non-Asian consulting resources is still involved in the delivery of this program or in the certification of lead instructors. All major delivery roles are currently filled by instructors who participated in the developmental courses, and program results have remained consistently high.

We believe that this is a sound approach for ensuring the "transfer of technology," and it sets an early desirable tone with department managers encouraging "ownership" of the developmental processes that can occur in a training intervention of this scope. When working with Asian client systems, we have found that such long-term developmental strategic planning is especially important, since many clients lack depth in the skills and management strategies characteristic of Western HRD/OD departments.

Obviously one program cannot change a whole system, or even a whole department. However, we believe that when key decision-makers are committed to the broad objectives of the intervention, the impact of a program such as this can be the start of the change process. One consideration will be how to ensure such an ongoing commitment to the program and an opportunity for a large number of employees to go through this training experience each year, resulting in waves of newly motivated, recharged workers returning to their jobs and interacting in a new spirit of teamwork. This front line cadre will be the supervisors and managers of the projected additional twelve to fifteen thousand employees expected to join CPA in the next five years. The potential impact of the 3C's program is enormous—it could act as a shot in the arm to stimulate the kind of leadership within the ranks of the employees that will be needed if CPA is to successfully meet the challenges of the future.

Another long-term aspect of this intervention relates to the department's desire to assume more control over what is taught and the costs of customizing the training programs it offers. Clients in the U.S. can choose between a wide variety of training program and materials vendors. There are a tremendous number of skilled professional resource people available to them to help fill in the skills gaps in their departments, so they can undertake the task of creating or customizing training programs quite easily. Asian clients, on the other hand, are vulnerable to training firms who arrange long-term contracts for delivering copyrighted training that they control. Clients are expected to pay a fee or a royalty for every one of their employees who attends the training, even when they have paid a design or consulting fee to have the content and materials customized by the vendor firm.

As consultants, we wanted to educate the decision-makers in the department about the process, as well as about the costs and benefits of creating program designs and materials that are the sole property of the client system.

By targeting the 3C's program to serve as the forerunner for this objective, we were able to develop a strategy for comparing the developmental and the long-term implementation costs of each of the two approaches in a very dramatic way.

We solicited bids from outside vendor firms specializing in "customizing" outdoor programs for clients, and then compared their numbers with the costs that we had projected for the first two years. In addition to the straight cost savings that this revealed, we were able to show that by developing the program "in-house" the client system would benefit by retaining all rights to the material through their own copyright, controlling the content and the design, never having to pay a fee to an outside firm to send their employees to their own training, and avoiding long-term contractual agreements with instructors regarding how many attendees and sessions they planned to commit to each year. We also introduced the department to a new, highly successful strategy for working with outside program vendors and other resource people and demonstrated the utility and cost savings that could be realized by using Macintosh computer technology to create and modify training materials.

As a result, training materials that until then had been sent out at great expense for production, or had to be developed by outside resources, are now being produced and upgraded in-house. The long-term effects of this are impressive, both in saving costs and in enhancing the skills and sense of pride and ownership of the in-house resource people.

While our project was the first one in the department to utilize this approach for the creation of training materials and participant manuals, Project Officers now take the initiative in making sure that the training materials used in their programs are visually attractive. Distinctive, graphically enhanced handouts and participant manuals are now the norm, and the department has invested in enough Macintosh equipment to ensure that everyone "catches the spirit." Had they been told that they had to modify their materials, or that they had to modify their current course designs or adapt their training strategies to reflect more highly experiential learning approaches, it is quite possible that instead of interest and receptivity their response could have been resentment and resistance.

In summary, the set of assumptions and intervention strategies that the authors of this article brought to the design and implementation of the 3C's training program allowed them to break through the "cultural differences" of their Asian clients.

Cultural sensitivity is central to any training effort. We believe that effectively adapting and transferring our "Western" approaches to training may be no more complicated than understanding the client's needs, developing trust and rapport, and successfully demonstrating that our ideas can solve their problems in new and creative ways that result in bottom-line savings.

Unsuccessful consultants and trainers who attempt to blame their poor results with Asian clients on "cultural differences" may experience the same poor results whenever they work with any "foreign" cultures, simply because clients want their problems to be understood in less stereotyped ways.

About the Authors

Phyliss Cooke is a consultant with a private practice based in San Diego, California. Before establishing her independent practice in 1988, she was employed for eleven years as a senior consultant with University Associates, Inc., a publishing and consulting firm. She completed her doctorate in Counseling Psychology at Kent State University. In addition to her work in the United States, for the past six years Phyliss has worked extensively with a number of major clients in Singapore and Hong Kong, and together with Ronnie Ng has recently established a new, Hong Kong-based firm called Training Design Consultants.

Ralph Bates is President, Bates & Associates in Annandale, Virginia. Previously, he was Vice President, Personnel and Organizational Development for TransCentury Corporation. He specializes in organizational development, teambuilding, and management development projects. Ralph has an MA in Latin American Studies and has worked extensively with clients in a number of Latin American countries. As a Peace Corps worker for five years, Ralph lived in Columbia and Costa Rica. He has more than fifteen years experience as a consultant and trainer, and has done extensive work on cultural issues and experiential approaches to training.

Ronnie Ng is a Senior Partner in Training Design Consultants in Hong Kong, serving clients throughout the Pacific Region. He specializes in projects such as the 3C's program. Previously, he was Senior Staff Development Officer at Cathay Pacific Airways. Ronnie is fluent in several languages. His partner in Training Design Consultants is Phyliss Cooke.

CHAPTER 27
Imperatives for HRD Concepts and Practices in India

Shyam B. L. Bharadwaj

Concern for people has been an integral part of the Indian ethos. Religious affiliations to Hinduism, Islam, Buddhism, Christianity, and other belief systems have deeply imprinted the Indian psyche with humanistic values of caring, compassion, and charity. However, the powerful impact of Western models of materialism and "pursuit of happiness," reinforced by internal poverty and scarcity of resources, has seriously dented this humanism. India has become today a country of paradoxes and contradictions:

- Stability coexisting with traditional states
- Spirituality juxtaposed with materialism
- Floods and droughts
- Scientific sophistication and illiteracy
- Constitutionally enshrined human rights coexisting with strong governmental interventions
- Affluence and poverty
- Brimming granaries while nearly one-third of the population has very poor buying power
- Entrenched traditionalism and revivalism, assailed by strong movement towards modernization and ambitious dreams of a glorious future

Underneath the visible dualism and turbulence lies a hard core of basic strength and resilience. The essential strength of India lies in her hoary wisdom and capacity to reconcile the contradictions inherent in a country of subcontinental proportions. Meanwhile, we take small but firm steps into the future. India bases her faith in her own destiny on

- The openness and *joie de vivre* of her pluralistic society
- The multi-dimensional talents and vigor of her people
- The traditions of craftsmanship and creative endeavor
- Her willingness to learn from anyone and everyone
- Her concern for the peace and well-being of global humanity
- Her readiness to join hands with others in pursuit of worthy causes
- Most especially, her capacity to reflect and introspect, to correct and make amends, and to combine dreams with vigorous action

India is a country in transition—everything about her seems to be in a state of flux. The centuries-old social structures and institutions are undergoing the trauma of remodelling and adjustments. The economy, despite turbulence, is acquiring a more confident and contemporaneous look, and some futuristic dimensions are emerging. The mass media are opening new doors to perceptions of "Indianness." They are creating a new world view, even in the remote villages and hamlets. A new awareness of the possibilities, relevance, and limits of science and technology is beginning to create new mindsets. An acute realization of the international, geopolitical, and economic realities has triggered a search for appropriate national policies and measures. New approaches to the governance of a pluralistic subcontinent within the framework of a democratic and equitable welfare-state are being conceived and tried. India is grappling with the twin phenomena of aspirations' explosion and population explosion. Yet, another challenge being faced and tackled by the country is the politically engendered assertion of sub-national identities based on geography, history, ethnicity, religion, and social stratification.

In the context of this scenario intensive questioning and self-critiquing activity has emerged over the past decade within and about the organizations concerned. It has taken the form of economic, educational, socio-political, scientific, and administrative operations within the country. Some major issues that have been raised, debated, theorized, and explored in the fields of management and public administration are

- Organizational ethos (culture and climate) in public systems and in enterprises in the public and private sectors in India (Higginbotham, 1975; Hofstede, 1980; Frost et al., 1985; and Singh, 1988)
- The values and styles of leaders and managers in the Indian context (Banerji, 1986; Ganesh & Malhotra, 1975; Bharat Ram, 1986; Virmani et al., 1988)

- The Japanese style of management and its relevance and effectiveness in the Indian milieu (Nakatani, 1986)
- Theories of leadership and their relevance to the Indian reality (King, 1990; Hassan, 1989)
- Attributes and approaches of successful "change masters" who have stimulated a high degree of innovation, enterprise, and initiative from their people (Kanter, 1985)

These issues reflect a recognition of the importance of people. They also reflect the talents and contributions of individuals and teams, their dominant values and styles of functioning. And they reflect the organizational ethos that stimulates them to create, to innovate, and to overcome serious blocks and threats. It appears that when organizations exist in stable circumstances, they ask people to fit themselves into the "system." As organizations face threats from their external environment and the danger of being overwhelmed, "people" occupy center stage and call for the "system" to fit them. This seems to be a global and fundamental truth.

Indian Organizations and Their Human Ecology

During the past two decades, organizational consultants and HRD advisers in India have been chiefly involved in enterprises in the public, private, and joint sectors. This includes ministries, departments, and statutory bodies of the central (federal) and state governments. It also includes education systems, research institutions, and governmental and voluntary bodies concerned with health, family welfare, population control, ecological issues, integrated rural development, public utilities, and adult literacy programs. These organizational and institutional systems present a scenario of hope and despair, dynamism and stagnation, dedication and alienation.

Public-sector enterprises
The public-sector enterprises, with some redeeming exceptions, do not generate profit. Prevailing stereotypes describe them as:

- Over-staffed; low in productivity
- Having poor market orientation
- Highly centralized; obsolete in technology
- Having poor cost-consciousness and low-capacity utilization
- Slow in responding to the changing environment
- Tardy in seizing opportunities; characterized by risk-avoidance
- Over-bureaucratized
- Lacking consistency and continuity at the Chief Executive level
- Displaying poor work ethics

- Having diffused (or nonexistent) accountability
- Poor in teamwork and lateral coordination
- Suffering from role ambiguity and identity confusion
- Poor in internal communication flow
- Having managers feeling powerless and helpless
- Having conflicts and power games
- Low in morale and commitment
- Suffering from dysfunctional labor-management relations

In short, people perceive the vast majority of public enterprises (owned by the central, state and local government) as stagnant, if not comatose. They are continuously bailed out with public funds, for political, strategic, or welfare-related reasons.

Government organizations
The government organizations are perceived as:

- Cumbersome; playing safe
- Cold and impersonal; over-staffed
- Unconcerned about the people they are expected to serve
- Hierarchy- and power-conscious
- Preoccupied with form and rituals
- Hamstrung by undue political interference
- More concerned with proprieties of methods, means, and procedures than with the quality and timeliness of outcomes
- Negligent of the people manning the system, leading to alienation, survival-mentality, and preoccupation with careerism
- Inefficient and wasteful
- Characterized by buck-passing, empire-building and a "psychology of entitlements"

Private enterprises
The private enterprises fare no better. They are often perceived as:

- Highly profit-oriented
- Using fair means or foul
- Insensitive to their social obligations
- Neglectful of R & D
- Highly market-oriented
- Poor in innovation; wasteful of non-renewable resources
- Heavily contributing to environmental pollution
- Cutting corners and bending the laws
- Engaging in unfair trade practices

- Encouraging corruption in dealings with regulatory agencies
- Unable to face international competition on their own (failing on criteria of quality, cost, delivery schedules, packaging, after-sale services, and market intelligence)

However, on the positive side, many large and small private enterprises are also perceived as:

- Dynamic
- Innovative
- Growth-oriented
- Deeply mindful of their human resources
- Offering attractive remuneration packages and growth opportunities.
- Nurturing, grooming, and using talent
- Concerned with the quality of life of their people and of the local community

The organizational entropy depicted above in the governmental organizations and the public and private enterprises may appear pessimistic and melodramatic. These descriptions have been culled from numerous "organizational health" surveys, reviews, reports, seminars, symposia and notes, articles, and editorials in many business and professional periodicals and journals. They also stem from debates in the boardrooms and discussions held in scores of management conferences. The reality is, perhaps, far less grim than that stated here, and there are shining exceptions offering hope and solace. Yet, the negative symptoms are serious enough to warrant diagnosis of prime causes and a prescription for remedial action. At the request of these organizations and enterprises, management consultants and HRD experts have analyzed the roots of ineffectiveness and organizational failure along diverse diagnostic dimensions. They have analyzed the following areas (there may be considerable overlap):

- Organizational design and structure
- Organizational mission, strategic planning, and goal setting
- Human ecology within the organization, QWL (quality of work life issues)
- Decision-making and problem-solving skills
- Work ethics and habits, task-management skills, work design
- Technology obsolescence, available alternatives and their compatibility
- Innovation, Research & Development
- Environmental analysis and coping strategies, public relations
- Management systems, including information system and control
- Issues in man-machine productivity, quality assurances
- Human Resource Management and employee relations
- Leadership contingencies and styles, team-building

- Management of change, organization development
- Human Resource Development (HRD)
- Financial Management and Resource Management, costing and pricing
- Marketing, sales, after-sales services, competition

It is in this context of the Indian organizational realities that HRD seeks its validation, content, and modalities.

HRD: The Term

The term "human resource development" appears to have become a part of the management and "organizational behavior" vocabulary in India in the early 1970s. Its usage gained further respectability when a Ministry of Human Resource Development was created within the central government at new Delhi. Recognition of the term by the Indian Society for Training and Development, Indian Management Association, National Productivity Council, the leading management institutions, and university departments of business management followed suit. By 1975, HRD was in use with both macro-and micro-connotations.

At the macro-level

HRD implied efforts in skill development and other educational activities, including welfare programs geared to improving the quality of life of people at the national level. These programs give special attention to youth, women, children, and vulnerable sections of the populace.

At the micro-level

HRD denoted value-adding—training, development, and education of the employees—by the employing organization. By the year 1978, Human Resource Development started being emphasized as a significant dimension of organizational philosophy in the annual reports of leading enterprises in the private and public sectors in India.

HRD in Indian Organizations: A Summary Report

HRD activities (labelled variously as "training and development," "manpower development," or "HRD") are reportedly being carried out in an organized manner in many government departments and agencies. They are also found in military, paramilitary, and police systems, large business and industrial enterprises, banks and financial institutions, and public utility agencies and corporations. However, such activities are not favored by small and medium-sized private enterprises, nor by one prestigious business house. Nearly two-thirds of the organizations that practice HRD appear not to have a formally stated HRD policy. Of the top 100 large enterprises in the private and public sectors (as nominated by the Economic Times in 1989), only thirty percent had a separate HRD department. Fifteen percent had an in-house HRD institution called Training Centre, Management Training Centers, Management Training Institute, Staff College, Management Development Institute, or OD cell. Some of these are regarded as centers of excellence with high professional recognition. Examples include Tata Management Centre, State Bank Staff College, Management Training Institute of Steel Authority of India, and the Human Resource Development Institute of Bharat Heavy Electricals, to name a few. In eighty percent of the enterprises where it exists as a separate function, HRD reports to the head of the Personnel function. Personnel is now called Human Resource Management in ten percent of these organizations. Indian subsidiaries of most multinational companies appear highly supportive of HRD activities.

The prime target groups of in-house HRD activities within business and industrial enterprises (and in government departments and agencies) are middle managers and supervisors. Senior level executives, managers, and administrators are most often sent to external HRD programs conducted by universities, management institutes, or HRD consultants. Staff members below managerial levels, including shop-floor workers, receive scant HRD attention. Like findings have been reported in an HRD survey done in the United States in 1987 (*Training and Development Journal*, 1988). They are summarized in Table 27.1.

Table 27.1: Resource Use in HRD Experience

Resource Use in HRD Experience Mean Score on a 5-point Scale			
1. University-based programs	3.40	2.65	1.51
2. Outside consultants and trainers	3.13	3.02	2.33
3. In-house HRD staff	2.45	3.67	4.15
4. On-job coaching and mentoring	2.53	3.06	3.40
5. Special task-force projects	2.32	2.41	1.93
6. Vendors of management training programs	1.76	2.36	2.40

In an instrument entitled "Exercise on HRD Culture" (Bharadwaj, 1990), I listed the following strategic interventions for Human Resource Development:

- Planned on-the-job development
- Formal in-house training and development
- Formal external training and development
- Performance feedback
- Development-oriented job rotation and career-track planning
- Coaching, guidance, modeling, counseling, and mentoring (at individual and group level)

- Study tours and observation trips
- Effective library and information services
- Documentation of organizational successes and failures in crisis management episodes
- Encouragement and help in individual efforts at self-development.
- Exposure to reputed experts and leaders in diverse fields
- Remedial learning for "low performers"
- Identification and grooming programs for talented employees
- Special, voluntary programs for about-to-retire people
- Assistance in developing avocational interests and pursuits, also voluntary basis
- Exposure to unfamiliar but learning-generating situations ("Action Learning" programs)

These are means. However, the challenge of HRD lies more in sustaining its spirit and ethos, its clarity of purpose and priorities, and its achievement of sharply defined outcomes. There is a real danger of "means" becoming "ends" and "form" becoming "function." This danger has been recognized by HRD professionals elsewhere who have started warning against "mechanical HRD" and advocating "integrated HRD" instead (Webster, 1990). In several HRD forums in India, the same danger of getting lost in mechanical HRD has been loudly articulated. One of the traps of being HRD practitioner within an organization lies in seeking personal visibility through a dazzling display of one's professional knowledge, including familiarity with the latest in educational technology and sophisticated information gadgetry and gimmicks. One comes across too many HRD professionals so deeply engrossed in "rituals" that they tend to forget to "worship."

Too often "innovation" is mistakenly perceived to be merely the business of the R & D establishment within an organization. Similarly, "people development, and human systems development" are wrongly regarded to be the business of the HRD establishment alone. Truly speaking, HRD involves a *network of accountability* within the organization. I spelled this out under the title, "Developing People: Whose Responsibility?" (Bharadwaj, 1980). It has been suggested that such accountabilities, diverse in content, lie at the *top management* level, the *HRD manager* level, the *line manager* level, and the *targeted employee* level. Unless these accountabilities are recognized at these levels, and unless they are smoothly interlinked within the organization, the HRD efforts are unlikely to achieve best results. Unfortunately, such awareness and networking of HRD accountabilities in people-conscious organizations in India does not always seem to exist.

There are HRD success stories, but also numerous instances of HRD inadequacies in Indian organizations. This was revealed in a series of HRD function-evaluation exercises carried out by external consultants over the past decade. However, most of the findings are derived only from business and industry. Another limit of the available data is their negative bias. External consultants are only invited to evaluate the HRD function when ineffectiveness is experienced or suspected. The following negative symptoms should therefore be interpreted cautiously:

- Very often the other functions view the HRD function as existing in ivory tower isolation, with narrow parochial perspectives. Its credibility in many organizations is low. Most HRD subsystems lack awareness of business functions and of the logic of economic decisions. They know little of their enterprise—its economic vicissitudes, challenges, threats, opportunities, technological nuances, and its place within the industry.

- The HRD function is often seen as not participating in formulation of organizational vision, plans, and strategies. This results in its being regarded as a "second class citizen" or "poor cousin" in the organizational family.

- HRD people tend to forget that they belong to a "staff function," and attempt to grab power and visibility by usurping the "line" role.

- In most organizations, there is no Corporate HRD philosophy nor a corporate HRD plan. Therefore, HRD subsystem operations are often perceived to lack a clear sense of purpose and direction. Thus, these activities are regarded as *ad hoc* and academic, arising from personal predilections of the head of the function. They may be seen as prevailing whims or fancies of the academic, blind imitation of practices in other organizations, or the result of marketing efforts by vendors of HRD packages. Or, they may stem from uncritical acceptance of the advice of some persuasive external expert or some private agenda of the HRD functionaries themselves.

- Top decision-makers in the organization misuse HRD activities as a soft way of manipulating the employees. The HRD functionaries succumb to this role without any resistance, thus committing an ethical transgression.

- Managers and other professionals assigned to the HRD function lack the values and competencies called for by the functions. Eventually, they become obsolete in knowledge, skills, and attitudes because they fail to update themselves periodically .

- HRD professionals in the organization often do not build rapport and a network of relationships with other departments and individuals, as well as with the professional world outside the organization.

- Usually, HRD functionaries neglect their responsibility for developing the follow-up mechanisms which are needed to ensure that gains in knowledge, skills, and attitudes resulting from HRD activities are transferred to the work situation. Without follow- up, these gains will be extinguished with the passage of time.

- HRD is equated merely with mechanically done training activities. This is role myopia.

- In designing HRD activities and interventions, the HRD manager and the team often fail to balance the needs and interests of the individual and the organization.
- HRD intervention programs do not recognize and accommodate individual and population differences relevant to these activities.
- The HRD manager fails to establish the relevance and utility of the function within the organization, and may further neglect to validate it from time to time with the users and the corporate decision-makers.
- The HRD operations, by their very nature, provide certain forms of organizational power to members of the function, and sometimes this power tends to be used inappropriately.
- Information acquired in confidence during HRD operations may sometimes be indiscreetly disclosed, violating the ethical code of the profession.

Guiding the HRD Ethos

It has been my experience that the presence of certain growth-oriented values in the organization seems to facilitate the achievement of HRD aims. Together, these positive values may be designated as the "Learning Climate" within the organization. The relationship between HRD operations and this climate of learning appears to be cyclical, as shown in Figure 27.1:

Figure 27.1: HRD and the Learning Climate

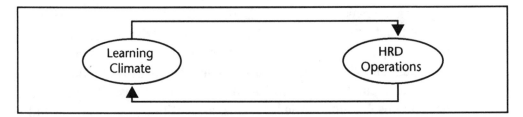

The Learning Climate facilitates the optimal impact of HRD activities, and in turn, the HRD operations help to build an organizational climate of learning and growth.

Some components of the Learning Climate are

- Basic trust, across and within the hierarchical levels
- Result-orientation
- Openness, information-sharing, and accessibility
- Willingness to seek help and to provide help-team culture
- Self-disciplined freedom of expression
- Positive work ethics
- Effective habits, skills and attitudes of working

- Authentic behavior-no "game playing"
- Consultative-participative culture
- Respect for expertise
- Respect for persons of ideas as well as persons of action
- A climate of high expectations
- A culture of equity and fair play
- Perseverance against heavy odds
- High value for self-propulsion and initiative
- Habits of looking at problems as wholes (not piecemeal)
- Focus on quality and excellence of outputs
- Sensitivity to and accommodation of individual and population differences
- High value for flexibility of approach
- Focus on innovations, improvement, and experimentation
- Habits of honest self-criticism, and willingness to change if necessary
- High value for time as a critical resource

This list of HRD-oriented values deserves to be further refined and ordered along a few factorial dimensions through empirical validation. However, the results of such empirical investigation may pose problems of interpretation, because of the cyclical relationship between HRD operations and the learning climate of the organization, as suggested above.

I have also experienced the *negative* impact of certain dysfunctional cultural phenomena in the organizational ethos that seem to hinder and nullify the effectiveness of the HRD endeavor. A few of the negative cultural phenomena are:

- Nepotism and favoritism
- Interdepartmental conflicts and uncooperativeness
- Inequities (real or perceived) in the recognition and reward system
- Serious doubts about the fairness of the performance appraisal system
- Negative "self-image" of the organization
- People-stagnation—poor prospects of vertical and lateral mobility
- Perception of the organization as impersonal or "heartless"
- Prevalence of the grapevine
- Power-hogging and clique formation

The Learning Climate and the negative cultural phenomena are, in essence, two sides of the same coin. They stress the integral relationship between HRD and other functions and realities existing within the organization.

The major point to be made about building an HRD ethos is that HRD is not merely a matter of sophisticated knowledge, logistics, support mechanisms, delivery technologies, and intervention strategies. It is also a matter of vision, faith, ethics, values, and ambiance. Culture is an input, as well as an output, for the HRD endeavor. HRD has both a "form" and a "spirit."

HRD: Challenges Over the Next Decade

The 1990s portend a decade of global, comprehensive, and fast-paced changes: economic, geopolitical, technological, ecological, and socio-cultural. Organizations that will survive and even flourish in this era of discontinuity, turbulence, and ambiguity will be those capable of anticipating and coping with the future that has already arrived. It is no wonder that the National HRD Network in India announced an international conference focusing on "Management of Change Through Human Resource Development." Change is the *raison d'être* of HRD.

In India, the 1990s may offer both threats and promises. The decade may be the turning point, commencing with crisis and anomie and leading to a renaissance and reintegration at both the macro-and micro-levels. In the expected upheaval and resurgence, the human factor would occupy center stage. The implications for HRD professionals and practitioners, working with human resources at the national level and in the organizational settings, will be serious and far reaching. The 1990's will challenge us to come out of our castle of theories, philosophies, rituals, and slogans. We must validate our right to exist in the real world of action and transformation. We have to integrate ourselves with other subsystems and functions in the organization. We will be called upon to invent, innovate, adapt, and anticipate. The 1990s may well witness a "paradigm shift" in the management, development, and optimization of human resources in India.

The issues

Specific issues and areas within the organization are likely to test to the limit the grasp, professional skills, creativity, ingenuity, and action competencies of the HRD professional and practitioner. They may well include the following:

- Debureaucratization of structure and style
- Efficient and involved work ethics
- Perceiving problems holistically
- Creating a climate of learning and growth
- Facilitating innovative processes, approaches, and outcomes
- Creating a culture of excellence and quality
- Assisting in installing technological changes and making them operational
- Team development, an ethos of lateral relations and consensus building
- Updating task skills and relational skills
- Creating a sense of urgency and value of time
- Contributing to the creation and internalization of an organizational vision
- Promoting an awareness of the environment, and customer-orientation
- Developing values and skills of resource optimization and cost reduction
- Helping to develop mature and constructive labor relations
- Promoting free flow of communication and information sharing

- Helping build ethos and action programs for self-development
- Innovative work design and decision structures
- Recognizing and positively utilizing individual differences and population differences
- Promoting community involvement and social responsibility
- Helping to build pride in the organization
- Enhancing productivity of all resources
- Integrating knowledge workers with the rest of the organization

The requirement

The HRD practitioner in the 1990s will have to be much more than a "trainer." We will be expected to create visions, be internal consultants and change agents, contribute to organizational planning and strategy formulation, solve real-life problems, and build bridges between the organization and its environment. To be able to do this, we will have to raise our caliber and stature; win acceptance from the top decision makers, the subsystems, and people in the organization; and validate our existence by producing results. Above all, we must grow—for "he who does not grow himself cannot help others to grow."

References

Banerji, U. "Macro Value Systems," *Economic Times*, May 31, 1986.

Bharadwaj, S. *Developing People and Spotting Talent: A Note for the Line Manager.* EHS Occasional Paper No. 1. Hyderabad: Effective Human Systems, 1980.

Bharadwaj, S. *Exercise on HRD Culture.* Hyderabad: Effective Human Systems, 1990.

Bharat Ram, V. "Torn Between Two Cultures." *Economic Times,* May 31, 1986.

Frost, P. et al. (Eds.). *Organizational Culture.* Beverly Hills, CA; Sage Publications, 1985.

Ganesh, S., and Malhotra, A. "Work Values of Indian Managers: Some Findings." *ASCI Journal of Management,* Vol. 4, March 1975.

Hassan, A. *Dynamics of Leadership Effectiveness in Indian Work Organizations.* New Delhi: Commonwealth Publishers, 1989.

Higginbotham, S. *Culture in Conflict: The Four Faces of Indian Bureaucracy.* New York, NY: Wiley, 1975.

Hofstede, G. *Culture's Consequences: International Differences in Work-Related Values.* Beverly Hills, CA; Sage Publications, 1980.

"HRD Survey: 1987, Fortune 500." *Training and Development Journal,* Jan. 1988, pp. 26-32

Kanter, R.M. *The Change Masters.* London: Unwin, 1985.

King, A. "Evolution of Leadership Theory." *Vikalpa,* 15 (2), April-June, 1990.

Nakatani, R. "Industrial Culture in Japan and India", *Management & Labour Studies*, 11 (1), 1986, pp. 48-55.

Singh, P., and Bhandarkar, A. "Cultural Ethos in the Organizational Milieu", *Indian Management.* October 1988.

Virmani, B. et al. *Indian Management Practices.* New Delhi: ASCI & Friedrich Ebert Foundation, 1988, Ch. 2.

Webster, B. "Beyond the Mechanics of HRD. " *Personnel Management,* March 1990, pp. 44-47.

About the Author

Shyam B. L. Bharadwaj is the Chairperson and Managing Director of Effective Human Systems Pvt. Ltd. in Hyderabad, India. Previously, he was director of studies and head of organizational behavior group at the Administrative Staff College of India. He has been a Fulbright exchange scholar and Visiting Professor at New York University. He holds a Ph.D. in Organizational and Industrial Psychology. He is a member of the New York Academy of Sciences and is National Coordinator of the Indian National Centre for Quality of Life and Work.

CHAPTER 28

Staff Development for Multinational HRD Staff

Ali M. Dialdin

This chapter begins by briefly describing the role of Saudi Aramco in providing HRD to the Saudi Arab work force. Then follows a brief description of Saudi Aramco's Training Organization (its HRD unit) and the comprehensive HRD system that has been established to provide HRD for Saudi employees. The focus of the chapter, however, is on the HRD programs that have been developed to provide learning for a multinational group of full-time and part-time HRD practitioners. The chapter also explains how these programs have improved the quality of HRD that Saudi employees receive.

As the national oil company of Saudi Arabia, Saudi Aramco is responsible for producing most of the country's oil and natural gas. Developing the national work force is one of Saudi Aramco's highest priorities—in fact, providing HRD ranks second only to the safe and efficient management of oil and gas operations. Reflecting this high priority, Saudi Aramco's HRD system represents one of the world's largest projects for the transfer of technology in the oil and gas industry.

The company emphasizes the development of Saudis at all levels as part of its comprehensive HRD program. In 1990, the company had approximately 44,000 employees in Saudi Arabia, including more than 31,800 Saudi employees. About 7,000 of these were involved in full-time and part-time learning programs conducted by the Training Organization. These programs are conducted at HRD centers in Saudi Arabia's Eastern Province and at Yanbu in western Saudi Arabia on the kingdom's

Red Sea coast. Some of these locations are now more familiar to readers in other parts of the world than they were before the United Nations action in Kuwait in 1990-1991. The exact locations are shown in Figure 28.1.

Figure 28.1: Map of Saudi Aramco Training Facilities

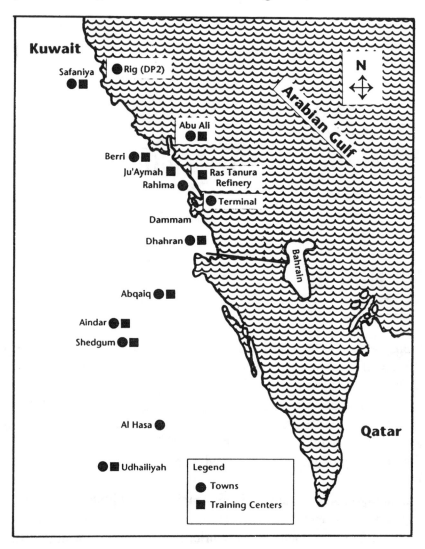

HRD Programs

The Training Organization conducts programs at different levels to accommodate the varying educational backgrounds of new employees. A variety of structured education programs provide preparation for entry level jobs and beyond, as well as college attendance and learning programs for people in higher level positions. Figure 28.2 shows the structure of this HRD system. Special management, professional, and technical programs are also offered to upgrade employees' job skills and to keep them informed of the latest technological developments in the company's diverse operations. As part of the effort to tailor the learning even more closely to job needs, a company-wide, computer-based tracking system has recently been established to maintain an HRD history for each employee. This system helps to relate HRD to those employees with high potential for advancement; individualized plans that specify further HRD programs are then developed for outstanding candidates.

The majority of Saudi new hires are high school graduates and these are enrolled in a two-year Apprenticeship Program. This program provides intensive academic worked mainly in English, Math, and Science, and job skills education for industrial and administrative jobs. On successful completion of this Apprenticeship Program, the process continues with line organizations providing on-the-job training (OJT). This enables the apprentices to meet the specific requirements for their targeted jobs. The Training Organization also provides advanced technical training courses for those employees who require them. Advanced technical training is given in areas like electronics and instrumentation, and in the use of new oil industry equipment and systems. The entire Saudi Aramco HRD System is depicted in Figure 28.2.

Current staffing

There are approximately 600 HRD practitioners in the Training Organization. As in other company departments, this is a multinational work force, of which 15 percent are Saudis, 35 percent are from Western industrialized countries, and about 50 percent are from the Middle Eastern and Asian countries.

In addition to administering the HRD centers, the Training Organization also has a Program Development and Evaluation division that develops and monitors programs and tests for academic and job skills learning programs. It also provides on-the-job training manuals for the company's various line organizations.

Recruitment and Selection of HRD Practitioners

Regular recruitment workshops and interviews are held in the countries from which the Training Organization recruits staff. Academic instructors must have a B.A. degree and a minimum of four years' teaching experience, and must have specialized in an area relevant to the subject and level assigned. English-language instructors must have TEFL/TESL experience and teacher certification. Math and science instructors must have new math or new science teaching experience and teacher certification. Industrial-skills instructors who work in job skills must have a degree or Higher National Diploma together with wide industrial experience in the craft to be taught.

To support of the recruitment effort, the Training Organization has produced a special recruitment video and booklets, which give HRD practitioners practical information about living in Saudi Arabia and working in the Saudi Aramco HRD centers.

Figure 28.2: The Saudi Aramco HRD System

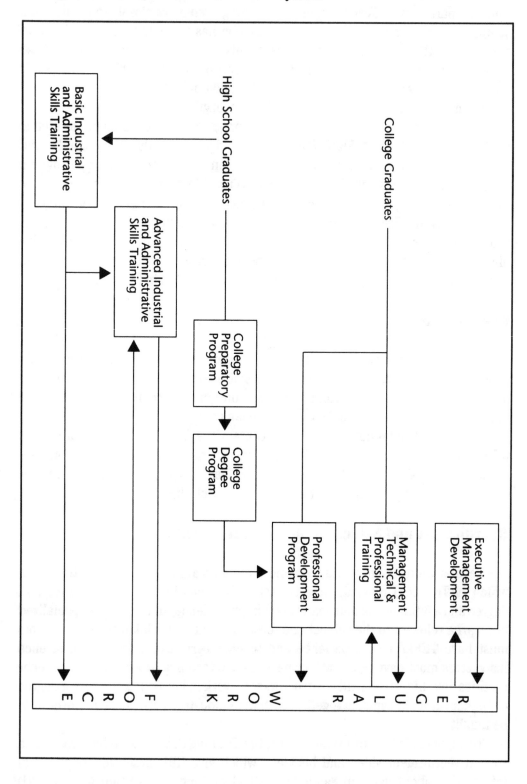

Investment in Staff Development

The Training Organization's investment in developing HRD staff is in three main areas:

- Staff Development Unit (SDU) Programs
- In-Service Day Conferences
- Refresher Training and Education

We will consider each of these areas in turn.

Staff Development Unit (SDU) Programs

The Training Organization's Staff Development Unit consists of six professionals with a Course Registrar and a clerk. The unit's mission is to provide courses to increase the effectiveness of HRD practitioners and HRD throughout the company. This means that as well as serving the Training Organization, the unit works closely with on-the-job trainers to help them develop instructional skills in their own specialist fields, such as computer operations, gas plant and refinery operations, medical services, and industrial security. SDU provides the following types of courses:

- Orientation for new HRD practitioners joining the Training Organization
- A Trainer Certification Program for young Saudi craftsmen and technicians who will become industrial skills instructors
- A Trainer Certification Program for experienced craftsmen and technicians assigned to be industrial skills and on-the-job instructors
- Developmental learning experiences for experienced HRD practitioners
- Mentor orientation and training for craftsmen and technicians who provide one-on-one instruction and coaching
- The annual SDU Seminar for HRD Coordinators and senior line organization HRD personnel

Orientations for new teachers and trainers

Studies have shown that a systematic orientation program can help new staff adjust more quickly and positively to their new working and living environment and become more effective employees. SDU assists with this orientation by providing:

- A one-day workshop for Training Organization supervisors and supervisors from throughout the company on how to plan and conduct in-house orientation programs
- Orientation checklists that can be used by HRD practitioners to support the local HRD center orientation
- A two-day orientation to the Training Organization

The orientation program involves orientation to the company, the Training Organization and the curriculum, and presentations on where the new employee's unit fits into the organization and where the new employee fits in. Potential problem areas and adjustments that the new HRD practitioner may need to make are discussed, and appropriate problem-solving activities are conducted.

Saudi trainer (instructor) certification program

SDU conducts an intensive instructional skills program for young experienced Saudi craftsmen and operators who are targeted to become instructors. Currently, 16 Saudi instructors are enrolled in this program.

It involves six months of classroom instruction and practice, and three months on-the-job training practice at the HRD center under the guidance of a skilled HRD practitioner who acts as a mentor.

The main objectives of the program are that learner should be able to:

- Prepare and conduct a variety of learning presentations
- Make a variety of craft demonstrations following the 3-Step OJT Method

In achieving these objectives, trainee instructors also learn how to:

- Develop and use learning materials
- Use learning aids, including the chalkboard and flip chart, the overhead projector, the film projector, and video
- Develop and manage learner-practice activities
- Handle classroom management situations
- Conduct safety talks and discussions
- Coach individual learners, using a six-step coaching method
- Prepare written and performance tests
- Complete HRD reports and documentation

From the beginning of the program, learner/instructors are required to prepare and conduct brief presentations and craft demonstrations. These sessions are videotaped so that participants can assess their own performance and identify areas for improvement. At the end of each of the five units of instruction, there is a written test to assess participant knowledge, and a performance test involving a presentation or demonstration.

Trainer (instructor) certification for industrial skills and on-the-job instructors

To teach advanced technical courses the Training Organization needs experienced craftspersons and technicians. They must not only be experts in their field, but also need the instructional skills to transfer their expertise. Company on-the-job

(OJT) trainers have a similar need. Typically, these are part-time trainers in their department, or craftspersons or technicians who may be assigned to HRD temporarily. As learners graduate from their HRD programs, they go to their departments and need to gain experience on their specific job and the equipment used at the job site. Consequently, there is a need for effective OJT trainers throughout the company.

However, craftspersons and technicians generally lack experience and knowledge of HRD techniques. They need help and guidance to make their learning effective and to gain confidence as HRD practitioners. In response to these needs, SDU provides a Trainer Certification Program designed to develop skills in the planning, preparation, conduct, and evaluation of training and education. The content of the certification program is shown on Table 28.1.

Table 28.1: Trainer Certification Program.

Workshop Title	1-on-1 OJT Trainer Track	Group/Class Trainer Track
Orientation to training & training by performance objectives	X	X
Oral questioning techniques	X	X
Effective use of audiovisual equipment		X
Using group work		X
Producing training plans and aids	X	X
Conducting demonstrations	X	X
Making training presentations		X
Developing tests		X
Evaluating hands-on performance	X	X
Coaching and on-the-job training	X	
Training management & motivation		X

When the program started in the early 1980s, the most of the industrial-skills and OJT HRD people were expatriates. Today, more than half of them are Saudis.
The program has a number of features that are worth noting in terms of providing professional growth for HRD practitioners of a multinational training staff:

Participation. Approximately 400 HRD practitioners graduated from the program by 1990 and the program is continuing. The HRD practitioners come from approximately thirty departments, covering every aspect of company operations, including computer operations, gas plant, oil terminal, refinery, communications, nursing, and industrial security.

Tracking. For the purposes of program development, SDU has grouped HRD personnel into two categories:

- One-on-one instructors/trainers who conduct programs for one or two employees at the job site
- Group/classroom instructors who teach in a classroom or workshop setting

Workshop content. The Trainer Certification Program is modularized, with each workshop focusing on a specific skill, such as demonstration. The learners attend different kinds of workshops, depending upon their needs. Most of these workshops are full-day. A one-on-one OJT trainer would have five days of workshops, while the group/classroom instructor would have nine days of workshops. Rather than being taken one after another, however, workshops are intended to be taken over time with the learning experience feeding into the work experience and vice versa. The modular approach also provides flexibility so that Training Coordinators and supervisors can fit the learning into their normal schedule. They can accelerate or decelerate the learning based upon operational requirements and the learning requirements of the learner.

Workshop methodology. The methods used in the workshop include the usual variety of techniques. The following are some particular elements:

- *Language*. Since English, is the business language of the oil and gas industry, Saudi Aramco conducts its business in that language. SDU courses, therefore, are conducted in English, but the use of bilingual instructors proficient in both English and Arabic allows for additional explanation or individual help where there is a language problem.
- *Mixed classes*. HRD practitioners from a variety of cultural backgrounds and Saudi Aramco departments attend SDU workshops. People learn about each other's work and HRD circumstances. This a valuable spin-off from the courses, as participants learn more about HRD and the company as a whole from their fellow participants.
- *Performance objectives*. Each workshop in the Trainer Certification Program has specific behavioral objectives for participants to accomplish and specific tasks to perform. Workshops often involve the production of learning materials (e.g., individual learning plans, some learning aids, a demonstration) which HRD practitioners can use when they return to the job site. The use of specific performance objectives for learning is particularly effective in a multinational setting where there are increased possibilities of misunderstanding and miscommunication.
- *Group activities*. SDU has found group activities to be very effective, particularly in working with participants from a variety of cultural backgrounds and experiences. Group work reduces the risk of information overload and ensures assimilation and application of the course material. What is more important

perhaps, is that group work helps the participants to work together in teams, reduces communication barriers, and improves intercultural communication.

- *Videotaping.* SDU uses videotaping, particularly in workshops where participants conduct demonstrations and make presentations. After a demonstration or presentation, the learner receives feedback from other participants and the SDU instructor, structured by an observation form. The learner then views his/her videotape privately with an SDU instructor, and they discuss the demonstration or presentation in terms of strengths and suggestions for improvement. The private viewing ensures that the session is nonthreatening and the learner can view his/her own performance without fear of criticism from peers. When SDU began to videotape demonstrations and presentations in the early 1980s, the process was unfamiliar and some participants felt anxious about the experience. Now participants are used to videotaping, are no longer nervous about it, and appreciate the private viewing and coaching session. In particular, inexperienced HRD practitioners respond well to the use of videotaping and the constructive feedback from the SDU instructor.

- *Custom-made videos.* SDU uses a mix of off-the-shelf and custom-made videos in the Trainer Certification workshops. Custom-made videos are obviously more expensive, but they do have important advantages. The language level is appropriate for a multinational group, most of whom are using English as a second language. Realistic situations can also be portrayed with a Saudi Aramco background and employees. For example, a video produced for a series of workshops for refinery employees shows refinery staff at the work site involved in craft training and coaching situations. When learning is being developed for fairly large numbers of staff, custom-made videos can provide a key element in a cost-effective learning package.

Evaluation. Evaluation in the Trainer Certification Program consists of three elements: performance checks in the workshops; structured observation with the learner's supervisor using a Performance Profile; and a final follow-up observation by an SDU instructor.

Performance checks are used in the Trainer Certification workshops to verify the achievement of workshop objectives. For example, learners participating in "Training by Performance Objectives" have to produce a satisfactory objective that includes performance, condition, and standard to get credit for completing the workshop. In "Training Plan Preparation" each participant must prepare a lesson plan for a topic in his/her area and at least one learning aid (overhead transparency, handout, flip chart pages) to support the learning session. In "Demonstration as a Training Method" and "Presentation Techniques," participants have to make demonstrations and presentations that meet the required standards. Checklists are used for discussions of the demonstration or presentation that include two staff HRD practitioners.

When a learner has completed the workshop program, SDU provides the learner's supervisor with a Performance Profile to conduct follow-ups on the learner. The Performance Profile booklet lists a series of competencies in the areas of instructional planning, the development and use of learning aids, demonstration techniques, presentation techniques, management of learners, and evaluation. These are the competencies that the HRD practitioner should have as a result of participating in the workshops.

After the supervisor has conducted a series of observations using the Performance Profile, and verified that the learner is ready for certification, an SDU instructor conducts a follow-up observation at the job site. There is a follow-up discussion with the learner after this observation and if the learner has met the required standards, he/she is certified. However, if the learner fails to meet the standard in a key area (e.g., use of the demonstration method), the learner will be scheduled to repeat this workshop and a further observation will be conducted.

Developmental learning experiences

The oil and gas industry is a rapidly changing environment, and HRD programs and methods must adjust to changing operational and work force requirements. HRD practitioners need to adapt to these changes and to stay current in their fields and in their instructional skills. Accordingly, SDU provides instructional-skills workshops for experienced HRD practitioners who may need a refresher. After these workshops, SDU staff people visit participants at the job site to ensure that learners are applying what they have learned and to give any necessary assistance.

Mentor orientation and training

As part of Saudi Aramco's overall HRD effort, the Training Organization has assisted departments in setting up their own master HRD plans for on-the-job learning. To provide systematic support and to standardize company on-the-job training, the Training Organization has developed Aramco Job Training Standards (AJTS): workbooks that provide tools for planning, conducting, and evaluating on-the-job training in craft, technical, and clerical job areas. Each AJTS workbook includes a job orientation checklist for the supervisor to use, guidelines for training, a job-task list including all the tasks the employee is required to perform, and a description sheet for each task. Each job task has very specific conditions and standards of performance. Finally, there is a record of certification verifying that the employee meets the requirements of the job.

To conduct OJT using the AJTS workbooks, each department has selected experienced workers to act as mentors for the new Saudi employees. Mentoring is defined as "work experience directed by an experienced fellow employee" and involves the experienced craftsman or technician transferring his knowledge and experience to the new employee. The mentor acts as an instructor for new or unfamiliar tasks, as a "coach" when the learner knows parts of the task, as a "monitor" when monitoring progress, and finally as an "evaluator" of the new employee's performance.

SDU conducts workshops to orient mentors to their department's on-the-job training program and to ensure effective use of the AJTS. Orientation workshops are also conducted for the department's administrative and supervisory staff, so they will know about their department's on-the-job training program, the AJTS, and how they can support the mentor in providing on-the-job training.

The workshops that SDU conducts for mentors are usually department-specific, and so far, workshop programs have been conducted for Power Distribution, Pipelines, and Utilities. Other departments are now requesting this service as their OJT programs and AJTS come on stream.

Annual SDU seminar

Every year SDU organizes a seminar for senior Training Organization and line-department staff involved in HRD throughout the company. The seminar provides a showcase for Training Organization activities and services, and an additional opportunity for HRD to communicate with other departments in the company and receive feedback. Different departments also make presentations on their own on-the-job training programs and can exchange information and experience with others. Recent topics at the seminar have included *Training Quality Assurance*, *Computer-Based Training*, and *The Organizational Development Program* conducted by management HRD staff. Presentations at this seminar are made both by Training Organization staff and staff from other departments, who describe their own OJT efforts.

In-Service Day Conferences

In the autumn of each year, the Training Organization conducts a one-day In-Service Day Conference. It involves guest speakers as well as presenters from different parts of the Training Organization. The purposes of the conference are to provide an overview of current HRD programs, to offer professional development opportunities, and to provide a forum for HRD practitioners to share expertise and experience.

The 1990 conference offered ten concurrent sessions, with participants able to choose from a variety of presentations, workshops, panel discussions, and technical demonstrations. The wide range of topics included Computer-Assisted Language Learning, Intercultural Communication, Time Management, Team Leadership, Learning and Training Styles, and Interactive Video. Familiar but highly practical topics like testing, class management, and teaching techniques were also covered in a number of sessions. There were also presentations on oil industry topics, to familiarize trainers with current developments in the industry as a whole.

Refresher Training and Education

The purposes of the refresher program are to provide professional growth opportunities for instructional staff and HRD administrators, and to enable staff to stay current with developments in their fields of specialization.

Since the early 1960s the company has sponsored the refresher program whereby HRD practitioners (including HRD administrators) earn one week of refresher experience for each year of service. HRD practitioners accumulate this paid time off and use it to attend summer courses in their specialist field at reputable learning establishments throughout the world.

In addition to the paid time off, instructors receive a per diem allowance to cover their living expenses for the duration of the course, as well as most of their expenses for tuition, textbooks, and stationery. Every year approximately fifty HRD practitioners go on refresher courses. Upon return, each learner submits a report describing the main features of the course attended. HRD practitioners also disseminate the information and expertise they have gained from the course through presentations and workshops—many of them given at In-Service day conferences.

Return on Investment in Staff Development Activities

Return to the learners in the organization
The employees benefit in the following ways from their HRD practitioners attending staff development courses:

- They receive more systematic and relevant learning.
- Instructor becomes more skilled and confident.
- Less learning time is wasted and there is less need for reinstruction, so the frustration that such additional learning can cause is avoided.

Return to trainer
Through participation in HRD activities HRD practitioners can benefit in the following ways:

- They are better equipped to cope with the company HRD environment and to work as part of a multinational work force.
- They learn not only from the SDU instructor but from the experience of the other workshop participants who are involved in company HRD programs.
- Industrial and OJT instructors who have little or no previous HRD experience gain in confidence as well as skills.

Return to the company and HRD system

The company and the HRD system benefit in the following ways from investing in HRD practitioner learning programs:

- A systematic orientation and good initial contacts are important for the retention of staff, continuity, and a return on the company's hiring investment.
- By providing in-service training, the company and the department show concern for the professional growth of their HRD staff. The motivational impact of this is particularly evident among those craftspersons and technicians who have been asked to become OJT instructors or mentors.
- Mentor training leads to improvements in OJT and effective implementation of Aramco Job Training Standards (AJTS). The transfer of skills and technology from expatriate craftsmen and technicians to Saudi employees is enhanced.
- SDU's development of Saudi HRD practitioners for the Training Organization and the line organizations contributes significantly to company and national human resource development goals.
- Improvements in HRD lead to greater safety, which is of vital importance in the oil and gas industry.

Future Outlook

Programs for HRD practitioners such as those conducted by SDU have proved to be extremely cost-effective in vocational settings. In particular, such programs have a "multiplier effect," with each HRD practitioner coming into contact with a number of employees in the classroom or job site and impacting on their job performance. For a relatively small investment in time and money, the effectiveness of HRD practitioners and therefore the whole HRD program can be significantly improved. The following factors are expected to impact on future activities for HRD practitioners.

Increasing need for on-the-job trainer and mentor training

More training is required in the OJT area to ensure that learners make a smooth transition between the general job skills training and education, and specific on-the-job requirements. The development of AJTS for more job areas means an increased requirement for supervisor and mentor orientation to the use of these job training tools.

Training quality improvement

Perhaps the hottest issue in HRD at the moment, and one that is gaining momentum, is quality improvement. The Training Organization has established a Corporate Training Quality Assurance Group that reviews HRD programs throughout the company and makes appropriate recommendations. In addition to promoting quality improvement through HRD programs and follow-up observations of learners, SDU assists Quality Assurance (QA) in conducting their QA reviews. In this way, any review recommendations that involve HRD can be addressed directly.

Quality improvement is likely to be a key issue in HRD through the 1990s and coordination between quality assurance and HRD functions is likely to increase.

About the Author

Ali M. Dialdin is General Manager of Training and Career Development at the Arabian American Oil Company (ARAMCO) in Dhahran, Saudi Arabia. Previously, he was ARAMCO's General Manager of Training and Director, Training Department. Under his direction, the organization provides HRD opportunities for 7,000 Saudi Arab employees in the various aspects of operation of the world's largest oil producing company. He has a B.S. in Geology from San Diego State University. He is an Associate Member Representative of the International Federation of Training and Development Organizations.

CHAPTER 29
HRD Consulting in Emerging East Europe

Michael Sandrock

Human resource development activities in Eastern Europe have dramatically changed since 1989. Before that, only lectures were used. After 1989, learning and consulting activities began to be practiced, mainly by West German HRD consultants and practitioners in the former Soviet Union and in former East Germany, to develop a change of mind and structure.

This is a basic task of consultants, if they understand that playing the role of change agent has been requested. HRD people are always aware of the opportunities to transform ideas from one culture to the other. But such a process of transformation between the East and the West is more difficult than, say, between the U.S. and the Netherlands. In those countries there is a common understanding about economics even if there are possibly different cultural approaches. Between Germany and the republics of the former Soviet Union, there is not only a difference in culture, but also a different understanding of economics. Even in a divided country, such as Germany until 1989, this difference can be seen in the use of language. In what was West Germany, the word "valuta" means a way of payment, a discount – for example, whether the supplier grants the customer 30 d/s ("valuta") or 60 d/s ("valuta"). In what was East Germany, "valuta" has an absolutely different meaning: payment in another currency. So, if an East German firm charged a Dutch firm and was paid in guilders, this was "valuta."

I participated in the process of HRD change from 1989 to 1990 in the USSR. I supplied consulting activities requested by East German firms and West German firms who wanted to establish activities there. I helped to establish an HRD consulting group in East Berlin. I gained some interesting knowledge about changes in the countries formerly in the USSR through membership in the German-Soviet Management Conference. I benefited from instructing then-Soviet managers and also from my membership in an international HRD consulting group with activities in Hungary and Czechoslovakia.

From Planned Economy to Market Economy, Between 1989 and 1990

In the autumn of 1988, some treaties were made between the West German and Soviet governments (President Gorbachev and Federal Chancellor Kohl), including support for Soviet management training and education. About six months later, the German-Soviet Management Conference took place in Moscow, designed to bring the requests of the Soviets into line with the possible contributions of the Germans. (Later, in the summer of 1990, training for over 600 Soviet managers began.) The German-Soviet Management Conference included experts from the administration, industry, and Chambers of Commerce. Parts of that group have become independent HRD consultants and practitioners.

The changes in East Germany began in November, 1989, when the border was opened between East and West Germany. Preceding this step was the economic breakdown of the former German Democratic Republic, beginning in 1988. The GDR government had rejected the ideas of President Gorbachev and did not implement them. The stagnation in the GDR did not correspond with the changes that happened elsewhere, such as Hungary, which also was in the Eastern system. The borders between Hungary and Austria were removed in the summer of 1989. East German people were allowed to spend their holidays in Hungary, and in the summer of 1989, there began a stampede via Austria to Germany.

After the 40th anniversary of the GDR in September, 1989, the structure of power became increasingly unclear because of the many changes taking place. On November 11, 1989, it became legal for East German citizens to travel to neighboring countries, including West Germany.

In fact, there had been many contacts between East and West Germany before that. East German managers of the State Industry were permitted to contact their West European partners, which was not such a risk for East German authorities since most of these managers ("Reisekadern") were obliged to be members of the Communist Party SED. Furthermore, they had to collaborate with the State Security. Before 1989 these contacts very often led to a stabilization of political conditions in East Germany. They also produced a monopoly of know-how for a few managers in East Germany. At this time, HRD consultants and practitioner groups already existed in

East Berlin. They were responsible for the support of East German Combinates (nearly a holy structure), which coordinated sales of East German products to West Europe.

The main process of changing structure and culture can be divided into five periods:

1st period: until about the end of 1989

During this period, East Germany employed many West German people, including HRD consultants and practitioners. Age was a factor. Older HRD people agreed immediately to the unification, and identified themselves with the people in East Germany. HRD people and managers born after 1950 had less affinity for the developments in East Germany and identified themselves less with the unification.

In the area of HRD consulting activities, this period was regarded as the time of charlatans. People in East Germany were willing to pay for anything coming from the West. For example, in Erfurt at a Conference House for People's Education, a West German representative for office machines held a management seminar. About fifty persons had to pay DM 20 (West German Currency) or M 40 (East German currency) for the two-hour seminar. The instructor directed the participants to write on their exercise books "MARKTWIRTSCHAFT" (market economy). They also had to speak in chorus every letter of this word. After that, they were taught about management structures. The reference was a paperback version of a general management text, titled "Management for Everyone Simplified."

2nd period: early 1989 to March 1990

The next time period is from early in 1989 until March 18, 1990, the day of the first general and free elections in East Germany. The periods overlap.

At this time, HRD consultants and practitioners exhibited either emotional or reserved behavior. Emotionally oriented consultants often confused help and self-help with a missionary mission, whereas consultants with a reserved behavior waited for a complete change in structures and the re-unification of East and West Germany.

During this period many private corporations were established. That meant transforming East German state-owned enterprises into enterprises with the usual European structure. But although the external structures of the East German enterprises changed, the acting and responsible persons did not. Very often Communist managers made contracts with West German enterprises in which they received a personal assurance. West German enterprises that wanted to make a "fast buck" entered into possible and impossible structures to be suppliers for the East. These deals were very favorable for West German enterprises, and the East German enterprises were the big losers.

There were many differences in management practices, as shown by the following example. When sending a shipment from Frankfurt to Leipzig, the supplier usually must bear all the risks for the shipment until it arrives at the customer site. It is also usual to give the customer four weeks to pay. However, West German enterprises explained to East German managers and stipulated in the contract that the East Germans must bear all risks for the shipment when it was loaded on trucks in West Germany. It was also stated that there was a period of only *two* weeks before payment was due. The usual discount was not granted to East German managers—in fact, West German enterprises denied any form of discount.

At that time, differences arose between the middle management and top management within an East German enterprise. Middle managers were angry because at the top of the enterprises nothing had changed. The top managers only feathered their own nests.

The activities of West German HRD consultants and practitioners in East Germany were often ineffective. Often, they did not understand that cultural differences existed in the other part of Germany, so they tried to transfer what they had done successfully in West Germany to the East. The result was that many middle managers felt they had been ridden over roughshod. Self-doubts could be noticed, combined with a loss of self-identity.

3rd period: March 1990 to June 30, 1990

During this period, East Germany relinquished its own currency and on July 1, 1990, agreed with West Germany upon an economic and monetary union.

After that, East German corporations were established. These are nothing but the former state-owned enterprises with superior holdings. At that time, the Trust Company (a kind of audit company) was owner of the East German enterprises. Until then East German enterprises had enough financial income to deliver their supply commitment with the USSR on the basis of East German currency.

Many East German enterprises were using West German HRD consultants and practitioners, who did very well because everything coming from the West found East German approval.

The following example should illustrate how the situation got out of hand. An East German firm producing tires, rubber goods, and similar products was unable to find a ready market for their products in East Germany. The managers arranged for a French company in the same line to supply the packing material for the East German firm's products. The East Germans then sold their products as French products successfully on the East German market. This example shows how grotesque the East German techniques of survival have been.

4th period: July 1, 1990, to October 3, 1990 (the day of unification of both Germanys)

Before October 3, 1990, lethargy was noticed in East German companies, because they had less income than before June 30, 1990. The simple reason was that many East European enterprises were no longer able to pay in deutsche marks (West German currency) and their own currency was not accepted for payment.

Many West German HRD consultants and practitioners acted for West German enterprises. These companies have established subsidiaries in East Germany or have plans to establish them. A great number of West German managers were active in East Germany. We wonder how the East German population felt about this development. A comment of the CEO of the Trust Company notes, "Many of them conduct themselves as colonial officers, having manners not accepted in West Germany."

5th period: October 3, 1990, until the present (unification of both Germanys)

In this period, East German companies were taken over by West German enterprises. Only a few East German enterprises showed courage and worked to change their structures responsibly. The employment of many West German HRD consultants and practitioners can be called job-oriented. The objective was to solve a task. But, the HRD personnel had to face difficulties in integrating people. Crowded air and railway travel on Monday morning and Friday afternoon from and to West Germany was a fact of life. East German hotels took on the character of places of refuge in the evening for the actors coming from the West.

Practices of HRD Activities in East Germany and the Soviet Union in Different Cultures

Some basic observations about HRD activities in East Germany are appropriate. These activities have been conducted in a region where everybody speaks the same language. But, as a result of 40 years of socialist government, a counter-culture had developed. It had been not only typical for the Communist leaders but in a manifold and different way for part of the population. This was evident when difficulties arose. We needed, but didn't have, the same understanding of language. This was illustrated earlier by an example of management terminology.

We will have to pay continued attention to techniques of coordination activities like deciding, planning, and controlling. Regarding leadership activities, the difference between motivation and vision which leaders need are illustrated in the following.

1. The Decision-Making Function

West German managers project creative and influence-oriented meanings into this term. As compared with the international level, West German managers are less decision-oriented than was thought. This was shown by an international management study done by Human Synergistics Inc. and Metabasis GmbH.

East German managers associate decision making first with possible consequences, and they usually project negative consequences. This is one reason why HRD activities in what was East Germany should refer less to decision-making processes and more to an individual analysis of factors.

2. The Planning Function

West German managers relate this term to management circles, as they have learned to associate the term with goal-setting and strategy.

East German managers associate this term rather with bureaucracy, bondage, and restraint.

3. The Controlling Function

West German managers have learned to define this as an information function rather than an act of authority. This was evident when managers were asked in management seminars to use another term for "controlling."

East German managers know that controlling is necessary and view it as an act of authority. Thus far, they have not experienced management control, but only what might be called "revision control."

4. The Coordinating Function

West German managers are presently learning the management of change and how important visions are (although they find it difficult to articulate them).

Although East German managers understand the basic idea of *coordinating*, their basic approach to it is underdeveloped. They really don't know what to do with this term. Instead of coordinating, they confine themselves to the sober transfer of knowledge, which is then to be measurably duplicated. They accept those functions that are measurable and based upon an already existing scientific understanding, but they still do not understand the need for having objectives. This is one reason why many East German companies were lethargic. Leadership means running a risk and having a vision. East German managers must learn to have a formal target and motivate people rather than just give orders.

5. The Motivatation Function

West German managers understand motivation to be direct contact with employees that stresses the personal factors. However, it cannot be denied that formalistic, technical motivation theories have found favor with West German managers.

East German managers think of motivation mainly in terms of the Hygiene Factors defined by Herzberg. Many East German companies had their own library, hairdresser, nursery school, and concert agency. At monthly conferences, management publicly explained the current situation. The form was friendly within the hierarchy, but it would be wrong to suggest that the understanding was also friendly.

West German HRD consultants and practitioners often had to face a strange problem. In both East Germany and the Soviet Union their ideas and knowledge were accepted simply because they were West German, and not because of conviction. The impression was that one hierarchy was exchanged for another. HRD messages have been accepted but rarely practiced. This unwillingness has little to do with lack of technology or understanding. It results from a cultural background. People survived in the East European planned economic systems because they were prevented under very difficult circumstances to implement their plans. This nonrealization spurred development of an individual freedom of a subculture. Obstruction instead of constructive participation in the process was seen as success. The latter would have meant to stabilize the system's starting points and this would have meant to accept the socialist planned economy.

Furthermore, people and managers have learned to put up with unavoidable restrictions. The result is a dependence that can still be noticed today. Networks were a compensation for finding one's way in an inflexible economic system. They were more important in East Europe than in West Europe. These social networks offered, and are still offering, protection and mutual approval. Decisions were made on the basis of group agreement and eliminating risks right from the beginning, because every risk meant possible non-approval of people in the social network. This attitude of counter-productiveness also preserved Communist managers from being dismissed.

West German and West European HRD consultants and practitioners need to examine this mentality. They have to learn that there are relatively independent social groups that can be infiltrated only by getting prior approval. This means that HRD practitioners must show formal competence but also leave time for informal communication so that East German managers can articulate their feelings. Deadline pressure, such as "We only have an hour at our disposal," does more harm than good because it confirms East German or Soviet ideas that this is a new type of hierarchy.

The following example will illustrate the interaction. In May 1990, I held a seminar for East German purchasers. I could show competence because I was familiar with all proceedings of purchasing and because I discussed them with the participants. Consultants often specialize in foreign exchange negotiation activities or business administration in purchasing in a purchasing department. Consultants with such an attitude could neither show competence nor get agreement. It was important to have complete command of all fields regarding the purchasing processes. During the first two or three hours, many questions were asked about various kinds of work. However, this situation led to the fact that the seminar's participants basically understood the previously existing reality, but needed more time to come up to speed. If the objective of the seminar was to discuss a specified matter in a certain time, it would face considerable problems regarding agreement. Such HRD activities have not only run for eight hours a day—but for more than twelve hours a day. Discussions were similar to comparable sessions being held in the East, lasting till late in the night. The need for information was rarely satisfied.

The Issues for Consultants in Eastern Europe Shown by the Example of East Germany

Western HRD consultants and practitioners need to fulfill their task of understanding leadership, commitment, authenticity, and a variable method.Usually, HRD consultants must limit themselves to acting only as change agents, and should not take on the tasks of their client groups. In East Europe they can do so of course. That is the reason their consulting activities are so difficult. Everybody who has had this leadership experience may run the risk of acting the same way in similar situations, even if they happen to be in Switzerland or in Austria, but you can be sure that the Swiss or Austrians would not accept this.

Leadership also means to act appropriately to the situation and, therefore, to demonstrate, to show, and to counsel without having agreed with the client on it. Leadership also means to reveal visions and to define them, to motivate all employees of the firm to act as entrepreneurs. Of course, it is required that the HRD consultant be available for certain periods of time to repeat respectively to confirm the postulated starting points.

In West Europe, as in the U.S., learner commitment is expected. This is not so in East Europe because of previous experience. In East Europe, one way instruction or orders can be very successful. If a West German HRD practitioner or consultant stays for a long time in what was East Germany, he or she runs the risk of accepting this technique and trying it in West Germany, where it would get neither approval nor understanding. So the HRD practitioner must vary his or her ways of acting according to those two cultures that have a different understanding of the situation.

Culture exists as a reference point for commitment, which the East German people can also copy. Today, everything about business administration is accepted and, therefore, also the full variety of contracts. It is also possible to combine contract and commitment, a structural component, and a psychological component. Managers on the East German side understand this.

To be genuine, West German HRD consultants and practitioners must work independently and should not be the instruments of their clients. They will find approval when they define their position emphatically and show that their own work has its ups and downs. They use West German examples to point out to East German managers that the West's understanding can also be wrong and superiority is only an external factor. This is the best method to brace up the East Germans' self-confidence and encourage them to take responsibility.

During the 1989 German-Soviet Management Conference, this result could be noticed. Many Soviet managers studied at business schools in Leningrad and Moscow, and have been taught the knowledge coming from the U.S. and from Canada. Thus, they had fewer problems in the knowledge field of management than was expected. West German HRD consultants and practitioners were asked to be a good example and to have the courage to hold free and independent lectures. Always when West German HRD experts were successful in doing so, Soviet managers started a creative and spontaneous discussion.

In training and education for Soviet managers, there were considerable difficulties regarding translation. Interpreters were skilled formally, but in the field of creative techniques could do nothing with the synergistic presentation of $1 + 1 = 3$. They corrected it to $1 + 1 = 2$, which is arithmetically right but has nothing to do with the synergistic starting point of a multiple process.

West German HRD people have to use a variable method if specific learning contents are to be accepted as an absolute. It is certainly understandable that East German and Soviet managers tend to go from one extreme to another. Thus, it is important to transfer knowledge and thereafter to employ different case studies to show the different uses of the knowledge. Most especially East German managers have to learn the meaning of situational leadership, that fact A in one situation is not fact A in another. Therefore, it is prudent to sensitize their understanding of rules. This means conveying that rules should show a standardization for actions but not automatically have to lead to an adoption of actions in everyday life. It is known that rule infractions can be starting points for new developments and changes.

Future Development – Assumptions and Visions

For the next few years, it will be important to work methodically with the model of experience groups (similar to the therapy model). The stabilization of such groups by former social networks is still important. The interpersonal network is the best possible means of encouraging realization that there is a new way of thinking. Finally, these experience groups can stabilize the attempts of the persons concerned.

If only for time and expense reasons, the form of cascade training should be chosen. This training starts with top managers and is transferred by them down to all levels of the firm. If all training activities were conducted by West German HRD practitioners, a new dependence would arise; this means it would produce a pipeline without an end. Therefore, training aims have to be combined in the future with train-the-trainer projects, which call for the seminar's participants to transmit the messages to colleagues and partners. This process is very effective, as it permits one to integrate Western techniques of management into already existing, experienced, and familiar starting points of culture. The only way to transfer knowledge effectively is to recognize that two cultures have developed in Germany. Finally, it is more important to accept the different types of being and thinking than to try to impose one's own ideas on them.

About the Author

Michael Sandrock is General Manager of Eloqu in Freiburg, Germany. Formerly, he was CEO of MetaSans Inc. Now a management consultant, he completed studies in law and political science. He is Vice President of the German Society for Seminars and Congress Activities, President of the European Videoconference Association, and a seminar leader of the European Network of Training Associations. He serves on the Council of the International Federation of Training and Development Organizations.

CHAPTER 30

HRD in the European Community After 1992

Robert Hersowitz

At first glance, Europe in the 1990s seems a very exciting place to be. Many commentators, including politicians and journalists, would have us believe that every opportunity is available. They say European business is ripe for the picking and everyone should jump on the enormous bandwagon that is hurtling along at an incredible speed. Upon further examination, rather than reflection or speculation, pragmatists will find that all is not quite so simple and clear. In fact, the situation can be compared to a newly chosen building site. The ground, rather than being flat and marked out ready for construction, needs an enormous amount of work to clear away the debris and unevenness that represents the current terrain. This is due to the long and checkered history of the political, economic and social life of Europe.

The industrial and commercial life of modern Europe has its roots in the Renaissance period, when art, innovation and discovery were blossoming. Alvin Toffler in his book *The Third Wave* refers to the near future as bringing with it another "Reawakening" or "Rebirth." This indeed seems to be part of a developing trend in Western Europe. The combined impact of social political, economic and technological change seems to have accelerated the process. The events of 1989, including the political revolution in the Eastern Bloc, have added to the complexity of this Third Wave of change.

Toffler's predictions were not all optimistic. He wrote about urban decay, the decline of the Second Wave mass-production society, pollution, terrorism, and war. He talked about political change. Although he did not specifically refer to the changes in the East, he alluded to a new age of diversity and choice—the global village where the world would get smaller but more diverse. This brings into question the whole concept of a united Europe. Many politicians still argue the case for maintaining different national identities in Europe. Yet, on a commercial and industrial front, the idea of a common market with no economic boundaries conjures up a picture of a homogeneous business culture. Most European leaders support the idea of an integrated Europe. Few, however, understand the impact that this will have on organizations and people, including managers and employees who will be intensely affected by this change.

Comparison of Industrial Second Wave and Third Wave Assumptions

In describing the different assumptions of the "old world order," or Second Wave and the "new world order," or Third Wave, Toffler offers this comparison:

Old: Most people want the same things out of life and for most of them economic success is the ultimate goal, so that the way to motivate them is through economic reward. *New*: Once basic subsistence needs have been met, most people do not want the same things out of life, so economic rewards alone are not enough to motivate them.

Old: The bigger a company the better, stronger, and more profitable it would be. *New*: There are upper limits to the economies of scale, both for a corporation and for governmental organizations.

Old: Labor, raw materials, and capital, not land, are the primary factors of production. *New*: Information is as important as land, labor, capital and raw materials—and perhaps even more important.

Old: Production of standardized goods and services is more efficient than one-by-one handcraft production in which each unit of output differs from the next. *New*: We are moving past factory mass production toward a new system of "handcraft" or "headcraft" production. It is based on information and super-technology, and the final output is no longer millions of identical, standardized finished units, but "customized" goods and services.

Old: The most efficient organization is a bureaucracy in which each sub-organization has a permanent, clearly defined role in a hierarchy—in effect, an organizational machine for the production of standardized decisions. *New*: The best way to organize is not bureaucratically, but *ad-hocratically*. Each organizational component is modular and disposable, interacting with many other units laterally, not just hierarchically. Decisions, like goods and services, are custom-made rather than standardized.

Old: Technological advance helps standardize production and brings "progress."
New: The advance of technology does not necessarily bring "progress" and unless
carefully controlled it may even destroy progress already achieved.

Old: Work for most people must be routine, repetitive, and standardized. *New*:
Work for most people must be varied, nonrepetitive, and responsible, challenging the
individual's capacity for discretion, evaluation, and judgment

These differences encompass the central debate that has been going on in
Europe. They point to two "camps," two schools of thought that divide European
attitudes toward organization and management development. These differences
have their roots in European social history.

Understanding European Cultural and Value Systems

In attempting to understand the complexities of modern European cultural and
value systems, it is worth referring to the work of Morris Massey. His ideas are useful
in understanding theories of motivation and leadership. He spoke about four categories: Traditionalists, In-betweens, Rejectionists, and Synthesists. Massey (1980)
asserted that "what you are is where you were when"— an attempt to explain how
each generation imprints its own value system and cultural heritage on individuals.
This imprinting process is also influenced by mega-events, such as war, revolution,
and massive economic change. Massey further refers to age bands and generational
influences. Table 30.1 is adapted from Massey's ideas.

The present generation of middle to senior managers falls within the range of
thirty to fifty years of age. This group of people was mainly influenced by the values
of the 1960s—freedom, fun, self-fulfillment, rejection of traditional principles. They
are part of the social revolution, products of the new opportunity society—where the
welfare states of Europe guaranteed a better life, more education, and continuous
growth and economic expansion to rebuild what the war had destroyed. With this new
generation came new values: the rights of individuals to be recognized, the ability to
compete, to question, to experience new things. To replace the old-fashioned
attitudes of traditional societies, new norms were set up. Anyone who could prove
themselves could forge ahead. Indeed, many European countries experienced a
direct challenge to centuries of Christian conformity.

Application to National Groups. In applying Massey's theory to national groups
of individual European managers, there are certain patterns that emerge. The main
influences are the generational value systems associated with prewar and postwar
European experience. When asked to identify with any of the above columns of data,
most managers over the age of forty-five will firmly identify "traditionalist" influences on their lives. Those below the age of thirty, often see themselves as "new
ager-synthesists," while those between the ages of thirty and forty-five identify
strongly with the "rejectionist" column. In addition, most women managers strongly
identify with the "rejectionist" column.

Table 30.1: Generational Influences

Born 1930s Age 50-60	1940s 40-50	1950s-60s 30-40	1970s 20-30
•Traditionalists	•In between	•Rejectionists	•New-Agers
•Group-Team		•Individualism	•High Tech
•Authority Figure		•Questioning	•Information
•Institutional Leadership		•Democracy	•Ambition
•Social Order		•Competition	•Success
•Puritanism		•Performance	•Materialism
•Workaholism		•Freedom	•Pluralism
•Facts		•Fun-Experience	•Self-Goaled
•Formality		•Informality	•Specialist
•Stability	•Change	•Synthesism	

When managers from different nationality backgrounds were asked to comment about their identification, there was an interesting split between Northern and Southern European cultures. Northern Europeans identified themselves more strongly with traditionalist values while those from the south saw themselves as rejectionists. In an attempt to understand the implications of these differences, research was carried out during several management-development programs. Teambuilding exercises reflected totally different working styles and preferences. For instance, where a team consisted of German, Austrian, and Swiss German managers, the attitude and approach to planning and organizing the work was based on traditionalist conforming work norms with strong leadership. Those teams made up of French, Italian, Spanish, and Portuguese managers behaved differently.

Application to Individuals. Individuals were far more questioning, they took longer to put forward ideas and make decisions, and the work norm was very nonconforming and individualistic, with a higher degree of leadership rivalry. When these experiments have been repeated, the same patterns emerge. However, research and exploration of organization culture and accompanying value systems seem to indicate that these patterns are not always reflected at subordinate levels inside corporations. There is an anomaly. Throughout Europe, most subordinates are influenced by social values that still uphold principles saying "employees should be seen and not heard." This comes from an inherent "parent-child" or "controlling" behavioral culture deeply embedded in the traditional European education system. This encourages obedience and conformity. In the Teutonic cultures as well as in parts of Britain and Holland, the Protestant work ethic reinforces this behavior.

In the Latin countries, especially in France and Italy, the values of self- expression are also linked to religious and social experience. They produce a reaction that encourages people to rebel against conformity and autocratic leadership. This rejection of authority manifests itself when the subordinate is promoted and often results in a wider gulf between management and staff levels. The political and industrial upheaval of "Latin" Europe in recent years is probably a direct result of traditional and rejectionist forces clashing. The rejectionist culture encourages individuality, creativity, and innovation. Provided that these energies are well-contained and managed, the future merging of traditionalist and rejectionist cultures at work could produce some outstanding organization and management models for the future. To paraphrase Peter Drucker: What managers do is the same the world over, HOW they do it is embedded in their tradition and culture.

To comprehend the challenges that face European companies in the future, it is important to consider the historical cultural differences that divide Europe and its ancient social order. It can be helpful in understanding the differences between management attitudes to explore the existing influences of the Catholic and Protestant faiths on individuals. Charles Hampton Turner (1981) refers to Protestantism, Scientism, Capitalism, and Max Weber's (1977) writing on religious character. Turner quotes the work of Michael Walzer (1965) and David Bakan (1966) in distinguishing the different value systems. The values presented here in Table 30.2 probably are responsible for the major divisions in working styles, values, and attitudes in modern Europe:

Table 30.2: Philosophical Influences

Anglo-Catholic Organicism	vs.	Puritan, Atomistic Individualism
•Communal mediated relationships	vs.	Private direct relationships
•Intercessionist God	vs.	Delegating God
•Salvation through communion	vs.	Salvation through work
•God experienced with many senses	vs.	The Word read, heard and enacted
•Other-worldliness	vs.	This-worldliness
•Human personality cultivate	vs.	Personality submerged in work

The above supports my own theory that there are three working cultures in Western Europe: Conformist, Individualist, and Synthesist. The Teutonic and Nordic cultures are more in line with the Protestant work ethic and emphasizes conformist values, while the Latin and romance cultures foster paternalism and concomitant Individualism and self-expression. If one studies the geography of Europe, one can draw a cultural line from north to south. Countries such as Germany and Austria fit very well into the Teutonic model, while parts of Britain, Switzerland, Holland, and Belgium fall between Teutonic and Latin. The term Synthesist can apply to a social system that represents the assimilation of a wide range of multicultural influence. It is typical of the Scandinavian countries where the exchange of ideas and the "team" experience are heavily promoted across all borders. On the other hand, France, Italy, and, more recently, Spain and Portugal are far more typical of the paternal/individualistic approach. Britain, Ireland, Holland, and Belgium are the "gray" areas of Europe where the cultural "systems" change according to the historical, geographic, and demographic make-up in each region. At this point, it may be useful to share some perceptions about specific regions in Europe. These perceptions have been gained over the past ten years during various assignments involving management development projects.

Spain and Portugal

One of the most interesting recent developments in Europe is the economic transformation of Spain and Portugal. Both countries have recently joined the European Community and both have undergone enormous political and social changes.

In comparing the working/managerial styles of Spain and Portugal with those in France or Italy, one finds a difference in the "maturity" of management styles. France and Italy are quite established in their approach to management, while Spain and Portugal are "rising stars" in the new European economic partnership. Many corporations are making huge profits in these countries, partly because of the change in attitude of the governments in these countries. As part of the EEC requirements, these countries have had to remove political and economic constraints that have been typical of their paternalistic outlook for centuries. This has broken down the feudal mentality and allowed modern management methods and new social and work systems to be introduced.

These new work practices are beginning to reshape the economies in both countries. The interesting fact is that while the systems and methods are changing quite quickly, the people are finding it more difficult to adapt their styles of work. Part of the instant success in these countries is attributed to the readiness of the working population to conform. In the short term, this reinforces new "feudal working habits" that were quite prevalent when both countries operated economic systems based on agriculture and a working peasant proletariat. Blind obedience to the *Patrona* (now manager) produces excellent working disciplines and results especially when the individual is well rewarded.

Sue Canney-Davison, a researcher at Oxford, has compared the meeting styles of different nationalities (1990). Her observations are adapted for this chapter. Generalizations about the Spanish are as follows:

Common Generalities About Meetings in Spanish Business Culture				
Purpose	Prepared	Time Frames	Inputs	Style
•To brief others	•Not really	•Informal & Formal •Challenging	•Spirited/ Empathetic	•Strong chairman

The arrival of new technology, expanding industries, and huge international investment has put Spain and Portugal on the economic map. Their short-term commitment to growth and development is certain. The long-term reality of such development requires a commitment to change. Spain and Portugal will have to catch up with their European counterparts when it comes to management practices. To manage change and cope with new technology and all the complexities that it brings, they will have to introduce new management methods as part of major Organization Development programs. Opportunities for training and development are wide open, especially for U.S. consultants experienced with Latin American culture. There is still a strong link between Brazil and Portugal, and the two countries often share management expertise. This is less prevalent with Spain, though many joint projects do exist with Mexico and Argentina. American companies are investing quite heavily in Spain. Language remains a problem, as most Spanish and Portuguese managers lack a good command of English.

In addition to the needs for training and retraining in these countries, there are also other long-term concerns. These include the effects of political change in Europe —reunified Germany and the breakup of the Eastern Bloc—all of which represent tough competition for the Iberian peninsula.

France

The French stand out as being somewhat individualistic in their attitude to the rest of Europe's management practices. As mentioned earlier, the French have been through massive changes over the past two and one-half centuries. The values of Liberty, Fraternity, and Equality are well espoused in their trade union movement that still wields much power in industry. The French worker is very conscious of rights, and the idea of expressing one's opinions is still cherished. Yet, despite this sense of democracy, there is an underlying traditionalism that dominates French politics and business. There continues to be a high proportion of family-owned businesses in France. In addition, the education system is still seen by some as elitist and nepotistic, with many senior positions in the top 100 companies being filled by the "old boy network"—people who went to the right sort of schools and universities. Most French corporations, in considering career development for senior managers, were very concerned about the Grand Ecole background and the consequent decisions in shaping Human Resource Planning and specific career paths. This "them and us" culture can produce heightened conflict, as has been witnessed many times in the past few years. In management circles there is a problem with team development and managing conflict. The team culture in France is made up of individuals who will find it difficult to conform. The stereotypical idea of emotional outbursts and vociferous exchanges at work is a daily reality in many companies. How do they cope with these characteristics?

Common Generalities About Meetings in French Business Culture				
Purpose	Prepared	Time Frames	Inputs	Style
• To bring ideas and defend	• Yes	• Lunch & Formal	• Critique and argued overall theory	• Strong chairman • Individual

In addition, the French have always been noted for their strong feelings of national identity. They have been called "chauvinistic imperialists." This is based on an attitude characterized as "ours is the best way and others should learn our ways." This characterization may well be resented by the French, but it represents the feeling of many non-Gallic nationals in Europe. However, because of the massive political and social changes in Europe, the French attitude is slowly changing. Increasingly, French managers are acquiring English and other language skills, and are now appearing at international conferences and seminars as participants.

Until recently there was a distinctive French School of Management which did very little embracing of American management principles. Outside of France, American management practices have always influenced European businesses. The work of Peter Drucker, Mouton and Blake, Hersey and Blanchard, Edgar Schein and recently Tom Peters, Rosabeth Moss Kanter and Peter Block, dominate the European management scene at every international HRD conference. In further research on European attitudes to imported management ideas, Sue Canney-Davison comments on different national attitudes. She observed that the French rejected the planning concept of Management by Objectives, and that the French rejected this system probably for the same reasons that Total Quality Management has had mixed results. It was seen as too controlling, too uniform, and too bureaucratic. Quality circles, on the other hand, seem to have been successfully applied, especially in the 80s. The idea of individuals being able to freely express themselves under the tactful control of a "strong" facilitator is probably what made quality circles appealing.

Italy

Italy is a country of management contrasts between north and south. This division has its roots in Italy's history. Centuries ago, Italy was divided into separate duchies. The reunification of Italy in 1848 and the Risorgimento embodying the visionary aspirations of the architects of present day Italy made the country a fully participating player in the European community.

In the 15th century, the Italian Renaissance inspired the world. The Florentine benevolent despots created a style of management that still leaves its mark on Italian business culture today. This paternalistic style has generated the opposite response in Italian political life. Like the French, the Italians value self-expression and uphold their right to challenge authority. This, combined with a zeal for creativity and innovation, produces an interesting mix of a society caught between two worlds: past and future. The future is often seen in the North, where Teutonic influence is strong and industry and commerce flourish. In the South, the country remains much poorer and accompanying social problems have caused a constant migration of Italians to other parts of the world, including the United States. The Italian governmental system since World War II, has seen the development of bureaucratic Christian Democratic Socialism. This was a reaction to the war and Mussolini's fascism. Still, many Italians complain of their frustration in being unable to manage political change. The same leaders have dominated Italian politics for years, despite several revolutionary attempts to shake them off. The anomaly of traditional leadership set against a country trying desperately to transform itself from an agrarian economy to a high tech international competitor has seen the fortunes of Italy change. On the one hand, Italy boasts many examples of corporations that have grown and succeeded admirably. Italy has also become a focal point in the EEC—indeed, it was in Rome that the original EEC treaty was signed.

But as far as management issues are concerned, there is still a wide gulf between management and subordinate levels in most companies. As in France, there are many corporations in Italy originally started as family enterprises that were then sold off, retaining the highly paternalistic style. Much work in OD consulting is needed in this area to help companies transform themselves into more workable team environments. Many Italian companies have espoused the Total Quality Management concept—but they have found difficulty with the process because it calls for a more "balanced" team approach where individuals as well as leaders and facilitators are empowered.

Common Generalities About Meetings in Italian Business Culture				
Purpose	Prepared	Time Frames	Inputs	Style
•To bring ideas and defend/ resolve	•Not really	•Informal & Formal •Two meetings	•Philo- sophical, complex	•Strong chairman •Individual

Germany

Postwar West German industry and enterprise are often seen as one of the latter-day economic miracles. Yet, if one compares the development of the former East German economy, the same miracle is absent. Many theorists have commented on German working culture. The focused attitude towards labor, the work ethic, and Teutonic obsession with planning and precision have influenced German management progress. In addition, Western investment (particularly American), technology, and management expertise has contributed greatly to Germany's success. The influence of a communist system and isolation from the West does not seem to have sparked off the same results in East German industry.

Events of the recent past seem to indicate that the principles of communism did not rest easily with the East German working mentality. The quest for excellence and constant striving to aspire to the higher standards of quality and service in the West first motivated East Germans to escape and then to rebel against their communist masters.

Germany, like many European countries, has its regions where cultural differences and attitudes vary. New demographic shifts are affecting the future even inside former West Germany, and the new reunification will definitely have a huge impact on the economy.

The sociopolitical changes in the Eastern Bloc as well as the development of HRD issues in this region are in Chapter 29 of this book. In understanding HRD approaches in Germany, one cannot ignore the effect that Germany's defeat in World War II had on its people. It clearly motivated most workers to be totally self-sacrificing in rebuilding their country. The bombing and mass destruction of German cities produced a social as well as a physical levelling. After the war, people were united by a common purpose—to rebuild and reestablish a new society.

This new society was inspired by visions of a peaceful democracy. Elitism was rejected and even the German trade union movement reflects this — there is much more sharing of power that is not evident in the highly polarized British, American, and French trade unions. In addition, the rebuilding process strengthened and reinforced existing work-ethic values. Although West Germany espoused a form of socialism, this quickly turned to a kind of "workaholic" capitalism where German goods became recognized as the best and most sought after in the world. The irony of capitalism in Germany is that people spend so much of their lives working for material goods and a better lifestyle that they hardly have time to enjoy the fruits of their labor. This is also true in Switzerland and Austria, where similar attitudes prevail.

However, close inspection of individual attitudes in Germany shows that this "workaholism" is changing. Individuals who work for non German-owned companies (especially U.S.-owned companies) prefer to remain in these "mixed culture" companies. "Once you have worked for an American company in Germany, it is very difficult to go back to a German company!" This statement is often heard from managers who have developed their careers in multinational companies. It reflects the anomaly of the work ethic. On the one hand, people are meant to aspire to success and excellence. But, in doing so, they must repress their individuality and desire for social approval and fulfillment. An example of this occurs when German managers working for a U.S.-owned company travel to Britain or America for meetings with their Anglo-Saxon counterparts. While in Germany they address each other formally, using business titles or Herr, Herr Doktor, or Frau so-and-so. While in the U.K or U.S. they use first names and become very informal—something that is difficult at first, but which they then begin to enjoy.

Similarly, German managers are surprised at the idea of acquiring counselling skills as part of a strategy for solving productivity problems where an individual is not performing because of being affected by "personal problems." German work attitudes are very task oriented, suggesting that home and work should be kept quite separate and that managers should not attempt to involve themselves in their employees' home lives. While this is true in parts of Holland, the U.K., and even France, the separation of work and social roles is much more emphasized in German working culture. Again, because of the transformation in Europe, these attitudes are beginning to change.

Switzerland and Austria share similar profiles. Switzerland is more complex because it is influenced by its French, Italian, and German roots. While the Swiss Confederation is much more cosmopolitan, business and industry are still dominated by a German management culture. Emphasis is placed on planning, precision, efficiency, and productivity. However, there is more awareness of cross-cultural issues in Switzerland, and the whole political system serves as a model for a well-integrated, culturally diverse social and economic structure. Austria is more tied to the German economy and functions as a microcosm of the German management model. Austria's role in the future will be much influenced by developments in the East.

Meeting processes have been observed as follows:

Common Generalities About Meetings in German Business Culture				
Purpose	Prepared	Time Frames	Inputs	Style
• To brief others	• Yes	• Exact	• Have to be timed	• Ordered
			• Bureaucratic	• Hierarchical
			• Must qualify to participate	

German goods are made to last. Germany's manufacturing companies hold a strong position in Europe, far ahead of their competitors. Whether the German obsession with control and efficiency will affect German management's ability to be flexible and tolerant of other European management cultures is a question that ranks highly on the new European HRD agenda.

The Netherlands

Today's Dutch business culture is rooted in the philosophies of the Protestant work ethic. To a large extent, work attitudes are similar to those in Germany, but Dutch society is far more homogeneous because the country is smaller, which makes it a lot less complex. The country is basically flat, with no remote regions. The people share a colonial history that goes back to the 15th century, when Holland was a seafaring nation that dominated world commerce. The "merchant" culture and spirit of free enterprise still exist in major centers throughout the country. The Dutch have links with many countries on all continents. They have strong links with the U.S. and all that American culture represents. In this regard, they are an outward-looking nation. Most business people speak English and German because Dutch is not as widely spoken internationally.

The Dutch were severely affected during World War II by great poverty and starvation. Recovery led to the rebuilding of the nation along Christian Democratic socialist lines. Although Holland is a monarchy, it retains an interesting balance between capitalist practices and socialist ideals, and is well known for its very liberal government, social welfare program, and consequent high taxation. The government also supports training and development with legislation that includes tax exemptions and subsidies for industry. In recent times Dutch industry and commerce seem to have been quite well managed. Inflation has been kept to a minimum and the Dutch have treaded a careful path between socialist and monetarist principles.

One of the anomalies of the Dutch system is that despite the strongly liberal political climate, the management culture in most corporations is very conservative, although this is slowly changing. This feature of management can be linked to the traditional Calvinist heritage. Leadership in Dutch companies often has a distinctly parental flavor. Where multinational corporations operate, especially those which are American owned, career opportunities are limited. Management can exploit this by wielding more power over staff. Many Dutch managers become frustrated with the lack of progress in their careers. Many are committed to a Dutch way of life—although they are quite comfortable in a multicultural business world, a large percentage of people, including managers, prefer to remain in Holland where their families can enjoy an excellent quality of life. However, career progress often means going to live abroad in another European country. It seems that apart from the very large corporations, most organizations maintain a "lean and mean" structure that severely limits choices in this area.

There is also a distinctive "family" culture that is often seen as parochial by visitors to Holland. The image persists of a small country with quaint little towns and canals where life goes on much the way it has for many years. Amsterdam remains the big shock to this perception. It is truly the rejectionist capital of Europe, and the one big anomaly in an otherwise "cozy" country. Amsterdam's radicalism includes a strong feminist movement, a highly politicized gay movement, and a stream of political movements that constantly challenge the establishment. This has caused side effects in big business, where the trade union movement is quite active. The system does encourage a "works council" approach, but as in Germany it is bureaucratic though less formal.

Common Generalities About Meetings in Netherlands Business Culture				
Purpose	Prepared	Time Frames	Inputs	Style
•To bring data and resolve/ defend	•Yes	•Yes	•Frank	•Democratic
			•Towards compromise	•Group

The idea of "familiarity breeding contempt" is a real issue in Dutch working culture. Because of the rather delicate balance of power that this brings, there is quite a growing demand for HRD professional services. Non-Dutch HRD consultants are quite sought after, provided they understand the anomalies of the culture. On the one hand, you have a social system that seems to represent an open, tolerant, and challenging society that welcomes change, progress, and innovation even for its own sake. On the other, you have a formidable and sometimes overbearing parental system that can be highly critical, dominating, and counterproductive.

Belgium

Belgium is a strange synthesis of cultures. Historically Belgium was divided into two regions, French in the South and Flemish or Dutch in the North. The two cultures sit uncomfortably side by side, although integration has begun to transform the country. This is probably because of the changing status and higher economic importance of Belgium as the gateway to Europe. It is the center of European government and NATO and together with Luxembourg plays an important part in the economic, legislative, and political administration of Europe. For this reason, Belgian industry has attracted investment from all over the world. There are numerous multinational companies operating in Belgium, many of them very successful. Belgian management serves as a model of tolerance. In one sense, the Belgians have had a head start in dealing with the integration of Flemish and French (Walloon) culture. In progressive industries, corporations have initiated cross-cultural development progress to break down barriers between the "mentalities" of each culture.

American management principles have always been well accepted in Belgium and there is a large expatriate American and British management presence in the country. In this regard, the Belgians are less chauvinistic. They share with the Swiss a relativist attitude to multicultural living: Every culture does things differently and has its share of the truth.

In the past, Belgian management has embraced concepts such as Quality Circles. This has been a slow process not without difficulties in family-owned businesses. This is similar to the experience in France, where managers are far more individualistic. The idea of measuring performance as a yardstick of successful work practices is appealing to Belgians, who tend to have a high work ethic. At the same time the quest for more responsibility and promotion can be stifled in much the same way as in Holland. Belgium is a small country with limited career opportunities. There is also evidence of rivalry in multinational companies, where in the recent past many top positions have been filled by American and British managers, although this has changed as a result of the high costs of keeping expatriate staff in Europe.

The benefits of "free cultural exchange" have lead to a more integrated management culture. Diminished cultural prejudice leaves managerial minds more open and willing to acquire new ideas and experience, so many consultants are used in Belgium's international corporate arena.

Scandinavia

In discussing the management and HRD issues of the Scandinavian countries, one must focus on Sweden and Denmark. In the past thirty years, both countries have contributed greatly to management know-how and training. The Scandinavian Service School, SAS, Volvo and names like Jan Carlzon and Klaus Moeller have come to represent hallmarks in progressive and successful management techniques. The Scandinavians—including the Norwegians, Danes, Swedes, and to some extent the Finns—are fortunate because of the homogeneous culture that unites them. Most Scandinavians understand each other, and their common language and culture create an environment with few barriers to managing change. Another positive factor is that Sweden, although affected by World War II, remained neutral while other countries in the region emerged relatively unscathed. All Scandinavian countries have small populations.

Sociologically, the countries share a similar heritage in an almost classless society. In Sweden, ninety percent of the people come from working class backgrounds. In the last century, the Swedes went through their own social revolution, challenging the elitist and rigid principles imposed upon them by traditionalist forebears in the guise of Puritanism and by a very controlled social system. The pattern is similar in Denmark. In reaction to conservative control, Scandinavians swung the other way to the principles of socialism and democracy. For some time, Sweden and Denmark boasted the most advanced socialist systems in Europe, with a very high per capita living standard and the highest tax rates in Europe. They are renowned for their socialized medicine, subsidized housing, open legal system, and liberal and tolerant attitudes—especially towards women and minorities.

This liberal political culture has greatly contributed to education and the management and business environment. Scandinavian governments are very supportive of training and development. Indeed, Jan Carlzon, a former Deputy Prime Minister of Sweden, was responsible for some of the most progressive approaches to human resource development. His links with Swedish companies, especially SAS and Volvo, have added to Sweden's reputation as one of the most advanced business cultures in Europe. Sweden is often called the "Japan of Europe." Its people are far less risk averse than other Europeans when it comes to trying out new ideas. There is a much better balance between "right brain" and "left brain" skills in Scandinavian culture and the concept of a balanced team approach is well accepted. Much of this is attributed to an education system that encourages creativity, experimentation and innovation at a very young age. At the same time, Scandinavians value high living standards.

As in many other European countries, there is still the lurking influence of right-wing traditional paternalism. Although the concept of Quality Circles in Sweden was seen as something quite positive, the trade unions were highly skeptical of them, considering them too hierarchical. This led to conflict in the early 1980s.

People are pressured to perform from a young age so they can compete for better prospects. These pressures are reflected not only in industrial relations but in social problems too. Alcohol abuse, a high divorce rate, and accompanying family problems are typical issues that confront HR people.

Scandinavians, while extremely hospitable, are quite inhibited. They suffer from a tendency to repress their feelings rather than express themselves openly. Managers find it difficult to be assertive. Sensitivity to criticism and strong values placed on politeness and respect often cloud issues in problem-solving discussions. The difference between Scandinavian and other European countries with traditional roots is that the Scandinavians have taught themselves to confront these issues. Managers are far more self-aware and willing to expose themselves to new ideas and methods of training, the results of which are well recognized in international HRD circles.

Common Generalities About Meetings in Swedish Business Culture				
Purpose	Prepared	Time Frames	Inputs	Style
• To gain consensus	• Yes	• Yes, but relaxed	• Use silence	• Group
			• Agreement	• Dynamic
		• Avoid conflict		

Swedes have a strong competitive advantage when it comes to customer-service training. They strongly emphasize performance through better working environments and productivity management; therefore, they have moved away from Quality Circles and much more towards Total Quality Management. In writing about Scandinavia, it is all too easy to blanket all the countries without indicating the differences. It can be said that Sweden is the dominating culture with a more "Teutonic" outlook—hardworking but also very democratic. Denmark seems to follow next, with Norway and Finland seen as more parochial with more informal management approaches.

Britain

To most non-Britains, the United Kingdom—England, Wales, Scotland, and Northern Ireland—appears to be fairly homogeneous, with shared value systems and a collective approach to doing things. That is not the reality: The U.K is made of several sub-cultures, the strongest of which is English in influence and dominance. Even in England there is a division between north and south. The hub of political life, industry, and commerce is in the southeast. English culture is in sharp contrast with Scottish culture, where language, accent, education, and legal systems are quite different, as they are in Wales and Northern Ireland.

The synthesis of different cultures in one geographic area has influenced this part of the world over the centuries. The Saxon, Norman, Viking, and Roman invasions probably have a great deal to do with the eclectic nature of culture in England. The English language, Britain's greatest asset, remains a very expressive language because of sharing its roots with Latin, French, German, and Danish. There are more words in the English vocabulary than in most other European languages. Even in post-1992 Europe, the common language will be English. All professional conferences—including international HRD conferences—are conducted in the English language.

It may be worth pointing out that although language is an important issue in European HRD circles, it is far more important for British, American, and other English-speaking consultants and professionals to know how to use "neutral" English in Europe. This means learning how to edit the spoken language, eliminating jargon, slang, and expressions that are only used in a local context. Also, speaking the language slowly and clearly with visual support such as flip charts and overheads is important for English-speaking trainers in Europe.

In the U.K, when an individual speaks, he or she is immediately judged in terms of social and educational background. Britain is still one of the most class-conscious societies in the world,which has been both its strength and its downfall. The roots of British leadership culture go back to ancient times, when British families lived as part of a "tribal" system. The monarchy and the aristocracy still play an important part in British social institutions and the concept of ranking, uniforms, and status still prevail.

However, a great deal has changed since World War II, and like most other European countries, Britain has gone through a complete social revolution. The post-war period culminating in the 60s saw people move away from the autocratic tenets of a cheap labor economy dominated by an elite, towards a much freer society where trade unionism, a socialist democracy, and principles of popular freedom were widely espoused.

Despite this, England—unlike Germany, Holland, and Scandinavia—remained polarized after the war. There is still a deep division between the "haves" and the "have-nots." This has been reemphasized during the ten years of Margaret Thatcher's rule and is probably one of the most common explanations given for her political demise. Ironically, Thatcher and her successor, John Major, hail from working, middle-class backgrounds, which indicates how much things have changed in the country since the war.

The polarization of British society has affected trends in management development and human resource development. Britain's major economic asset has always been its cheap labor. Even after 1939, the Second Wave industrial culture of Britain which had grown up out of the Industrial Revolution was able to thrive on assembly-line industries. Working conditions were primitive and people were expected to put in long hours for low wages. Even at management and executive levels, the U.K is still notorious for its poor compensation. This is beginning to affect the U.K.'s ability to attract and retain high caliber management. In the 1970s, Britain suffered a major "brain drain" when thousands of professionals were attracted to jobs in the United States. Today Europe is opening up and many career-minded Britons are looking to the Continent for better career, job, and salary prospects.

Despite Thatcher's attempt to consolidate Britain's political and economic position in Europe, the country still enjoys the reputation of being one of the most democratic in Europe. The electoral process and the U.K. system of government always championed the right of freedom of expression. This has been true in the industrial setting as well. Before "Thatcherism," the "people power" trend was leading to widespread industrial disputes, and the country was threatened with economic decline. The sharply divided "them and us" management culture has taken its toll on the British work force's ability to innovate and respond to challenge. Even though the U.K. has an excellent track record of innovation and creativity, it has always been restricted to pockets of individuals and small groups.

One of the biggest growth industries in the U.K. is Do-It-Yourself Hypermarkets. This demonstrates the ordinary person's enthusiasm for craftsmanship and creativity. Even in the grayest urban areas in industrial Britain, one will always find high standards of workmanship and individual expression. This seems to be a direct reaction to the mass conformity so often expressed in the physical and social architecture of the people.

On the other hand, Britain has always looked west towards its ally, the United States, for political inspiration. Many of Thatcher's policies in the 1980s were influenced by the free-enterprise culture of Ronald Reagan and his monetarist high investment, low government spending, low taxation policies. Thatcher's policies were largely an attempt to reverse Britain's fortunes by removing the system that had cocooned the population to expect everything from the welfare state. The idea of the state providing everything from jobs to socialized medicine had filtered through to business. In the U.K., the majority of workers have always "worked to live" and not "lived to work" as in countries like Germany and even certain parts of the United States. The U.K. work ethic has always been about what bosses, the company, and ultimately the state can provide. Conditioned by many years of socialist work principles, British managers and workers do not take easily to the concepts of creating initiative, asserting oneself, and changing things.

Common Generalities About Meetings in British Business Culture				
Purpose	Prepared	Time Frames	Inputs	Style
• To bring ideas and compromise	• Maybe	• Can amend	• Mixed and pragmatic	• Middle of the road • Can be hierarchical

Many corporations who have been influenced by their multinational status or foreign ownership have responded positively to progressive management ideas. This has proved the potential for U.K. management, and there is now a whole new set of prospects in Britain. In the 1990s Britain seems to have reached a turning point. Will the country continue to look west or has the Anglo-Saxon U.S./U.K. pact weakened and will the U.K now become a full-fledged member of the United States of Europe?

In management and HRD circles, it is quite clear that the Anglo-Saxon tradition will continue to prevail. This is mainly because of the fact that the English language dominates. At least eighty percent (some would argue more) of the ideas of management are imported from the United States. Often, materials are transliterated to suit local markets—but the American approaches still dominate. In the U.K., HRD practitioners are very receptive to American HRD practices but find it difficult to "sell" them to corporate executives and decision-makers. The complaint has always been that the packages were "too American" for British audiences. In turn, Europeans sometimes complain that there are too many British consultants projecting British ideas that are parochial and not applicable in Europe. What is clear is that there are not enough HRD professionals who can demonstrate a broader knowledge of international management practices, including the use of a wide range of examples.

Americans seem to be better at marketing their ideas worldwide. Names such as Drucker, Peters, Hersey, Blanchard, Kanter, Block, Naisbett, and McCormick are well-known in Britain and Europe. Rarely do you find the same prestige attached to British or European writers. In Europe, the problem is language. Many countries do have their own management "gurus," but their ideas are not marketed or exported.

The American Management Association's Management Centre Europe in Brussels does convene HRD and Personnel Management Conferences each year. These are prestigious events in Europe and slowly, for the first time, European contributors are beginning to emerge. The conference is always dominated by U.S. speakers. The European Speakers are never as dynamic as the U.S. "big names," who remain the ultimate crowd pleasers.

As indicated, British HRD practitioners are not great innovators. They are good at adopting U.S. material, and have pragmatically imported such planning concepts as Management by Objectives from the U.S., faithfully linking the "HAY MSL" method of performance appraisal to MBO principles. The 1980s saw a tidal wave of Total Quality Management inspired by Tom Peters, which many successful consultancies have developed in the U.K. The Crosby school is still considered one of the best.

Quality circles still hold sway, but often fail because of the traditional top management's failure to follow through on "bottom-up" initiatives. The current focus for most service industries is "customer care" training, with British Airways leading the field very successfully. In addition, the Thatcher regime introduced performance-related pay and accountability measures as part of its massive privatization scheme.

HRD Issues in Europe

To sum up, HRD issues in Europe are reflected in the inherent cultural differences that can broadly be stated as follows:

European Cultural Differences		
• Assertive	vs.	Passive
• Individuality	vs.	Conformity
• "Right Brain" Mindset	vs.	"Left Brain" Mindset vs. "Brain-balanced" Mindset
• Strategic	vs.	Tactical Approaches
• "Big Picture"	vs.	"Small Picture"
• New Age	vs.	Traditional Outlook
• Heterogeneous Society	vs.	Homogeneous Society
• Decentralized Power	vs.	Centralized Power
• Informal Communication Methods	vs.	Formal Communication Methods

At a recent HRD convention in Brussels, research was carried out among delegates to identify the HRD focuses. Participants represented a wide spread of companies and nationalities. The following list of issues is in the order of how they were rated by delegates:

List of Priorities in HRD
- Training to Support Change
- Making Managers Responsible for Training
- Customer-Focus Quality (Training)
- Vision and Strategy
- Teaching the Organization How to Measure Results
- Synergizing Across the Organization
- Managing Change
- Anticipating Future Changes
- Concern for External Social and Ethical Issues
- Empowering Employees
- Measuring Quality Improvements
- Producing Return on Investment
- Communicating
- Developing Leadership
- Improving Creativity
- Institutionalizing Change
- Cultural Differences
- New Skills Development

On further exploration of key issues, the following subjects were mentioned on different topics:

Managing Change
- Dealing with moving targets
- Prioritizing dynamically
- Learning to thrive on chaos and change
- Developing useful models of understanding
- Developing key management competencies
- Working on critical success factors
- Clarifying the roles and tasks of experts/technician managers

Vision and Strategy
- Vision and culture
- Strategy development and execution
- Establishing a consistent approach

Empowering Employees
- Empowerment not control
- Empowering employees

Recognizing Cultural Differences
- Cross-cultural training and teaching skills
- Cross-cultural communication and cooperation
- Diverse work force issues

Working Across Cultures
- Raising the level of understanding of cross cultural and international management
- Multicultural team building
- Developing cross-cultural effectiveness
- Meeting the need for people to network
- Globalization vs. local cultural characteristics
- International impact (global village concept)

This collective feedback matches up quite well to current thinking in a wider European HRD arena. It must be said that many of the participants at the HRD conference were strongly influenced by their multinational, and indeed, U.S. parentage. The semantics, buzzwords, and HRD jargon show clearly that much American "HRD culture" has been imported into Europe. This is no bad thing, but it does point to how much more innovative American HRD practitioners are than Europeans.

Europe is still a culturally fragmented continent. Language is one of the biggest problems but so is the lack of homogeneity and consequent sharing and pooling of ideas. However, major corporate initiatives are trying to move things forward. ICI, headed by Britain's Sir John Harvey Jones, is one such European pioneer. He is an example of the excellent managerial talent that is scattered about Europe. What is needed is a cohesive body similar to the ASTD that would help assimilate, coordinate, and disseminate HRD ideas, initiatives, and programs. As one TV comedian recently put it: "If we in Europe do not get our act together soon, then we will indeed have a single European market, but it will meet once a week in Amsterdam on a Thursday afternoon!"

References

Bakan, D. *The Duality of Existence*. Unpublished manuscript, 1966.

Canney-Davison, S. *Managing in Different Cultures*. Presentation at MCE International Training and Development conference, Brussels, 1990.

Massey, M. *Theories of Motivation and Leadership*. Presentation at American Society for Training and Development conference, Anaheim, California, 1980.

Turner, C. *Maps of the Mind*. London: Mitchell Beazley, 1981.

Walzer, M. *The Revolution of the Saints*. Cambridge, MA: Harvard University Press, 1965.

Weber, M. *The Protestant Ethic and the Spirit of Capitalism*. London: Allen & Unwin, 1977.

About the Author

Robert Hersowitz is a management development consultant at International Management Development, his own consulting business, in London. Previously, he was General Manager of Cegos Management Development, Ltd. in London. He holds a B.A. in Industrial Sociology and a Postgraduate Diploma in Marketing and Advertising Studies from Watford in the U.K. He has worked with managers in 26 countries. His focus is on cross-cultural management issues in Europe.

CHAPTER 31

HRD in Ghana

Ralph R. Keteku

One important factor in the development of Third World countries has been the quality of their human resources. Ghana is no exception, even though its situation may not be as serious as it is in some other Third World countries. There is no doubt that the development and utilization of Ghana's human resources have been given much serious thought. This chapter outlines the process of HRD in Ghana and the role played by HRD consultants and practitioners.

The Nation and Its People

Ghana, formerly the Gold Coast, is an independent republic within the British Commonwealth of Nations, having become independent on March 6, 1957, after being ruled by the United Kingdom as a colony. The country lies on the West Coast of Africa. The Greenwich Meridian runs through Ghana, so the time there is the same as Greenwich Mean Time.

The vegetation of Ghana ranges from tropical forest in the Southwest, West, and Central portions of the country to savanna grasslands in the Southeast, East, and North. The climate is tropical with two main seasons: a wet season that usually runs between March and October and a dry season that runs from November to March. Temperatures range from low night temperatures of 70°F during the harmattan dry season to a high of 85°F during the days during the month of January. Rainfall varies from a moderate 80 inches per year in the tropical forest areas of the Southwest, West, and Central areas of the country to a low of 35 in the Northern Savanna grasslands.

The people of Ghana are of the Negroid descent, with a few Fulani elements in the North. There are numerous tribal groups within the country, but they can be broadly classified into five groups: The Akan who are in the majority, the Ewes (who are also found in Togo and Benin Republics), the Ga-Adamgbe, the Dagbani, and the Hausa/Fulani tribes in the North. Thus, there are five main local languages with some dialects. The official language is, however, English and all business is conducted in English throughout the country. The population of Ghana today is about 15 million.

The Economy

Ghana, like many developing nations, exports mainly primary products. More than 55 percent of the GDP is derived from agriculture. Cocoa, the largest agricultural product, accounts for 65 percent of exports and is still the biggest foreign-exchange earner for the country. Until 1981, Ghana was the world's leading producer of cocoa, but is now second to the Ivory Coast—and the industry faces a new challenge from the cocoa-producing countries of Southeast Asia. Other Ghana products include timber, coffee, cassava, corn, yam, rice, and various vegetables.

Total output of food crops has grown more than 65 percent since 1983. Although Ghana is not self-sufficient in food production, it is certain that food imports soon will be greatly reduced. Animal husbandry had been given varied degrees of attention in the past, but since 1983 renewed efforts have been made to increase animal production. Poultry farming, piggeries, and cattle rearing have received new investment and attention.

Mining has long been an important activity in the country. Indeed, the oldest existing mine is about 100 years old. Ghana produces various minerals, but the most important is gold, which has been found in the area since ancient times. The name of the country before independence (The Gold Coast) suggests that gold was available as a commodity for trading with European merchants even in the eighteenth century. There are six Ghana gold mining companies, which produced over 600,000 ounces of gold during 1989/90.

Other minerals produced are bauxite, manganese, and diamonds. Aluminum is produced in Ghana, but the plant depends on imported alumina rather than the vast bauxite deposits in the country. A massive injection of capital into the mining industry in the past three years has made it possible to sharply increase the production of all minerals.

Industrial development policy in the country had been based on producing of goods to replace imported goods. Over the years—as a result of lack of spare parts, poor management, and unavailability of raw materials—industries declined so much that some were producing only at twenty percent capacity. However, since 1983, when the Economic Recovery Program (ERP) was launched, new capital has been injected into the sector and many plants were rehabilitated and modernized. The capacity utilization of most of the industries has increased significantly, and some industries, mainly in the textile and wood-processing sectors, have even started exporting modest amounts to neighboring countries.

The School System

British colonial administrations had a policy of developing indigenous manpower to help in the administration of the country, and Ghana was no exception. Schools were established, first by the missionaries and then by the government. By 1957 when Ghana became independent, it had some twenty-five secondary schools and nineteen colleges. Ten technical colleges educated artisans and craftspersons. A university college was founded in 1948 as a college of the University of London—it attained full University status in 1961. A college of technology was founded in 1952 to raise the system of technical education to a higher level. This college also became a full-fledged University in 1961.

Independence brought an expansion of the Civil Service and the public service. This, coupled with the drive for industrialization, led to the realization that the existing facilities were not adequate for the development of needed manpower. The response to this realization was the establishment of Polytechnics in Accra, Kumasi, and Takoradi; the expansion of the Universities to include courses in business management; and the expansion of the engineering educational facilities at the University of Science and Technology.

By 1966, some 1,500 students of different disciplines were graduating from the three Universities (the University College of Cape Coast was added in 1962).

National Development and Human Resource Development

The transformation of Ghana from a purely agricultural "primary product" economy into a diversified economy became a major goal of the government soon after independence. The cornerstone of that objective was the implementation of the Volta River Project. This hydroelectric project was conceived by the government as the important requirement for the industrial take-off of the country. It was to be the source of cheap and abundant electricity. This has turned out to be true. But, with the start of the project in 1960, came the realization that qualified manpower was needed to ensure the effective implementation of the programs. Mechanical, electrical, and civil engineers were needed for the Volta River Project to continue successfully. Architects, surveyors, quantity surveyors, accountants, and other professionals were needed for that and all other industrial projects to be effectively implemented.

It was also quickly realized that some specific skills in management and administration were needed if the industries and various institutions were to be developed and run effectively and efficiently. This prompted a new Human Resource Development policy within the country. The facilities of the existing universities were expanded and modernized to ensure that they produced the required graduates in the relevant professional areas and in the needed numbers to meet the human resource needs of the country.

University of Ghana, Legon

The University of Ghana added a medical school in 1960 to educate medical staff locally and more readily. In the same year, it added a faculty of agriculture to ensure the production of agricultural graduates for the sector. Clearly indicating the new strategies of the government was the establishment of a school of administration at the university. The school was charged with the education of accountants, finance experts, managers, and administrators for the economy. Simultaneously the enrollment of the university was dramatically increased. Before 1964, no more than 300 new students entered the university each year. In 1964, it admitted 825 new students.

University of Science and Technology

The university started as a College of Technology in 1952, with the aim of developing competent technician and middle-level manpower for the country. The first few batches of students were composed of accounting staff, student teachers, and mechanical, civil and electrical engineering students. They took courses leading to diplomas that enabled them to take jobs in the Public Works Department or industry, notably the motor vehicle maintenance firms, as technicians and supervisors. By 1960, it was obvious that the nation's industrial and scientific revolution depended very much on the caliber of its human resources. The College of Technology was identified as a crucial link in the achievement of the objectives. To make sure that the architects and mechanical, civil, and electrical engineers were available to carry out the planned projects, the college was upgraded to a full university. It now has a new pre-university studies department created to ensure that young school leavers (high school graduates) passed their university entrance in the shortest possible time. By 1962, the university population was three times more than in 1960.

University College of Cape Coast

The University College of Cape Coast was conceived purely to educate science teachers. The need for science education was felt to be of paramount importance and it was rightly decided to develop an intuition that would educate students in the basic science subjects. The college developed into a full university in 1970 and has since produced many graduates in the basic sciences.

HRD Consultants and Practitioners: State Organizations

The earliest attempt to introduce HRD consultants and practitioners services into Human Resource Development in the country was in 1966, when the Productivity

Centre was established. The purpose of the Centre was to provide HRD service to industry and commerce to improve their effectiveness and efficiency.

In 1970 the Centre was adopted by the International Labor Organization to be developed into a first-class management consultancy institution. For five years the ILO provided experts in the fields of general management, accounting, marketing, training (HRD), and operations research to train and educate Ghanaians in various practices of HRD consultants and practitioners. The Centre's name was changed to Management Development and Productivity Institute (MDPI). With ILO help, it developed various training and education programs, which it then sold to the public and conducted for those who were interested. An essential part of the Institute's work was to develop HRD practices and capabilities within the country. The private HRD firms that developed later in the country drew their HRD consultants and practitionners from former employees of the MDPI.

Enterprises that have problems—usually state-owned enterprises—call on the MDPI. It then assigns HRD consultants and practitioners to the enterprise to investigate and diagnose the problems and prescribe solutions. The Institute organizes HRD programs on its premises for client organizations and has been very successful in developing managerial skills in many areas of operation. It has courses ranging from Industrial Engineering to General Management to Accounting.

A second institution providing human resource development services is the Ghana Institute of Management and Public Administration (GIMPA). Unlike MDPI, GIMPA, was set up primarily for public-sector development. In its early stages it concentrated on the development of bureaucrats for the Civil Service, Public Boards and Corporations, and the Armed Forces. Since 1983, however, GIMPA has de-emphasized the public sector and has developed a viable HRD practice in which properly qualified HRD consultants and practitioners employed by GIMPA are now available to client organizations for studies into various areas of organizational development and organizational effectiveness.

Private HRD Companies

Before 1979, there were no private HRD companies in Ghana. Those companies that existed were mainly for accounting and auditing purposes only. HRD practice with private companies started with the arrival of Project and Management Consultants (PMC) Ltd. Industrial and Management Services (IMAS), and a few others after 1979. This brought a new dimension to HRD practice in the country.

These companies, together with local branches of U.K.-based companies like Price Waterhouse and Co., and Coopers and Lybrand, undertake the kind of HRD assignments earlier reserved for the two state-owned institutes, MDPI and GIMPA.

The private companies operate similarly to MDPI and GIMPA. They advertise at the beginning of each year the HRD programs they intend to run for the public. They sell their services to client organizations that need to develop specific programs to take care of identified needs of the organizations. In such cases, the HRD consultants and practitioners do the usual preliminary survey and follow the normal procedure for executing such jobs properly. An example will illustrate this practice.

Project and Management Consultants (PMC) Limited were contracted by Social Security Bank Limited to take care of their HRD needs. PMC did a survey to determine these needs and then developed a series of learning programs covering specific staff levels. Other companies have been involved in similar situations in recent times.

The Economic Recovery Programme introduced in 1983 with World Bank Assistance arrested the downward decline in the Ghanaian economy. This created a need for competent management and technical expertise. The massive "brain drain" of the 1977-83 period reinforced this need for the training and education of human resources so that Ghana could maintain the kind of economic growth that was expected.

As a result, all packages for economic and project aid had an HRD component. This work usually went to external HRD companies and by the end of 1987 there was some dissatisfaction among the Ghanaian professionals that jobs they could easily carry out were given to external HRD consultants and practitioners. This led to the formation of the Association of Ghanaian Consultants early in 1988, with the objective of developing the expertise of Ghanaian HRD people to enable them to handle the jobs that the foreign HRD people were given.

This objective was spurred when in 1989 the United Nations Development Program (UNDP) started a program to develop local expertise in various fields. An HRD practitioner was appointed to assess the needs of the local HRD consultants and practitioners and to develop suitable training and education programs for their development.

Apart from these efforts, it has become the accepted practice for local HRD firms to seek partnerships with foreign HRD resources to undertake joint projects and help them in the programs that they run locally. Establishing working relationships with foreign-based firms, allows the knowledge of the foreign HRD practitioners to be used while maintaining the assignment with the local HRD firms. If the UNDP assistance program turns out to be successful, there will be a crop of local HRD practitioners able to fulfill the requirements of top-level performance on all the jobs available within the country.

A new development in the past two years is that the School of Administration of the University of Ghana has entered the HRD field rather strongly, developing short courses in Executive Development and other General Management areas that they conduct for the public. These have successfully filled a gap created by the other private and public HRD institutions, and have also allowed the use of foreign HRD practitioners without much difficulty. They come in as external lecturers and therefore can conduct and teach sessions and do studies needed for the success of whatever project they were invited for.

The Future of HRD

The National Development Program has very clear objectives: the rehabilitation of the country's economic infrastructure, the provision of essential amenities for the social well-being of citizens, and maintenance of a healthy GDP growth rate. The result of these objectives, judging from the past two years, will be the execution of various projects and the introduction of new ones, notably to rehabilitate highways, railways, and ports, and expand existing electricity supply to many more areas. Judging by the experience of the past decade, new plant and equipment will also be introduced, with new technologies previously unfamiliar to the people of Ghana.

For the program to succeed, therefore, existing personnel will have to be trained in the use of new technologies. However, it is doubtful if the existing HRD institutions and organizations are equipped and ready to take on these responsibilities.

As part of the recent development effort, computer hardware and software has been introduced into the country—unfortunately, without any effort to ensure that people are capable of not only using the technology but also maintaining the equipment that goes with it. It is rather disheartening to see the quantity of equipment idle because of lack of maintenance, itself the result of lack of knowledge and skills necessary to do the job.

Thus, it will be necessary for HRD institutions to introduce new courses in the fields of data processing, microcomputer technologies, and the maintenance and servicing of personal and mainframe computers. This can best be done by either entering into partnership agreements with various HRD firms in the United States and Europe or encouraging foreign HRD firms to develop and run HRD programs in the country. The best results will be achieved by those firms who will first familiarize themselves with the needs of the country as well as the level of knowledge and skills of its people. Very often programs are prepared outside the country or imported wholesale, and only then is it discovered that they must be modified extensively for them to be meaningful and effective.

For example, recently an HRD firm brought a database program to run accounting and materials management programs. During the learning activity it was found that whereas expenditures in billions of cedis (local currency) are not unusual, the U.S.-based learning program did not provide for those kinds of figures. Had the HRD practitioners familiarized themselves with the needs of the company and the country before they came, everything would have been simpler and easier.

Foreign HRD practitioners face another problem because they are unfamiliar with the educational/school system and the level of education in Ghana. They automatically assume that people have very low educational standards or very low skill levels. That this is not so is illustrated by the following incident. Two foreign HRD practitioners came to instruct a group of Ghanaians in project appraisal in 1985. When the practitioners entered the lecture hall for the introductions and preliminary entry exercises, one of them found that some participants had been his classmates in graduate school. It is not unlikely that the effectiveness of that particular program was greatly affected by this coincidence.

The main areas of need in HRD in the next decade, as evidenced by the Economic Development Program and the Planned Investment Profile, will be the following:

Maintenance management

Because most project loans to Ghana are tied to products from the donor countries, the country has a variety of plant and machinery equipment. While some may be familiar, some are completely new and call for new knowledge and skills. Planned maintenance, so important to the life and efficiency of any plant and machinery, is given fragmentary attention at best. It is therefore absolutely necessary to ensure that personnel involved in the maintenance of plant and equipment are thoroughly familiar with the maintenance management needs of this plant and equipment. Given the lack of any planned-maintenance culture within the country, it is important that those who know the need for and effectiveness of planned maintenance management should develop and run courses on the subject.

Mining technology

The future of this economy lies in the effectiveness of the mining sector. The mines, especially the gold mines, not only provide employment for large numbers of workers, but also contribute almost 35 percent of Ghana's foreign exchange earnings. To keep the mines going, especially as rich ores get exhausted and less rich ores are discovered, new technologies must be adopted. This means that new plants will need to be built and new systems of mining may have to be developed and used to ensure efficiency and effectiveness. But, the only assurance that any new technologies introduced will be effective is the ability of people to use them. This requirement can only be met by providing appropriate HRD programs.

Since these will be new areas, it is unlikely that the expert knowledge required for developing people in the needed skills and knowledge will be available within the country. This means that qualified foreign HRD practitioners knowledgeable in the field of mining technology in this country will be needed—probably for the next decade and possibly beyond.

General management training

There has been a shortage of competent managers in Ghana since the massive brain drain of 1979-1983. Many industries that might have survived were unable to make any headway because of poor management. In the cases of Tema Food Complex Corporation and Pomadze Poultry Farms Limited, the appointment of competent management teams reversed years of losses and poor output within very short periods. It is obvious, therefore, that competent managers are needed if the gains of the Economic Recovery Program are to be sustained. This calls for properly planned and executed management HRD programs organized by highly qualified and experienced management HRD practitioners. Since such experience may be lacking in Ghana, foreign HRD practitioners will be required either in partnership with local HRD firms or through bilateral arrangements.

Computers in management

As mentioned, there is a rush to acquire computer hardware and software in Ghana. Several dataprocessing education institutions have sprung up throughout the country. However, many of them are not equipped for the type of education needed for effectiveness in this area, so foreign HRD practitioners are needed to setup education and training in the dataprocessing field if the country's computerization program is to succeed. They are more likely to have the necessary equipment and resources for the comprehensive in-depth programs that will create the human resource base for an effective computerization program.

Ghana's is a clear example of the common misconception that exists in the Third World about economic development. There is no denying the fact that plant and equipment, capital, energy, proper infrastructure, and appropriate policies are essential for the development of a nation. It must be remembered, however, that plants and equipment are operated and maintained by people, capital and energy are managed by people, and infrastructure collapses if there is lack of proper care and maintenance. The human resources of a nation invariably make that nation great or small, developed or underdeveloped. It is therefore paramount that efforts to develop qualified, well-trained, and educated human resources for the nation be continued and maintained. As now, the local efforts are limited. It is essential to encourage foreign HRD practitioners and consultants to join the effort to develop a solid human-resource base for Ghana.

About the Author

Ralph R. Keteku is Manpower Development Manager of the Ashanti Goldfields Corporation (GH) Ltd. in Obuasi, Ghana. Previously, he was Consultant to the Project and Management Counsel, Principal Personnel Officer of the West African Exams Council, and Training Manager of PZ (Ghana) Ltd. He has studied at the University of Ghana, University of Cape Coast, and completed the M.Ed. in psychology at the University of Ottawa in Canada. He is President of the Ghana Association for Training and Development and a member of the Council of the International Federation of Training and Development Organizations.

CHAPTER 32
HRD in Zimbabwe

Alistair Black

Zimbabwe is a landlocked country in the middle of Central Africa, lying within the tropic of Capricorn. It is bounded on the east by Mozambique, to the north by Zambia, to the west by Botswana, and to the south by the Republic of South Africa.

The country is approximately two and a half times the size of the United Kingdom. It is split into five major provinces: Matableland, Mashonaland, Midlands, Manicaland, and Masvingo. Some provinces are further subdivided into north, central, west, etc.

A Brief Historical Overview of Zimbabwe

In order to understand the current human-resource situation and how human-resource influences grew, it is necessary to deal with the history of Zimbabwe.

In 1888 Lobengula, the King of the Matabele, granted a concession—called the Rudd Concession—to Charles Rudd, who was acting for Cecil John Rhodes. In 1889 Queen Victoria granted a charter to Cecil Rhodes to occupy Mashonaland, an area to the northeast of Matabeleland. The Charter was similar to those which had been granted by earlier British monarchs to the East India Company and the Hudson Bay Company of Canada. It allowed Rhodes to form a company, the British South Africa Company (now the Anglo American Corporation) and to raise an expeditionary force to occupy Mashonaland. The expeditionary force—called the Pioneer Column—and set out in 1890 from Macloutsie in Bechuanaland, now Botswana, which was a British protectorate.

In September of 1890, the Union Flag was raised on a hill outside of Salisbury, named after the British Prime Minister, Lord Salisbury.

Zimbabwe's history has always been turbulent, and during this period the Matabele *Impis* (war parties) continued their practice of raiding the Shona or Mashona tribes in Mashonaland, stealing cattle and women and killing the men.

The following is a chronological sequence of events to give the reader a broader outline of the country to help in understanding the human resource position:

- **1889:** British South Africa Company chartered.
- **1890:** Mashonaland occupied by the Pioneer Column.
- **1893:** First Matabele uprising.
- **1894:** Lobengula and the Matabele defeated and Matabeleland occupied.
- **1895:** Territorial boundaries identified and country named Rhodesia after Cecil John Rhodes.
- **1900:** Rhodesia's population estimated at only 400,000. First piece of H.R.M. legislation passed, the Master and Servants Act which was designed to regulate the contracts between Masters, (Tradesman) and Apprentices. Was also used to regulate the conduct of domestic servants (black) and their employers (white).
- **1923:** Referendum for self-governing status inside the British Empire but outside the Union of South Africa. Blacks not included in the referendum. (Up to this time the country had been administered by the British South Africa Company.)
- **1934:** First Industrial Conciliation Act passed by Parliament to control collective bargaining between employers and employees.
- **1940:** Commonwealth Air Training Scheme brings many British, Canadian, and other commonwealth personnel to Rhodesia to learn to fly so as to fight the Germans in the 1939-1945 war. The country at this time flourishes under British protection and develops a sound agro-industrial base. Rhodesia becomes a major grower of tobacco and citrus fruit, and a major exporter of cattle.
- **1945:** Many of those who trained for the war in Rhodesia return to the country at its end. Industrial Conciliation Act amended to take into account apprenticeship training for particular industries.
- **1953:** Rhodesia joins the Federation of Rhodesia and Nyasaland, consisting of the countries of Southern Rhodesia, Northern Rhodesia, and Nyasaland. (These countries are now Zimbabwe, Zambia, and Malawi). The legislature passes a new Industrial Conciliation Act which governs more effective collective bargaining between employers and employees in industry and commerce. The agro industry is not covered and domestic workers are still covered by the Master and Servants Act.

- **1959**: The first political riots occur in Salisbury, now Harare, demanding black enfranchisement within the political system. Apprenticeship Act to regulate apprentice training into law.
- **1960**: Nyasaland gains independence from Britain and becomes Malawi.
- **1961**: Tanganyika, now Tanzania, gains independence and Joshua Nkomo, now Vice President of Zimbabwe, forms the Zimbabwe African People's Union (Z.A.P.U.).
- **1963**: The Federation of Rhodesia and Nyasaland is dissolved and Britain refuses independence to Rhodesia. In Rhodesia, the Zimbabwe African National Union is formed by disaffected Z.A.P.U. members. Parliamentary select committee meet to discuss and make recommendations on technical and skilled manpower training.
- **1965**: The first grouping of personnel managers, mainly white, form a Personnel Management Institute. Ian Smith, then Prime Minister of Rhodesia, issues a unilateral declaration of independence from Britain, which responds by applying selective sanctions against Rhodesia. Northern Rhodesia gains independence and becomes Zambia.
- **1968**: United Nations imposes comprehensive mandatory sanctions on Rhodesia. Commerce and industry become isolated from the outside world and respond by building a sophisticated agricultural and mining sector and becoming the largest exporter of flue-cured tobacco in the world. The country also becomes the largest exporter of beef in the Third World and the largest producer of white maize in the entire world. Apprenticeship Training and Skilled Manpower Development Act promulgated by Parliament.
- **1972**: Rhodesia finds itself in a guerilla war with Z.A.N.U. and Z.A.P.U. cadres. All whites are called up for some form of military or police service and have to undertake 180 days service per year. The effect on skilled manpower is tremendous.
- **1974**: Manufacturing sector expands and contributes thirty-two percent to the G.N.P.; agriculture accounts for eighteen percent and mining only eight percent. Antonio P. Salazar overthrown in Portugal, which causes a shift in political status in Mozambique and Angola. Nationalist movements make moves to become governments in those countries.
- **1975-79**: Black political pressure increases inside Rhodesia. Rural area suffers immense damage as internal war is fought on three definitive fronts—1600 rural schools destroyed, more than 20,000 rural people killed, many more injured. Over one million people displaced and flee the country to Mozambique. One-third of all rural health facilities are destroyed and agri-sector loses more than one million head of cattle. Farms are prime targets for attack and some incidents occur in urban areas.
- **1979**: Ian Smith and his government begin talks at Lancaster House in London to prepare for the transition to independence under the authority of the British Government.

- **1980**: Independence elections held and Z.A.N.U., under the chairmanship Robert Mugabe, wins an absolute majority. April 18, 1980, sees Zimbabwe become an independent nation with Mugabe as Premier.
- **1981**: Government introduces salary and wage legislation to freeze salaries and wages of those earning over $24,000 per year and to increase wages at the lower end of the scale by a minimum of eighteen percent on a graduated scale. Government sets a minimum wage for industry and commerce and the agricultural and domestic sectors. Apprenticeship becomes a Government responsibility and apprentices become bonded to the State for the period of their training and an equal period thereafter.
- **1985-90**: Government introduces new Labor Relations Act and Regulations which prohibit the dismissal of employees without the authority of the Ministry of Labor. The Ministry creates Labor Relations Officers and Hearing Officers to hear and mediate disputes. Government continues to legislate on minimum wages and ceilings.

Zimbabwe has two histories: The history of the colonial period from 1890 to 1980 and the post-independence period, 1980 to 1990, the first decade of a new country situated in the heart of Central Africa.

In 1890, very few white men had ventured into the interior. David Livingstone had taken an expedition inland and discovered the Victoria Falls and Sir Henry Stanley had been sent by the London Missionary society to find him. Arab traders and Portuguese settlers had navigated the mighty Zambezi River as far as Tete, but little or nothing was known of the interior beyond.

The Pioneer Column left Bechuanaland and crossed into the interior at the Sashi River on July 1, 1890. A historian of the time, Wilfred Bussy, described this expedition as, "a march of less than 500 venturesome Britishers through 400 miles of trackless desert infested by hostile savages and marked at every stage by drifts; barred by great rocks, mountain walls through which a practicable road had to be cut; long torturing stretches of country that held no water, or well-nigh impenetrable bushveld. Such an undertaking had to be carried out before the object of the expedition could be achieved—the occupation of Mashonaland and the establishment of Rhodesia."

Those familiar with Central and Southern African history will be aware of the famous, or infamous, Jameson Raid, the Boer War, and various rebellions that occurred around the turn of the century, as well as Cecil John Rhodes' dream of building a railway from the Cape of Good Hope to Cairo in Egypt. It is sufficient for this chapter to say that until World War II, Central Africa was as far away as the moon is from the earth today.

After that war, Britain embarked on immigration schemes to the colonies. Vast numbers of people from Britain went to Canada, Australia, South Africa, Rhodesia, and elsewhere. The subcontinent had a line of rail stretching from Cape Town up through South Africa, through Bechuanaland, through Rhodesia to Northern Rhodesia. Towns sprung up along this line and became the focus of industry, commerce, and farming centers.

Both blacks and whites drifted to the towns, looking for work and to improve their situations. Joan May's introduction to her book, *Where Do We Go From Here?* typifies the situation: "Rhodesian society has been described as exhibiting the classic characteristics of a 'plural' society, characterized by two main racially defined groups, European and African (and two minority groups, Asian and Colored, usually for administrative purposes put together as one), each having its own basic institutions." She goes on to say that the superordinate group, the Europeans, are a distinct minority, only 4.5 percent of the population, and are preoccupied with the problems of maintaining and controlling the African majority.

From 1945 until 1965, the bulk of the labor force was commonly housed by employers on tneir property. In the agricultural industry, the farmer had his compounds. In the towns and cities, the large employers had their factories and compounds with single quarters and married quarters. These compounds sometimes had a school, a beer hall, a recreation hall where films were shown, ran a football team, and a clinic.

There were two distinct work forces: the whites, who held down the skilled, supervisory, and managerial jobs in government, commerce, industry, and agriculture, and the blacks, who were the semi- and unskilled and gathered at the factory gates looking for work. They could be fired at will because for every employed black, there were twenty outside waiting to be hired.

It is interesting to note that in 1966 Senator Robert Kennedy in his report to the National Advisory Commission on Civil Disorders stated: "The crisis in Negro unemployment, therefore, is significant far beyond its economic effects – devastating as those are. For it is both measure and cause of the extent to which the Negro lives apart —the extent to which he is alienated from the general community." Further on in his report he said, "What Negro teenagers are not inclined to accept are dead-end jobs that pay little and promise no advancement or training."

This was the situation in Rhodesia in 1965 when a group of Compound Managers decided to form an Institute of Personnel Management to deal with the human-resource problems of the day. They, of course, did not realize just how important their decision was and the effect it was likely to have.

When Prime Minister Ian Smith declared U.D.I. (Unilateral Declaration of Independence) from Britain in November of 1965, Britain applied selective sanctions.

The UDI Years and Human Resource Management

The effect of sanctions upon Rhodesia was dramatic. Being surrounded to the north, east, and west by independent black-controlled countries meant that these countries could control the flow of imports and exports, thus effectively blocking goods to and from Rhodesia. The British blocked the port of Beira, the principal port through which exports and imports had previously been channeled. This forced Rhodesia to turn to South Africa for both political and economic strength during the early period of sanctions.

The effects of the sanctions have been well documented. They did not work, and instead had the effect of uniting the country. True, there was a certain amount of emigration of skills but the white community rallied round the Rhodesian Front Government and built an effective economy using South Africa as a means of trading with the rest of the world. The economy grew but the effect on human resources of the country was devastating. While manufacturing output grew and became very innovative in order to circumvent sanctions, there was a reduction of labor in the manufacturing and commercial sectors. Many people were made redundant and businesses closed. As a result, many skilled people moved to South Africa.

Population estimates based on the 1969 Census returns shows that the population of Rhodesia was approximately 6,200,000. The breakdown was 5,900,000 African,(92%); 274,000 white (4.4%); 19,900 classified as colored (that is,Afro-European or Afro-Asian); and 9,900 classified as Asian. The other groups represented .48 percent of the population.

Joan May states that the word "Colored" is used in South Africa and Rhodesia to denote people of African descent. The Beadle Commission of Enquiry regarding the Social Welfare of the Colored Community (1946) attempted to define the word "Colored" but could only make what it felt was an unsatisfactory suggestion because "the term is not capable of a precise definition."

At this time fewer than one million people were formally employed in the public and private sectors of the economy. The remainder were employed in the agro-industry or in the rural and peasant farming sectors. These latter sectors had to be self-sufficient or the tribesmen would starve. White Rhodesians became paranoid during the early years of sanctions and found many ingenious ways to break the sanctions.

Although human-resource management was in its infancy, it recognized that if the country was to succeed, it had to develop its human resources. In 1972 the independence war began to heat up. Guerillas attacked a white-owned farm. This marked a very decisive phase in the war. A National Service Act was passed subjecting European and colored citizens to an initial period of national service and so many days per year thereafter until age fifty-five. At the height of the war the call-up periods were a maximum of 180 days out of 365.

Human-resource management thus began to come into its own as organizations looked to this discipline to assist in developing skills to keep commerce and industry turning. Programs were designed to develop the semi-skilled work force, which was mostly black and not involved in "call-ups." Commerce and industry staggered from one crisis to another but continued to survive.

Military commanders reportedly told Ian Smith that the war could not be won militarily and that it required a political solution. During the 1970s, whites became tired of the war and began an exodus to South Africa.

In 1979, talks began at Lancaster House in London at Lancaster House in preparation for majority rule under British authority. The pre-independence elections were held in February of 1980 and Robert Mugabe swept to power despite assurances that Bishop Abel Musorewa, a moderate black, would win.

There was a further exodus of whites from the country to South Africa. From a total of 274,000 in 1969 to fewer than 100,000 in 1981 was a skills drain of immense proportions. The competition for the remaining skills was fierce, particularly in the engineering and electrical fields.

During the war, many young blacks had fled the country and had received training in countries all over the world, including universities in America, Britain, Russia, Cuba, East Germany, West Germany, Sweden, and Canada. After 1980, they came flocking back to the newly independent Zimbabwe.

The Colonial Era

It is impossible to attempt to define human-resource management in Rhodesia due to differences in attitudes between whites and blacks. At the turn of the century, Rhodesian blacks lived as tribes. Each tribe was ruled by a chief who had absolute authority. For each subunit there were subchiefs and village headmen. They were responsible for running the villages that made up the chief's area. The country was divided into two basic regions by whites; Matebeleland in the South and Mashonalland in the North and East. There are, however, over forty tribes represented in the country, and each tribe has as many differences in culture and heritage as the clans in Scotland.

At the time of colonial occupation, the tribes were basically farmers. They tilled the land, tended to the cattle, and built their houses with poles from trees daubed with mud, which hardened in the harsh African sun. There was no industry, no currency, and any trading between tribes was on a barter basis.

The coming of the white man changed the course of the country. In Salisbury (now Harare), industry sprung up as the whites moved away from the capital and began to occupy the best arable land. The blacks began to drift into the towns looking for work, so labor was cheap.

In 1931 the government passed the Land Apportionment Act, which divided the country into racial areas: African areas, European areas, and National and Unreserved land held by the government.

Mason states that while the original intention of the British South Africa Company and the Legislative Council in apportioning the land into racial areas was to protect the "native" until he could be assimilated into European society, in practice the European settler was opposed to the principle of competition with the African and moved more and more toward total segregation based on the needs of the two races. However, each African farmer was given only a few acres, while each European farmer was given hundreds or thousands of acres. This had the effect of forcing the blacks into the towns to look for work.

In their book *Education, Race and Employment in Rhodesia*, Murphee et al. tell us that, "from the beginning of European rule in 1890 the African was prevented from competing with the European on equal terms. A very early act of the British South Africa Company was to establish a separate department to handle African Affairs."

The first piece of human-resource legislation was the Master and Servant Act. While this legislation was supposed to control the terms and conditions of apprenticeship, it also dictated the relationship between any "master" (employer) and "servant" (employee) and contained clauses very similar to what might have been contained in American legislation dealing with slaves. If a servant ran off, he could be charged for desertion.

In 1934, the government passed the Industrial Conciliation Act. Its purpose was to control the collective bargaining process and conditions of employment in commerce and industry, but it was seriously flawed in the eyes of Africans. Firstly, Africans were not given a break in terms of apprenticeship. They were not allowed to join trade unions or to become skilled workers.

Murphee et al. also tell us: "The control over unskilled African wages was largely in the hands of government and these were kept low largely through a policy of alien migrant labour. These measures stifled African advancement, succeeded in limiting economic progress to a few individuals and prevented the natural emergence of a sizable African middle-class."

They go on to tell us that the selective immigration policy, the practice of job reservation, and the pervasive racial insecurity had created a European society that was not only highly stratified but which exhibited a remarkable political solidarity which minimized ethnic and class differences.

In the post-war period Africans became disenchanted and there were a number of strikes for better wages and conditions. At the same time, African Nationalism was beginning to make demands for a political voice.

In 1945, the Industrial Conciliation Act was amended to give industries the chance to look after their own apprentices. However, this was not successful and fourteen years passed before a separate Apprenticeship Act was passed in 1959. Behr and MacMillan point out that a similar piece of legislation was passed in South Africa as far back as 1922—so Rhodesia was some thirty-seven years behind other economically viable countries in the area of skilled manpower.

It may seem that we are discussing human-resource management from a very narrow standpoint. Unfortunately, in Rhodesia that was the situation. Basically, there was no human-resource management. Labor was cheap, because it was black, unskilled, and could be fired at the drop of a hat. Recruiting replacements involved merely a walk to the factory gate where unemployed blacks sat waiting for an opportunity in the world of work.

In 1962, the white electorate became alarmed at the rapidity of African advancement and rejected the United Party's policy of moderation and gradual integration in favor of the more racial policies of the Rhodesian Front. By 1965, three years of negotiation with Britain had not brought independence, and in that year Rhodesia issued a unilateral declaration of independence. This brought about the imposition of sanctions from Britain and, in due course, from the rest of the world.

At this time, a group of personnel practitioners, under the aegis of the Rhodesian Institute of Management, formed a professional association of personnel managers in recognition of the need for a more formal approach to human resource management. In due course, this became the Institute of personnel management of Rhodesia (now the Institute of Personnel Management of Zimbabwe).

A major problem was that the Industrial Conciliation Act mitigated against blacks. The act enshrined the principle of verticalism—that is, that only one union could be registered for a given set of employees in an industry, thus dividing union strength. The 1959 amendment of the act stated that it was to be applied nonracially. However, by this time the already registered white unions were very strong and did not take kindly to new black unions emerging. Thus, black labor leaders turned to political action in trying to gain their objectives.

The U.D.I. early years saw economic gain in Rhodesia. At the same time, human-resource practitioners began to realize that if manpower was to be used successfully it had to be on a nonracial basis, using other forms of criteria in order to achieve economic objectives.

Between 1965 and 1970, the economy of the country became very sophisticated. In agriculture and mining, gains were made that would not have happened had U.D.I. not taken place. As a result of U.D.I. and the resulting sanctions, Rhodesian whites rallied around the flag and made great efforts to break the sanctions. The country became the largest exporter of beef to the rest of the Third World and the largest producer of white maize in the whole world.

But on the horizon was looming the war of liberation. Many of the blacks had left the country. Younger ones had crossed into Mozambique or Zambia and from there had been taken to "refugee" camps in Tanzia, where they were trained in guerilla warfare by Chinese, Koreans, Russians, and Czechoslovaks.

From 1966 onwards, if any white had lost his job because of sanctions, the government offered him or her employment as full-time reservists in the armed forces or the police until the sanctions problem had been resolved. But this was not offered to the blacks. If they lost their jobs, they were paid off and left to go back to their tribal area. Many of them left the country and joined their colleagues in the camps of Mozambique, Zambia, or Tanzia.

The start of the war of liberation brought its own particular problems to human-resource management. Early on, the war was contained by the Police Force with the assistance of the Army and Air Force. However, escalation of the war led to many strains in the industrial and commercial sector, although the agricultural sector was worst hit because it was considered a soft target.

In the mid-1970s military service became compulsory and those who had not done any form of military service were called up for an initial period of two years. This caused many white families to emigrate to South Africa. In addition to the initial two years service, everyone between the ages of twenty-one and fifty-five years who was fit was called up to the Army, Police, or Air Force for a period of 180 days per year.

The drain of skills to call-ups and emigration took its toll. Many companies were left without skilled manpower, not just in engineering skills such as fitters and turners, but across a broad spectrum of skills. Organizations were required to continue to make a profit, but the skills drain was creating tremendous problems.

In 1972, the Institute of Personnel Management set about professionalizing its membership by introducing a two-year, part-time Diploma course at the local polytechnics. The first students graduated in 1974.

Elsewhere, other organizations became very proactive in the area of training and development. One organization, African Associated Mines, purchased a franchise from the U.S. for criterion-referenced instruction and pushed its semi-skilled staff through these programs in order to overcome their skills deficiencies. Another organization, Hunyani Paper and Packaging Limited developed learner-centered instruction programs for all types of operator training and succeeded in increasing the skills and productivity of what was a semiliterate work force. There are many such examples.

HRD Practices

Prior to Rhodesian independence, HRD practices were dictated by the Industrial Conciliation Act and the agreements published under that act. Industry and commerce were self-regulated. Breaches of the agreements were reported to the police by designated agents for the industry and were passed on to the Prosecutor's Office. Some penalties were imposed and fines levied, but prosecutions were few and far between. The biggest number of offenses were, in the construction industry, usually underpayment or nonpayment of wages.

The blacks believed that the Industrial Conciliation Act was unfair to them. The process of setting conditions of service for an industry were two-fold. If the industry was judged representative of employers and employees, then the employers were required to form an employer body and the employees a trade union. If this was achieved, they formed an Industrial Council to regulate the industry, with equal representation from employers and unions. Agreements reached by the Industrial

Council were sent to the Minister of Labor for scrutiny and approval. When published they became binding on all employees within the industry whose jobs were designated in the agreement. In this way, employers were not regulated for those senior and skilled jobs mainly held by whites.

If an industry was too small to form a Council then the Minister of Labour could direct that an Industrial Board be formed. This Board, whose Chairman and independent member were appointed by the Minister, together with equal representation from employers and employees, set out the recommendations to the Minister. The Minister published regulations in terms of the Industrial Conciliation Act. These were binding on all employees covered by the regulations for those jobs detailed in the schedule to the regulations.

These pieces of legislation governed human resource practices in commerce and industry but did not cover domestic workers or agricultural workers, who were still under the Master and Servants Act.

Disputes within an industry or commercial organization were handled in different ways. Disputes arising in an Industrial Council area of control were handled by the Council unless they reached an impasse. In that case, the Council requested that the Minister appoint a mediator or send the dispute to arbitration. This could not be done without a request from the relevant council. In the case of regulated industry where Boards had been appointed, the Minister had the right to directly intervene through officials within the Ministry, and mediation and arbitration could be mandatory.

After independence, the first directives from the new regime were for the formation of Workers' Committees in every organization, as part of the new socialist culture that was to developed within Zimbabwe. These Workers' Committees were to have a say in how the organization was to be run. However, great conflicts arose between the Workers' Committees, who saw themselves as all powerful, and management. The formation of Workers' Committees had no formal legislative backing, but was based on a publication put out by the new Ministry of Labor, Manpower, Planning, and Social Welfare. Many employers saw the formation of Workers' Committees as interference in the running of their business, while the more progressive saw as an opportunity to improve communication within the organization.

In December of 1981, the Ministry of Labor, under the Emergency Powers legislation, published the Emergency Powers (Control of Salary and Wages) Regulations. By using the Emergency Powers legislation, which had been passed during the U.D.I. years, the Minister had devised regulations from which there was no right of appeal. The regulations froze salaries and wages at a maximum of Z $24,000 per year and gave workers two things: move to a minimum salary or wage and graduated increases from nineteen percent at the lowest level to one percent at Z $23,500 per year. The effect was dramatic . The cost of living, which had been rising throughout the late 1970s, would now have the greatest effect on those earning over Z $2,000 per month because the legislation prohibited them from getting any adjustment to their cost of living.

There were other effects as well. Skilled employees, who were in short supply in the labor market, saw this as an opportunity to hop from job to job, gaining increases along the way. While this was forbidden, the legislation, there was no way of policing it. However, employers could retain their skilled employees by redefining the job, adding extra responsibilities, and changing the job titles. Unscrupulous employers did this without any thought to real changes in job definition or content, while progressive employers saw the need for improved personnel practices, and job engineering and enlargement provided logical and defensive personnel policies to retain their existing skills and advance their other skills.

The government also published "no dismissals" legislation, again under the Emergency Powers Legislation, whereby any dismissals, particularly of lower-level staff and members of the Workers' Committees, had to be approved by the Ministry of Labour. This meant that an employee guilty of an infringement at work, who in the past could be dismissed at the whim of his or her manager or employer, could now not be dismissed without formal hearings.

There was some confusion over the role of the Workers' Committees. Many Workers' Committees believed that they had to be consulted on every aspect of the business, that they should have more say in the factors of production, that control of business was being passed on to them, and that management should listen to what they have to say.

There arose conflict between them and the unions. The Zimbabwe Congress of Trade Unions (Z.C.T.U.) was formally recognized by the government. The roles of the trade unions and the Workers' Committees became very confused despite the fact that the roles of the Workers' Committees and the Workers' Councils within an organization had been laid down in the guidelines.

The Institute of Personnel Management became crucial. Before 1980, it had been white-dominated, but many of its members left the country for South Africa. At independence, the personnel profession suddenly became black-dominated, with many graduates returning from Britain and the United States, where they had undertaken scholarship programs.

In the newly independent government, the Minister of Labour seemed to see the Institute as a colonial hold-over, and considered developing a new Institute of Human Resource Management to fill the needs of the new and emerging personnel practitioner. However, when the Institute broke away from the Institute of Personnel Management of Southern Africa and became wholly Zimbabwean, the government changed its attitude and has used the Institute as a professional sounding board for human resource practices.

In 1985, the government published the new Labour Relations Act. Although there were many radical departures from the old legislation, the new Act retained some important features. Industrial Councils became Employment Councils, and Industrial Boards became Employment Boards.

The biggest changes in the Act, leading to changes in personnel practice, were legislating the role of Workers' Committees and their right to bargain at shop-floor level, and setting out the concept of tripartite negotiation practices. The legislation provided for three types of bargaining. At the national level, bargaining on minimum wages, conditions of service, etc. would be done by government, the Employers Confederation of Zimbabwe (EMCOZ) and the Z.C.T.U. At the industry level, bargaining would be between the employers' body and the union at employment council level. But government had the right to dictate what was required and the right to promulgate agreements reached under this process – which was not much different from the process under the previous legislation. At the shop-floor level, the Workers' Committee had the right to bargain with its employer for conditions of service not covered by the industrial agreements.

The other major provision in the new Act defined unfair labor practices and protected workers from them. Giving less than ninety days maternity leave per confinement was declared an unfair labor practice, as was recruiting or promoting on the basis of race, creed, religion, or ethnicity.

The mechanism set up to control these practices was cumbersome. Any issue involving the Act or its regulations could go in front of a Labor Relations Officer who could give a determination. The employee or employer could then appeal the determination to a Hearing Officer. Appeals could continue to a Regional Hearing Officer, to the Labor Relations Board, to a Labor Relations Tribunal, and finally to the Supreme Court. In practice, an employee who took this lengthy appeals route found that it might two to three years for a final determination. During this process, the employee could be in place at work or on suspension receiving no income.

Two other government labor initiatives—while good for employees in principle —were slowly strangled by bureaucracy. First, the government set up a central manpower registry for the enrollment, control, and development of apprenticeship. All apprentices would enroll with the central Apprenticeship Authority. Employers would receive their apprentices from this authority. The apprentices would be employed by the state, paid by the state, and after completing their four-year training period be bonded to the state until they had repaid in time the money expended on their training.

Because employers had no longer any say in who they employed as apprentices, there was a decline in the numbers of apprentices entering industry. In 1990, the government relented and encouraged employers to again begin to recruit their apprentices, provided they were registered with the Apprenticeship Authority and had the correct entry qualifications.

The second initiative was to quantify skills within the engineering, iron, steel, and electrical industries. Government contended that there was no such thing as an unskilled person and to this end set up centers where semi-skilled persons could receive a trade test. The concept was very revolutionary for a Third World country. Skills were broken into four classes: Skilled Workers Class 4, 3, 2, and 1. A Skilled Worker Class 1 had journeyman status. There were two routes to reach that status. You could become an apprentice for four years, one of which was in a technical college, or you could join an organization as an operative and over the years skills tests to improve your position until you attained the Skilled Worker Class 1 status.

The problem was that people took trade tests, came back with skilled-worker certificates, and demanded increases in pay and position when there were no such positions in the organization. Once again bureaucracy took hold and it is now almost impossible to obtain a trade test at any of the government centers due to the long waiting lists and a shortage of skilled testing personnel.

The government has begun to realize that intervention at a central level causes blockages and backlogs that it cannot deal with, and to this end has recently issued regulations which in part state that if an employer has a code of employment conduct that has been ratified by a Works Council, (equal numbers of management and Workers' Committee representatives sitting as a collective bargaining body) and registered by the Ministry of Labour, the employer does not need approval from the Ministry to dismiss employees for major breaches of discipline.

This move away from total central government control has been resisted by the trade unions as an appeasement to the trade liberalization policy recently announced by the government. Stringent price controls are in force and organizations have had to apply to a government committee for permission to increase prices as a result of increases in input costs. These committees can take up to two years to agree to increases in the mean currency allocations to purchase raw materials outside the country. Meanwhile, the organization tries to cope with a work force that theoretically cannot be dismissed and an ever-increasing inflationary spiral.

The last and most important issue Zimbabwe faces at this time is AIDS. Government in its wisdom has for many years been tight-lipped about the numbers of Zimbabweans who are HIV-positive and those who have died with the full-blown disease. Only recently are statistics becoming available. Some experts have estimated up to forty percent of the work force has HIV infection, and by the year 2000, over 600,000 will be dead or incapacitated. This human tragedy will create immense problems for the human resource practitioner.

Recently the trade unions have fallen into disrepute because the workers see them as ineffective and because of their insistence that all members of a Workers' Committee should be union delegates. This country does not have shop stewards as union officials in the same way that Europeans and Americans have. The power currently is in the hands of the workers at the front line, and they are unwilling to give it up.

The government has indicated that in the future, collective bargaining will be the order of the day and that it will not continue to legislate wages and conditions of service. It has seen the wisdom of leaving negotiations to the organizations themselves, because of legislating for wages and salaries each July. A number of progressive organizations would give annual increments at other times of the year, but when the July increases came along, the work force demanded these as well, under the impression that the government was actually giving them the increases with its own money. Progressive employers then stopped giving annual increments, because after giving an annual increment of say, ten percent in January, they would be forced to give another increment of say, fifteen percent in July. Not many organizations can afford such wage increases, especially when their output costs are affected by price controls.

In 1990, the government insisted that all industries enter into collective-bargaining negotiations over wages and conditions of service and have indicated that it is well pleased with the results. Organizations are now moving towards full collective bargaining for the years ahead.

References

Behr, A.L., and MacMillan, G.H.L. *Education in South Africa.* Pretoria: Van Schaik, Ltd., 1971.

Davies, R. "Who Will Pay the Price of A.I.D.S.?" *Executive Magazine,* 1990, pp. 29-31.

Gould, J., Gould, J., and Smith, B.K. *Report on CIMS Feasibility Trip.* Zimbabwe: Y.M.C.A., 1982.

Labour Relations Act. Harare: Government Printer, 1985.

May, J. *Where Do We Go From Here?* Association of Round Tables in Central Africa, 1978.

Mothobi, B. *Training for Development.* Association of Round Tables in Central Africa, 1978.

Murphee, Cheater, Dorsey, and Mothobi. *Education, Race, and Employment in Rhodesia.* Association of Round Tables in Central Africa, 1975.

About the Author

Alistair Black is Chairman and Chief Executive of M.B.B. (Private) Limited in Harare, Zimbabwe. Previously, he was Personnel Director, Hunyani Paper and Packaging Limited and Personnel Manager of Rhodesian Pulp and Paper Industries Limited. Previous to that he was Assistant for Staff Officer Training to the Commissioner of Police, British South Africa. He has a Diploma in Personnel Management from Harare Polytechnic and a Bachelor of Education degree in Adult Education from the University of Rhodesia. He is a Fellow of the Institute of Personnel Management of Zimbabwe.

CHAPTER 33
Spirit of Quebec

Denis Ouimet

HRD is of great importance because it will allow people to make a meaningful contribution to their organization or enterprise. During turbulent times, changes occur at a very fast rate, so it becomes essential to help the organization adapt to the contexts and issues with which it is confronted. Consequently, much energy is invested in HRD. It is easily understandable, since human resources use all the other resources.

Therefore, we need strategies, methods, and techniques that will achieve a successful training, education, or development intervention. A particularly important need is to facilitate an easy transfer of learning, behavior, and practices from classroom exercises to daily work activities.

I have been working in HRD for more than fifteen years. These years have revealed a great deal of talking and some good techniques and suggestions for designing an HRD intervention. Much material is available about needs assessment, planning, design, learning techniques, leader's role, and evaluation. Yet it is difficult to find extensive coverage of

- Adjustments needed during an intervention that take into account new input brought by the participants after exposure to some new ideas or reflections, new learning, and awareness of their own situation
- How to guarantee support of new knowledge and behavior and assure that everyone in the organization agrees to the "new ways" of doing things

Because of the familiar Mercator projection maps, you may not be aware that Quebec is the largest province in Canada. Quebec stretches from Hudson Bay to south of the St. Lawrence River. The first permanent settlement dates from Champlain's founding of a trading post in 1608 at the site of what is now Quebec city, the province's capital. Today, about eighty-five percent of our population are urban dwellers, most of them the descendants of seventeenth-and eighteenth-century French settlers. French Canadians constitute eighty percent of our population and Roman Catholicism is the dominant religion. There are separate radio and TV stations and newspapers in French and English. The French Language Charter of 1977 made French the official language of education, business, and government, and in 1988, the Canadian Parliament recognized Quebec as a "distinct society."

Our Quebec-based HRD practice had to develop a method to answer the HRD concerns just mentioned *and* fit the local situation. That led to development and use of an approach called E.S.P.R.I.T. in Quebec HRD interventions.

First, I will describe how this approach was developed for Quebec. Several chapters in this book point out the importance of cultural differences. Only the most naive person would expect to simply import anything from another culture and have it work. One cannot just import ideas willy-nilly. Nevertheless, HRD practitioners often consider using certain worthy ideas that come from other countries. Sometimes they must be adapted. In other cases, an idea can successfully pass substantially intact to another country.

I want to point out some of the influences we considered—most of them foreign. The literature we reviewed was mostly from the U.S. Many of the foreign principles were considered for local adoption and several were accepted. Today, they are at the very heart of HRD practice here in Quebec. It may prove valuable to describe those ideas in some detail here. They include:

- The need to be participant-oriented
- Having facilitating conditions in an intervention
- Having the superior's support

Participant-Oriented

After a needs assessment in which the future participant has played a major role, the intervention design must consider the participants themselves, their opinions, and their willingness to get involved.

As put forward by Plessis (1984, p. 62), it is important to "give the individuals opportunities of cultural learnings which seem to fit best to their perception of the situation."

Beside opportunities, one must make sure of the participant's willingness to get involved. As Farnsworth believes (1975, p. 4): "No man can be taught anything, even by the most gifted speaker, unless he is willing to learn and can see that by doing so he will achieve his own personal goals."

You may share his opinion about the acquisition of knowledge when he says : "Little that is new will be retained unless it is discovered by the man himself—unless it clarifies or codifies his experience, or provides him with a new vantage point from which to reassess his existing judgments and opinions" (Farnsworth 1975, p. 5).

According to Varney (1976, p. 31), the success and efficiency of a HRD effort starts from the "individual's own awareness, efforts to change his or her work relationships and climate and feedback from those involved with him or her in this effort."

Regarding learning, Apgar and colleagues (1982, p. 2) observe: "It is assumed that adults can and do want to learn, that people learn best what they are most involved and interested in, and that learning must be a cognitive and effective experience."

They share Tracey's (1974, p. 4) viewpoint in focusing on the person: "If training is to be personal, specific knowledge of and sensitive concern for the individual and the environment in which he will live and work are essential. Training must also be supportive and it must allow for freedom of expression."

Nonetheless, you must be attentive to the need to protect one's self-image as suggested by Vaught and colleagues (1975, p. 70):

"Everyone concerned with employee development (trainers, supervisors, etc.) must be constantly aware of the tendency of trainees to become defensive. Learning is unlikely to happen with this type of dysfunctional attitude, either in the classroom or back on the job. Employee defensiveness is the natural tendency for people to protect their ego and self-image."

According to Dyer (1983), participants in a good training program:
- Feel a need to change
- Are supported by their superior and by experts
- Prepare action plans to be implemented in their actual workplace
- Are able to assess their own progress resulting from HRD activities in terms of well-being and personal pride
- Are able to link the learning to daily activities
- Consider learning objectives important for them personally

Dyer (1983, p. 210) also believes: "It is important that the organizational work group support the HRD effort; if old social ties resist the new behaviors, the impact of the learning is in danger of being washed out. . . . Joining an HRD program just to please the boss or because "the company wants me to" offers less possibility of change than engaging in the activities because of personal commitment to the program and the change goals."

Facilitating Conditions

Porras & Anderson (1981) suggest reasons for poor results in development interventions. They point to conflicts between cognitive components and behavioral orientations and difficulty in transferring learned behaviors to work.

In a management development program, Parry & Robinson (1979) identified two categories of objectives: those concerning values, attitudes, perceptions, and understanding and those about behaviors related to the job in terms of procedures, rules, and technicalities.

Varney (1976, p. 31) believes that "Any development effort is most effective if it helps people act on current organizational issues, particularly those in which increased problem solving and collaborative team skills are needed in order to link up dispersed and specialized knowledge throughout the organization."

So, Plessis (1984, p. 63) suggests: "An intervention design should not seek an 'ideal solution' that we must try to understand but should be designed in terms of 'ideal ways of doing' transferable to the social, technical, and economical reality of the enterprise." In so doing, he shares Tracey's (1971,p. 11) opinion that: "Training should be strongly oriented to practical, work-unit based, training interventions, to short workshops tied to actual practice and to skill building rather than information giving."

However, training activities could disturb labor relations between partners of different levels in the hierarchy. According to Reynolds (1972), when only peers are involved in training programs, you will find resistance to collaboration between different levels in the organization that could be difficult to overcome. But, when everybody gets involved in a specific issue while participating in a HRD program, these barriers will no longer exist.

According to Campbell and colleagues (1970), an HRD activity has greater chances of success if the following conditions exist:

- The activity stretches over a period of time
- The activity is given in a modular format
- There is intrinsic and extrinsic reinforcement
- The objectives are clearly stated
- The participant is motivated to learn
- The examples and activities are easily related to the workplace situation
- The participant is given the opportunity to practice in his or her own work environment

Concerning the length of the training program, Wallis (1978) suggests: "Educational and training opportunities are more effective if they are targeted to those most likely to use them in their work, especially if time between exposure and application is minimized" (cited in *Work in America Institute Studies in Productivity*, No. 29, p. 2).

About the participant's motivation, Vaught and colleagues (1975, p. 63) believe: "It is unlikely that unless the individual trainee is truly motivated to learn the material and apply it to the job, long-term improvements will be made."

As Plessis (1984, p. 89) puts it, an appropriate intervention must satisfy simultaneously three conditions: "The motivation to participate to a work group, the efficiency criteria on group functioning and the influence criteria of the group on its environment."

Superior's Support

Plessis (1984, p. 53) strongly affirms that the transfer of learning depends on the superior's support:

"It is not enough to train individuals to new know-how or behavior. Training must be associated to a willingness in doing or being. Also, it must feature the accessibility of doing or being available through management implications in allowing trainee necessary opportunities."

Farnsworth (1975, p. 50) talks about the key role of the superior:

"The essential single factor in determining a manager's post-course performance is the behavior and attitudes of his immediate superior. If the boss has attended the same course and is enthusiastic about its teachings, the probability is that the pace of improvement will be accelerated greatly. If he has not attended the course but is eager to evaluate its effect, he must be ready to play a more patient, subtle role."

According to Porras and Anderson (1981), there will be poor results without reinforcement mechanisms to sustain the use of new behaviors. Vaught and colleagues (1976, p. 68) share that opinion:

"Often, line managers may want to support training and resulting behavior but simply do not know how. They do not have the interpersonal skills needed to reward behavior adequately, help establish organizational and employee goals, and apply reinforcements for successful job performance. It is quite likely that training in interpersonal competence will be needed for all line managers if they are to support employee development adequately in their respective departments."

Varney (1976, p.153) puts it even more strongly, arguing that "they [the managers] do not recognize that real development takes place within the context of their relationship with their subordinates."

From the employee viewpoint, Vaught and colleagues (1986, p. 71) consider: "It makes very little sense to design elaborate HRD programs that will not be supported by the organization. Employees are unlikely to try newly learned behavior in an organizational atmosphere that is characterized by low trust, conformity, poor communication and other variables associated with authoritative management."

To remedy the difficulties of learning transfer, Plessis (1984, p. 97) suggests "training or development design should be elaborated in such a way as to involve multilevel participants."

An Alternative Approach

Our survey of the literature suggested changes in HRD methods to bring about adequate results. It is possible to design a learning program enabling the individuals involved to visualize themselves in more desirable situation and, thus, be motivated to pursue that goal on their own.

Performance goals can be established by the individual performers themselves or by other people. There is usually a big difference between showing people a particular performance goal and having them accept and attain it.

To better understand the behavior of a person in an organizational setting, you need to identify what he or she wants to do and how. Let us look at three situations in which I am involved in a vacation trip, a business venture, and an HRD program. In each case, let us look at the similarities and differences in making decisions on the "what" and the "how."

When I decide to take a vacation: I make all the decisions. I decide where to go. I choose the means (car, train, bus, plane, etc.). I can ask for advice, but I am the one who will decide in the end.

When I decide to get involved in a business venture: I also make all the decisions. I decide what venture. I choose the means: money, size, location, etc. I can ask for advice, but I am the one who will decide in the end.

When I am involved in an HRD program: I have much too often been told to participate by the training director or others. I am told why, where, when, how, with whom, etc. People have done things for me that they think are in my own interest, inside the organizational setting.

This comparison of the decision-making processes in three areas reveals a basic discrepancy in who makes decisions for whom. I believe that it is the external decision-making process in HRD which jeopardizes learning programs.

Figure 33.1 shows how the organization generally looks at its employees in terms of improving performance, efficiency, and minimizing cost—all common organizational goals. The organization relies on its Human Resources Department or HRD consultants to let the employees know that "they are lacking in something."

Figure 33.1: Organizational View of Employees

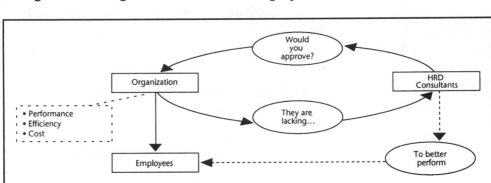

After first sharing these concerns, the trainers hurry to respond to them by asking for organizational support and asking how and why such things ("My staff is lacking in....") could happen and what solutions could be developed to help correct the deficiencies.

This organizational view has very meaningful implications:

- The organization judges its employees.
- The HRD department or consultants judge employees.
- Employees realize that they are being observed, analyzed, and evaluated.
- Employees realize that somebody else is organizing their own future.
- Employees feel they are being told that they are not good enough.

Much too often, the result of such a situation is, total failure for everyone:

- Employees resist, refuse, drop out.
- The HRD department or consultants become frustrated.
- The organization wastes much money.

The key to success in any HRD action depends upon the employees themselves. You need to help employees to

- Look at themselves
- Find out what is best suited for themselves and the organization
- Be more satisfied with the results of a learning program

We must find ways to help employees discover their own objectives, the objectives of the organization, and their place in the organization as they see it and as the organization sees it. After having discovered where they currently stand and where they would like to be, our experience shows that they will act like the person who has decided to take a vacation trip or has decided to get involved in a business venture. They will feel that they have chosen the means that suits them best to correct their problem as they perceive it.

To choose that corrective step, the employees must have clarified in their own mind their

- Opinion of themselves and of themselves versus the environment
- Value system
- Needs
- Interests
- Expectations regarding peers and superiors
- Employee's, peer's, and superior's expectations about their job

The learning program designer who wants to discover what will trigger an individual to take a particular action must have answers to these six questions as seen by the participants themselves through their own personal perception of the world.

For the vacation trip or the business venture, only the person could judge, at any moment, how well a goal is being achieved. In the same way, in a learning program, only the participants who have chosen a particular action can evaluate the effectiveness of that action, by comparing where they were and where they are now, what they knew and what they know now. They will evaluate the action through their own judgment mediated by such things as: stereotypes, halo effects, expectancies, projection, selective perception, and perceptual defenses.

Through our own experimentation in Quebec, we believe that a learning program will better lead to appropriate change of behavior and satisfactory achievement of performance goals if it has the following features:

- It is based on needs perceived by the employee.
- It is aimed at ways of satisfying these perceived needs.
- It triggers the interests of the employees and their willingness or desire to continue to search for new learning and effort.
- It is set up so that employees will be able—at any stage in the learning—to perceive the new learning as their own doing.

This means that before designing an HRD program, any human resources department or HRD consultant must validate information about the individuals in the organization with specially designed tools, to assess:

- How each employee is considered as a human being: value system, interests, needs, expectancies, etc.
- Where the employee sees the organization going.
- Where the employee sees his or her place in that organization.

After having designed an HRD program, any human resources department or HRD consultant should be able to answer YES to the following questions:

- Have we found, during learning activities, the needs perceived by the employees?
- Are there methods available to satisfy these needs?
- Are the training activities designed so that the employees will want to continue on their own without being asked to do so?
- Are the learning activities closely related to the employees' personal concerns?

S.P.I.R.I.T.

From the preceding analysis, we conclude that the design of any HRD intervention aimed at a transfer of knowledge and behavior change must essentially emphasize five important elements:

- Individual self respect
- Personal interest
- Possibility of expressing one's opinion
- Willingness to get involved
- A desire to continue afterward

We are convinced that such a design can be achieved by using S.P.I.R.I.T., an alternative approach to conventional design that undergoes six critical phases before attaining tangible results.

This approach works for us here in Quebec. We emphasize the participants' position and perception and the involvement of other organizational members as support to the transfer of knowledge and behavior to the workplace. Figure 33.2 identifies each phase, explaining the activities involved and the motives and reasons of such activities.

Statement of interests

Starting from the other person's viewpoint and perception of reality, and having an open attitude, the consultant who neither confronts nor puts the person in a defensive position can more easily bring him or her to new areas of concern.

The consultant will avoid the attitude of "you are right with what you perceive, but I would like to show you something more important." Instead of taking such a position before anything "official" goes on between the consultant and the client, why not give the client the chance to adjust his or her perception while undergoing the intervention?

Proposals

Since we all live in a world full of changes, we must try to gain new knowledge and behavior so we can better adapt to the changing world. It is then quite easy for both managers and workers to identify common concerns in the organizational context.

Themes of seminars and workshops are chosen by the consultant, modularly, based on knowledge of the organization and its context. These workshops will take place over a period of time not exceeding one year, since a longer period would cause lack of interest from the less tenacious participant.

Naturally, it will always be possible for the participant to delay or cancel the intervention at any point without anybody feeling bad about it.

The workshops happening over time create a type of "ritual" and a need to get together to think, discuss, and share experiences long after the intervention is finished.

Figure 33.2: The S.P.I.R.I.T. Model: An Alternative Approach to Designing a HRD Intervention

1. Statement of interests	Formulation of specific concerns by members of a functional entity inside an organization.	Respect individual personality. Have a sense of autonomy and responsibility. Allow everyone to keep their "little secrets."
2. Proposals	Suggestions by the consultant of themes to be explored concerning their daily life.	Find out common concerns. Give opportunity to share ideas about subjects difficult to introduce when it does not seem appropriate. Allow the opportunity to look for a better well-being at the individual and organizational levels.
3. Individual preparation	Simple exercises and questioning in order to get ready for the workshop activities.	Help to bring about reflections on a specific matter. Provoke exchanges and discussions. Allow psychological preparation.
4. Reflection workshop	A one-day workshop activity with much questioning, validation, information gathering and interaction between the participants and the consultant.	Minimize chances of "dropping out." Suggest the expression of opinions in front of others. Validate assumptions and perceptions with superiors and colleagues.
5. Identification of action plans	During the workshop, individual and collective action plans are formulated concerning the matters at hand to improve organizational life from the individual and group viewpoints.	Aim everybody towards action. Develop cooperation between partners. Give opportunities to identify what they want to do and to take charge of their life.
6. Transmission of action plans	Transmission of ideas, intentions and actions to everybody concerned: superiors, colleagues and employees.	Make the intervention very visible. Develop pride in what is happening. Increase the willingness to get to ACTION.

Individual preparation

The consultant gives the participants some material before each of the workshops to help them prepare for what will be discussed and to gather some data.

Even if some participants have not had a chance to work on the suggested material for whatever reason, the consultant manages to get them involved in the workshop discussions without their feeling apart from the group.

During the time the participants have to prepare for the next workshop, their subconscious mind is well aware of what the discussion subjects will be. A colleague may bring up a specific question about the preparation material during a meeting, a coffee break, or daily activities.

Reflection workshop

Since the discussion subjects are brought up by a consultant familiar with the topic but is not involved with the group in daily life, the reflection workshop discussions can begin in a nonpartisan manner between all the participants, including the manager—who is considered as a member of the group without having a superior position. This is useful, because many subjects of the workshop cannot possibly be discussed in regular meetings even when the superior is skillful in facilitating processes.

During the workshop, the consultant's main concern is the interest and motivation of the participants. The consultant's task will be to elaborate original activities that involve everybody, without too much effort on their part since it is easier to learn in a playful environment.

The consultant's imagination is the only limit to the gathering of vital information needed to provoke discussions and exchanges to find solutions to the participants' concerns.

Identification of action plans

Individual and collective action plans will be developed during the reflection workshops and reported to the consultant by the participants. This information will be written on a flip chart or other media so it can be seen by the participants all day long. At the end of each activity, the consultant will decide whether to ask the participants for "concrete actions" or "suggested behaviors," according to the evolution of the situation.

After the workshop, a particular activity related to the identification of personal and collective action plans is suggested. Part of the individual action plan should be revealed by the participants and another part kept "secret."

When the participant tells fellow group members what he or she proposes to do, it becomes a kind of moral engagement based on "honor" and "personal pride." It is like saying: "I promise to do this and I am telling you it is important!" Doing so, in the weeks ahead, a comment or a joke will serve as a reminder of what he promised to do.

The "secret" part of the action plan will become a motive of special interest during the "transmission phase" of this approach.

Collective plans are the manifestation of the group's willingness to transfer into action what it believes would benefit the whole organizational setting at its own specific level. The consultant's role is to help the group identify the implementation process and the checkpoints that will bring forward the group's willingness to adjust to the new reality.

Transmission of action plans

Shortly after the workshop, the consultant prepares a summary of all the relevant information gathered and distributes copies to the participants. These documents are not censored by any organization member. The main reasons for sharing the information are to give everyone tangible proof of the decisions made during the workshop, to bring these decisions back to daily activities, to continue the suspense of finding out "who said that, who made that promise" and to sustain the desire to go on with the process.

When the manager of a specific group gives the summary to his or her boss, it tends to be seen as an "official opinion" of what the group believes to be the best way to satisfy individual and collective well-being. Naturally, this transmission needs the approbation of the workshop participants, and the consultant plays a major role in explaining the reasons for doing so. To have even greater impact, colleagues from other departments must also be aware of what is happening and which action plans and decisions have been accepted. It will then be easier for them to understand the changes that will occur. Even though they might not be directly involved, they will have to live with the different habits or behaviors. Spreading information about this ongoing process at the personal and collective level will promote a stronger mutual support. Therefore, it will be possible to hear someone say to a colleague or a member of another working group: "Don't you remember, we had decided that...." or "I'm not alone in...."

Cultural Comments and Analysis

We have been using the S.P.I.R.I.T. approach with French-speaking Canadians in Quebec. Here are some of the things we have learned from our experience, which extends both to the public and private sector with large and small businesses and organizations.

We don't know if it is a French-Canadian cultural trait or not but the participants are generally more "talkers" than "doers." They like opportunities to talk about what they do and how they do it, provided they feel someone is listening to them.

In a multilevel design, bosses must have a participant's role no different from the others. It's the consultant's role to ensure this and to guarantee freedom of expression in a nonconfronting manner oriented toward a "better workplace."

The management and leadership style of a superior has much to do with the involvement of the participants during the workshops. Sometimes the boss is excluded from the first session to allow the participants to become aware of their own behaviors in relation with their boss. On occasions, during special meetings with the consultants, bosses have been briefed to pay attention to their behavior related to certain issues.

In large organizations it is better to make the participants relate to smaller units, such as divisions or departments, because they often tend to refer to the organization as a whole. Confusion can be generated by different signals and contradictory positions. It is better to start with a congruent unit and proceed afterward to a larger level to be sure to deal with the people's actual concerns.

Members of large service organizations tend to be more talkative than their counterparts in smaller production enterprises. It is easy to get participants of large service organizations to *talk* of new ways of doing things, but when it comes to making moves their interest quite often seems to fade away as though they were overwhelmed by the work to do and the small possibility of making an important contribution.

On the other hand, participants in smaller enterprises, mainly those working at the production level, are less talkative and don't feel the need for detailed explanations and analysis. They want to get quickly into action and the consultant must bring them back to analyzing of constraints and consequences of what they want to implement.

The impact of the S.P.I.R.I.T. approach is directly related to the importance attached to the intervention in terms of publicity and exposure of the activities in the daily life of the organization. Publicizing the positions taken by the participants about values, attitudes, behaviors, and the proposed action plans can make the difference between a successful intervention and one that fails to produce results. The more everybody knows about the intervention, the likelier there will be results because the participants usually want to stand for what they believe in and decide to do.

For example, participants in one medium-size production company put in writing a set of values and beliefs. They wanted to live by them to improve the quality of working life and the overall efficiency of the company. Each of the eighteen middle managers signed the document and presented it to their boss with the intent to have it accepted by the board of directors and shared by all employees. The directors accepted their code of conduct and granted them some money to have the document laminated. They posted it in strategic areas of the plant while copies made on fine paper were distributed to all the employees. Many changes occurred since everybody knew which behaviors were praised. It took some courage on the part of these middle managers because they were confronted by their employees on behaviors they had told them were not admissible. For instance, one manager told us he had a meeting with an employee to talk about his work performance. During the meeting, the employee was continually looking at the wall behind the boss. The boss was wondering "What is he looking at?" when suddenly he remembered two sentences of the code of conduct: "Stop blaming" and "Accept mistakes on a first trial." These were the messages the employee wanted to get through to his boss without saying it bluntly. This manager assured us that the conversation changed from that point on.

There are also situations following the application of the S.P.I.R.I.T. approach where the participants who were very enthusiastic about a particular action get together and change their minds. In a particular case, the participants were authorized by top management to do whatever they decided to improve a specific area of behavior. Following the S.P.I.R.I.T. approach, they decided to build an attitude survey of what their employees believed would be the best attitude for a superior to adopt in a specific context.

The consultants formatted the survey according to the decisions of the participants. They had it checked by the participants for conformity to what they wanted to know. The consultants then gave them the final version of the questionnaire to distribute to the employees. Two days before the distribution date, the participants decided not to proceed as planned. They tried to explain to their superiors, in a confused manner, their sudden change of mind; they were afraid of something. From that decision, the intervention started over.

Conclusion

There is no doubt that the S.P.I.R.I.T. approach brings about side effects at the personal and organizational levels far beyond the conventional needs-assessment method, since it starts with a "statement of interests" instead of a problem-solving approach.

It is an intuitive "trial-and-error" approach in which the consultant wishes to control neither the input nor the output—but only the process. This approach is the opposite of a more conventional and rational approach based on logic and reason, in which the consultant is trying to control the output of a HRD intervention by having a strong hold on the input and the process as well.

In the S.P.I.R.I.T. approach, controlling the process is done in a nonconfronting and subtle manner. The consultant uses the eastern philosophy that he or she is receptive to what will emerge instead of "fighting against," while being totally aware that his or her role is to "provoke events."

Our approach to HRD puts considerable emphasis on the value system and on the organization practices challenged by new learnings and new behaviors.

We started using this approach for the design of a HRD intervention in 1983. There has been a growing need for an open system approach. Not only the participants in an intervention but everybody in the organization or enterprise want to share the trend started by a design intended to bring changes in the way things were. This need will grow stronger in the years to come.

Of course, the S.P.I.R.I.T. approach must be adapted to specific contexts. Nonetheless, this approach can make a difference in cultures other than that of French-speaking Canadians in Quebec. We believe that the consultant with great flexibility and ingenuity can adapt the approach to whatever need is expressed along the way in an intervention. This is why we are more concerned with the process itself than with controlling the output, because some changes will occur if the S.P.I.R.I.T. approach is used.

I have not made cultural comparisons between French-speaking people and other Canadians. Neither have these comparisons been drawn with Americans. I leave it to you to make your own.

References

Apgar, K., et al. *Life Education in the Work Place.* Family Service Association of Am., 1982.

Campbell, J., Dunette, Lawler III, E., and Weick Jr., K. *Managerial Behavior Performance and Effectiveness.* New York, NY: McGraw-Hill, 1970.

Chalofsky, N., and Lincoln, C. *Up the HRD Ladder.* La Jolla, CA: University Associates Publishers Inc., 1982.

Dyer, W. *Contemporary Issues in Management and Organization Development.* Reading, MA: Addison-Wesley, Publishing

Farnsworth, T. *Developing Executive Talent.* Maidenhead, U.K.: McGraw-Hill Book Company Ltd., 1975.

Ouimet, D. "Motivating People in Training Contexts." *N.S.P.I. Journal.* XVII, No. 6, July 1978.

Ouimet, D. "E.S.P.R.I.T.: Methode alternative de realisation d'une intervention de formation ou de developpement," *INFO Ressources Humaines.* IIV, No 6, Feb. 1991.

Parry, S., and Robinson, E. "Management Development, Training or Education?" *Training and Development Journal.* XXXIII, July 1979.

Plessis, J. *Concevoir et gerer la formation dans l'entreprise.* Les Editions d'Organisation, 1984.

Porras, J., and Anderson, B. "Improving Managerial Effectiveness Through Model-Based Training." *Organizational Dynamics.* IX, Spring 1981.

Reynolds, M., "The Effects of Training Interventions on Management Relationships." *European Training.* I, Spring 1972.

Tracey, W. *Designing Training and Development Systems.* New York, NY: American Management Inc., 1971.

Tracey, W. *Managing Training & Development Systems.* New York, NY: AMACOM, 1974.

Varney, G. *An Organization Development Approach to Management Development.* Reading, MA: Addison-Wesley, 1976.

Vaught, B., Hoy, F., and Buchanan, W. *Employee Development Programs.* Westport, CN: Quorum Books, 1985.

Wallis, W. "Educating Future Managers" *Managers for the Year 2000.* Newman, W. H. (Ed.). Englewood Cliffs, NJ: Prentice-Hall, 1978.

About the Author

Denis Ouimet is a HRD consultant for the Bureau de Recherche et de Formation en Gention Integre in Quebec. Previously, he was a Lecturer at the Department of Industrial Relations, Laval University and Professor of Administrative Techniques at the Levis-Lauzon Community College. He studied at Sherbrooke University and Montreal University and completed his doctoral studies in Social Sciences at Laval University. His memberships include L'Enterprise de Demain, Association of Human Resources Professionals of Quebec—where he received a special award for contribution to the advancement of Human Resource Management—and the American Society for Training and Development. He is the author of two books and more than thirty articles.

CHAPTER 34

Bringing Learners to the Technology-Source Country

Serge Ogranovitch

For many years, corporations, government agencies, and foundations have been sending employees and students abroad for study and instruction in technical and managerial skills. Often, they arrange such HRD activities in countries where needed technologies are available.

Corporations usually pick these employees for their technical skills and their long-term job potential. By contrast, nonprofit organizations and government agencies usually select employees for their educational achievements. The aim is to build a cadre of persons with special skills for the industries targeted for development in the home country.

Until recently, most "technology transfer" programs have concentrated on technical learning. Few have considered the effect on the individual. Yet program managers should realize that the aim of HRD is not only to help the learner become an effective technician or manager. It is also important that learners feel positive about themselves and satisfied with their cultural, social, and professional experiences. Corporate sponsors, for example, want learners to return not only technically qualified, but motivated to use their newly acquired skills to benefit the company. As the vice-president of a multinational corporation recently told me, "We have invested a great deal of time and money in the development of these employees. We would like to see some returns. They are our future."

The Problem

Unfortunately, corporate sponsors have learned that badly managed HRD programs may lead to hardships for learners. Disgruntled newly-trained employees usually leave the company or are less effective than expected.

Some prospective learners have a negative self-image because of their cultural and religious environment and their lack of education. A poorly planned and implemented HRD experience can easily strengthen of that negative self-image. This problem is particularly acute when HRD happens in a foreign setting.

What can we do to prevent this? How can firms better choose employees for HRD? Most important, how can companies better train and support workers both during the HRD period and after they return to work? These are questions we must explore and answer.

The Solution Strategy

Let's look at what you can do to improve the prospects of HRD success in a foreign environment. We have used the proposed process during the past ten years in training over 5,000 foreign nationals from Europe, Africa, the Middle East, the Far East, and Central and South America. It provides specific parameters for

- The planning and execution of an effective program
- The particulars of each element
- The selection of participants
- The training necessary to achieve the desired results

People undertake HRD abroad for many reasons. For illustrative purposes, we will look at a corporate-sponsored HRD program (the guidelines proposed will apply to a broad range of HRD programs). Assume, for example that a corporation wishes to bring a national from an overseas division to the home office. Or, a company is sending an employee abroad to a vendor's office or plant for technical training. In our example, an employee is brought to the home office. We assume that this firm has a policy of promoting from within and of developing the skills of its "nationals" whenever possible.

The employee-learner, Mr. Yaz, is from the Middle East. Like most such selectees, he was picked for training based on his technical knowledge, positive attitude, and company loyalty. Comprehensive pretesting was not done, nor were other major factors considered in making the selection. As the HRD director for the plant, you are responsible for choosing and overseeing the training needed.

Proposed Model of Action and Responsibilities

The proposed model starts and ends in the home country. It incorporates technical and non technical areas into a single HRD program that considers the needs of both the company and the employee.

Figure 34.1 illustrates seven important elements in a well-organized HRD operation. It begins with pre-departure, pre-program information and ends with follow-up after the instruction is complete.

Figure 34.1: Design Steps

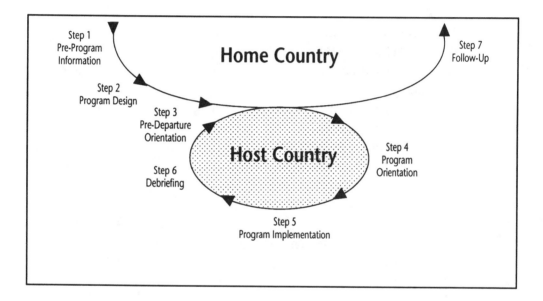

Pre-Program Information

As with any HRD program design, the more useful information you have about the participant(s) the better the design. Before the learner's arrival you should seek the following information:

- HRD Program's Purpose(s)
  1. Company's stated objectives (short-and long-term) in arranging for the HRD
  2. Skills to be acquired
  3. Expected or desired program length
  4. Participant's purpose in participating
  5. Estimate of learner's commitment to company

- Technical
  1. Previous technical experience
  2. Types of work performed and positions held

- What HRD Activity
  1. Formal, including vocational programs
  2. On-the-job training
  3. Level of related relevant skills
  4. Copies of any tests and evaluation
  5. Language skills (if relevant)

- Personal
  1. All learners are identified by age, sex, etc.
  2. Health (problems that may relate to HRD, travel, or work)
  3. Marital status. If married, what are implications of travel, absence from the home?
  4. Previous out of country travel? Where, when, length, purpose, experience, difficulties?
  5. Cultural or other bias
  6. Motivation to live abroad for an extended time

Program Design

One key to a successful HRD program is the planning before start-up. The design must permit flexibility, estimate problems, and allow for contingencies. Two tactics call for particular attention when designing programs.

The first tactic

The tactic that most managers understand is to focus on the nature of the technical training. This is usually straightforward. You examine the pertinent information from Step 1 and decide what will be needed to achieve the objectives.

However, we propose that you start backwards. Consider first the skills the participant should have at the end of the instruction. Then build a curriculum to achieve those goals, considering the learner's current skills levels.

HRD managers often attempt to teach too much in the time available. Try to avoid this situation. First, pick an instructional method that (at least at the beginning) is compatible with the learner's previous educational and cultural experiences. Second, consider previous experiences and proposed HRD programs after eliminating redundancies, and combine skills with HRD efforts that are supportive. For example, you can teach language and technical concepts simultaneously. You can also combine tool use and basic mechanical skills. Third, blend classroom and plant (or office) HRD so they reinforce one another. Foreign nationals in a host country often need consistent hands-on reinforcement. The combination will bring two important results:

- Better understanding of data, especially when provided in small segments
- Better monitoring of progress when facilitated by more frequent checks on skills achieved

In designing programs, state your assumptions, contingencies, and evaluation criteria clearly.

The second tactic

The most overlooked tactic in HRD program design is the personal support of the participants. Often, a key to success is how we receive and treat the participant during instruction. Put yourself in the learner's place. You have just been selected to go to another country for special learning. It's an honor. Your peers are envious. You are marked for success, advancement, and security. You're willing to suffer personal hardships if necessary, such as being away from your family and home. It's crucial that you succeed. However, you don't control what happens during the instructional period. As a result, uncertainty and lack of accountability may be major pitfalls.

Let's look at Mr. Yaz and two separate scenarios.

Scenario 1

He arrives in your city on a Sunday afternoon. He has been told that after going through customs, he is to take a taxi to a local motel near the plant. He will be picked up in the morning at 7:30 A.M.

Your assistant picks him up. She tells him that you have to attend a staff meeting that starts at 8:15 A.M. She will take him to the plant to register and take care of the paperwork. From the time he arrives at the plant until lunch, Mr. Yaz fills out forms in a small room. At noon you arrive to introduce yourself, apologize for the delay in meeting him, and you and your assistant take him to lunch. You tell him that he has a week to find lodging, and give him a list of potential apartment options.

In the afternoon you have your assistant show him around the plant. You then encourage him to look for an apartment and tell him to report back to the plant the next day for the start of the program. Throughout the day he is treated courteously.

Scenario 2

Mr. Yaz is met at the airport, by a plant employee appointed to his "host contact" during his instructional period. He is taken to a hotel where he has already been checked in. Then at the plant you explain how the "host contact" program works, and what his schedule for the next few days will be and how it fits into the overall HRD program.

The next day the "host contact" picks up Mr. Yaz at the hotel. The contact takes him to the plant, shows him around, introduces him to people, and helps him fill out the paperwork. All involved and interested parties review the HRD program, starting with the purpose and expectations of both the company and the participants.

Let's look at the differences in these two scenarios. In the first, Mr. Yaz is treated courteously, but is often left alone and is not made to feel comfortable with his new situation.

In the second, he is treated courteously and is in the company of peers or supervisors throughout the day. At an early opportunity he is given an explanation of what is expected of him.

Pre-Departure Orientation

As much as possible, learners should be oriented to the program before their departure. As the person responsible for the HRD program, you should involve yourself in the design and planning of the pre-departure orientation (that is, content, format, and delivery mode). The pre-departure orientation should include:

- Purpose of the program
- Criteria for selecting employee(s)
- Travel and arrival logistics
- Tentative instructional schedule
- Role in corporation after successful return
- Emergency contingencies
- Local and plant culture

This orientation is best done two to three weeks before departure. This allows the learner to adjust to the idea of the trip, ask questions, and take care of last minute changes and arrangements.

Program Orientation

Preferably, program orientation is done right after arrival, in one or two days. The topics covered are almost the same as pre-departure orientation, but from a different angle and in more detail. During the orientation you should signal to the learners that they are special, and make it clear that the organization has carefully arranged this program to suit their needs.

During these sessions, managers should cover the purpose of the program, outlining the design and schedule. Each part should be described in detail and cover the new skills and capabilities the learner is expected to acquire. Explain the support system and social activities available. Try to make the learner feel a part of the company work force, and not an outsider.

The orientation should include a presentation of cultural imperatives, including similarities and differences between the relevant cultures and the two working environments. Use this opportunity as a learning experience for the people of your plant. You need to identify idiosyncrasies of "the plant" and the community. The orientation should also include a trip around town to point out points of interest (places of worship, banks, supermarkets, etc.). Also explain any laws and regulations that the learner needs to know, such as driver's license requirements.

Program Implementation

The HRD program we describe is in two parts: the technical training and the support services. Each part is critical to a successful outcome.

Technical training

We recommend that the design of the technical training program should start at the end and move back to the beginning. The reason is this. The only thing you know before you design the program is what you want the learner to be able to do at the end of instruction. Just imagine that, as shown in Figure 34.2, you are building a brick pyramid and you know what the top brick is. Now you need to identify the two bricks to support it, and so on until you reach the learner's existing skills level. You only include the bricks needed (i.e., only cover the skills the learner does not have).

Figure 34.2: Program Design

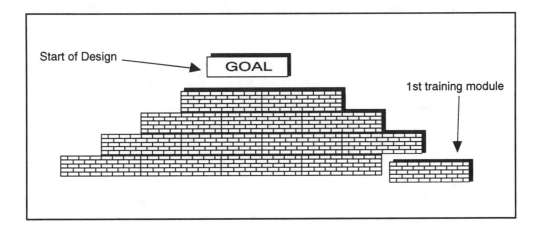

Technical training techniques should incorporate extensive hands-on reinforcement. Adults, especially those who have not spent much time in formal learning, learn best by doing. This practical experience will have two added benefits. First, it helps you check what learning is really taking place. Second, it helps the learners to become more a part of the plant, which makes them feel that they are contributing to the local operation or company team.

Support Services

Most programs only look at the technical side of HRD, and do not consider the personal needs of the learners. This contributes to failures and results in high turnover. That's why a "host contact" support system is so important. The purpose is to give foreign learners a personal contact, aside from you—someone who will introduce them, show them around the stores, explain various activities, and help them in the event of trouble. This concept helps relieve personal anxieties, and should make the learner feel more comfortable. Mr. Yaz, for example, will be able to concentrate on his main purpose: the acquisition of skills.

The "host contact" program also has beneficial by-products. It helps to globalize your company and enhances the business relationship between operations in different regions of the world.

The more you integrate the learner into the plant life, the better. In preparing the support system, develop a program-specific checklist of items to consider. These include:

- Residence (apartment)
    1. utilities
    2. telephone
    3. laundry
    4. where, how food to be prepared
- Residence (hotel)
    1. cooking
    2. laundry
    3. available services
- Food
    1. shopping distance
    2. ethnic foods
    3. restaurants
- Transportation
    1. public
    2. cars
    3. driver's license
    4. insurance
- Medical and Dental

- Social Activities
    1. cultural events
    2. sports
    3. company or plant
    4. tourism
- Banking and Legal

Another item to consider is non-HRD counseling. Most learners, will have problems with homesickness, interaction (miscommunication) with staff or social acquaintances, study habits, and expectations. The learner can best be counseled by the "host contact" if they have a close relationship. If not, it will become your role.

Program Conclusion, Debriefing, and Reentry Preparation.

Corporations around the world have learned that culture shock also happens when someone returns home after spending time in another culture. To help the learner prepare for return, you can plan a short debrief and reentry program. The topics covered should include:

- Culture shock – handling expectations and disappointments
- Program goals and whether they were met (from both points of view)
- Where learners will be assigned in the organization
- In-depth discussion of their experience (negatives as well as positives)

This session will not only prepare the learners to reenter their culture but will also help you improve future programs and prevent problems. Remember, you have a lot invested in the learners and their success reflects on you and your organization.

Follow-Up

This is another often forgotten step. To improve future programs you need to do periodic follow-ups. During follow-up, you can find out what skills learners use frequently, which areas need more detailed coverage during instruction, and which areas were superfluous. You can also utilize the learners for future pre-departure orientation and program designs.

A well-planned program considers not only the technical skills to be acquired, but the whole individual. Every learner wants something out of the program aside from the technical skills that the corporation is providing. By taking care of the whole person, you can design an HRD program that provides a "win-win" situation for all involved.

About the Author

Serge Ogranovich is a Partner in The Potomac partnership in Vienna, VA. Previously, he was President, International Support Services. Earlier he was General Manager, DYN Training Division of Dynalecron. He had been President of Systran and Marketing Manager of Telemedia. He studied at the University of Paris and New York University. He has taught or managed HRD projects in twenty-four countries and provided consulting on HRD design to foreign governments and multinational corporations.

PART FOUR

Conclusions

CHAPTER 35

Lessons for International HRD People

Angus Reynolds
Leonard Nadler

Juan Sebastian del Cano completed the first voyage around the world in 1522. It took him two years, eleven months, and seventeen days. In 1873—351 years later—Jules Verne wrote an improbable, fictional account called *The Tour of the World in Eighty Days.* We suppose it reflected what was potentially possible then. Less than 100 years after that, anyone could fly around the world on a routine commercial Pan American Airways flight in approximately four days. Yuri Alekseyevich Gagarin completed a circumnavigation of the world in 1961, alone in the spacecraft *Vostok*, in 89.1 minutes!

Speed of travel is no longer an obstacle to the interaction of people from different cultures. The speed of mail is essentially unchanged in recent years. Telephone communications improve consistently and are almost universally available. FAX communication has made quick exchange of information simple and reliable at reasonable cost.

Some Key Guidelines for Global Consultants and Practitioners

This chapter does not try to summarize the content of this book. We suggest that to fully appreciate the book, you must examine each chapter yourself. Neither do we try to speak for these distinguished professionals. Each of them has done very well on their own behalf. In fact, we see no serious difference between these writers' views. Many themes recur consistently throughout the book and we feel that they are common to other operative professionals in the field as well. Many ideas in the book provide guidance. Let's explore several guidelines that we feel are key to successful international work.

Be culturally sensitive

Cultural sensitivity is pivotal in every HRD project conducted in another country. In global HRD, each situation calls for a culturally sensitive approach. This involves two cultures: yours and theirs. We cannot divorce ourselves from our own cultural baggage. If you are really lucky, the host-country people may try to learn something of *your* culture beyond stereotypes. More probably they won't. It is well to understand your own culture— it will help you avoid culture shock. But, ethnocentrism (focusing on your own culture as *right*) will prevent the development of a more global perspective. On the other hand, you must try to learn as much as possible about *their* culture. Not one writer in this book, and no one of any merit we have met, downplays the importance of culture in global HRD.

For example, the Chinese are not just the Chinese. Chinese from the People's Republic of China, Taiwan, Hong Kong, and Singapore differ in ways important enough to make a difference in HRD activities. Culture is a powerful force in *all* global arenas. An interpretation of the biblical Joseph's understanding of the importance of culture and its implications for success in another country suggests that expatriate consultants are not a recent development.

You *can* overcome cultural differences. There is adequate proof that "Western" approaches can be adapted and transferred effectively to other countries. "Eastern" ideas have moved west as well. However, we must *never* impose them. You must always apply a process we call "cultural filtration." In any HRD-related project in another country, we ask that you examine the relevant cultural factors—please.

Use HRD terminology consistently

The distinctions among training, education, and development are extremely important. Yet, we lack an important tool for approaching the global arena. There are still global HRD programs without a specific focus. As a result, proper utilization and evaluation are difficult.

When HRD people call all programs "training" they do no one a service. If training means more than one thing, it becomes meaningless as a descriptive tool. In consequence, the HRD profession loses the impact that it can have when learning experiences are clearly differentiated as training, education, or development.

Prepare yourself for global work

Several points have been suggested to help you prepare to enter or continue in the global HRD arena. A fundamental point is that proper preparation for such work is your own responsibility. We know that people in different countries are significantly different. The differences are more accurately characterized as many and large than as few and small. Ignoring them is to take a "bulldozer" approach to your interaction. Somehow a fatal sort of "macho" seems to be involved—like a factory worker who feels that a safety helmet and safety shoes are only for the weak. We have assembled a stellar group of chapter authors who reiterate the need for understanding the differences. You can only be a global HRD professional when you are not ashamed to acknowledge those differences.

The characteristics needed to achieve success differ from country to country. It is absolutely necessary to adapt to the host-country people and their culture. Remember, they have no need to adapt to you. Adequate preparation can dramatically reduce your likelihood of failure, as well as that of any other expatriate.

One sure difference between success and failure for a global HRD consultant or practitioner is human concern. Unfortunately, this is not always present, and there is no real way to generate it. International work isn't for everyone. There is no shame in deciding not to engage in it. We sincerely hope that anyone who doesn't feel comfortable in this work will not attempt or continue it.

Employ your consultant skills

Much of this book focuses on consultant skills. We cannot repeat all of the suggestions here, but we can refocus your attention on several areas.

Hiring expatriate consultants. Considerations were suggested for those who hire expatriate consultants. You might want to consider these from the consultant's side of the table:

- Define the consultant-related problem clearly.
- Define your mutual obligations.

Planning an intervention. Let's assume that you are successful domestically. Without proper preparation you will certainly *fail* in the host country. Here are a few of the notably large number of considerations:

- Know the basis of the HRD field, including research.
- Examine your own values and assumptions.
- Carefully analyze the problem or situation.

- Know the dominant activity for your population.
- Adopt varying styles, postures, and competencies.
- Empathize with the client.
- View the project from alternative perspectives.
- Work in harmony with local consultants.

Addressing learners' nontechnical needs. Technology-transfer projects tend to concentrate on technical learning. But is also important to address the learners' need to feel positively about themselves and satisfied with their cultural, social, and professional experiences.

Termination and withdrawal. A wise person said, "All good things must come to an end." A well-done project must do the same. In fact, a good ending is one mark of a professional. The relationship you establish should lead naturally to withdrawal. Ideally, at project end the client will have become autonomous—and remain your friend.

Appropriately adapt personal and alternative methods

In all HRD projects, you must be responsive to the problem or situation. To be effective in global projects, you must develop appropriate knowledge and skills.

When working through interpreters, you must properly perform the functions related to

- Selection
- Briefing
- Speaking properly and only in English
- Avoiding unusual words
- Providing your outline
- Creating feedback

When adapting media for foreign users, you should follow these guidelines:

- Develop an accurate learner profile.
- Do not adapt "somebody's baby."
- Use professional translators exclusively.
- Develop standard procedures for translation.
- Don't be "egotistical."
- Focus on cultural sensitivity.
- Use a "friendly" text layout.
- Include an instructor's guide.

When adapting technology-based instruction for foreign users, you should follow these guidelines:

- Keep it simple.
- Insure clarity.
- Anticipate foreign use.
- Think screens vs. pages.
- Anticipate display format.
- Consider text characteristics.
- Deal with system- and application-generated messages.
- Avoid cultural bias.

Ensure learning transfer

Learning transfer is a relatively new HRD concept. Transfer of learning is not the process of measuring transfer. It is the name we give a system of structured and pre-planned activities to ensure the effective on-the-job application of knowledge and skills gained in HRD activities. We wouldn't take issue with the idea that it is the single most important aspect of any instructional program. We feel it essential that global HRD people ensure incorporation of a complete learning transfer system— including managers, instructors, and learners—before, during, and after training. We hope to see responsible HRD people take this important step.

Where Do We Go From Here?

More indigenous HRD systems
Global joint ventures are on the increase, and with them the need for global HRD will increase and be added to the HRD needs of the many multinational organizations. Providing the necessary HRD will be the key. Who will develop the appropriate systems?

Formerly, host-country HRD managers have often used imported HRD systems, models, techniques, and consultants. Currently they are increasingly developing indigenous HRD systems using local people. This positive trend will presumably continue in the future, so the multinationals and joint ventures can base their programs on the local systems.

A global business culture?

Is a global corporate culture developing or likely to develop? Perhaps a limited answer can be seen in the European Community. Former intensely national cultures may be subordinated to economic interests. Should this be proven possible in Europe, a global business culture could follow. We can even consider an opposite example to support this notion. Two cultures developed in Germany when it was divided, suggesting that the underlying culture *can* be overcome, at least in certain situations. Can we expand this notion to include making changes when it is in enlightened self-interest to do so? The answer is unclear, but even if people only vigorously attempt to understand how other people think, the world can be a better place.

The future for global consultants and practitioners

We wish all global consultants, and practitioners, (as well as those who would be active in those areas) success in their chosen endeavors. We have already testified that the global arena is bigger, incredibly complex, diverse, and intensely satisfying. Many countries are increasingly autonomous in HRD. Local HRD practitioners are increasingly capable of meeting domestic HRD needs, and local consultants eagerly await an invitation to consult. They want the opportunity to demonstrate their competencies and advance the HRD development in their country. The need for foreign HRD practitioners will decrease.

HRD is not an old enough profession to have developed many "proverbial" statements. But we feel that it will eventually be classed among the most noble of human endeavors. More people will have encountered caring HRD professionals and will remember them with the same fondness currently reserved for a select few of their school teachers. Since we know many people had bad experiences in school, the dedicated HRD professional may be the first and only caring learning-related person some ever meet.

The world seems headed toward a better era than has been true in our lifetimes. Peaceful interaction between countries seems more likely than ever before. Global communication makes this possible on a total scale never before attainable. The importance of global focus is now recognized in organizations. Simultaneously, HRD is becoming respected for the magnitude of its contribution to these organizations.

All of these developments leave us poised on the brink of professional victory. You, in fact, may be today's Juan Sebastian del Cano, fixed on the rolling deck of the small but indomitable *Victoria*. You are bravely sailing into uncharted waters, and we wish you every success great and small. When you ultimately prevail in completing today's voyage, the world will be again smaller. If you do your job well, it will also be better!

Author Contact Information

The author's names and addresses are provided here to facilitate reader contact. In every case an indication of gender is provided to assist communication.

Professor (Mr.) Tadashi Amaya – Chapter 17
        Teikyo University of Technology
        229-1 Hirata, Ichihara-Shi
        Chiba Ken 290, Japan
        Tel.0436-23-7314

Mr. Ralph Bates – Chapter 26
        Training, Organization and Management Development,
        6818 Murray Lane
        Annandale, VA 22003
        USA
        Tel. 703/354-0669

Dr. (Mr.) Shyam B. L. Bharadwaj – Chapter 27
        Effective Human Systems Pvt. Ltd.
        Plot 398, Road #22B, Jubilee Hills
        Hyderabad-500 034
        India
        Tel. 248555

Mr. Alistair Black – Chapter 32
        No. 6 Arun Close, Vainona
        P.O. Borrowdale, Harare
        Zimbabwe
        Tel. 708512/722453

Ms. Chalintorn Burian – Chapter 25
        River Mansion 5A 23 Phra Athit Road
        Changsongkram District
        Bangkok 10200
        Thailand
        Tel. (662)282-5012

Mr. Eduardo Q. Canela – Chapter 25
The Foundation for Entrepreneurship and
Appropriate Technology
P.O. Box 44, UP Diliman Campus
Q.C. 1101, Metro Manila
The Philippines
Tel. 90 08 19

Dr. (Mr.) Dunstan Campbell – Chapter 13
CAEP
Ministry of Agriculture, Castries
St. Lucia
Tel. 809/452-0172

Dr. (Mr.) Pierre Casse – Chapter 9
Professor, Director
IMD, International Institute for
Management Development
P.O. Box 915, CH 1001 Lausanne
Switzerland
Tel. 41 21/618 01 11

Dr. (Ms.) Hui-Chuan Cheng – Chapter 19
Partner, Princeton Software
372 Devon Street
Kearny, NJ 07032
USA
Tel. 201/991-4983

Dr. (Ms.) Phyliss Cooke – Chapter 26
9755 Mesa Springs Way, #132
San Diego, CA 92126
USA
Tel. 619/693-0757

Mr. Ali Dialdin – Chapter 28
General Manager
Arabian American Oil Company
P.O. Box 8283, Dhahran
Saudi Arabia

Mr. Robert Hersowitz – Chapter 30
　　　　　　　　　11 Arden Road
　　　　　　　　　London, N3 3AB
　　　　　　　　　England
　　　　　　　　　Tel. 081-346-6528

Ms. Florence Ho – Chapter 20
　　　　　　　　　Human Resources Officer
　　　　　　　　　The University College of Cariboo
　　　　　　　　　343 Arrowstone Drive, No. 221
　　　　　　　　　Kamloops, B.C. V2C 1P9
　　　　　　　　　Canada
　　　　　　　　　Tel. 604/828-5458

Mr. Masaaki Imai – Chapter 18
　　　　　　　　　Kaizen Institute of Japan, Inc.
　　　　　　　　　c/o The Cambridge Corporation,
　　　　　　　　　Kowa Bldg. No. 3, 1-11-45 Akasaka, Minato-ku,
　　　　　　　　　Tokyo, Japan
　　　　　　　　　Tel. 81(3)3582-8931

Dr. (Ms.) Zulaiha Ismail – Chapter 24
　　　　　　　　　School of Business and Management
　　　　　　　　　Institut Teknologi Mara, 40450 Shah Alam
　　　　　　　　　Selangor, Darul Ehsan
　　　　　　　　　Malaysia
　　　　　　　　　Tel. 03/5564145

Mr. Ralph Keteku – Chapter 31
　　　　　　　　　Manpower Development Manager, Mine Office,
　　　　　　　　　P. O. Box 10, Obuasi,
　　　　　　　　　Ghana
　　　　　　　　　Tel. 0582-475

Dr. (Mr.) Robert Kohls – Chapter 4
　　　　　　　　　Institute for Intercultural Leadership,
　　　　　　　　　Suite B, 1362 Vallejo Street,
　　　　　　　　　San Francisco, CA 94108
　　　　　　　　　USA
　　　　　　　　　Tel. 415/474-0552

Mr. Jeff Len – Chapter 12
School of Government Business Administration
George Washington University
Washington, DC 20036
USA
Tel. 202/994-4988

Dr. (Mr.) Michael Marquardt – Chapter 10
Vice President, The World Group
1688 Moorings Drive
Reston, VA 22090
USA
Tel. 703/437-0260

Ms. Sandy Mayers-Chen – Chapter 15
International Instructional Systems Design
129 East 63 Street, Suite 4F
New York, NY 10021
USA
Tel. 212/371-0769

Dr. (Mr.) Leonard Nadler – Chapters 1,2,3,11,16, & 35
Partner, Nadler Associates
9209 Dewberry Lane
College Park, MD 20740-3906
USA
Tel. 301/935-5229

Dr. (Mr.) Neal Nadler – Chapter 12
Director, Corporate Learning Institute
Box 321, Peabody College
Nashville, TN 37203
USA
Tel. 615/322-8414

Ms. Zeace Nadler – Chapter 5, 11
Partner, Nadler Associates,
9209 Dewberry Lane
College Park, MD 20740-3906
USA
Tel. 301/935-5229

Mr. Ng Peck Ho – Chapter 23
69 Saraca Road
Singapore 2880
Tel. 2359766

Mr. Ronnie Ng – Chapter 26
Sr. Partner, Training Design Consultants
2/F, No. 8, DD215, Lot 1000,
Dui Hai Village, Sai Kung, Kowloon
Hong Kong
Tel. 852/791-0577

Mr. Serge Ogranovich – Chapter 34
Partner, The Potomac Partnership
P.O. Box 405
Vienna, VA 22180
USA
Tel. 703/761-3030

Mr. Denis Ouimet – Chapter 33
Bureau de Recherche et de Formation en Gention Intégré
11, rue Nobel, Lévis (Quebec)
Canada G6V 7C6
Tel. 418/833-0761

Mr. Michael Pellett – Chapter 6
President, M² Limited
P.O. Box 2342
Gaithersburg, MD 20879
USA
Tel. 301/977-4281

Dr. (Mr.) Angus Reynolds – Chapter 1,2,3,7,21, & 35
P.O. Box 585
Central Islip, NY 11722
USA
Tel. 516/234-4514

Dr. (Mr.) Don Roberts – Chapter 22
                        School of Education & Human Services
                        Marymount University
                        2807 N. Glebe Road
                        Arlington, VA 22207
                        USA
                        Tel. 703/522-5600

Mr. Michael Sandrock – Chapter 29
                        Geschäftsführender Gesellschafter, Eloqu
                        Mozartstrasse 5, 7800 Freiburg i. Br.
                        Germany
                        Tel. 0761/36497

Dr. (Ms.) Cheryl Samuels-Campbell – Chapter 13
                        c/o D. Campbell, CAEP Ministry of Agriculture,Castries
                        St. Lucia
                        Tel. 809/452-0172

Dr. (Mr.) Mel Schnapper – Chapter 14
                        President, Melvin Schnapper Associates, Inc.
                        2522 West Fitch
                        Chicago, IL 60645 USA
                        Tel. 312/262-2113

INDEX

A

E

F

T

Z